Implementing Change

Implementing Change

Alcoholism Policies in Work Organizations

Janice M. Beyer
Harrison M. Trice

THE FREE PRESS
A Division of Macmillan Publishing Co., Inc.
NEW YORK

Collier Macmillan Publishers
LONDON

The Free Press
A Division of Macmillan Publishing Co., Inc.
866 Third Avenue, New York, N. Y. 10022

Collier Macmillan Canada, Ltd.

Library of Congress Catalog Card Number: 78-54127

Printed in the United States of America

printing number

1 2 3 4 5 6 7 8 9 10

Library of Congress Cataloging in Publication Data

Beyer, Janice M.
   Implementing change.

   Bibliography: p.
   Includes index.
   1. Alcoholism and employment--United States. 2. Civil
service--United States. 3. Alcoholism--Treatment--United
States. I. Trice, Harrison Miller   joint author.
II. Title.
JK850.A4B49   658.38'2   78-54127
ISBN 0-02-903460-4

TO THE MEMORY OF

RALPH "LEFTY" HENDERSON

Who Pioneered in Helping

Problem Drinkers in the Workplace

Contents

List of Figures

List of Tables

Acknowledgments

AS WE LOOK BACK on the research project described in this book we are impressed by the number of people who have contributed to its completion—if one can use such a final phrase about any research effort. Certainly one of the great joys, and occasionally one of the great frustrations, has been fitting the diverse skills and personalities of our co-workers into the research mosaic. There are very few persons who can contribute equally well across the entire range of such an effort. Nonreactive field interviewers, adroit at getting to respondents and securing their cooperation, are rarely equally skilled at telling the computer what to do. Even fewer can also take pencil in hand and write a readable account of results for the typist. Consequently we must acknowledge first the invaluable assistance of those who have "walked the long mile" with us, contributing in some fashion through much of this effort.

Because research on work organizations is impossible without unfettered access into them, we must first express our appreciation to Patricia Allen of the U.S. Civil Service Commission. Certainly there were others in the commission who gave us the formal "laying on of hands," but it was she who—to use a good sociological term—routinized our formal access. She contacted more than eighty-five installations (this includes pretest), explained what we wanted to do, and then set the stage for our contacting them; this was no mean feat. Also remarkable, she immediately grasped the reasons for our sampling design and never questioned the inconvenience of random sampling. Moreover, she remained our chief feedback contact as preliminary data emerged and as we increasingly faced demands by the world outside our ivory tower to know "what we had found." She remains in this role even at this moment, for we suspect that research of this type is never truly finished, and we certainly intend to continue with our analyses and with disseminating our results.

Picking up the contacts that Pat made for us, Cynthia Coppess arranged for our visits to the various federal installations in our sample and then traveled to many of our sample installations with her crews of trained interviewers. Her sense of logistics, of sensitive situations, and of timing got her teams where they were supposed to be, at the time they were to be there. We sustained our sample largely because of her diligence. Cindy began with us at the practical beginning of the project (after funding), and her contributions are evident not only in the quality of the fieldwork, including pretesting, but also in ideas and suggestions for items for our instruments, in her library research on the policies and on innovations in organizations, and later in her help with interpretation of results.

Although impending fatherhood kept Richard Hunt from the field experience until much later, he bore the brunt of initially managing the large amounts of data brought back from the field each week to Cornell. From the first, he was the data management specialist at Cornell. He took the major responsibility for supervising the arduous task of coding all of the data. Later he supervised and performed most of the data analyses in Ithaca. Through this whole, long process he patiently dealt with temporary coders, computer budgets, and the inevitable disappointments of runs that "bombed." He dignified the whole process by getting a Ph.D. out of it, and finally wrestled with the mundane, but necessary, problems of storing data for future reference. His good humor and indefatigability throughout helped make this book possible. He was especially valuable in contributing his ideas and knowledge about labor unions.

John M. Stevens performed many of these same functions in Buffalo. Although he joined the project later, he was the first to carve a Ph.D. from it, and he brought to the entire effort his strong dedication to research. Jack set up the data files at Buffalo and was especially important in refining our conceptualization and the data analyses that led to the construction of the scales that measure receptivity—a major emphasis in his dissertation. His comprehensive knowledge of the literature was often very helpful. He was a joy to work with, was always there when he was needed, and deserves substantial credit for his efforts.

Our efforts were also aided by those who were with us for shorter periods but nonetheless provided reliable and quality inputs. Jean Sparacin was as adroit with a respondent as with a codebook, and her care and intelligence gave a solid base to our statistical analyses. Pam Swieringa was far more than a typist; she was a highly skilled and sensitive person whose competence at arranging codebooks and being generally and intelligently helpful was unparalleled in our experience.

Peggy Bailey also began to work on the project immediately after funding. She was valuable in the early stages of the research, helping with instrument construction, pretesting, and the very early phases of fieldwork. She ended her work with us during the coding phase, applying the determined accuracy and intelligence of a fledgling lawyer to the coding of structural and census data. Jonathan Reader contributed his sophistication and experience with the federal sector to refining our instruments in the early stages. Linda Fischer on more than one occasion carried out "crisis missions" for us, making it possible for us to remain on schedule. Diana Barhyte gave us part of a summer and efficiently managed a field crew during the time of maximum data collection effort. Richard Katamay helped us with much-needed background library research. Mona Schonbrunn assisted with early data management. Gary Whaley ably performed later phases of data analysis at Buffalo. At the very end, Andrea Lodahl labored for weeks to produce a useful index. We are grateful to them all.

Undoubtedly the liveliest time during this research project was when we were in the field collecting data. We thoroughly enjoyed the experience, partially because of the remarkable cooperation of the federal managers and others with whom we made contact, but mostly because of the good humor, competence, and professional conduct of our interviewers. In addition to those already mentioned, we thank Michelle Lissner, Andy Bernstein, Hilda K. Meyers, and Allen Freedman for their conscientious and intelligent efforts. They cheerfully put up with horrible motel room décors (Cindy saw to it that rooms were otherwise quite livable considering the restrictions of state rates), met the dress and appearance requirements we had imposed with style and flair despite the hot summer weather and a continuous travel schedule, and generally were a pleasure to work with.

In addition to specific individuals, we also acknowledge the aid and support of organizations. The National Institute on Alcohol Abuse and Alcoholism provided us with a generous research grant (No. 5R01 AA00492), including a supplement when our traveling and personnel costs were the heaviest. The U.S. Civil Service Commission, through the cooperation of Harvey Rehn, Thomas T. Campagna, and especially Donald Phillips, provided formal background support. Our respective universities also deserve mention. Facilities for the project were originally provided by the Department of Organizational Behavior, School of Industrial and Labor Relations,

Cornell University, joined approximately a year later by the Department of Organizations and Human Resources, School of Management, State University of New York at Buffalo. We owe much to these groups for their administrative support and for the provision of other resources when money ran short. In addition, we have enjoyed the steady backup support of the Christopher D. Smithers Foundation and its generous president, R. Brinkley Smithers. His encouragement and support helped us deal with the numerous problems that could not be met by more bureaucratic means.

Many colleagues have supported us in various ways during the execution of this research, but some have made special contributions with their advice to us about specific issues or with their insightful comments on earlier drafts of the material presented. We would like to acknowledge the valuable advice of R. Danforth Ross, Richard Schoenherr, and Paul Lohnes on various methodological issues. Peter Feuille gave us helpful comments on chapter 1, and William Ouchi also gave us a telling comment on part of that chapter.

We also wish to thank our editors at Free Press—Robert Wallace, who encouraged us to begin the book, and Ron Chambers, whose help and continued encouragement enabled us to bring it to completion.

No acknowledgments would be complete without recognition of those who convert almost illegible scribbles into readable text. The patient typing and retyping of Patience Minor and Shirley Foster at Cornell, and Sabina Schneider and Jeanne Lewis at Buffalo helped to make this book possible.

We also want to thank our students, who responded positively when we exposed them to some of these findings in class and who bore patiently our short tempers as deadlines neared. They have respected our plight in trying to meet conflicting role demands, and perhaps this effort will somewhat justify any inconveniences and neglect that they may have suffered at our hands.

But our biggest debt we have reserved to the last. This is our acknowledgment of the tremendous cooperation we received from the federal managers who were involved in this study. Hundreds and hundreds of them received us warmly, cooperated with us fully and intelligently, and shared with us their personal experiences, feelings, and reactions. Other federal managers at various levels within the nine executive departments helped us gain access to specific installations or made a variety of other data available to us. We give them all our heartfelt thanks. Social science of the type reported here is highly dependent on such cooperation, and we hope that those who cooperated realize how important their help has been and will feel that the results of the study make their cooperation worthwhile.

These remarks would not be complete without our acknowledgment that our collaboration on this research brought us to a deeper personal collaboration. We cannot say that without the research, that outcome would not have been possible. But we do acknowledge that it provided the occasion, and for that we are most grateful.

Finally, we must admit that, even with all of this help, there are still certain to be shortcomings in what we have presented here. We must take the responsibility for any deficiencies that are found. We hope they are not so numerous as to outweigh what we believe will be positive contributions to the literatures on change in organizations and on occupational programming in the field of alcoholism.

Introduction

SOCIAL CHANGE HAS undoubtedly always been part of the human condition, but perhaps at no time in history so much as today has social change been engineered on such a massive scale. Much of the social change that occurs today is the result of deliberate attempts at change—attempts that involve many persons and that are legitimated and sanctioned by large segments of the society as at least intended to bring about desirable results in society. Many of these changes are legislated, and much of this legislation follows a strategy of involving existing formal organizations in the implementation of the desired change.

Examples abound. Head Start, occupational health and safety regulations, equal employment opportunity legislation, state legislation aimed at requiring basic competency levels for high school graduation, environmental protection legislation—these are just a few of the types of legislation that are intended to require or otherwise induce formal organizations within the society to adopt and implement various programs and policies designed to bring about social changes. Formal organizations that are on the receiving end of such legislation must find ways to implement it. Sometimes implementation is discretionary; sometimes it is mandated. Either way, it is the responsibility of those in the top administrative posts within these organizations to find ways to ensure that implementation occurs.

This is no easy task; the social science literature and common knowledge show that there are more instances of resistance to change efforts than of easy implementation. If organizational leaders are all too aware of resistance to change, policy makers often seem to be unaware of the same problems and frequently put the onus for any failure of implementation on the administrators of the programs. Administrators, on the other hand, may be only too happy to blame

1

the policy or program itself as basically defective in strategy, level of resources, or some other feature, when the desired changes fail to materialize.

Who is right? What can the social sciences contribute to our understanding of change, and how and why it is or is not implemented? How to deal with and to account for social change has been a pervasive concern in sociology and the other social sciences. In the applied fields of organizational behavior, public administration, management, and the policy sciences, there has also been concern with the problems of managing and encouraging innovation and change. Since change is endemic in present-day society—a constant, rather than an exceptional, occurrence—social scientists cannot claim any lack of the phenomenon to study. Despite the centrality and pervasiveness of the issues posed by change, there is little known about the processes by which change is deliberately brought about. Much past scholarly work has centered on the origins of change. It seems equally important to understand how change attempts are planned and implemented, how they are received, how they are resisted, and what factors contribute to success or failure of such attempts. The research reported in this book focuses on the implementation of legislative change within formal organizations and thus is a step in the direction of filling this gap in our knowledge.

Change is often the result of a problem that has been sensed by some interested parties,[1] who then advocate relevant legislation as a means to deal with the detected social problems. The interested parties and others then want to know how successful these laws have been in achieving the changes envisioned. Often evaluation of the changes is mandated by the same legislation that formally initiated them; sometimes the evaluation follows later. The research reported here has direct bearing on the process of evaluation of change efforts, for evaluation of outcomes means little without consideration of the implementation that produced the outcomes.

THE FOCUS OF THE BOOK

This book reports on a study of a legislated change effort. On December 31, 1970, the U.S. Congress passed the so-called Hughes Act (P.L. 91-616), which was concerned with setting up programs to deal with problems of alcoholism among employees of the federal government. The Civil Service Commission was delegated to oversee the implementation of these new programs and issued an insertion to the Federal Personnel Manual (FPM Letter No. 792-4) on July 7, 1971.

In 1972 Harrison M. Trice applied for and was awarded a research grant from the National Institute on Alcohol Abuse and Alcoholism to study this change effort. The study began in 1973. Janice M. Beyer, then a graduate student at Cornell, began work on the project almost immediately, first as a methodological consultant, but soon as a full-fledged collaborator.

Although alcoholism is a pervasive social problem in the United States and elsewhere, we recognized early that the effects of the provisions of the Hughes Act would not be immediate and that we could not expect full-fledged programs throughout the employing organizations of the executive departments such a short time after the initiation of the change. Also, there were no data indicating the pervasiveness of alcoholism-related problems among federal employees. If we accepted the most pessimistic estimates (which lack substantial empirical bases) of 6 to 8 percent of the working population as problem drinkers, and assumed that the rate would be similar for federal employees, the opportunities to use the provisions of programs designed to help such persons would still be severely limited by the relatively small number of employees likely to evidence need for the programs. In addition, the recency of the formulation of the program both limited the number of cases of alcoholism that could have been detected and suggested the possibility that the change would not be fully diffused, never mind implemented, through the relevant populations.

These considerations led us to two conclusions that affected our research design: (1) that we were dealing with a change that would be difficult to measure because of the infrequency with which the suggested new behaviors were called for, and (2) that we should focus on the entire process of the change, not just on the ultimate behaviors intended to deal with alcoholic employees. Thus we decided to focus on what we called the implementation process—those behaviors and other changes needed to bring about the changes envisioned by the legislation. This focus was made additionally attractive by our awareness that the implementation process had been neglected in past studies of change.

For this reason, it was not clear how our investigation would compare with past studies of change and innovation. It was clear that studies of innovation, especially those that had focused on innovation in formal organizations, would be relevant to this investigation. How relevant was not easy to determine. This innovation had unusual aspects, and it was not likely to directly affect all federal employees. Moreover, the impetus for the change did not occur within the organizations involved, as is typical of many studies of organizational innovation; instead, the change was mandated from outside the organizations we would be studying.

In addition, because of the formalistic nature of the alcoholism policy as it was diffused by the Civil Service Commission in compliance with the Hughes Act, we wondered if this change should be viewed as an issue of formalization rather than as one of innovation. After all, the strategies for bringing about these changes were also determined by those outside the implementing organization and formalized within a policy before the FPM letter was sent to any implementing organization. Thus the policy could be viewed as a type of control mechanism similar to the many other rules and regulations that are so common in government bureaucracies.

Despite our uncertainties about exactly how this type of change would operate within formal organizations, we made two basic decisions relevant to the research design: (1) that the focus would be on the entire implementation process within individual federal installations, and (2) that we would need to develop a model of this implementation process in order to measure the process itself. In developing this model, we would begin with models of innovation and change proposed by other writers.

The third basic decision that needed to be made about the research design concerned issues of sampling. Where were we going to measure the implementation process? From whom would we collect data? What behaviors were relevant to this process and therefore needed to be sampled? And, finally, would a sample of behaviors relevant to the implementation of this policy enable us to come to any conclusions about change in formal organizations?

We decided to undertake a comparative organizational study, with a relatively large number of different federal organizations in our sample so that we would be able to explore a variety of independent variables at the organizational level of measurement. We were also interested in how individuals implemented the policies. Here we identified three key roles relevant to the policy: the head or director of the installation, the coordinator appointed to implement the alcoholism program, and supervisors, who were in the best position to detect deteriorating job performance that was to be the occasion for the use of the policy as an intervention. The range of behaviors to be sampled would be dictated by the model of implementation that we would devise and also by a series of hypotheses we would develop about those factors that might be expected to influence either implementation or innovation in organizations. Most of these hypotheses would be based on the organizational literature or the literature on change and innovation. Finally, we would also sample from various common demographic and other variables that so often affect social science findings that they might be considered appropriate control variables.

The issue of the generality of our findings was the most difficult to resolve. Since we were unaware of any other studies of a comparable implementation process, we realized that all of our measurements of the implementation process—our dependent variable—would have to be devised from scratch. This circumstance suggested that we should be quite thorough in our attempts to measure implementation—that a few questions would not suffice, and we would have to collect quite a lot of data just about the implementation process itself. In addition, the organizational and innovation literatures suggest a large number of variables that might be expected to affect the diffusion, adoption, or use of these policies. These variables would also have to be measured. Thus, while it early occurred to us that it would be desirable to compare the implementation of this change with other changes that had occurred or were occurring in these organizations, it was also clear that we would not have the resources, nor would respondents be likely to be able to give us the time and cooperation, to study more than one additional change.

We then set about investigating other possible changes that we could study in these federal organizations. We early decided to use another change in policy that had been promulgated through the Civil Service Commission. This would control some of the possible sources of differences between the changes being compared. For the same reason, we also decided to choose a change that had been in effect for a somewhat similar period of time. But we wanted to study a change that would affect a larger number of employees in these federal installations, so that its measurement would yield a larger range of responses than we were likely to obtain for the alcoholism policy. We surveyed all portions of the Federal Personnel Manual that had been issued since 1970 and finally decided that we would use the equal employment opportunity policy as our comparison policy. This policy was designed to implement changes legislated through the passage of the Equal Employment Opportunity Act of 1972 (P.L. 92-261) and issued by the Civil Service Commission in FPM Letter No. 713-17, dated November 3, 1972.

Here was a policy that was clearly intended to be applicable to a greater number of federal employees. Its content and intent were controversial, like those of the alcoholism policy. It thus involved possible changes in norms and values within the employing organizations. In addition, it had certain formal prescriptions that were similar to the alcoholism policy, especially the designation of certain

functionaries to assist in implementation of the policies. These similarities would facilitate comparable measurements for the two policies, and yet the clear differences in content and breadth of the
policies would enable us to discover what factors were common to
implementation of both (and thus perhaps more general factors
related to change) and which were specific to each policy (and
therefore affected by policy content).

Having made these design decisions, we developed a general
model that would guide research efforts, given in figure I.1. In this
model the relevant legislation is seen as the precipitating event that
set in motion the implementation processes that were the focus of
this study. The impetus for change thus came from outside the
implementing organizations—in this case, individual government installations. Two other major components affecting the implementation process were identified from the literature. The first of these,
shown in the right-hand side of the figure, is the most obvious.
Certain members of the installations would be involved in behaving
relative to the formal prescriptions of the policies under study, and
their behaviors would or would not serve to implement these policies
as intended by the policy makers in Washington. Three important

Figure I.1.   Diagram of Overall Design of Study of Policy Implementation Within
Federal Installations.

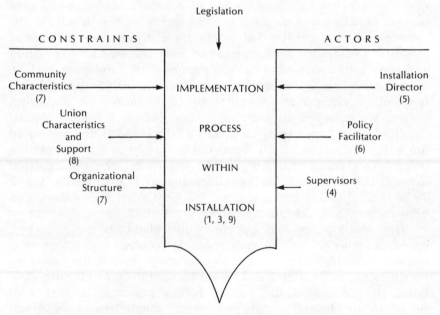

NOTE: Chapters of book focusing on each part of diagram are given in parentheses.

classes of actors were chosen for study: the installation director, who was responsible administratively for the overall functioning of that installation; the policy facilitator, who was supposed to be appointed to lead and assist others in the implementation of a given policy; and the supervisors, whose role was crucial if the provisions of these policies were going to be applied to employees in the installation.[2] Also, three classes of factors that might be expected to affect the behaviors of actors seeking to implement the policy within these installations were identified from the organizational literature and our knowledge of the policies. The first of these—community charac-teristics—might be expected to affect implementation in at least three ways: (1) through community norms and values that would be favorable or not to the content of the policies; (2) through the personnel and other resources the community provided that were needed to implement the policies; and (3) through the demand for implementation of the policies generated by these above factors and by the characteristics of the work force coming from that community. Unions, when present, are always crucial to the implementation of personnel policies. Local unions can act to support or interfere with the implementation of such changes. We knew that unionization was relatively new in many federal government installations and suspected that unions might vary widely in their power and effectiveness as agents representing employee interests. But, where present, unions certainly had the potential to affect how these policies were implemented. Finally, the structure of organizations has been widely investigated as a constraint on organizational change and innovation. Many research studies have found relationships between the adoption of change and various structural attributes in organizations. An organization's structure can be viewed as providing both opportunities and constraints that set limits on the range of behaviors of individual actors involved in implementing change.

The systematic consideration of all of these elements relative to the implementation of the two policies under study became the overall objective of this research. In keeping with the general systems framework that guides much of the research in organizations today, we expected that these elements would interact to affect the implementation process. In the chapters that follow, we shall focus on research results relevant to each of these elements, as indicated by the chapter numbers given in figure I.1.

But we must first examine the change process in more detail and then focus specifically on the elements of the implementation phase of change. These tasks are undertaken in chapters 1 and 3. Chapter 2 sets the stage for presentations of research results by outlining the methods and procedures used in carrying out the study.

LACK OF RESEARCH ON IMPLEMENTATION

The processes by which policy innovations and changes become operational has received less empirical attention than commonly is asserted in much of the relevant literature. Although some writers conclude that "the stage of implementation, the actual mechanics of managing the changes . . . has been the subject of another large body of literature" (Zaltman et al., 1973:59), much of the literature they cite is opinion and impressionistic rather than data-based (Kahn, 1974). This is especially true of the literature on what is called "organizational development." Moreover, more attention has been given to how changes are initiated than to the processes and mechanisms involved in actually putting them into place.[3] One classic treatment (Lippitt et al., 1958) gives only brief attention to the implementation process. Others offer opinions about what they believe should be involved, yet present no data to support the opinions (Bennis, 1966). Although there are exceptions (Greiner, 1967; Gross et al., 1971; Berman and McLaughlin, 1975a, 1975b; Schultz and Slevin, 1975b), the emphasis in studying implementation of change in organizations has been upon subjective experience of change agents or upon advocating particular change philosophies. Only infrequently are hypotheses about implementation tested or theoretical proposals put forward for testing. More often, the process is reduced to a single problem, namely overcoming initial resistance to change by organizational members. Many of these treatments rely heavily on the Lewin (1947a, 1947b) formulation of unfreezing past behaviors and attitudes, changing behaviors, and then refreezing so that new behaviors will persist—a conceptualization that remains "not only unelaborated and untested, but really unused" (Kahn, 1974). Sensitivity or T-group training is often recommended and used for altering resistance to change (unfreezing) and encouraging problem-solving orientations and cooperative behavior seen as facilitating change efforts (Argyris, 1962; Argyle, 1967; Bennis, 1966). Such singularity of focus tends to ignore the numerous factors within an organization that are outside individual resistance to change, particularly structured factors like resources, slack, and existing role demands. Until very recently the social science research community has largely overlooked the processes involved in putting a new policy or program into operation (Williams, 1971). Moreover, program analysts in complex bureaucratic structures have also ignored, or treated lightly, how policy changes and innovations will be put into effect (Etzioni, 1976).

Fortunately, there is a current trend in conceptual treatments, at least, to incorporate implementation processes into the general innovation process, usually as one of three stages (Hage and Aiken, 1970; Zaltman et al., 1973): ideas enter the organization and are considered, adoption decisions are made, and implementation occurs. According to such models of innovation, the implementation process should receive as much research attention as the idea and adoption stages. An example of this awareness is the work of Pressman and Wildavsky (1973), which concentrates the conceptual analysis of processes designed to carry out policy innovations. Another example is Bunker (1972), who focuses on the power and influence processes involved in implementation strategies. Two other approaches to the implementation of public policy should be mentioned: Bardach's analysis of the implementation process as "the playing out of a number of loosely interrelated games" (1977:57- 58), and a conceptual framework by Van Meter and Van Horn (1975).

However, as Kahn so aptly puts it, "the mill of science grinds only when hypotheses and data are in continuous and abrasive contact" (1974:487). Unfortunately, the empirical literature on the implementation of change is still small. A relatively quantitative and comprehensive study was done by Kaplan (1967), who investigated actual changes occurring in forty-two welfare agencies over a ten-year period. While Sapolsky (1967) is often cited as an empirical study of implementation, this study is of limited generality because of the impressionistic nature of the data and, more important, because it is not clear that the changes studied were ever adopted and intended to be implemented by upper management (Sapolsky, 1967:507). Hage and Aiken (1970) interpret their results on social service agencies in terms of implementation (for example, on pages 37, 44, 52, 57, and 101) but have actually studied "program change," which is measured in terms of whether or not new programs were begun and the rates at which they were begun. Thus their study is more appropriately viewed as one of the adoption, rather than the implementation, of change. Two other case studies can be mentioned. Gross, Giacquinta, and Bernstein (1971) focused exclusively on the implementation of innovation in a single school, and Pressman and Wildavsky (1973) reported on a case of failure of an innovation under organizational circumstances of support.

The most notable exception in the recent literature is a study of educational change carried out by the Rand Corporation (Berman and McLaughlin, 1975a, 1975b; Berman and Pauly, 1975; Greenwood et al., 1975). This study collected empirical data by both survey and case study methods on several different innovative programs in a large sample of schools and districts. Furthermore, the study team developed a rather comprehensive and sophisticated model of the implementation process (Berman and McLaughlin, 1975a:19), including for investigation various levels of actors and constraints from both inside and outside the school organizations studied.[4]

Also relevant are the studies of the implementation of operations research—a managerial technique plagued with problems of adoption and implementation. However, the same lacks have tended to occur in this literature in the past—more impressionistic reporting and conceptualization than empirical data (Malcolm, 1965). But a volume of papers presented at a recent conference (Schultz and Slevin, 1975b) illustrates a recent trend to remedy the paucity of empirical data in this field: while seven papers are purely conceptual, eight others are research papers with quantified, systematic data collected relevant to specified models of the implementation process. These models vary in their inclusiveness and generality for other change processes. Also, when the eight empirical papers are assessed, only four deal with actual behaviors involved in implementation; the others use subjective measures of intention or willingness to adopt or use, or focus on the researcher rather than client behaviors (Schultz and Slevin, 1975b:16-17).

Moreover, recent trends in evaluative research underscore the mounting emphasis on including implementation in assessing policy and program effectiveness. For example, Bernstein and Freeman (1975) document increasing attention among evaluative researchers to "process evaluation" as well as to outcome assessments.

Turning to the literature on the specific changes that are the focus of this study, we found little of relevance to this research. We did not locate any empirical studies of the implementation of the Equal Employment Opportunity (EEO) or Affirmative Action programs, although journalistic accounts are plentiful. While some studies of the outcomes of job-based alcoholism policies have appeared, they have largely ignored the implementation phase despite the relatively early identification of the "policy-practice gap" in this field (Trice and Belasco, 1965:37). One exception in this literature uses a randomized four-way design to study the training of work supervisors about alcoholic and other problem employees, focusing upon what types of information diffusion produced attitudes and behavior most consistent with an alcoholism policy (Trice and Belasco, 1968; Belasco and Trice, 1969). Since the preparation of key personnel such as supervisors for understanding the innovation and their role in it is clearly a facet of implementation, this study is one data-based effort directed toward policy implementation in the occupational alcoholism field.

Why the relative neglect of implementation processes? Although systematic data are not available to answer this question, some speculations seem reasonable. The predominance of the goal attainment model in assessing organizational effectiveness probably accounts for a sizable amount of the neglect. Such an orientation tends to focus attention on outcomes of collective effort rather than upon mounting the effort in the first place. Reinforcing this emphasis is a larger societal emphasis upon pragmatism and "getting results." Thus, in the evaluative research field, the focus has remained on the goal attainment model despite the appearance and obvious need of other approaches (Trice and Roman, 1973). Apparently a focus upon the outcomes of innovations is more simple, straightforward, and obvious than one upon the processes that supposedly brought them about. Furthermore, efforts to study implementation require an examination of the complex process of organizational behavior, and it is easier to concentrate on measuring the concrete outcomes of these processes than to try to measure the processes themselves. This is because outcomes look seductively simple and provide "hard" measures; processes are obviously complex and require approaches to measurement that are "soft."

NEED FOR ASSESSMENT OF IMPLEMENTATION

Gross, Giacquinta, and Bernstein concluded from their research on the implementation of educational innovations in a ghetto school: "The major implication of our inquiry for educators and social scientists who conduct evaluative studies is that it underscores the need to ascertain whether the innovation under examination has in fact been implemented before they attempt to make assessments about its effects" (1971:206- 207). Bernstein and Freeman (1975) conducted a study of 236 federally funded evaluative studies. Based on their data, they believe that reasons for analyzing implementation processes are obvious: "It is critical to know that what presumably was paid for or deemed desirable was actually undertaken" (1975:19). That is, assessment of these processes provide data on the extent to which an innovation goes forward as designed. Moreover, initial acceptance, even optimistic and enthusiastic acceptance of an innovation at first introduction, fails to ensure implementation of organizational change. Other processes either emerge to carry the change into operation or they fail to materialize, leaving initial acceptance but nothing else. Thus the focus of many past studies on the adoption of innovation failed to illuminate whether the innovation involved has ever had the chance to create the outcomes envisioned in its adoption.

Furthermore, data on the outcomes of innovative policies need to be interpreted in the light of information about the extent and effectiveness of the implementation process. It may well be that outcomes from innovative policies may be directly related to processes present in attempting to implement. For example, in the implementation of alcoholism policies in work organizations, selective factors may operate that bring the most responsive employees into the program, producing a very high outcome. Or, alternatively, the strategy in the policy may be largely bypassed, causing the problem-drinking employee to be rushed into treatment rather than processed under the strategy known as constructive confrontation. This, of course, will also affect desired outcomes.

Another reason why it is necessary to assess the implements available to execute policy innovations such as the EEO and alcoholism policies studied here is that original program goals are typically unstable. The entire program may "slither out of carefully constructed categories" (Weiss, 1972:33). To overcome these tendencies, organizational changes need regular and prudent scrutiny of the processes and implements used, and available for use, in carrying out original intents and strategies. This is especially true of a policy such as the federal alcoholism one. This point is graphically portrayed by a federal manager who fell into our sample. He described the policy as an "infinitesimal speck in a bureaucratic cosmos buried on a supervisor's desk." He was angry that the policy had so little chance of intervention impact, so little chance of competing with the swarm of other formal norms for behavior that surround the supervisor—unless it received the attention, administrative support, and other resources for careful, thorough implementation.

QUESTIONS ADDRESSED

To summarize, our research differed from most of the past studies of change and innovation in three ways:

1. The research focused on a deliberate and planned change rather than a spontaneous or relatively unplanned change.

2. The changes studied were mandated by legislation and thus by elements outside the formal organizations in which they were to be implemented. This meant that the adoption and presumably the implementation of these changes were not a matter of discretion for the organizations involved. This nondiscretionary aspect differs from much of the research on organizational innovation, which has tended to focus on instances when the changes themselves or at least the decisions to adopt specific changes were internally generated.

3. This study focused on the implementation process, whereas most past studies of change and innovation have dealt with the adoption, diffusion, or evaluation of outcomes of change efforts. Because the changes studied were designed to be implemented by formal organizations, the theoretical and conceptual approaches de-

veloped for the study of formal organizations would be available to guide the study, as well as the wealth of past empirical findings from studies of other aspects of the change process in organizations.

The organizational literature is replete with suggestions that bureaucracies are not well adapted to change because of internal rigidities (Burns and Stalker, 1961; Bennis, 1966; Victor A. Thompson, 1969). Government bureaucracies are often considered to be among the most rigid and resistant to change. Since this study deals with organizations within the U.S. federal government, it will focus upon a sector of American society that might be expected to manifest significant barriers to the change processes envisioned in the policies under the study. Through this study we hoped to be able to provide at least partial answers to such questions as:

1. How can the change process within formal organizations be delineated and described?
2. What are the barriers to change within formal organizations?
3. What characterizes a successful change effort?

Another unique feature of this research is that it was designed to *compare* the implementation of *two* policies within federal government installations. We did not attempt to assess outcomes—that is, whether or not these policies actually succeeded in solving or ameliorating the problems they were designed to attack—but instead attempted to discover the degree to which these policies were actually implemented in the organizations studied, and how this implementation varied according to the following factors:

1. Characteristics of incumbents of key roles within the organizations
2. Organizational supports provided to these roles
3. Structural characteristics of the organization
4. The characteristics of the communities in which the organizations were located
5. Pressures from local unions

The study thus investigated possible psychological, social role, social structure, environmental, and interorganizational correlates of the implementation process.

ORGANIZATION OF THE BOOK

The first chapter presents a general model of the change process, identifies some relevant dimensions of change, and then relates these to the two policies studied. Further history and description of the two policies are also presented.

Chapter 2 presents the research design in more detail and deals with issues of sampling, data collection, statistics, measurement, scaling, reliability, and validity.

Chapter 3 returns to a portion of the model of change presented in chapter 1 and further develops that portion of the model relevant to the implementation process. Three stages of implementation are identified. Using data from supervisors on the two policies, path analysis is used to assess the viability and strength of the three-stage model of implementation used.

Chapter 4 further explores the data from supervisors, first presenting data that indicate the general levels of implementation characteristic of each of these policies across all of the installations. Next, hypotheses are advanced and tested about factors expected to affect implementation of these policies by individual supervisors. Factors considered include individual characteristics and attitudes of supervisors, characteristics of their supervisory roles, and characteristics of the organizations in which they work. Similarities and differences between findings for the two policies are discussed.

Chapter 5 follows a similar approach in assessing the role of the directors of the installations in the implementation of these policies. First, general attitudes and levels of implementation as reported by directors are described for all installations; then, specific hypotheses are tested to expose factors facilitating or inhibiting policy implementation.

In chapter 6 the roles of the two policy coordinators are analyzed and discussed. This role analysis first defines their role as internal change agents crucial to the implementation process and then analyzes their connections with other relevant roles. Five basic elements of their role are identified and explored for both the alcoholism coordinators and EEO functionaries. The coordinators are then compared with supervisors along a variety of dimensions: individual characteristics, relevant attitudes, and organizational locations. Other factors investigated include segmentation of the role, formalization, work overload, resources, and organizational size.

Chapter 7 presents data at the organizational level of analysis. Initially, the organizational and environmental characteristics of the seventy-one federal installations we studied are presented and discussed. Hypotheses are then advanced and tested for organizational and environmental factors expected to influence the implementation process.

In chapter 8 we move into the area of interorganizational relations. The impact of the public sector unions present in these installations on the implementation of these two policies is investigated. The supervisor's awareness of the union and the activities of the union are investigated as factors affecting the implementation process.

Chapter 9 brings together the findings of the previous chapters, identifying common themes in the findings and tying them to the original models of implementation and change presented in the first chapters. An exploration of the Mertonian paradigm of adaptation (Merton, 1938) is then applied to the data on implementation. Organizations that are conformists relative to the policy prescriptions and those that deviate in some sense are identified. Discriminant analysis is then employed to identify factors that distinguish each of the deviant types from each other and from the conformist installations. Finally, the relevance and importance of the findings of this study for the issues of evaluation of change efforts are discussed.

An Appendix is included to give details of how the variables used in this study were measured. The wording of the items in questionnaires or other pertinent specifics of operationalizations are given, as well as procedures and statistics relevant to combining single items into scales.

Before proceeding to report on our findings, we would like to remind readers that our data was collected during the spring, summer, and early fall of 1974. The formal policies studied were only three years old (less in the case of the EEO policy) at that time. Our results are therefore most appropriately considered as applicable to relatively early stages of change efforts of this scope. We do not expect that the levels of implementation that we describe in this book still characterize the federal installations studied. Many events have occurred in the federal government and wider society in the time interval between when we collected the data and publication of this book. The time lag was necessitated by the usual tasks of social science research—organizing and coding data, analysis and interpretation, and finally the difficult task of writing this report and others. During this interval we provided feedback to the Civil Service Commission, the U.S. Congress, and others on the preliminary results of this research. We are unable to comment with any authority on the effects of this feedback on the system we studied or on the shape that any resultant changes may have taken, but we hope that they and other factors have produced improvements.

Because of the complexity of the issues under study, we have treated many different types of variables in this book. Our general analytical strategy was to employ multivariate techniques of analysis whenever possible so that the unique effects of variables could be assessed. Our choice of variables was guided by the existing literature on change and innovation, by the organizational literature, and by the knowledge we gleaned from initial contacts with the organizations studied. We tried to design our research so that the results would be meaningful both theoretically and practically. This is also our aim in writing this book.

1. The Policies as Processes of Organizational Change

CHANGE IN FORMAL ORGANIZATIONS

WITH THE ADOPTION of the open systems perspective, organizational change has come to be accepted as part of the everyday state of organizations. Organizations are currently conceptualized as ongoing systems responding to and interacting with an active environment. Within system boundaries, other levels of interaction create internal pressures toward change. In surviving organizational systems, these processes produce a dynamic equilibrium in which adaptive mechanisms arise to deal with the continually changing demands made on the system.

Kast and Rosenzweig list six sources of the impetus to change within organizations: the environment, goals and values, the technical system, the structural system, the psychosocial system, and the managerial system (1974:575–78). From this perspective, change is seen as the result of forces that can emerge from any element or variable defined as relevant to the study of organizations.

Despite the pervasiveness of change in organizations, the terminology for discussing change has not been standardized. Consequently, the meaning of terms is ambiguous, and it is frequently hard to know if different authors and researchers are discussing the same or different phenomena. For example, we have used the term "adaptive" in the first paragraph to refer to changes made by an organizational system in order to survive in a changing environment and under changing internal pressures or demands. The term "adaptation" has become popular with the systems view of organizations, but authors also refer to organizational "change." It is hard to

16

discern how large a change must be before it is organizational change and not organizational adaptation. Or perhaps the magnitude of the change has nothing to do with differential use of the terms and they are interchangeable. This might resolve the issue, except that there is another term in wide use: organizational "innovation." Although there seems to be an underlying dimension of size or magnitude defining some boundary between change and adaptation, the dimension underlying the difference between innovation and change appears to be novelty versus routineness. It is also possible to fit all three terms along that one dimension, with adaptation referring to a routine change, innovation referring to a really novel change, and change itself somewhere in the middle. Alternatively, organizational change may encompass both innovation and adaptation, which represent only subsets of change: the novel and routine instances, respectively.

All of the above possibilities seem almost equally plausible, given the use of these terms in the literature. But none of the "solutions" presented above is really satisfactory. Each term has a range of meanings and connotations associated with it that the "solutions" fail to capture. It seems that the dimensions of organizational change must be identified before we can decide on a more precise use of terms. Some dimensions seem implicit in past use of different terms, but comparison of theoretical and empirical findings has been hampered by the lack of a consistent and precise terminology based on explicitly defined dimensions for discussing the concept of organizational change.

DIMENSIONS OF CHANGE

Various attempts have been made to define types of change or innovation in organizations. Rogers and Shoemaker (1971:8-9), for example, proposed a typology based on where the recognition of the need for change occurred and where the new ideas for change originated. Either of these dimensions is classified as internal or external to the social system in which the change occurs, leading to a fourfold typology with four categories of change. Although this is an interesting way to categorize change, their typology does not address the kinds of dimensions of change identified above as perhaps determining the differential use of terms. What they have done is categorize changes on the basis of the location of key behaviors early in the change process.

The same authors have identified five attributes of innovations: relative advantage, compatibility, complexity, triability, and observability (Rogers and Shoemaker, 1971:137- 72). Zaltman et al. (1973:32- 45) have extended this list to nineteen attributes. Have-lock (1970) identified three attributes related to the communicabil-ity of an innovation: complexity, visibility, and demonstrability. As the term "attribute" implies, all of these are lists of characteristics of an object or thing—for example, a new seed, drug, device, practice, program, product, or technology. These lists of attributes describe something about a thing called an innovation,[1] which is then related to individual, organizational, or other characteristics and behaviors.

From the beginning of this study, our interest was in behaviors involved in a change process. None of the approaches already dis-cussed seemed to illuminate our attempts to grapple with the differ-ences between the changes embodied in the two policies we intended to study. Eventually it became evident that one problem with the categories already developed was that they were not descriptive of behaviors involved in the change process. Also, they described rela-tively peripheral aspects of change and innovation—characteristics that might have implications for behavior in dealing with the change or innovation but that somehow did not address the central issue of how much of a change (or how much of an innovation) was involved. What we needed for this study were dimensions along which we could characterize the intrinsic quality or nature of the process involved in the change effort.

We were thus forced to identify for ourselves some dimensions of the behaviors involved in a change process. We quite easily identified four: pervasiveness, magnitude, innovativeness, and duration.[2] These dimensions are intended to measure change as a process rather than to characterize some object involved in a process.[3]

Pervasiveness of a change process can be defined as the propor-tion of total behaviors occurring within an organization[4] that will be affected by the change. This proportion will be determined by at least two factors: how many persons within the organization are expected to change their behaviors because of the change, and how frequently or how much of the time these involved persons will be behaving in new ways. A possible measure of this dimension would be the number of persons in the organization involved in the change process multiplied by the proportion of their time involved in activi-ties affected by the change process. Such an approach could be as useful in studying the adoption of a new procedure in a hospital, or the use of a new computer system, as it would be in differentiating between the two policies studied here.

The second dimension is magnitude, which can be defined as the degree of displacement of existing organizational states that the change will entail. Various aspects of ongoing organizational life may be more or less displaced, including member attitudes, member behaviors, structural arrangements, and allocations of resources. A good way to measure magnitude of change is to assess the costs involved in the change as reflecting displacement. What personal or organizational resources will have to be reallocated? What new resources will have to be generated? What past advantages will be lost versus gains to be expected? How much will attitudes have to change to be consonant with new behaviors expected?

Innovativeness can be defined as the degree to which past behaviors provide routines or programs useful in the change process. Such routines or programs may be part of the individual organizational member's repertoire, or they may be stored in collective memories, that is, stored in files of the organization or available from other persons or organizations in the environment.[5] Clearly, the implementation of even a massive change (in terms of both magnitude and pervasiveness)—for example, a change in operating technology such as a new process for making steel—will be easier if the firm involved can profit from the experiences of other firms who have adopted the same or a similar technology in the past than if it is the first adopter of this technology. It will be still easier if the adopting organization belongs to a corporate group where the change has been implemented elsewhere in the overall organization and the information about past adoption and implementation efforts are available through organizational channels. This is true whether past efforts were successful or unsuccessful. On the other hand, the adoption of even a small change—such as a new tax form for the personnel department—will be highly innovative if forms have never been used before in that organization and if organizational members have never even encountered the use of forms to record such information; such a situation could occur in attempts to transplant administrative technologies to developing nations. Other changes may be quite routine; they are similar to past changes, and programs and solutions already used can be adapted readily to the new change. An example of this is personnel changes. In most organizations, routines and solutions exist for the bulk of changes of personnel, including training and various initiation activities and ceremonies. Such changes can be considered routine until they involve a new job description, a level of responsibility that has implications for many participants, or a new type of organizational member, since all of these additional elements tend to make past solutions and programs less applicable to the induction of the new member.

The fourth dimension of change is its intended duration, which can be defined as the period of time to which the change is applicable and intended to persist. Some changes that occur in organizations are temporary, either responses to events viewed as cyclical or responses to emergencies that are seen as unusual, must be coped with, but are not likely to occur in the same way again. In such instances the organization intends to return to previous patterns of behavior after the particular occasion to use the focal change has passed. The heavy snows, cold weather, and fuel shortages of the winter of 1976-1977 entailed such temporary changes for many organizations. In other circumstances, organizations make changes that they intend to be permanent into the foreseeable future; that is, they do not intend to return to previous practice, and the particular change instituted will direct future courses of action until another change is deemed necessary. Thus, many organizations have instituted energy conservation programs that are presumably intended to respond to the "energy crisis" and accompanying higher energy costs on a continuing basis.

ROUTINIZATION OF CHANGE

If organizational change is a regular part of ongoing organizational life, then organizations must find ways to make such changes part of ongoing processes; change must be somehow converted from the exceptional to the everyday. Individual changes must be routinized as they are incorporated into organizational life.

How is this done? Organizations have both formal and informal means at their disposal to achieve organizational control, including control over change processes. Since organizations are purposive systems, members tend to initiate or respond to various changes with some intent or goal, which must then be translated into means for action. A common mechanism for the translation of social or organizational goals into procedures for the realization of those goals is the use of policy.

Policy thus often becomes the interface between various organizational or social goals and the prescribed means to those goals. It is a formalized mechanism by which organizational change ideally can be initiated, implemented, and routinized. However, actual attempts to implement policy can elicit various kinds of responses, identified by Merton (1938) as modes of social adaptation: Members of the organization can conform to policy, accepting the goals and complying with the prescribed means, or they can fall short of conformity by failing to accept the goals and/or the means of the policy. Innovators will devise new means that they feel are better suited to accomplish policy goals. Ritualists will comply with prescribed means with little attention to whether this meets policy goals. Rebels will formulate alternative goals and means. Retreatists will try to ignore the whole thing.

Considering the implementation of policy in terms of both means and ends does two things:[6] (1) it provides a method by which the completeness of implementation of a given policy can be assessed, and (2) it provides a way to distinguish between various kinds of incompleteness. In some cases, the ends of policy will not be met even though prescribed means have been followed. In other cases, the desired ends may be reached by locally invented means, and thus the prescribed means will be missing. Although implementation may technically be incomplete in both instances, the overall effect of the policy will be very different in these two examples, and it would be still different if the other types of responses envisioned by Merton occurred instead.

Kelman's (1961) approach to the processes of opinion change can also be applied to the behavioral changes dictated by policy. He identified three processes of social influence—compliance, identification, and internalization—and then specified both antecedents and consequents for these processes. The primary distinctions in his model concern the issues of whether changes are externally induced and enforced (compliance), incorporated into role behaviors and expectations that are highly salient to the actor (identification), or incorporated into some changes of values and perceptions of the actor (internalization). Mere compliance could lead to ritualization, in Merton's terms, while identification and internalization would lead to either conformity or innovation. Internalization is most likely to lead to innovative behavior, because it involves the reorganization of means-ends frameworks, which may lead, in turn, to the adoption by the innovator of means that he decides are better suited to the ends than those prescribed, as mentioned above. Merton's most deviant types—the retreatists and rebels—are examples of unsuccessful attempts of social influence, which Kelman does not treat.

A MODEL OF THE CHANGE PROCESS

Table 1.1 presents our view of the stages in a completed change process. This model does not present any startling or new approach toward change, but is instead an attempt to synthesize the elements of a variety of approaches to change found in the literatures on innovation (Smith and Kaluzny, 1975; Zaltman et al., 1973), on policy formulation (Dror, 1968), on organizational change (Hage and Aiken, 1970), or on planning and decision making in organizations (Kast and Rosenzweig, 1974:356- 464). The brief explication of the

Table 1.1
Necessary Stages in a Completed Change
Process Within a Purposive System

1. Sensing of Unsatisfied Demands on the System

Some part of system receives information indicating a problem or potential problem with organizational functioning. For example, some part of the system becomes internally imbalanced, subsystem relations become imbalanced, new demands are made on the system, or the relation between inputs and outputs is unfavorable.

2. Search for Possible Responses

Elements in the system consciously or unconsciously set about finding alternative ways of dealing with the issues sensed in the previous step. Alternatives can involve programs that are preexisting, are readily available, are located with difficulty, or must be invented.

3. Evaluation of Alternatives

A comparison is made between desired outcomes, probable outcomes of alternatives located, and costs. Probabilities are derived for alternative actions (means) leading to desired outcomes (goals). The values of outcomes are more or less explicitly assessed relative to systems of values. Costs of means are also assessed relative to systems of values.

4. Decision to Adopt Course of Action

An alternative is chosen from among those evaluated. Goals, operative goals, and means are more or less specified, i.e., a strategy for dealing with the demands is adopted.

5. Initiation of Action Within the System

A policy or other directive for implementing the change is formulated. This involves a choice of tactics based on the strategy already chosen. The initial diffusion of information about the change takes place within the system. This information is more or less explicit about the policy or directives that have been developed, the demands that have made the change desirable, the connection between desired outcomes or goals and the means prescribed, and the general rationale behind the strategies and tactics chosen to implement the change.

Table 1.1 (Continued)

6. Implementation of the Change

Further information is diffused to all involved members. Resources are allocated toward implementation efforts, e.g., training, hiring, new equipment, reallocation of time. Attitudinal reactions occur relative to prescribed means, including changes in role expectations and definitions. Role behaviors change as specified, i.e., compliance with prescribed means occurs.

7. Institutionalization of the Change

Attitudinal reactions toward goals occur relative to values held. Values are modified to accept goals. Goals are internalized into modified value system.

stages is intended to highlight the distinction between goals and means, and the interaction of both with values. The model thus encourages consideration of the approaches of both Merton (1938) and Kelman (1961) to the change process.

Most of the models of the innovation process that have been advanced by writers have included a series of stages or steps.[7] Perhaps the most widely used approach to change in organizations is that originally advanced by Lewin (1947a, 1947b) and later elaborated by Schein (1964) and others. This model seems best suited to the executors and initiators of change processes and has thus been used most extensively by practitioners and researchers concerned with organizational development. It emphasizes the forces resisting change efforts and specifies three stages: (1) unfreezing of past behaviors and attitudes through the introduction of some disequilibrium into the present stable equilibrium; (2) changing by exposure to new information, attitudes, and theories; and (3) refreezing through processes of reinforcement, confirmation, and support for the change (Sorenson and Zand, 1975:217).

While this approach was not consciously used in the formulation of the model presented here, some correspondences can be noted. The unfreezing stage suggests stage 1 of our model, although the application of the Lewin model usually involves a change agent who deliberately introduces disturbance into the system, while our approach implies that the disturbance may arise from a wide variety of sources. Their second stage—the change stage—seems to incorporate elements of our model's stages 2-6, but without clear specification of details of how the change is brought about, and especially without the same emphasis on conscious decisions to adopt the change. The Lewin model thus seems to emphasize a more emergent, evolving process of attitudinal and behavioral changes—a model well suited to the practices of external change consultants, but one that seems less applicable to other types of change, including the use of policy. The final stage of the Lewin model clearly corresponds to the final stage on our model.

More recently, writers have advanced models that emphasize the more deliberate and rational aspects of innovation and change. For example, Smith and Kaluzny (1975) proposed a four-stage model of innovation: recognition, initiation, implementation, and institutionalization. The stages of their model correspond to stages 1, 5, 6, and 7 of our model. In a similar vein, Hage and Aiken (1970) identified four stages in the change process in their work: evaluation, initiation, implementation, and routinization, corresponding to our stages 3, 5, 6, and 7. In the most recent attempt of this kind, Berman and McLaughlin (1975a) focus on the implementation stage and suggest a three-stage process of innovation: support, implementation, and incorporation. Their description of the support stage includes stages 3- 5 of our model, and their later stages correspond to our stages 6 and 7.

In the most complete model to date Zaltman et al. (1973) suggested a two-stage model, with substages specified within the major stages.[8] The two major stages in this model are the initiation stage and the implementation stage. Their initiation stage includes three substages: the knowledge-awareness substage (corresponding somewhat to our stages 1 and 2), the formation of attitudes toward the innovation substage (which would be incorporated in our stage 3 along with attitudes toward other alternatives), and the decision substage (our stage 4). Their implementation stage includes two substages: the initial implementation substage and the continued-sustained substage. These correspond roughly to stages 6 and 7 on our model, except that the approach of Zaltman and his associates makes special provision for innovations that are given a first, trial implementation to determine whether additional implementation will occur.

We agree that initial implementation efforts may be seen as a trial by organizational participants, and their failure will probably lead to termination of the change effort. However, other alternatives are possible as a result of the feedback from early efforts at implementation of a change, or indeed from feedback from such efforts at any point in time. In our view, effects of the implementation are better seen as providing feedback that can have a range of results, including

continued implementation and movement into the institutionalization stage of our model, or the stimulation of a recycling back to
some earlier stage, which might then involve a decision to terminate
or a decision to modify the change. We thus present our stages
without the usual arrows implying a step-by-step and uninterrupted
progression. It seems clear to us that the process of change is not
such a clear-cut and linear process and that it is better to consider
stages as alternative types of behavior to which the organization and
individual decision makers within it will turn as they feel it is
appropriate or necessary. In a sense, then, no change process is ever
completed for all time, since decisions made at earlier times are
always open to reconsideration. Such a model of change seems more
appropriate to the idea of organizations as open systems, needing
both adaptive and maintenance mechanisms (Kast and Rosenzweig,
1974:117).

It is clear from this brief summary that some models of change
tend to stress the later stages of the model we have advanced, while
the earlier steps in our model are skipped over or defined as outside
the change process. While this is less true of the model offered by
Zaltman and his associates, it does not treat the early stages of the
innovation in quite as general terms as we have used. Part of the
reason for this is that they limit their perspective to cases where the
organization senses a performance gap, and thus they ignore the
change mandated from outside the organization. In order to find
models relevant to the decision-making processes that better characterize the early stages on an organizational change, we turned to the
literature on policy formulation and on decision making in
organizations.

Dror (1968) presented an extensive analysis of various models of
decision making as applied to public policy making and incorporated
what he considers the best features of each into what he calls an
"optimal model." His model has eighteen phases, broken up into
three major stages: meta-policy making, policy making, and post-
policy making. The first stage is really concerned with the process of
establishing policy making on policy making, and thus has no coun-
terpart in our model. What is notable about this stage is the emphasis
that Dror puts on values, as well as upon problems, resources, and
strategy. His second stage corresponds, with more detail, to our
stages 2–4; in this policy-making stage are included the establishment
of goals, the search for alternatives and their evaluation, and the
choice between alternatives. The last stage of the Dror model corresponds best to our stages 5 and 6 but has a somewhat different
emphasis. Dror refers to "motivating the execution of the policy,"
which places more emphasis on the use of techniques of influence

than is suggested in our model. Finally, he suggests an evaluation of the policy making after policy execution and also suggests a fourth separate phase that includes provision for a feedback effort to interconnect all phases. We have suggested that recycling through stages is likely whenever unsatisfied demands are sensed within the system, but we have not specified the necessary formation of feedback channels because we do not believe that organizations always set up such channels for the specific purpose of obtaining feedback about all change processes.

Various models of decision making have been advanced, and that discussed by Kast and Rosenzweig (1974:412–16) presents a good example of this approach. In their model, three periods are identified. In the first period the decision maker uses existing idealized goals to select an action goal that becomes the aspiration level. This period can be compared to the problem-sensing stage of our model, except that their emphasis is on goals while ours is on problems, with perhaps the inferred goal being to solve or otherwise deal with the sensed problem. The second period of decision making is concerned with a limited search for alternatives relative to a limited number of outcomes (stage 2 of our model), and the third period involves further search among the already identified alternatives to find one that is satisfactory in terms of a comparison of outcomes with the aspiration level set earlier. This last period is similar to our stages 3 and 4.

Our purpose in constructing the model given in table 1.1 was to provide a framework within which we could consider the particular policy changes to be studied. However, since we wanted our work to be comparable to other kinds of organizational change, we sought to construct a model that was as general as possible, in order to analyze the specific changes with which we were concerned as examples of the more general change process. Undoubtedly the work of others than those mentioned above has also been incorporated into our model in this effort toward generality. Besides its generality, we feel that our model offers other advantages.

Since our model proposes steps that are seen as necessary to a completed change process, it permits assessment of change efforts that are not completed and the factors that may have led to the interruption of the complete change process. The dimensions of change already proposed will affect the elaborateness with which the various stages are carried out. Relatively routine or small changes may involve a quick progression through the stages with little elaboration necessary, while more pervasive, large, or innovative changes may require a more extensive set of behaviors within each stage for successful completion of the change, or even recycling through stages if prior decisions are found to be less effective than deemed desirable or necessary. All changes that are intended to be of relatively long duration would require the final stage of institutionalization in order to ensure some permanence within the system.

A consideration of some specified model of the change process is important to any assessment of purposive change efforts. How can we know if a change has been successfully implemented without some specification of what is expected to happen in the change process? How can we assess the outcomes of a change effort in a rational way unless we know whether or not the change process has occurred? Unless we assess outcomes relative to the implementation of the change process, we cannot know whether outcomes can be attributed to the change process undertaken; perhaps the process was interrupted or altered and the outcomes that we assess are actually a result of processes not prescribed within the change effort. Conversely, if outcomes fail to materialize as envisioned, is this due to a faulty decision or to the lack of implementation of the decision? We can only know if we have a relatively systematic way to assess the change process itself. Outcomes of change processes can be evaluated independently, but the *meaning* of those outcomes will not be clear unless the degree to which all stages of the change process actually occurred is also known and evaluated.

HISTORY AND DESCRIPTION OF THE POLICIES UNDER STUDY

The model presented here was developed to guide our study of the implementation of two personnel policies within U.S. government organizations: the alcoholism policy and the equal employment opportunity policy. Both were mandated by federal legislation. The histories of these two policies are similar, although the exact timing of the stages from their initial impetus to the formulation of present policies varies somewhat. The respective histories of these two policies will be traced using the model of the change process presented in table 1.1 in order to determine the applicability of the model to the changes under study and also to determine how far along in the change process these policies were when our research program began.

History of the Alcoholism Policy

As we have analyzed the history of the alcoholism policy, a variety of factors combined in the mid-1960s to sensitize the U.S. Civil Service Commission to the problems of alcoholism among federal employees. Clearly, a central factor was the issuance of a presidential order in 1965 directing that health service programs for federal employees be expanded (Macy, 1968). Occupational health programs were seen, in the words of the then chairman of the Civil Service Commission, John W. Macy, Jr., as "good business" (Macy, 1968:4). From this perspective came an increased concern for safety and environmental health within federal installations, including "the new challenge of physical fitness programs and development of practicable methods to deal with employees who have drinking problems" (Macy, 1968:4). Approximately a year earlier, Macy had stated in the introduction to the program schedule for a conference sponsored by the Civil Service Commission on problem drinking: "The Federal Government, as the nation's largest employer, must fulfill its obligations to employees and management, and to the whole nation, by including in its personnel and occupational health programs a realistic and workable Federal alcoholism program which can serve as a model for all progressive employers" (U.S. Civil Service Commission, 1967:1).

The commission assigned the responsibility to explore an approach to alcoholism problems among federal employees to the Bureau of Retirement, Insurance, and Occupational Health, which held a conference in 1967 and published its proceedings under the title *The First Step* (U.S. Civil Service Commission, 1967). Andrew Ruddock, then director of the bureau, wrote that "as we looked for a plan of action, we quickly found how little we knew about alcoholism and its treatment" (1967:1). In effect, a series of new demands were made on the federal establishment; these grew out of an intensified emphasis on occupational health in general from which "we became aware of other areas that needed attention because nothing at all was being done about them. One such area needing attention was that too little was being officially done to help employees who had developed drinking problems" (Macy, 1968:5).

Sporadic efforts within the civil service had, however, preceded this formal expression of the realization of unsatisfied demands to help alcoholics within the entire system. The Naval Supply Center, Civilian Manpower Region, had established a formal policy and program in 1965 (U.S. Civil Service Commission, 1967:22-24). The Social Security Administration, through its medical officers, had begun to practice the outlines of a formal alcoholism policy in the early and mid-1960s (U.S. Civil Service Commission, 1967:20-22). In large measure these early efforts were fashioned after policies in the private sector, taking advantage of past innovations and inventions that were now readily available to deal with the growing sense of a major health problem. Moreover, these models from outside the federal bureaucracy were apparently considered sufficiently successful and applicable to minimize any search for alternatives and their evaluation.

In essence, the presidential order and the First Step conference together enunciated the principle of two socially held values: that occupational health was a responsibility of employers and that alcoholism was a health problem. If the initial sensing of the problem of alcoholism among federal employees had taken place in another framework of values, other solutions and other kinds of policies toward problem drinking could have emerged. The alternative was always open to view problem drinking and alcoholism as a disciplinary problem similar to other problem behaviors and thus to develop a policy that would intensify the disciplinary sanctions against problem drinking. But the problem-sensing phase of this change occurred within an ongoing and burgeoning concern with alcoholism as a health problem. Thus the search for alternatives was made within this definition of the problem, and the solutions adopted were readily available from an array of programs developed within the private employment sector to deal with a similarly defined problem. Thus the intervention strategies typically present in policies of the private sector were also adapted: the use of impaired job performance to confront an employee; the offer of rehabilitative help; and, if the employee should refuse and performance remain poor, the precipitation of a crisis through the use of disciplinary procedures, including termination as the last resort.

Available documents make it clear that the evaluation stage led to a decision to adopt a course of action that assumed alcoholism was a form of disease, but to retain traditional disciplinary procedures as an available alternative should it be necessary. With these decisions made, the commission published its second statement, *The Key Step* (U.S. Civil Service Commission, 1969). This document contained a preliminary and suggestive policy model, combined with practical suggestions regarding how a program based on the policy might work. The role of line supervisors was emphasized, but the role of the union, frequently emphasized in the earlier *First Step*, was ignored. Although the phases of alcoholism and program strategy are discussed at length, this document was not yet a policy statement for the commission; rather it contained some of the main themes of one, presented as suggestions for agency action. It did, however, establish one overall policy position: that the government would make no provision for paying the cost of rehabilitation, the employees being considered responsible for the costs of treating their drinking problems just as they are for any other health condition.

The events summarized above took place within the five-year period 1965 to 1970, with a concentration of action between mid-

1967 and early 1969. By 1970, this particular change process had reached stage 4 of the model in table 1.1, but no clear adoption of a course of action to solve the sensed problem—alcoholism among federal employees—had taken place.

Given a system as large and complex as the federal bureaucracy, the change process might well have stopped at this point. External forces, however, especially social pressure groups such as the National Council on Alcoholism, the Alcohol and Drug Problems Association, and the Christopher D. Smithers Foundation[9] working with and through Senator Harold Hughes of Iowa, secured the passage of the Comprehensive Alcohol Abuse and Alcoholism Prevention, Treatment and Rehabilitation Act in 1970 (P.L. 91-616). This act provided for a variety of actions, such as the formation of the National Institute on Alcohol Abuse and Alcoholism in the Department of Health, Education, and Welfare; project and formula grants to the states for prevention and treatment programs; and a clear mandate to the Civil Service Commission to develop policies and services for the prevention and treatment of alcohol abuse and alcoholism among federal civilian employees. Thus the earlier efforts of the commission received active support from a congressional act providing that the commission shall be responsible for developing and maintaining appropriate "prevention, treatment, and rehabilitation programs and services for alcoholism and alcohol abuse among civilian employees" (U.S. Civil Service Commission, 1971). The so-called Hughes Act became law on December 31, 1970; on July 7, 1971 the commission issued FPM Letter No. 792-4, a twelve-page document entitled "Federal Civilian Employee Alcoholism Programs." It directed that "the head of each department and agency with Federal civilian employees shall issue implementing internal instructions consonant with these guidelines by December 1, 1971" (U.S. Civil Service Commission, 1971). Step 4 of table 1.1 had been completed. A summary of the policy's contents follows.

Summary of the Alcoholism Policy

In attachments to the letter, the commission outlines the background and purpose of the alcoholism program in terms of policy statements that limit the concern of the federal government to those cases where the use of alcoholic beverages results either directly or indirectly in a job-related problem. A drinking problem is defined as existing when the use of alcohol negatively affects an employee's job performance: "when [it] interferes with the efficient and safe performance of his assigned duties, reduces his dependability or reflects discredit on the agency" (U.S. Civil Service Commission, 1971:2). In such cases, two types of action are suggested: nondisciplinary procedures to offer rehabilitative assistance or, if the employee fails to respond with acceptable work performance, disciplinary procedures (U.S. Civil Service Commission, 1971:2).

The FPM letter goes on to define alcoholism, an alcoholic, and a problem drinker. Alcoholism is defined as a chronic disease characterized by repeated excessive drinking that interferes with the individual's health, interpersonal relations, or economic functioning. An alcoholic is an individual who has the illness of alcoholism, while a problem drinker is any employee whose use of alcohol frequently affects his work adversely.

Agencies are urged to bring the problem "into the open," with top management issuing official statements designed to demonstrate full management support and to elicit understanding and support "all the way down the supervisory line" (U.S. Civil Service Commission, 1971:3-4). Specifics of elements for inclusion in the policy statement are then given. These include the recognition of alcoholism as a treatable disease and statements that an employee's job performance is impaired as a direct consequence of the abuse of alcohol, that employees with the illness or related problems should receive the same consideration as employees with any other illness, that the agency is not concerned with use of alcohol unless it affects job performance or efficiency of service, that employees may not have job security or promotion opportunities jeopardized by requests for counseling or referral under the policy, that records will be preserved with the same confidentiality as other medical records, that sick leave will be granted for purposes of treatment or rehabilitation as in any other illness, and that employees should be encouraged to voluntarily seek help under the program.

Unions are to become involved in policy formulation and kept informed through training of union representatives and open lines of communication. Management should make it clear to unions that the employer will extend maximum assistance toward rehabilitation, but that failure to raise job performance to acceptable levels will result in appropriate actions.

Roles are then defined to carry out the administration of the alcoholism program. A program administrator should be designated at each headquarters to direct the program on an agencywide basis, while each field installation should designate an individual to coordinate the program on a local basis. These individuals are to be allotted sufficient time to effectively implement the policy, including education and information of the work force, supervisory training, developing and maintaining counseling services, establishing liaison with relevant community facilities, and evaluation and reporting on program effectiveness. Personnel directors and their staffs are given the responsibilities in program development, implementation, and review consistent with other personnel management functions. The letter also suggests the use of and coordination with community resources involved in the treatment of alcoholism. To this end, current information on local resources should be maintained and be available to individuals providing counseling services to employees who may have drinking problems. The medical department, similarly, should have the capability to provide assistance to both supervisors and affected employees in terms of consultation and counseling, respectively. Medical staff should be provided with specialized training.

The letter discusses the key role of the supervisor in some detail as "the only representative of management who has a close enough relationship to the employee to realize the existence of a problem that may be caused by drinking" (U.S. Civil Service Commission, 1971:7). In this section of the letter, the supervisor's role in monitoring work performance is stressed, and specific suggestions for supervisory behaviors are given: be alert to changes in the work and behavior of assigned employees; document specific instances where work performance, behavior, or attendance fails to meet minimum standards or where the employee's pattern of performance appears to be deteriorating; consult with medical or counseling staff for advice on probable causes of employee problem; conduct an interview with the employee focusing on poor work performance and informing him of available counseling services in the event poor performance is caused by any personal problem; if the employee refuses help and performance continues to be unsatisfactory, give him or her a firm choice between accepting agency assistance through counseling or professional diagnosis of the problem, and cooperation in treatment, if indicated, or accepting consequences provided by agency policy for unsatisfactory performance. The supervisor does *not* diagnose the problem as alcoholism.

The alcoholism program supplements, but does not replace, existing procedures for dealing with problem employees. In practice the alcoholic or problem drinker should be dealt with little differently from other problem employees. It is most important that the alcohol program be carried out as a nondisciplinary procedure aimed at rehabilitation of persons who suffer a disease. However, if the employee refuses to seek counseling and/or if there is no improvement or inadequate improvement in performance, disciplinary actions should be taken, as warranted, solely on the basis of unsatisfactory job performance.

The letter goes on to provide for confidential record keeping on employees referred under the program and for the filing of periodic reports on the program with its agency and annually with the Civil Service Commission (CSC). Finally, the letter discusses specifics of the use of sick leave, eligibility for disability retirement, the financial responsibility of the employee for rehabilitation costs, and employment considerations surrounding the employment of persons who have a history of alcoholism or problem drinking.

History of the Equal Employment Opportunity Policy

Like the alcoholism policy, the formulation of the present federal EEO policy followed a series of steps taken in recognition of changing social values relating to a recognized social problem. The Equal Employment Opportunity Act of 1972 (P.L. 92-261) and its section on nondiscrimination in federal employment culminated a series of efforts to establish fair employment procedures within the U.S. Civil Service labor force. In terms of the steps in table 1.1, it could be argued that the sensing of unsatisfied demands relative to equal opportunity in employment occurred long before the passage of the 1972 legislation. Numerous efforts to prevent discrimination based on race, color, religion, sex, or national origin preceded it, reaching back to the issuance of Executive Order No. 8802 on June 25, 1941. Subsequent executive orders in 1948 and 1955 attempted to ensure that the socially held value of equality of opportunity would be realized within the federal employment system. Various alternatives were tried, such as a Fair Employment Practices Committee within the federal service and the extension of regulations against discrimination to private firms with federal contracts, but no enforcement powers were provided, so that compliance was voluntary. The same problem crippled Executive Order No. 10925, issued in March 1961, although it increased the pressure on federal contractors by specific requirements to hire without discrimination. Subsequent orders in 1963 and 1964 extended the coverage of equal opportunity to federally assisted construction contracts and to prohibit discrimination based on age. Title VII of the Civil Rights Act of 1964 set the stage for a statutory basis for fair employment practices throughout the American economy, but even this legislation failed to provide for direct enforcement powers. In August 1969, Executive Order No. 11478 directed that equal employment opportunity be an integral part of personnel policy and practice relating to civilian employees of the federal government.

All of these measures were presumably taken to do something about the sensed problem of unequal treatment of minorities and others in employment. Members of these groups were demanding changes, and considerable social and political support existed for such change. However, the eventual passage of the later EEO Act of 1972 suggests that each cycle of search, evaluation, decision, and initiation of action was followed by the sensing of still unsatisfied demands within the system. Thus the EEO change process had proceeded through steps 1- 5 several times, but steps 6 and 7 were seen by the proponents of this change as deficient. There are two likely possibilities: (1) that the last two stages were inadequately carried out, and the changes envisioned were thus never completed, or (2) that the changes incorporated in those steps were not sufficient to meet the demands within the system. Since subsequent legislation put heavy emphasis on measures to ensure enforcement of compliance, it seems likely that the change processes that were begun had been short-circuited in the implementation stage.

The Equal Employment Opportunity Act of 1972, which amended Title VII of the 1964 Civil Rights Act, put teeth into the earlier legislation and broadened its applicability. Perhaps the most important feature of this legislation was the creation of enforcement mechanisms under the direction of an Equal Employment Opportunity Commission. Mechanisms to ensure compliance placed major emphasis on administrative sanctions, formal complaint systems and hearings, and the possibility of lawsuits. The most relevant portion of the 1972 act to this study was Section 717, which directed that positions in federal employment be made free from any discrimination based on race, color, religion, sex, or national origin. Moreover, it gave the Civil Service Commission authority to enforce a policy of equal opportunity in employment through appropriate remedies, and directed the CSC to conduct an annual review of EEO plans, evaluate each agency, publish progress reports, consult on the policy with interested individuals, groups, and organizations, and provide training and education programs designed to establish opportunities for employees to realize their potentials. It is this last act, and the CSC policy stemming from it, on which we focus in this book.

Although the emergence of the EEO policy incorporated in the form of FPM Letter No. 713-17 does not neatly follow our conceptual stages for the change process straight through from beginning to end, the model does fit the history of the policy, if allowance is made for a recycling through the stages as various decisions and subsequent actions (or lack thereof) were found inadequate to meet the unsatisfied demands within the system. There was, for example, a long sensing-of-demand-for-change stage. Ever since the early 1940s, repeated signals indicated that problems of discrimination existed within the private and federal employment sectors. These signals were transmitted to the Civil Service Commission through executive orders that increasingly spelled out the form the change should and must take. Thus, one part of the system—the chief executive (president of the United States)—repeatedly served as the communication channel used to make new demands on the civil service system. Additional pressures to produce a substantive change came from congressional sources and active segments of the public.

The original 1964 Civil Rights Act did not authorize the CSC to work against employment discrimination in federal employment. Many members of Congress believed this should be added. Not only did executive orders indicate a need for a formalized policy and procedures for combating discrimination in hiring, but congressional opinion reflected a deep concern for the achievement of a socially held value—equality of opportunity for all citizens. Moreover, the federal government was seen as a model employer and hence should be the leader in the changes necessary to effect equal employment opportunities. Both congressional opinion and presidential action were, in turn, strongly influenced by the fear of violence and civil disorder—a fear already justified by the mid- and late-1960s. The influence of this anxiety cannot be overestimated. In all likelihood this one force alone generated a search for alternatives that would concretely demonstrate how equal opportunity in employment could be realized. The obvious place for such a demonstration was in government employment (Bickel, 1964; King, 1964; Hill, 1968).

Yet alternatives did emerge. In the early 1970s Title VII was reconsidered. Three clear-cut possibilities were proposed: (1) leave matters as they were, (2) vigorously execute existing policy, or (3) enact new legislation. Given the climate of the time, the first alternative was advanced by only a handful of ultraconservatives. The realistic choice was between the last two. Either of those alternatives would affect policies used with federal employees as administered by the Civil Service Commission. Interestingly, some advocates of the second alternative argued that the employment amendments should apply only to federal employment and to those employed under federal contracts. This alternative would have left many workplaces in the private sector not covered by EEO. Those who favored narrow application of EEO cited the desirability of limiting federal power, avoiding government by injunction, and appealed to fears of a tyrannical government (Bureau of National Affairs, 1973:23; *U.S. Code Congressional and Administrative News*, 1972:120–24). The question most under debate was the extent to which the changes would encompass the private sector as well. Since the pressures for and against were equally strong, the final political decision to move ahead centered instead around the issue of enforcement, with the advocates of cease-and-desist means of enforcement aligned opposite those who believed that enforcement could best be done through the courts (Bureau of National Affairs, 1973).

The Title VII Amendment resulted from a compromise that incorporated both enforcement devices and included both the private and public sectors of employment. With this resolution, the amendments to the Civil Rights Act of 1972, including specific directives to the Civil Service Commission, became law. Thus, in March 1972, the change process we call the federal EEO policy had once again reached the end of stage 4 in table 1.1.

At this time, the Civil Service Commission began work on the actions needed to apply the new law to federal employees; in November 1972 the CSC issued FPM Letter No. 713-17, which marks the beginning of stage 5 of this change process. This document explicitly stated the regulatory changes made in an effort to implement the EEO Act of 1972 (P.L. 92-261), spelling out the details of the commission's policy as it existed prior to Public Law 92-261 and the specific additions and deletions that must be made to the policy to conform to the new law. The summary that follows provides an overview of the updated policy.

Summary of Equal Employment Opportunity Policy

The EEO policy for federal employees was promulgated by the Civil Service Commission through Chapter 713 of the Federal Personnel Manual, and details of this policy are so numerous as to take up four subchapters of the manual. Thus, FPM Letter No. 713-17 represented detailed revisions to EEO regulations previously circulated. The summary that follows presents only the major features of this policy and the subsequent revisions.

The overall purposes of the EEO policy were to provide equal opportunity in employment for all persons, to prohibit discrimination in employment because of race, color, religion, sex, or national origin, and to promote the full realization of equal employment through a continuing affirmative program in each agency. The specific purposes of the revisions were to implement the EEO Act of 1972 and to strengthen the system of processing complaints of discrimination.

Generally, the provisions of the EEO policy are to be combined with those providing for employment based on merit and fitness and must be an integral part of every aspect of personnel policy and practice in the development, advancement, and treatment of employees. All personnel actions affecting employees or applicants for competitive positions in executive agencies, military departments, the U.S. Postal Service, the Library of Congress, units of the government of the District of Columbia, and the legal and judicial branches of the federal government are subject to this policy. The Federal Women's Program shall be integrated with this policy. Efforts toward implementation of the policy should include disciplinary actions against personnel who engage in discriminatory practices.

Plans and efforts to carry forward this policy will contain actions designed to utilize fully the skills of employees. When feasible, this will involve the redesign of jobs for maximum skill use as well as efforts to identify underutilized employees. Furthermore, maximum opportunities for employees to enhance their skills through on-the-job training and work-study programs will be made in order to encourage advancement according to ability. Agencies and their installations should communicate their programs to all sources of personnel recruitment without discrimination. At the community level agencies will cooperate with other employers in efforts to improve employment opportunities.

The policy goes on to require that the various agencies and their installations will inform all of their employees and appropriate employee organizations about the provisions of the various EEO programs. They shall also provide counseling for employees who believe that they have been the subject of discrimination in an effort to resolve the matter informally. In addition, formal procedures for prompt and fair consideration and disposition of formal complaints should be devised and used. Provisions for complaints are strengthened in the revisions to the policy (FPM 713-17) in various ways. Counselors, for example, are specifically prohibited from attempting in any way to restrain a person from filing a complaint of discrimination. In addition, time limits for filing complaints are extended, while time limits are placed on the counseling period, after which time employees must be informed of the right to file a formal complaint. Further provisions deal with rights to formal hearings, remedial actions, and case reviews—all of these designed to strengthen the affected employee's rights to obtain redress for grievances.

As with the alcoholism policy, the Civil Service Commission is given the major responsibility for implementation of the EEO policy. However, the CSC role specified in this policy is broader and more active. It is required to (1) provide leadership and guidance to agencies; (2) prescribe requirements for agencies to follow and establish guidelines for implementation; (3) maintain a continuing review of all aspects of the federal personnel system so as to detect impediments to the EEO program; (4) operate a training program for agency and CSC officials with EEO responsibilities; (5) review and evaluate agency operations; (6) require corrective action for program improvement; (7) operate a data-gathering system; (8) provide a system for the prompt, fair, and impartial consideration of complaints; (9) consult with other organizations having a particular interest in EEO matters; (10) report to the president on the progress of the program as appropriate; and (11) operate an information system to heighten awareness of the federal EEO policy and program efforts.

Each federal agency determines its own EEO program and operation, subject to CSC review. Heads of agencies are given the responsibility for general implementation and administration of the EEO program within their agencies, including providing maximum feasibility for upward mobility, coordination with relevant community agencies, providing recognition for superior accomplishment by supervisors in using EEO, informing employees about EEO, providing counseling and complaint services, providing a self-evaluation system, announcing relevant plans, procedures, and regulations, and setting future goals in plans of action that are to be revised every twelve months. Within each agency, several functionaries are to be designated to assist in program implementation: a director of EEO, and a Federal Women's Program coordinator (or committee) at the agency-wide level, and as many EEO officers and counselors as are needed to carry out EEO functions in all of the organizational units and locations of the agency. Officers so designated are under the immediate supervision of the installation head where they are located, and their duty is to assist the installation head in implementing the EEO program, especially in the affirmative-action aspects of the program, and in the processing of complaints. The counselors are to be separated from the formal complaint process so that they can function effectively on an informal basis. The names of all of these functionaries should be posted so that all employees may be informed of who they are. While there are no set numbers of counselors required, the policy suggests one for every 500 employees in locations with large concentrations of employees, and all installations with fifty employees or more are urged to have at least one counselor.

Agencies are also required to keep a statistical system to maintain information on employment by race and national origin. Such data is to be collected only by visual identification and disclosed only in the form of gross statistics. These data are to be used to report to the CSC, for periodic censuses of the federal work force, for commission inspections, and for internal self-evaluation. However, the establishment of quotas for the employment of persons on the basis of color, religion, sex, or national origin is prohibited.

As can be detected from even this brief summary, the EEO policy is less attentive to suggesting roles and behaviors for supervisors and others in implementing its policy and instead relies on a more regulatory approach. Unlike the alcoholism policy, provisions are included for both rewards and sanctions to be used to encourage implementation by supervisors and others.

Comparing the Two Policies

In comparing these policies, various similarities emerge:

1. All agencies and field installations must establish programs for each policy.
2. The CSC will review the programs and operations.
3. The CSC will provide leadership and guidance in establishing the programs.
4. Agency heads are responsible for the establishment and implementation of programs; both are intended to become an integral part of personnel policy and practice.
5. All employees of all agencies are to be informed of the programs.
6. Individual installations are to establish counseling services for each program.
7. Specific functionaries are to be appointed at the agencywide level and within each installation to help to implement the programs.
8. Relevant community resources are to be used in program implementation.
9. Records must be maintained, and periodic reports to the commission must be issued.
10. In both policies, work performance is a central issue, putting the supervisor into a key role in policy implementation.
11. Both are personnel policies.

The policies, of course, also have important differences. The most obvious is that EEO is intended to apply to all employees, whereas the alcoholism policy only applies to employees with drinking problems. It is also clear, just from the relative size of the civil service documentation, that the EEO policy has been given more "teeth." Reporting requirements are more stringent, and reference is made to remedial actions that may be required in cases of noncompliance. Also, the number of functionaries designated by the two policies suggests that the EEO policy is expected to be used more frequently. Finally, compliance with the EEO policy is suggested as worthy of formal reward; no such rewards are suggested for those supervisors using the alcoholism policy.

In the next section of this chapter, the question of differences between the two policies will be addressed more systematically. Although there are certainly large differences between the two policies, in content, applicability, and other features, it was the structural similarities as well as their differences in content that led us to study these two policies in a comparative way. We felt that an adequate study of change should examine more than one change, so that it would be possible to assess which results tended to be generalizable across changes and which were specific to the content or other features of a particular change.

Considerations of practicality limited this investigation to just two policies. Since we wanted comparable data, but at the same time wanted to investigate changes that were not too similar, we chose two policies that specified similar formal mechanisms yet differed in other ways. With this strategy we could develop parallel instrumentation to assess implementation of the policies, yet we would be able to investigate whether our models and hypotheses fit each of two disparate changes equally well.

In this process of comparison, the alcoholism policy served as our model for conceptualization and for instrumentation. The original purpose of the study was the investigation of the implementation of that policy, and it therefore received the most attention initially. Once the strategy of making a comparison was decided upon, the EEO policy quickly became its foil in our deliberations, and the contrast between the two policies helped to sharpen our thinking about the implementation process. Because of the complexity and number of issues raised in the EEO policy, this study may not have covered that policy in the same detail and with the same comprehensiveness as the alcoholism policy, although the measurements used are as comparable as we could make them. A policy as extensive and comprehensive as EEO would require many studies to explore fully its implementation, and some of these features would have carried us far beyond any possible comparison with the alcoholism policy.

THE FOCAL POLICIES AND DIMENSIONS OF CHANGE

The two policies can also be compared by using the dimensions of change defined earlier in the chapter. The first of these—pervasiveness—was defined as the proportion of total behaviors occurring within an organization that will be affected by the change.

Since both the alcoholism and the EEO policy are personnel policies that apply to all federal employees under the jurisdiction of the Civil Service Commission, these policies are potentially quite pervasive. Every supervisor of federal employees should apply these policies when the occasion for their use arises. However, since many supervisors may not have employees with drinking problems under their supervision, the most that can be expected is that such supervisors should be ready to apply the policy, and not that they all should personally have done so. The situation with the EEO policy has some similarities. While ideally the policy should ensure opportunities for all federal employees who deserve promotion or hire, the economic situation of the past few years has made hirings and promotions more limited than they have been at some times in the past. Thus, not all supervisors have had the opportunity to either hire or promote one of their employees, although a greater number may have had some opportunity to recommend employees for promotions when appropriate vacancies occur. On balance, it seems clear that both the potential and actual pervasiveness of the EEO policy is greater than that of the alcoholism policy. Our data indicate this: Only 11 percent of supervisors reported some use of the alcoholism policy since its inception, whereas 59 percent of supervisors reported some use of the EEO policy. In using t tests for correlated variables (sometimes called paired comparisons), it was found that this difference is significant at the $p = .000$ level.

In another sense, however, both policies are relatively low on pervasiveness. The central missions of these installations and the carrying out of these duties are not centrally affected by either policy. Supervisors do not spend all of their time on personnel matters, but presumably on getting some job done. Supervisors reported spending an average of 3.3 hours in the previous month on matters related to the EEO policy, but only 0.5 hours on matters related to the alcoholism policy ($p = .000$). While both policies may indirectly affect unit work performance, they do not do so directly, the way a change in operating procedures or technology would. An example of a highly pervasive change in these organizations was the institution of a new national computer system within the Social Security Administration after that agency was given broadened responsibilities. Because of the centrality of computerized records to all aspects of the functioning of the Social Security system, this change greatly affected the way in which many employees carried on their jobs. (Incidentally, this change was quickly routinized, since it had little magnitude and innovativeness.) The personnel policies studied are obviously less pervasive. If we combine the two indicators of pervasiveness—percentage of supervisors using the policy and amount of time spent on policy-related matters—by multiplying them to form a rough index, EEO receives a score of 1.947, while the alcoholism policy receives a score of 0.055. By contrast, a change that occupied 50 percent of supervisors only one hour daily (20 hours monthly) would have a score of 10, while one that involves 80 percent of supervisors for the same amount of time would have a score of 16. These last two hypothetical estimates do not seem unreasonable for the sort of pervasive change that occurred with the new national computer system in the Social Security Administration, nor for other large-scale technological changes.

Considering the magnitude of the change behavior, the EEO policy can be expected to cause more displacement of ongoing activities than the alcoholism policy. To the degree that EEO programs involve the allocation of resources, time, and attention of both supervisors and specially designated functionaries, our data show that the EEO policy has relatively high behavioral magnitude. When the two functionaries were asked about the amount of time and money they had to devote to the respective policies, only one alcoholism coordinator had any money budgeted to work on the policy, while the EEO functionaries reported an average budget of over $8,000 and spending an average of over $12,000 yearly on EEO implementation. The figures for the time spent on each policy were similar, with alcoholism coordinators spending an average of 51 hours of their time in the last year on the alcoholism policy, and EEO functionaries reporting spending an average of 934 hours on the EEO policy. This figure is an underestimate of actual differences, because most installations had several EEO functionaries (an officer and counselors), while no installation had more than one alcoholism coordinator, and many shared their alcoholism coordinator with other installations.

However, when it comes to changes in attitudes and values, the alcoholism policy equals or slightly exceeds the EEO policy in its magnitude. Supervisors are somewhat more reluctant to accept the idea that the problem drinker is a sick person who deserves and needs help than they are to accept the values underlying the EEO policy. Supervisors were asked about the degree to which they agreed with eight parallel issues related to each policy. The mean values of agreement with statements in accord with policy provisions were significantly higher for the EEO than for the alcoholism policy ($p = .049$ to $.000$). While consistent, these differences in attitudes are not large (overall means $= 4.84$ and 4.52, respectively), and therefore the EEO policy must be seen as involving a change of greater magnitude overall than is called for by the alcoholism policy.

The question of the innovativeness of the policies is harder to judge. Retaining and helping employees who have "caused trouble by their own behavior" may be seen as different from past programs of

T A B L E 1.2   Summary of Dimensions of Change as Related to Two Policies

	ALCOHOLISM POLICY	EEO POLICY
Pervasiveness	Low	Medium low
Magnitude	Medium low	Medium
Innovativeness	Medium	Medium high
Duration	High	High

action. The "fitting in" of minority group members may also be seen as requiring innovative behaviors, as will the presence of women in some jobs previously considered only for men. The alcoholism policy stresses an accepted role of supervisors—assessing job performance and then acting to deal with employees who have poor job performance so as to improve that performance. Techniques to be used include counseling, medical referrals, and possible disciplinary actions. None of these are totally unique to this policy. The EEO policy suggests an assortment of programs to help previously disadvantaged groups improve their employment status and to enable others to achieve employment with the federal government. Although counseling and complaints are not unique to this policy, the suggestions of restructuring jobs, on-the-job training, and providing opportunities of outside training may well involve innovative behaviors at some work sites or for some classes of employees. Specific techniques in training both supervisors and employees about these programs had to be developed, though training activities are not new per se. Both programs also demanded some interaction with the environment of the installation, the alcoholism policy for resources for treatment and the EEO policy for sources for minority recruitment and training. Since some private industries were also instituting similar policies, the policies were not without precedent. We would thus judge that they were at some moderate value in their innovativeness. When asked their assessment of how large a step these policies were for the government to take, supervisors responded with a mean of 5.16 for the alcoholism policy and 5.67 for the EEO policy on a semantic differential scale with $1 =$ minimal step and $7 =$ giant step. Thus they also saw the EEO policy as significantly more innovative $(p = .000)$.

The two policies do not differ on intended duration, both presumably being permanent changes in policy.

A summary of the considerations just discussed is presented in table 1.2. Neither policy is judged as high on any dimensions of change except for duration because many other changes could be envisioned that would involve greater pervasiveness, magnitude, and innovation than these two personnel policies. Future research could attempt to measure these dimensions of change more precisely, but for a first attempt perhaps these approximations will suffice to indicate whether the approach has any value.

SUMMARY

In this chapter we have tried to present an overview of various conceptual issues that were important in the design and execution of the study reported in this book. We have argued that change must be considered as an ongoing and pervasive aspect of organizational life and that policy is one mechanism by which change can be routinized. We have pointed out the confusions arising from the use of various terms to denote change and have advanced four dimensions along which the behavioral aspects of a change process may be located. These dimensions were distinguished from earlier ways of characterizing the attributes of innovations: (1) as being more process- and behavior-oriented and (2) as being concerned with the intrinsic nature of the change process.

In routinizing changes through policy, various deviations in behavior can occur. These can be seen as occurring in either prescribed means or ends, thus allowing us to characterize behavior not in conformity with policy intent and provisions in terms of the familiar Mertonian types: innovators, ritualists, rebels, and retreatists.

A seven-stage model of a completed change process was presented and subsequently used to analyze the history of the two policies studied: the federal alcoholism and EEO policies. Summaries of the contents of the policies were also given. Finally, the policies were compared in terms of their content and then in terms of the four dimensions of change presented earlier in the chapter. The two policies have some structural and other similarities, but the EEO policy is judged to be higher on three of the four dimensions of change.

In the chapters that follow, results will be presented that further document both similarities and differences between the two policies. But first it is necessary to describe the research design and methods employed to study the implementation of these policies.

2. The Research Design: Focus and Methodology

THE RESEARCH FOCUS

WHEN THIS RESEARCH EFFORT began in early 1973, the changes involved in both of these policies were already under way. In the last chapter we summarized the histories of both policies in terms of a general model of the change process. To recapitulate briefly, each change process was in stage 5 of the model given in table 1.1 when the relevant legislation was passed by Congress. Since both were personnel policies applying to federal employees, the Civil Service Commission was responsible for diffusing the policies it developed to comply with these laws to government installations throughout the country; this was done formally by issuance of the sections of the Federal Personnel Manual summarized in chapter 1. For the purposes of this research, we shall consider this initial diffusion as the culmination of step 5 in our model of change. It thus became the task of this research effort to analyze the two subsequent steps of the model—the sixth and seventh stages of implementation and institutionalization of change. These became the dependent variables of our study.

The purposes of the research, however, went beyond the mere description or evaluation of the extent to which these policies had been implemented and institutionalized. The primary objective of the research was to test hypotheses about how the factors shown in figure I.1 could be expected to either facilitate or hinder policy implementation and institutionalization. Data were collected on a wide range of possible impetuses or barriers to change, guided by the previous literature on organizational innovations already discussed and by general discussions of organizational change (for example, Kast and Rosenzweig, 1974; Hall, 1972).

RESEARCH DESIGN AND SAMPLE

The research began with an analysis of the history and content of the policies. From this base we developed the general research design given in figure I.1 in the Introduction. Our analyses suggested that we should center our investigation on supervisors working in federal installations, since they were the ultimate users for whom the policies were intended. Thus their role behaviors were crucial in implementing both policies. Other members of these organizations also were important for policy implementation: the head of the installation and a functionary who was created by each policy to facilitate implementation.

A search of the relevant literatures produced a wide range of possible independent variables, falling within the general categories given in figure I.1. Other independent variables, like those related to the union, were selected because of our general knowledge of organizations and the workings of personnel policy, although they had not been treated in related studies. Where possible, existing measurements of variables were obtained and scrutinized for relevance to this study. Some existing scales were used, some were modified, and many measures were devised entirely for this study. Issues of measurement will be discussed in more detail later in this chapter, and further information is given in the Appendix.

A substantial effort was then launched into four waves of preliminary interviewing and pretesting. Four different research instruments were devised, pretested, and developed for the four types of organizational members, whom we called the director, the EEO functionary, the alcoholism coordinator, and the supervisor. When pretesting began, most questions in the instrument were open-ended. Using responses to these initial waves of interviewing, we were able to gradually develop and pretest appropriate response formats so that most questions could have a specified range of responses. The final instruments consisted primarily of such closed-ended items, with open-ended questions included to probe for additional information where desirable. In addition, a form was devised to collect some of the data on the structure of each installation; since most of these data were available from the personnel manager, this instrument was dubbed the Personnel Information Summary. Finally, census data from the *County and City Data Book* (U.S. Bureau of the Census, 1973) were used to measure aspects of the communities in which the federal installations were located.

In order to give maximum generalizability to our study, we sampled as inclusively as possible from among the federal installations in which civilian employees worked.[1] We therefore obtained a list of all the nonmilitary installations within the Boston, New York, and Philadelphia regions under the jurisdiction of the Civil Service Commission. The sample was restricted to the Northeast to keep travel time and expenses within reasonable bounds. Agencies involved in covert operations (e.g., CIA, FBI) were eliminated because of practical difficulties involved in eliciting cooperation and contacting random samples from their population of supervisors, but all other executive departments with numerous installations were retained: Agriculture; Commerce; General Services Administration; Health, Education, and Welfare; Housing and Urban Development; Interior; Treasury; Justice; and Transportation. Finally, installations with fewer than 50 employees were eliminated. Once the list had been modified in terms of these three restrictions, it served as the sampling frame, or population, for a two-stage sampling procedure.

First, a stratified, random sample of installations was drawn, with strata determined by installation size (small = less than 150; large = over 150), the nine executive departments included in the study, and the three civil service regions. The resulting sample design was a $9 \times 2 \times 3$ matrix, with a total of 54 cells. Where possible, two installations were randomly drawn from the stratified list of eligible installations to fit into each cell of this design. Because of the distribution of the stratified characteristics in this population, we were unable to fill all 54 cells of this design with two installations, but we maintained the sampling design in all instances where it was possible—well over 80 percent of the cells involved—to yield a final sample of 71 installations.

The second stage of sampling occurred within each of the installations, when a systematic sample (McCarthy, 1957: 293-94) of supervisors was drawn from within the installations, with the size of the sample inversely proportional to the size of the installation. These procedures yielded responses from 634 supervisors,[2] 65 alcoholism coordinators (some served more than one installation in our sample), 71 EEO functionaries, and 71 installation directors. Structural and environmental data were collected for all installations.

Both samples were sustained so that representativeness can be claimed.[3] Only one installation declined cooperation, pleading a reorganization, and had to be replaced; six supervisors refused and were replaced (all potential respondents were explicitly offered the opportunity to refuse at the beginning of the interview). Changes in the number of employees within installations are continual, and some are substantial in size. Despite continual checking and updating of the population lists used, two installations that had fewer than 50 employees at the time of the data collection ended up in the final sample.

DATA COLLECTION

As mentioned earlier, different research instruments were designed for supervisors, directors (heads of installations), and each policy coordinator or functionary—a role specially designated in the formal policies. The instruments were a combination of questionnaire and interview items using a variety of data-generating techniques to measure the wide range of variables required by the study design. Items included self-reported behaviors, perceptions, and attitudes measured by Likert scales, semantic differentials, and other response formats.

As mentioned earlier, each instrument was developed with the aid of four separate phases of pretesting. These phases progressed from very general open-ended questions to more close-ended questions as we learned appropriate response categories from subjects similar to those who would be included in the final sample. All pretests were carried out in federal installations that did not fall into the final sample design. Fourteen installations were visited during the pretests, and approximately 75 supervisors, 25 functionaries, and 14 directors were interviewed. During the pretests, sampling and other procedures within the installations were similar to those used in the final data collection, and every phase of the data collection effort was pretested, including drawing the systematic sample of supervisors, maintaining rapport with subjects, and the standardized introduction that interviewers used to introduce themselves and explain the study to each subject.

Each interview-questionnaire was administered face to face by a trained field interviewer[4] in a private location, typically the respondent's office. In addition to the quantifiable data generated by the instruments, two methods of gathering qualitative data were used. The formal instruments contained some open-ended interview items so that the same field interviewer could also generate some qualitative information. Secondly, interviewers were provided with special forms to record observations, unsolicited comments, and their subjective impressions of rapport, organizational climate, and anything else that might be relevant. Finally, the pretest interviews provided a rich source of qualitative data.

Data from the 71 installations in the final sample were collected between April and October of 1974. Entry to installations was obtained with the help of the Civil Service Commission and a series of contacts that the commission set up within each executive department and region.

MEASUREMENT

Measurement of dependent and independent variables included all types of measurement: dichotomous, nominal, ordinal, and interval. Response formats were developed to be logical and complete to respondents and to achieve the highest level of measurement judged feasible for that item. Examples of dichotomous items included whether or not something had occurred; for example, whether a supervisor had ever used one of the policies, or whether he had received a particular type of information about it. Nominal measures were infrequent but included such things as descriptions of work, major in college, name of the union at the installation, or professional associations of which the respondent was a member. Ordinal measures included most of the attitudinal items, and other items such as G.S. rating of the respondent. Finally, interval measures included the number of cases handled under each policy, the number of subordinates, the number of hours spent in training relevant to each policy, the number of employees within the installation, and so on.

All of the items measuring the dependent variables were developed for this study. Past research on change and innovation failed to yield items that would be relevant to the content of these policies and the circumstances of their implementation. Measurement of many of the independent variables, on the other hand, was based upon past research and measures developed by other researchers. Measures of various work-related attitudes were derived from past research: organizational commitment (Ritzer and Trice, 1969*a*, 1969*b*), job involvement (Lodahl and Kejner, 1965), work overload (Roman and Trice, 1972; Kahn et al., 1964), and attitudes toward change (Hage and Dewar, 1973; Neal, 1965). In addition, many of the measurements of organizational structure were based upon or adapted from the study of Blau and Schoenherr (1971) on bureaucracies in state government. Other measures of attitudes, of factors related to the work role, and of structural aspects of organizations were developed for this study. Finally, measures of community characteristics followed the lead of Blau and Schoenherr and were obtained from U.S. Census data. Further discussion of measurements occurs in the text as we discuss the data analyses and their interpretations, with details of all measurements given in the Appendix.

SCALING

Many of the variables used in this study involved multiple sets of measurements. In all cases, the individual items in the questionnaires that formed multi-item scales were designed to measure particular variables. The homogeneity of these items was checked through correlational techniques and with Cronbach's alpha statistic; factor analysis was also employed to determine which items might profitably and justifiably be combined into one scale. Sometimes the factor analyses confirmed our conceptual assignment of items; other times sets of items that were originally conceived as falling under a single construct were subdivided into separate variables on the basis of the factor analysis results. In all cases, items were eliminated that had substantial loading on more than one factor, only items were included that loaded heavily on one factor ($> .40$), only as many factors were extracted as were indicated by eigenvalues over 1.00 in the principal components solution, and varimax rotations were employed if the principal components solution failed to yield a single factor.

Where factor analysis had been employed, items were combined by averaging single items after each had been standardized on its own mean. No differential weighting was employed. The only exceptions to this procedure were scales that had been developed by others; here the aim was to ensure maximum comparability with past research, and we therefore replicated the procedures of the original investigators. Details are given in the Appendix.

Some of the measures used in this study are what Mansfield (1973) has termed scalar quantities, as opposed to vector quantities. That is, the measures represent mass but do not imply a direction. For example, we cannot argue that a business organization must have a certain type of specialist, say one in union relations, before it has one in quality control. But if an organization has both, we can argue that it is more specialized than one who had only one or neither. The example illustrates that the number of different job titles, as used in this study, is a reasonable measure of division of labor. Another example concerns information diffusion of these policies. We cannot argue that a supervisor should have received a brochure on one of the policies before attending a meeting dealing with the policy, or vice versa, but we can argue that an employee who has done both has received more types of information than one who has done only one or neither. The primary test of such items is their face validity in terms of logical consistency and construct validity in terms of agreement with relations expected from past findings; traditional scaling procedures are not appropriate since they involve assessments of direction as well as mass.

STATISTICS

The statistical procedure most generally used in this research to investigate relationships between variables was multiple regression. Other techniques based on the regression model, such as path analysis and discriminant analysis, were also employed.

We recognize the classical statistical assumptions of multiple regression—interval levels of measurement, normal distributions, homoscedasticity, and nonsystematic residual errors—are not always met by the data presented here. However, this is far from a unique problem in social science research, and most researchers and methodologists have preferred recently to gain the explanatory power and versatility of parametric statistical techniques even while recognizing that some restrictions may have to be placed on the interpretations of results. Labovitz (1967) and Kerlinger and Pedhazur (1973) have been particularly convincing in arguing the merits of the use of parametric regression techniques even when all assumptions cannot be fully met.[5] These writers feel that the assumptions that are violated do not tend to create large errors because the F and t tests are relatively robust tests, and the use of ordinal measures as if they were interval measures gains more information.

Other parametric and nonparametric statistical techniques were also employed for specific purposes; these will be mentioned in text and tables when data are presented.

Throughout the results, we have chosen to report findings as significant at the $p = .10$ level or less. We have adopted this inclusive practice for three reasons: (1) We did not want to discard suggestive findings that might be valuable in suggesting directions for future research, since this is in many ways an exploratory study. (2) We have a fairly large proportion of the relevant population in our sample, and thus the usual tests of significance based on a model of small samples within large populations would be conservative tests with our data. The 71 installations in our sample comprise 22 percent of all installations in the three Northeast regions from the nine executive departments included. They represent 18 percent of all installations in those regions. (3) In the instances where specific hypotheses have been advanced, the .10 level of significance would be equivalent to the .05 level of significance for a one-tailed test.

VALIDITY

In carrying out this research, a variety of techniques were employed to ensure the validity of the data. There is always some question about the accuracy of self-reports of behavior compared to behavior actually observed by the experimenter. The concerns boil down to three questions: (1) whether subjects were influenced to alter their responses by others; (2) whether subjects altered responses because of their own notions of what the experimenter expects to find; (3) whether subjects can accurately recall or know the answers to questions.

To deal with the first two problems, as well as is possible in this type of field research, a variety of cautions were undertaken to try to minimize outside influence on the responses of subjects. First, the samples of supervisor respondents were not chosen until we had reached the research site. They were then chosen from alphabetized lists of supervisors provided by the person acting as personnel director in the installation. Depending on the number of supervisors in the installation, every second, third, fourth, or fifth name on the list was selected using a random starting point. Thus no individual supervisor knew for certain in advance that he or she would be interviewed. Interviews in most installations were completed in a single day; a few larger installations took two days. This minimized the time available for respondents to discuss the instruments with future respondents. In addition, respondents were asked not to discuss the questions or their responses.

Second, the usual effect that could be expected from prior knowledge of our research plans would be that supervisors and others would bone up on policy provisions and would be otherwise inclined to take steps in their preparation for our visit and to try in their responses to make their installations "look good" in the matter of implementation of these policies. Although we cannot be sure, we feel that this effect was also minimal. For one thing, the results show extremely low levels of implementation of the alcoholism policy. Many supervisors just told us flatly that they knew little or nothing about it. Many coordinators also admitted they had done nothing. All respondents were interviewed in private locations, so they were free to speak without fear of reprisal from superiors. In addition, since interviews were conducted by members of our research team, including the two authors, in a face-to-face situation, the interviewers were in some position to gauge the honesty and frankness of respondents' answers. We initially expected some tendency to cover up poor performance relative to the policies and were quite surprised at the willingness of respondents to report unfavorable attitudes or lack of action. The interviewers used a standard introduction that stressed the independence of Cornell University from the Civil Service Commission or the respondents' employing agency and that promised both protection of their identities and the aggregation of responses so that individual installations would not be identified. These promises may have helped to make respondents feel free to respond honestly; they have been scrupulously kept.

Third, entry to the installations was gained for study of the alcoholism policy. Supervisors were generally unaware that we would also be asking questions about the EEO policy. They therefore did not have any warning to prepare any responses or position relative to that policy in advance of our visit. We did not detect any differences in ease of responding to the EEO questions, and generally reports for that policy, as expected, indicated more activity, but not always more favorable attitudes.

Other steps were taken. In order to avoid possible contamination of the data, Harrison M. Trice refrained from public statements on the subject of alcoholism during the period of data collection, notably when asked for interviews by several news magazines of large circulation and when asked to testify at congressional hearings. We attempted to enter and leave each region as quickly as possible, so that the interviewing teams exhausted one region, then moved to the next, then moved to the third. This was done to minimize communication about the study among agency directors in the same region.

The third problem of whether respondents "know the answers" to report was also considered. The major device that was employed to deal with this problem was to make response formats and questions as specific as possible and to ensure through pretesting that response formats were relevant and clear and included a sufficient range to permit subjects to respond accurately. For example, we did not ask respondents whether or not they were familiar with the alcoholism policy, because that is a difficult judgment to make overall. We asked instead whether or not they were familiar with specific policy provisions, for example, with sick-leave provisions or with the definition of alcoholism. Such specificity, we felt, would ensure more accurate responses from subjects. Similarly, we did not ask how much information they had received but specifically whether they had received an insertion for the policy manual, a brochure, a letter. Also, we did not ask them about the behavior or attitudes of others. We instead asked them about what they had done, experienced, or felt—issues that they were in the best position to report accurately. In addition, we avoided asking questions that would be "reactive" to subjects, in the sense of making them apprehensive or hostile. Finally, interviewers were trained to maintain a "professional" manner toward subjects, pleasant but objective. Any contacts outside the scheduled interviews, such as lunches and rides to transportation, were refused.

Our findings repeatedly demonstrate the degree to which our various devices were successful. For example, time spent learning about the policies as reported by supervisors was highly consistent with the amount of time they had reported they spent in training. These items were asked several pages apart in the instruments, and we would have observed if respondents checked one answer against another; they did not. The responses indicate that learning time, as might be expected, is consistently somewhat greater than training time. Such logical consistency of responses are indicators of internal validity in the data. Numerous other examples could be given, but only a few will be mentioned here: the consistency of relationships between various means of information diffusion and the familiarity with policy provisions reported by various respondents; the fact that staff-type coordinators report that they administer more different policies than line administrators; and a high correlation between the length of time that a coordinator has been serving in that role and the number of policy-related cases in which he has been involved.

Two other issues that are relevant to the validity of data from field studies such as this one are the issues of possible bias introduced into the data by the research itself and by the interviewers collecting the data. The first of these we will call research effect. Here the fear is that the very fact of the research being carried out will lead to changes of behavior on the dimensions being measured; this effect is likely to increase over time as more of the potential subject population learn of the activities and interests of the researchers. In order to assess the amount of effect that our research effort was having through time, all interviews were coded with the date on which they were done. Responses could then later be divided into an early group, a middle group, and a late group in terms of when the interviewing took place. Selecting twenty items at random from the supervisor file of data, we ran one-way analyses of variance by these three groupings to see if the early responses differed significantly from later responses. Of these twenty tests of significance, only six indicated significant differences ($p < .05$) between early, middle, and late respondents. Three of the variables producing significant differences concerned the alcoholism policy, and results were contrary to what might be expected: The last group of interviews showed less expected use, less activity, and less familiarity with the policy than earlier groups. On four measures of the EEO policy, the data collected in the middle of the field effort—the middle group—were significantly different from those from the early and late groups. Because the differences found showed such similarity of pattern for each policy, yet differed across policies, it seemed likely that the differences that we were picking up in these analyses were genuine differences attributable to region rather than to research effect. As mentioned earlier, as much interviewing as possible was done in each region in turn, and therefore regional effects are confounded with the time that the data was collected. Subsequent analyses by region demonstrated many differences between regions, including many consistent with the differences found here. The issue of regional effects will be discussed in more detail in chapter 7.

The second possible source of bias is what we will call interviewer effect. Here the fear is that something about the interviewers will affect responses. For example, some interviewers may lead subjects to be generally agreeable and give positive answers, while others may engender hostility and elicit negative responses. Another possibility is that subjects will respond differently to interviewers on the basis of sex, status, or age of the interviewer and how that compares with the same attributes of the respondent. In order to assess the degree to which our interviewers may have obtained systematically different responses, we also ran one-way analysis of variance on the same randomly selected twenty variables to ascertain whether responses differed significantly by interviewer. Despite the fact that interviewers ranged in status from freshly graduated college students, through professional employees with advanced degrees and graduate students, to a full professor, ranged in age from about twenty-one to the midfifties, and were about equally male and female, there were only two statistically significant differences ($p < .05$) in the twenty tests performed. Since one significant difference could be expected by chance, the results show that there is little evidence to suggest that interviewer effect was present in our data. We feel that two factors helped to minimize interviewer effect: (1) the fact that the instruments were largely closed-ended and fairly objective in tone, and (2) the careful and extensive training given to the interviewers and our later checks on their performance in the field.

Content validity was enhanced by our attempts to conceptualize the implementation process prior to the design and writing of instruments. Details of a three-stage model of implementation will be presented in the next chapter. This model guided our formulation of questions, and we used it to ensure that we would have a reasonable sampling of information about various phases of the implementation process. Within the framework of the model, we relied heavily on the policies themselves, as expressed in the relevant sections of the Federal Personnel Manual, to give us the full range of attitudes suggested by the normative content of the policies, and specific administrative and individual behaviors expected in implementing the policies.

Discriminability was greatly aided by the use of factor analysis in the scaling of many of the measures, especially those related to attitudes. This technique also enabled us to assess the amount of variance captured by the factors. In all cases, the amount of variance explained was satisfactory, and in many instances, remarkably high.

Our examination of the same issues with several types of respondents may be considered as a way of attaining some notion of convergent validity. The general similarity in the patterning of these results from supervisors, coordinators, and directors supports their general validity. We could not expect exact correspondence, since each type of respondent was asked to report primarily on his own behaviors, experiences, and attitudes.

The overall validity of our measures can perhaps best be judged from our results relative to our predictions and to what can be expected from the past literature on change and innovation. Many of the findings reported here agree with results of past studies. These issues will be better exposed as the results are presented in subsequent chapters.

3. Application of the Change Model to the Implementation Phase

IN ORDER TO STUDY the implementation of the alcoholism and EEO policies in federal installations, it was necessary to specify in greater detail the particular phases of the change process that were relevant to this study. Accordingly, stage 6 of table 1.1 was broken down into three hypothesized stages of implementation that we call (1) diffusion, (2) policy receptivity, and (3) policy use.

These stages are expected to occur in the *majority* of instances in the order given, implying a weak causal order. That is, we expected information diffusion and training activities to precede knowledge of the policies and attitudinal reactions to them. We also expected attitudinal reactions to occur before actual policy use. Since these policies were relatively recent, we did not expect them to be fully implemented, and it was our intention to assess the level of implementation in any given installation in terms of these stages.

We did not, however, expect that activities corresponding to any single stage would ensure success in the next stage. As Coe and Barnhill (1967) have noted, it is quite possible for a change to be subsequently abandoned, even though it was formally adopted earlier. Every stage of the change process carries the hazard of omission, total abandonment, or return to an earlier stage. This is because changes—even adopted changes—are likely to encounter considerable resistance to actual use (Thompson, 1967).

Between the time of the formulation of our model and the writing of this book, other authors have advanced similar models of the implementation process. Zaltman et al. (1973) identified two stages in the implementation process, each of which has two sub-stages. Thus, their initiation stage is composed of the substages knowledge-awareness and formation of attitudes toward the innovation. Their implementation stage is made up of an initial implementation stage and a continued-sustained implementation stage (1973:58–70). Their first two substages are similar to what we have called diffusion and receptivity; their last two substages correspond to what we have called policy use.

Schultz and Slevin (1975:12–13) summarized twelve models corresponding to various articles in their book, but only two of these involved any steps or stages in the implementation process. The Schultz and Slevin model (1975a) has intended use leading to actual use. These two variables are similar to our last two stages, receptivity and use. The Lucas (1975) model has attitudes leading to individual use—again similar to our last two stages (Schultz and Slevin, 1975b:17). The omission of any information diffusion stage in these models is noteworthy and somewhat puzzling. Surely users of operations research programs have to be informed about them before using them, as Schultz and Slevin themselves recognize when they mention "diffusion of an innovation" as part of the implementation process (1975b:xiv).

Berman and McLaughlin (1975a:19) advance a rather complex model of educational change but focus their discussion of stages on those preceding and following the actual implementation effort (1975a:16–18). Also, the variables used to measure implementation in this study focused on outcomes rather than steps leading to those outcomes. Their implementation measures included percentage of goals achieved, the amount of teacher change, difficulty of implementation, and to what degree implementation proceeded as laid out. They also measured continuation of the project after federal funding stopped and project diffusion to other schools (Berman and Pauly, 1975). It is only in their more qualitative case studies that "activities that characterized the process of implementation" are investigated (Greenwood et al., 1975). For example, they concluded that training (a component of the diffusion stage in our model) greatly benefited implementation efforts (Greenwood et al., 1975:33).

Thus the model advanced here seems to agree quite well with the conclusions of other researchers. In order to bring about the implementation of a change, the persons expected to do the implementing must have some information: they may receive written or oral communications, attend meetings designed to inform them, participate in training sessions, study specially prepared materials. As this new information is encountered, at least two kinds of internal reactions can be expected. Recipients of information are likely to experience cognitive and attitudinal changes as they learn new facts, weigh new value systems, and are generally the objects of attempts at persuasion. As Gibson (1975:70) pointed out, implementation can be conceived of as a process of influence in organizations, and attempts to influence will begin with (or accompany) the diffusion of information.

Finally, someone must act if the outcomes of the intended change process are to be realized. The behaviors required to carry out this final stage of implementation will vary with the goals or content of the change. In the case of the policy change studied here, the policy-mandated behaviors varied with the position of the person within the federal installations. Supervisors were expected to use the policies in different ways than policy facilitators or directors. But in each instance, we could identify specific behaviors envisioned by the policies. We expect that this would be possible to some degree with any relatively formalized change process—that desired behaviors could be identified and measured in the process of studying the implementation of the change.

It seems obvious that the actual behaviors of organizational members will be affected by what they have learned and how they have subjectively reacted to information received about the policies. Behavior will also be affected by the quality, quantity, and content of the information itself. Thus it is reasonable to posit the stages in the order that we have. Our model is not without difficulties, however.

The prime difficulty is one of feedback effects. Use of a policy, for example, will probably lead to acquiring additional information about it, and some attitudinal reactions to what has happened. We recognize the likelihood of such feedback effects, and in the chapters that follow we frequently mention that possibility in interpreting the findings. We prefer, nevertheless, to begin with the model as already mentioned. Our reasons are twofold: its relative simplicity, and its coherence with prior literature. The identification of the discrete stages is, by itself, an advance over past work. The question of the causal connection between stages will now be addressed by an empirical test of the model.

The Test

Since this three-stage model of the implementation process was a basic part of the design for this overall research effort, we decided to assess its viability using path analysis on the data from supervisors ($n = 634$). This technique would expose the underlying assumptions and interrelations posited by the model, and results could demonstrate whether the approach captured any significant amount of the variance in behaviors and attitudes that had been measured.

Path analysis has frequently been used to try to investigate processes when the data are actually cross-sectional, as was the case in this study.[1] Also, such results would tell us how much of the variation in policy use we could account for using just the three-stage model, before investigating the many independent variables that we had hypothesized would affect policy implementation (i.e., environmental, structural, work-role, and psychological variables).

Several measures were collected for variables relevant to each stage of the implementation model. Diffusion among supervisors included the following variables for each policy: the amount of diffusion to supervisors (those of six types and six sources of possible information actually received), the diffusion to their subordinates (computed similarly), the hours each respondent spent in training on that policy, the number of specific topics relevant to the policy covered in such training, and the amount of administrative emphasis that the policy has received in diffusion compared to other policies (three-item scale). The policy receptivity variables included scales derived from several multi-item questions designed to assess the respondents' familiarity with specific provisions of the policies; their agreement with the prescriptions of the policy; and an assessment of the benefits to be derived from the policy, the need for it within the installation, its general social usefulness, and so on. Scales were constructed from the receptivity and the administrative emphasis items on the basis of factor-analytic procedures (Stevens, 1976). Further details on all measures are given in the Appendix.

Three measures of policy use were collected: (1) whether or not respondents had used the policy, (2) how many times they had used the policy, and (3) how much they expected to use the policy in the future.

In the path analyses, the diffusion variables were treated as the exogenous (or independent) variables, while the receptivity variables (stage 2) were treated as first-level endogenous (or dependent) variables—all of equal priority in the model. The use variables were treated as the final, third-stage endogenous (or dependent) variables for each policy. Since there are three use measures for each policy, the final results of the path analyses yielded six path diagrams.

Two of these diagrams are presented in figures 3.1 and 3.2: those analyses for each policy of whether or not the supervisors had ever had occasion to use the policy. In these diagrams, only paths that yielded statistically significant coefficients were included. All other paths were also tested and can be presumed to be not significant statistically unless given here.

Path analysis builds on the results of multiple regression analyses that are performed by stages. Thus, in the models given here, all of the variables in the second stage (the receptivity variables) were analyzed as dependent variables with all of the variables in stage 1 included as independent variables in the regression equation. These

Figure 3.1 Path Diagram of Three-Stage Implementation Model: Past Alcoholism Policy Use.

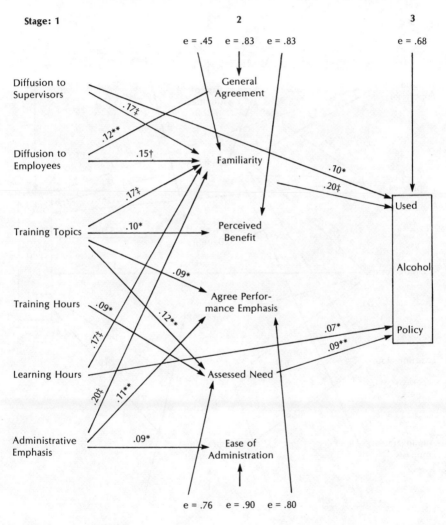

*p   .10
**p   .05
†p   .01
‡p   .001

results gave the paths of direct relationships between stage 1 and stage 2 variables. The next step was to run regressions with the stage 3 variables as dependent and all preceding variables in the model as independent variables included in the equation. These results yielded the paths of direct relations between stage 1 and stage 3 variables, or between stage 2 and stage 3 variables. By combining the results of

Figure 3.2   Path Diagram of Three-Stage Implementation Model: Past EEO Policy Use.

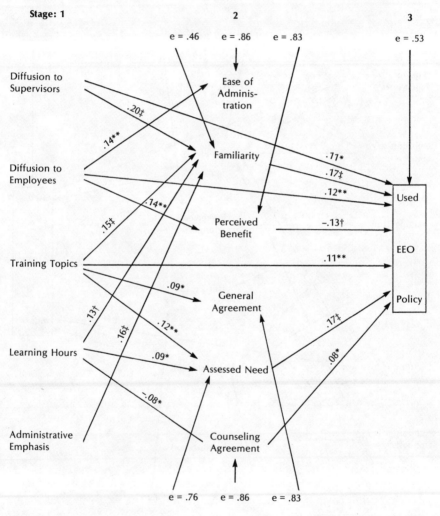

*p   .10
**p   .05
†p   .01
‡p   .001

these analyses in a single diagram, we can assess both the direct and indirect effects of each variable on the final dependent variables.

Numbers on the paths correspond to the standardized regression coefficients (betas) obtained in the regression runs. The numbers associated with the vertical arrows that point to the various endogenous variables in the model represent the residual or unexplained variance.[2]

Results

The results, on the whole, give encouraging, if not overwhelming, support to the three-stage implementation model. The analyses accounted for between 4 and 13 percent of the variance in the use variables for the alcoholism policy, and between 2 percent and 22 percent of the variance in use of the EEO policy. For both policies, the number of reported uses of the policy produced the least supporting results. Perhaps this was because the frequency of actual use is dependent on factors not included in the present model because they are hard to measure, control, or predict: for example, the amount of hiring going on, how many employees with drinking problems the supervisor encounters. For both policies, whether or not the policy has been used by the supervisor in the past and his expected level of future use yield similar amounts of variance explained.

The results generally document that both diffusion and receptivity variables are important in accounting for use of these policies, and this supports the notion of a model based on such stages. The diagrams also show the importance of the receptivity variables as intervening variables in the process model. For example, in figure 3.1, many of the training and diffusion variables are positively related to past use indirectly through assessed need and familiarity, but only two are directly related, and then only modestly. This suggests that diffusion and training efforts produce cognitive and attitudinal changes that raise the receptivity of organizational members toward behavioral change consonant with the training and diffusion efforts. Clearly, familiarity with the policy is the most important factor relating to whether or not a supervisor has used the alcohol policy. Somewhat the same pattern prevails for past use of the EEO policy (figure 3.2), except that the diffusion variables have important direct as well as indirect effects for this policy. These findings agree with those of the Rand study, where the more training of whatever form, the better the implementation of educational changes was judged (Greenwood et al., 1975:33), and suggest some intervening variables through which the training in those schools affected implementing behaviors.

The comparison of all six diagrams indicated that the most important predictor variable for use changes with the type of use of the policy. For past use, familiarity is the most important predictor (figure 3.1), or equally important (figure 3.2) with assessed need, whereas for future policy use, assessed need is clearly the most important predictor. Alone it accounts for 9.6 percent of the variance in future use of the alcoholism policy and 7.8 percent of the variance in future use of the EEO policy. While both need and familiarity are also somewhat important in predicting the number of alcohol policy uses, neither is related to the number of EEO policy uses.

Administrative emphasis is clearly an important variable in both models, but especially for the alcoholism policy. While it is positively and indirectly related to alcoholism policy use through familiarity, and through agreement with the performance emphasis (for expected use), it also has a negative direct relationship with the number of alcoholism policy uses. This suggests that administrative pressure that does not produce appropriate cognitive and attitudinal changes can create a backlash effect—perhaps by raising anxieties, perhaps by creating other resistances. Whether these trends are strong enough to be termed a form of deviance, in terms of policy prescriptions, is open to question; it surely is a pattern of "rebellion" familiar to many authoritarian supervisors and parents.

Across the three types of use, diagrams for the alcoholism policy are similar. Learning hours are not directly related to use except for past use (figure 3.1). As mentioned earlier, administrative emphasis has a direct negative effect ($-.10$, significant at the .05 level) with number of uses, and the agreement with the performance emphasis on the policy has direct effect on future alcoholism policy use (.08, significant at the .05 level).

For the EEO policy, the path diagrams are simpler for number of uses and expected use than is figure 3.2, representing past use. Only ease of administration and diffusion to supervisors are related to the number of EEO policy uses. Diffusion to employees is the only predictor, in turn, of ease of administration of this policy. For the EEO policy generally, diffusion and training have more direct, as well as indirect, effects compared with the alcoholism policy. Also, assessed need and familiarity are more evenly balanced for the EEO policy in determining past use, and familiarity is more important for this policy than for the alcoholism policy in determining future use.

Finally, the most important difference between the analyses of the two policies is that perceived benefit of the policy has two negative and significant relations with EEO policy use, while it is not significantly related to alcoholism policy use. Apparently, persons who use the EEO policy do so despite their relatively low assessment of its benefits, or persons who do not use the policy perceive it as more beneficial than those who have used it.

ASSESSING RESULTS IN TERMS OF THE DIMENSIONS OF CHANGE

As indicated on table 1.2, the alcoholism policy was judged to have less pervasiveness, magnitude, and innovativeness than the EEO policy. The two policies were considered to be similar in terms of duration. Differences along the first three dimensions can perhaps help to explain the variations in the results obtained for the two policies.

Considering the pervasiveness of a policy or other change suggests that variables in any model should be more tightly joined when pervasiveness is substantial than when there is little pervasiveness. If the change affects much of what a supervisor does, it will have greater salience for attitudinal and cognitive change, and for diffusion efforts. When pervasiveness is low, the amount of emphasis given to each of the stages of the model to which a given supervisor could be exposed may be more haphazard. The stages of the model are more weakly connected, because of competing claims of other activities and policies of greater salience. Thus we see that the alcoholism policy, with relatively low pervasiveness, yields results that account for only a modest amount of the variance in use. The EEO policy, on the other hand, with more pervasiveness, yields results that are more substantial in accounting for the variance in use.

Turning to the magnitude of the change involved, we note that the paths in the diagram for the alcoholism policy show predominantly positive coefficients. (The one negative path has already been discussed.) This suggests that the process of diffusion-receptivity-use flows relatively smoothly for this policy. Results show that more training and diffusion lead to more positive attitudes, and that familiarity and some positive attitudes lead to more use, as the model would predict. For the EEO policy, on the other hand, the results of diffusion are partially negative. Only diffusion to employees is related to perceived benefit of the policy, and perceived benefit is negatively related to past and future use of the EEO policy. This suggests that heavy information diffusion to employees can set up some attitudinal resistances to this policy among supervisors, probably because it is seen as having the potential for diluting some of the accustomed sources of power for supervisors, e.g., promotion and training opportunities. The data seem to suggest that a significant proportion of supervisors use the EEO policy and are skeptical of its benefits, while others view it favorably yet don't use or plan to use the policy. One type of supervisor is thus resisting the normative prescriptions of the policy, while another type is resisting by not using the policy. It seems reasonable to argue that a change of greater magnitude is more likely to encounter and provoke such resistance than a change that is seen as having very small magnitude. While there was also a negative path for the alcoholism policy, it did not involve an attitudinal component of the receptivity phase, and thus the types of resistance set up by the two policies appear to be different.

Generally, it can be seen from the path diagram that the EEO policy exhibits more significant relations between the stage 2 (receptivity variables) and the use variables. This finding also supports the notion that changes of greater magnitude may set up more attitudinal reactions than changes that require less behavioral or attitudinal displacement. Finally, the more innovative EEO policy requires the invention or development of new patterns or programs of behavior to a greater extent than does the alcoholism policy. This could weaken the connection between attitude and behavior.

ORGANIZATIONAL DEVIANCE AND IMPLEMENTATION

In using path analysis to test our three-stage model of implementation, we were forced to make certain assumptions. We have already mentioned the weak causal order that must be assumed to make the use of this technique appropriate. But another important assumption in the analysis already presented is that the stages of the process are monotonically related—in this case, that the more the diffusion, the more likely it is that receptivity will be high, and the more likely that use will be high. Furthermore, it is assumed that this is how the process of implementation usually proceeds. There is no provision in the analyses already performed for exceptions to this process—for reversals or interruptions in the process for some supervisors, except that these individual cases of behavior that do not fit the model become part of the unexplained or error variance. This was a reasonable model to advance, and one consistent with the past literature on change and the approaches of other writers to analyzing implementation, as summarized earlier.

Now, while it is likely that successful implementation processes often proceed as the model specifies, there is also the possibility that the process does not always proceed so smoothly—that is, it is possible that implementation may take forms other than diffusion leading to receptivity leading to use. The familiar Merton typology of deviance (1938), already mentioned in chapter 1, provides a way in which such interrupted or "atypical" processes might be categorized. Applying this typology to the federal installations in this study, for example, we would consider those installations that are above average on measures of all three stages of implementation are conformist installations. These cases fit the monotonic assumption of our three-stage model. Those that were high on diffusion but low on receptivity or use would be considered ritualists, attending to means but not achieving goals. The installations that are high on receptivity and/or use but are relatively low on diffusion would be considered innovators; that is, these installations have managed to achieve objectives of the policy without complying with the usual prescribed means of information diffusion and training. Neither ritualists nor innovative forms of implementation "fit" the assumptions of the three-stage model, and therefore such adaptations to policy prescriptions would contribute to error variance. Finally, those installations low on all three stages would be considered retreatists—organizations that have largely ignored the policies and have gone their own way without implementing them. Like conformity, this mode of adaptation fits the monotonic assumptions underlying our three-stage model. Once such distinctions are considered, it becomes clear that the analyses presented could only capture and explain conformist or retreatist forms of implementation.

We can combine both approaches in this study because we can identify through the three-stage model which behaviors might be considered the means to the end, in Merton's terms, and which are the end itself. In the paragraph above, we have considered diffusion and training as a means to an end, while receptivity and use are considered as goals or ends of the policies. With a combination of the two approaches, we can assess whether the "atypical" or deviant forms of implementation are associated with any of the independent variables considered in this study. Since this seems to be the first empirical application and operationalization of the classical Mertonian schema in studies of organizational behavior, it seemed desirable to pursue the more straightforward model already presented and then perform additional analyses to ascertain whether the application of the Merton typology would lead to meaningful refinements on the more usual approach to innovation and change. We shall present the results of our analyses using the Merton typology in chapter 9. Meanwhile, we shall proceed with a series of further investigations within the framework of the three-stage model tested in this chapter. In these analyses, we shall investigate how individual, work-role, organizational, and environmental variables can help to explain differing levels of diffusion, receptivity, and use of these policies.

SUMMARY

In the first three chapters we have identified and discussed three aspects of the change process in organizations: the dimensions of change, the identification of various modes of compliance and non-compliance using Merton's familiar schema, and the phases in the change process. We have applied these concerns to our study of the implementation of two personnel policies within federal government installations. We feel that the results are encouraging and give promise of explicating issues involved in change processes that have not been discussed or researched much in the past.

We have argued that policy is a mechanism for routinizing change, by specifying means and both operative and official goals for desired changes. A general model of a completed change process was advanced, and a three-stage model of one phase of that process—the implementation phase—was proposed and applied to data from supervisors.

One of the values of the model of change and the subsequent three-stage model of implementation advanced here is that they balance prior emphases on diffusion in the literature on change and innovation with consideration of the cognitive and attitudinal changes that are expected to result from diffusion efforts, and with consideration of the actual use of the change. The results presented in this chapter suggest that all types of diffusion do not have equal efficacy, and that some may even set up reactions opposite to those intended. They also demonstrate that positive attitudes toward a specific change are not a necessary condition for greater use of the change—in this case, the EEO policy.

4. The Key Role in Implementation: The Supervisors

THE IMMEDIATE SUPERIOR of an affected employee has a key role in the implementation of both of the federal policies studied. In the case of the alcoholism policy, it is the immediate supervisor who is supposed to detect any deterioration in work performance and then constructively confront the affected employee with evidence of this decline. In the case of the EEO policy, supervisors have key roles in detecting employees who should qualify for promotion or for additional training, and they have the responsibility of supervising work groups into which women and minority employees who are newly hired or promoted must be incorporated. In their general leadership role, they will also have impacts on the ways in which the normative changes incorporated in the policies will be viewed by their subordinates. A supervisor who is in clear and active support of a policy may lead his subordinates into better acceptance of the policy. Conversely, a supervisor who is in opposition or who feels no positive support for a policy is likely to inhibit support for the policy on the part of at least some of the subordinates.

In addition, supervisors have some role in disseminating information about the policy to subordinates, both in a general way and in response to situations where further information on the policy would be sought by a subordinate.

Thus supervisors can be seen to have both a formal and an informal role in policy implementation, including all of the phases of the process: diffusion and training, attitudinal receptivity and change, and actual use of the policy.[1] In order to assess the levels of implementation of these policies within the installations studied, we will therefore begin with an examination of what the supervisors in these government organizations reported relative to implementation of these two policies. Such data will enable us to do two things: (1) assess the general levels of implementation of these policies, and (2) compare these levels of implementation across the two policies.

GENERAL LEVELS OF IMPLEMENTATION AMONG SUPERVISORS

Information Diffusion and Training

Supervisors were asked about the types of information and the sources of that information from which they had learned about both policies. These data are presented in table 4.1. Generally, supervisors had received more written information about the EEO than about the alcoholism policy; memos or letters, insertions for the policy manual, and special brochures were received more frequently for the EEO than for the alcoholism policy. The differences in information diffused to these supervisors were even greater for oral forms of communication, with more than twice as much oral discussion (meetings and word of mouth) about EEO as about the alcoholism policy. Information on bulletin boards was even more discrepant across policies. Nine percent of supervisors admitted that they had received no information at all about the alcoholism policy, while only 1 percent of these supervisors had received no information about EEO.

Clearly, information on the alcoholism policy was relatively scanty. Many supervisors had received some formal written communication about it, but only about a third had had the opportunity to learn about the policy in situations such as a meeting where they could ask questions. They repeated that pattern with their subordinates, with only 27 percent reporting that they had given information about the alcoholism policy to their employees. Seventeen percent of these supervisors reported that their employees had received no information about the alcoholism policy. By comparison, 70 percent of supervisors had attended a meeting in which EEO was discussed, and 49 percent had, in turn, participated in informing their employees about the EEO policy, with the result that only 2 percent reported their employees had received no information about the EEO policy.

Furthermore, the frequency of sources of information for the alcoholism policy followed the bureaucratic pattern of communication downward through the hierarchy. Washington headquarters and the regional office were seen as the most frequent sources of information, while the installation head and alcoholism program coordina-

TABLE 4.1 Comparison of Diffusion to Supervisors for Two Policies

| | PERCENTAGE RECEIVING[a] | |
	Alcoholism Policy	*EEO Policy*
Forms of Information:		
Memorandum or letter	60%	85%
Insertion for policy manual	33	57
Special brochure on the policy	39	61
At a meeting	31	70
Word of mouth	20	42
Posted on bulletin board	11	54
Other	13	18
No information	9	1
Sources of Information:		
Washington headquarters	43	68
Regional office	43	75
Installation head	27	62
Program coordinator	16	51
Fellow worker	9	20
Public media	7	18
Other	8	11
Policy-related Training	19	54

[a] All differences between percentages for alcoholism and EEO policies are statistically significant at $\leq .01$ using the t test for correlated variables.

tor were less frequent informers. For the EEO policy, the amount of information did not tend to decrease so markedly at lower hierarchical levels. More information was received for this policy than for the alcoholism policy at all levels.

When asked about how the introduction of the alcoholism policy and program compared to other policies, the majority of supervisors reported that they had received less than typical exposure (54 percent), less than typical administrative emphasis (50 percent), and less than typical the number of techniques used to inform (52 percent). Ten percent or less reported that they had received more than typical exposure, emphasis, or informational techniques. The situation for the EEO policy is more than reversed, with 65 percent reporting more than typical exposure, 66 percent more than typical administrative emphasis, and 59 percent more than the typical informational techniques.

Additional data on information received by subordinates reinforce the findings: Clearly, the alcoholism policy was underdiffused as compared with the EEO policy. Training followed the same pattern, with almost three times as many supervisors reporting that they had attended training programs related to EEO as to the alcoholism program. For those who participated in training, five hours, on the average, had been spent in such training on alcoholism compared to eighteen hours for EEO. Overall, supervisors reported having spent an average of four hours learning about the alcoholism policy and thirty-one hours learning about the EEO policy.

One result is that only about half of the supervisors felt adequately familiar with the four provisions of the alcoholism policy most likely to affect their supervisory role: the situation in which the policy applies, the definition of alcoholism, disciplinary actions and procedures, and reporting procedures. Most supervisors were somewhat to totally unfamiliar with provisions of the alcoholism policy relating to medical benefits, leaves, union relations, treatment alternatives, or grievance procedures. Similar data for the EEO policy showed that the same supervisors felt at least adequately familiar with nine different aspects of that policy: formal complaint system, EEO action plan, community action program, incentives program, disciplinary actions and procedures, statistical reporting system, agency self-evaluation, training program, and recruitment program.

Clearly, the alcoholism policy did not receive as much attention in the diffusion process as did the EEO policy. This trend is evident in every facet, level, and type of communication about which we sought data. The obvious explanation of these differences is the wider applicability of the EEO policy—its pervasiveness, as we termed it in chapter 1. Also, the greater magnitude of the changes envisioned by the EEO policy made additional training and information diffusion desirable for that policy as compared with the alcoholism policy. Finally, the greater innovativeness of EEO probably makes the need for additional diffusion and training more evident to all concerned. The findings thus fall into a pattern that was expected. The magnitude of the differences found between the two policies, however, is another matter. The data suggest that the diffusion of information, the training activities, and the levels of familiarity for the alcoholism policy are very low—so low that it is hard to see how this policy could be expected to be implemented in terms of either appropriate attitude change or policy use when we view the implementation process in terms of the three-stage model discussed in chapter 3.

Attitudinal Reactions to the Policies:
Receptivity and Readiness to Use

A series of items was used to assess supervisory attitudes toward the two policies. Cognitive changes were assessed using the items on familiarity, already mentioned above. It was not possible to actually measure changes in attitudes with this cross-sectional study, but we asked supervisors about various types of attitudes toward the policy so that we might assess their general levels of receptivity toward the policies, which we felt would indicate their state of readiness to use the policies. As explained earlier, we could not assume that all supervisors had appropriate occasions to use either policy, and we therefore wanted to assess, as best we could, whether or not they were likely to use the policy when an appropriate occasion for its use did occur. One way in which we did this was to assess their attitudes toward the policies and their use. (The second method was to ask about possible future use, which we discuss in the next section, along with other measures of policy use.)

Two questions were asked about each policy.[2] The first asked respondents how much they agreed or disagreed with eight statements relevant to policy provisions and goals. The items were worded so that some were in accord with the intent of the policy, as specified in the insertions for the policy manual, and others were in disagreement with or exceeded policy intent. It was therefore necessary that these statements differed for the two policies; we attempted to make their content as nearly parallel as possible. The second question asked the supervisors to tell us their assessment of each policy in terms of identical semantic differentials, consisting of 7-point scales with each end anchored by a phrase that indicated an unfavorable assessment at the low end of the scale and a favorable assessment at the high end of the scale. We will call these the assessed benefit items.

Generally, supervisors were not as discriminating as the policies were in dealing with issues involving the details of provisions and their implementation. Many supervisors endorsed statements exceeding the formal written intent of the policies. Thus 91 percent endorsed the statement "Supervisors should try to identify employees who may be developing drinking problems," although the policy itself is concerned with the identification of employees whose drinking problems interfere with job performance. Trying to anticipate future problems that employees may have seems beyond the legitimate role of a supervisor. Similarly, 48 percent of supervisors agreed to some extent that "supervisors should concern themselves with employees' off-the-job drinking." Again the statement exceeds the legitimate domain of the supervisor and the policy prescriptions. It seems likely that overzealous endorsement of these statements was partially a result of the relatively low levels of diffusion and training for the alcoholism policy. Without training, in particular, supervisors are not likely to make fine discriminations about their role and will assume actions are desirable that may be beyond the intent of the policy. Because they remember the policy only in terms of the general social norms embodied within it, their actions respond to those norms rather than to specific policy content. Although this might always occur, the extent of its occurrence with this policy suggests that additional training was needed to adequately inform the supervisors about the policy provisions and the boundary conditions of their application. This interpretation is strengthened by the fact that only 17 percent of supervisors agreed with the statement "A drinking relapse indicates that treatment is a failure." This statement is clearly contrary to policy intent, and most supervisors failed to agree with it, indicating that not many were opposed to all aspects of the policy or likely to be led into endorsing a statement contrary to policy intent through some general tendency to agree with all statements.

Three other statements reflecting key items of actual policy content were overwhelmingly supported by the supervisors: a definition of alcoholism (87 percent agree), the provisions that alcoholics should be granted sick leaves (94 percent), and a statement that "alcoholism is a treatable illness" (96 percent). A key provision of the alcoholism policy, however, failed to receive more than minority endorsement, with only 43 percent of supervisors agreeing that "supervisors can best help employees with drinking problems by concentrating on their work performance." Clearly, this part of policy strategy is not understood or not accepted by many of these supervisors, probably because of low levels of training.

Finally, the attitudes of many supervisors regarding counseling seem likely to interfere with the role of the alcoholism coordinator, as specified in the policy. More than 80 percent of these supervisors felt they should counsel an employee with a drinking problem who came to them, while the policy strongly suggests that they be sent to the coordinator for counseling and/or appropriate referral to other counseling services.

Generally speaking, levels of agreement were greater for similar normative and judgmental issues relative to the EEO policy. Both appropriate and overzealous statements were more heavily endorsed for this policy. On the zealous side, 99 percent of supervisors felt they "should try to identify employees who may qualify for promotion"; 60 percent thought that "supervisors should concern themselves with identifying cases of discrimination"; and 65 percent agreed that "minority members should be sought out for employment vacancies." In conformity with policy intent, 96 percent endorsed a broad definition of discrimination, and 75 percent agreed that "discrimination in hiring and promotion can be eliminated." Surprisingly, the focus on performance was more accepted for the

EEO policy, with 79 percent of supervisors agreeing that concentration on performance would "best help minority employees." In regard to the propensity of these supervisors to feel they should counsel, only 75 percent felt they should do counseling relative to EEO problems, reflecting a slightly greater recognition of the formal roles assigned to EEO counselors in the policy, or perhaps more reluctance to get involved with this sort of problem than was true for supervisors (80 percent) regarding the alcoholism policy. In the statement contrary to this policy's intent, "A poor employment record by a minority employee hurts the EEO program," more supervisors (55 percent) endorsed the statement than the parallel statement for the alcoholism policy (with only 17 percent). Thus the overall pattern of responses for the EEO policy was for higher endorsement of the statements, without any greater discrimination as to their content. The results suggest a generally greater concern with the EEO than with the alcoholism policy, and a greater willingness to agree with statements relative to it. Apparently the greater administrative emphasis that the EEO policy received and the greater amount of diffusion and training that accompanied the introduction of this policy led to its greater salience to supervisors as compared with the alcoholism policy. They responded with concern and general public agreement, but also with some overzealous reactions and with some strong reservations about the policies. These responses may indicate *not* that they are in greater agreement with the EEO policy than with the alcoholism policy, but that they are more aroused about EEO. Thus supervisors more strongly agree and disagree with policy provisions in the case of the EEO policy.

The second set of items designed to assess attitudinal reactions to the policies produced more similar responses for the two policies, as shown in table 4.2. When asked their assessment of the policies, supervisors were equally favorable to the two policies in terms of their benefit to their installation, their benefit to society, their social usefulness, and that they were a good idea. The supervisors saw the EEO policy as somewhat closer to a giant step than they did the alcoholism policy, but this difference, while statistically significant, is small. Much larger differences were obtained in their assessments of the need for the policies within the installations and the ease with which they could be administered. Fewer supervisors felt that the alcoholism policy was needed than felt the EEO policy was needed in their installation, probably because of the greater pervasiveness of the EEO policy. Supervisors were also more likely to feel that the alcoholism policy would be "hard to administer."

An interesting difference was also reflected in the number of nonresponses to these items. The alcoholism items produced 46 to

TABLE 4.2 Comparison of Assessed Benefit of Two Policies

| | MEANS | | |
Assessment of the policy[a]	Alcoholism Policy	EEO Policy	p[*]
1 = negative . . . 7 = positive			
Not needed . . . widely needed in installation	2.71	4.50	.000
Hard . . . easy to administer	3.73	4.31	.000
Harmful . . . beneficial to installation	5.78	5.73	n.s.
Socially harmful . . . socially beneficial	5.78	5.95	.006
Minimal . . . giant step for government	5.16	5.67	.000
Useless . . . useful to supervisors	5.68	5.65	n.s.
Bad . . . good idea	6.05	6.08	n.s.

n.s. = not significant.

[a]Response formats were expressed as semantic differentials, with the negative phrase or adjective anchoring the low end of a 7-point scale and the positive phrase or adjective anchoring the high end of the scale.

[*]As determined by t-tests for correlated variables.

79 (7-12 percent) missing values for these items, with the lowest and highest nonresponses occurring in response to the need and administration items, respectively. The same items produced only 7 to 16 (1-2 percent) missing responses from supervisors relative to the EEO policy.

In advance of these results, we expected much greater attitudinal resistance to the EEO policy, largely because of the magnitude of the changes in behavior and attitudes that it involved. These results suggest that changes in attitudes may be as problematic for the alcoholism policy as for the EEO policy, and that in addition, the alcoholism policy is not accepted as needed in the installations and is seen as more difficult to administer. This last finding is surprising in comparison with the EEO policy, which has surely led to a plethora of rather difficult procedures in most employing organizations. Perhaps the presence of civil service regulations makes EEO easier to implement in the federal sector. Finally, the larger percentage of nonresponses for the alcoholism policy, which largely represent refusals to answer the item on the grounds of lack of knowledge, indicate the low degree of any kind of attitudinal reaction to this policy by many supervisors. They cannot react to specifics they have not been informed about.

Use of the Policies

About 11 percent of the supervisors reported "an opportunity to use the alcoholism policy procedures" with employees they supervise as compared to 59 percent for the EEO policy. When asked about the number of cases of such use, both the range and mean number of cases was greater for the EEO policy: the average number of subordinates involved in the use of EEO was over twelve per supervisor, while an average of only one employee for every four supervisors was involved in cases of use of the alcoholism policy. The great majority of the supervisors (70 percent) using the policy had only one employee that they had dealt with under provisions of the alcoholism policy. For the EEO policy, the median number of cases dealt with was three employees.

Considering the 85 cases of use of the alcoholism policy from our sample installations in more detail, we found that immediate supervisors most often initiated the consideration of an employee within the alcoholism program. The most frequent triggering events were poor work performance, excessive absenteeism or tardiness, and visible signs of drinking on the job—sometimes in combination. These are all appropriate reasons to apply the alcoholism policy. In 11 cases (13 percent) there was no triggering event, but the employee was believed to have a history of problem drinking. In five other cases (6 percent), some incident off the job led to the employee's being handled under the alcoholism program. It is not clear that these last two types of cases fall under the scope of the policy, although they are consonant with its general intent to provide treatment for problem drinkers.

Thus far, the actions of supervisors are in substantial agreement with the intent of the policy. When we considered other specifics, however, we found that the actual handling of employees who are considered problem drinkers deviated substantially from the intent of the policy.

Supervisors tended to both counsel and refer their subordinates for medical or other help without the involvement of the alcoholism coordinator. In only 9 cases (about 10 percent) were employees referred to the alcoholism coordinator, while in 34 cases (40 percent) the supervisor reported counseling the employee himself.[3] In 12 cases supervisors did nothing, and in 11 cases they used actions detrimental to the employee (dismissal or disciplinary measures).

Administratively, the predominant tendency was to do nothing official ("keep it between ourselves"); this happened in 33 cases, or 39 percent of the total. There were also cases in which the employee was fired, was transferred, was disciplined, voluntarily retired, or quit

ask potential latent functions of this approach (e.g., leverage over employee)

the job; these cases totaled about the same number as the cases in which "nothing official" was done. Only 27 cases (32 percent) eventuated in some treatment, counseling, and/or use of sick leave by the employee—all courses of action suggested by the policy. The remaining two-thirds of the cases were handled in ways not consonant with the provisions or intent of the alcoholism policy. The outcome of about 50 percent of these cases is uncertain, with supervisors unwilling or unable to tell whether there has been a change in drinking behavior. For the other cases, positive results are slightly more frequent than negative ones; that is, in 29 cases there is less drinking or no drinking evident as compared to 25 cases where the employee refused or could not stop drinking. In 36 cases there is also some improvement in work performance, as compared with only 16 cases where work performance has not changed or changed for the worse. In another 27 cases, supervisors were uncertain about present work performance.[4]

When we asked supervisors what happened when they applied the EEO policy, 30 percent of the 371 supervisors who reported using the policy failed to define the groups to whom it had been applied, while another 26 percent just used the term "minority." Only 5 percent specifically mentioned blacks, 23 percent mentioned women, 10 percent mentioned other ethnic groups, 4 percent mentioned other nonethnic minorities (part-time workers, older workers, the handicapped, etc.), and only 2 percent mentioned application to nonminority employees. Some supervisors mentioned more than one of these groups. Most of those (82 percent) who failed to define the groups mentioned that they felt the EEO policy applied to all employees and thus had a broad definition of the policy. Thus the data suggest that only about one-quarter (82 percent of 30 percent = 24.6 percent) of the supervisors who had reported using the policy interpreted the policy as applying to all employees; this is 14 percent of all of the supervisors in the sample.

The types of actions taken by these supervisors in using the EEO policy tended to concentrate in the classic personnel functions of hiring (49 percent of those who had used the policy), training (44 percent), and promotion (44 percent).[5] Recruiting was the next most frequent activity, with 12 percent of supervisors reporting recruiting and 8 percent interviewing activities. Only 3 percent reported counseling employees, and 7 percent reported being involved in grievance actions. For 39 cases supervisors mentioned either negative or mixed outcomes, such as the resignation of an employee who failed to obtain a promotion or the decision not to file a complaint by an employee who could have done so. In 18 cases outcomes were still pending or uncertain. But overall, the supervisors seemed to feel that the outcomes of the use of the EEO policy were positive (positive outcomes were mentioned for 102 cases). Thus, 64 percent of those who mentioned outcomes had positive as compared to 25 percent with negative or mixed outcomes. If the same proportions applied to outcomes of all cases, this would indicate very favorable results for the EEO policy.

In assessing use of these policies, supervisors were also asked questions about their future use of the policies. These items were important because we could not easily learn or know whether any given supervisor had had the opportunity to use either policy. Supervisors responded that they felt the alcoholism policy would be used relatively infrequently in their unit: 63 percent responded with 1 on the 7-point scale ("almost never"), and another 19 percent responded with the next lowest value. Only 2 percent of the supervisors gave a positive response (above the midpoint) on this item. By comparison, 45 percent of supervisors felt that the EEO policy would be used relatively frequently in their unit, giving responses above the midpoint. Another 23 percent chose a neutral response at the midpoint, and 31 percent responded that the EEO policy would be used relatively infrequently. Of these, 17 percent gave the lowest response, "almost never."

Summary

In all of these data, the trend is clear: supervisors report more use and more policy-consistent use of the EEO than of the alcoholism policy. Perhaps because of the lack of information, training, and general administrative emphasis, the alcoholism policy was not often used as the policy intended. At best, shortcuts of the policy provisions occurred. At worst, the policy provisions were circumvented altogether. However, supervisors did report that something was done about 164 cases of problem drinking in these seventy-one installations. Projected to all supervisors in these installations, the data indicate an estimated prevalence or occasion to use the alcoholism policy of 473 employees—3.3 percent of all employees in these installations. Using statistical procedures, we can be 95 percent certain that the actual prevalence of cases of problem drinking detected by supervisors falls between 1.9 percent and 4.6 percent. The upper figure conforms closely to conservative estimates of the prevalence of problem drinking from the private employment sector, indicating substantial use of this policy even though its implementation was deeply flawed in many ways. Since the policy had been adopted only three years before our data collection, a less-than-maximum level of implementation is not surprising. As our discussion proceeds, some of the shortcomings of the implementation present when we collected the data will be more fully explained.

Returning to the details of how the detected alcoholism cases were handled, because of the presence of civil service regulations, it is unlikely that any number of these employees were fired without cause or otherwise unfairly treated. What is more likely is that they were not processed through all of the formalized steps envisioned in the alcoholism policy; especially notable was the rare use of coordinators. Perhaps the presence of the policy led some supervisors themselves to function relatively effectively in these cases, offering the proper help in obtaining medical help or other assistance, sick leave, and other benefits. What is interesting is the obvious tendency of the supervisors to handle the matter themselves, as evidenced by their propensity to counsel and their tendency to refrain from doing anything official about the problem. Since many of the outcomes of these cases were uncertain, and few were definitely positive, this circumventing of the policy cannot be interpreted as an innovation that will result in outcomes similar to those intended by the policy. What is clear from the data is that such employees have seldom been confronted in the formal manner that the alcoholism policy recommended. Clearly, more training and appropriate changes of attitudes may be required before this policy is fully implemented.

In the case of the EEO policy, it is difficult to assess the actual levels of use relative to some desired level of use. Clearly, few supervisors gave a broad interpretation of the policy as applying to all employees, and this meant that a substantial number did not anticipate much use of the policy in the future. Since the policy should always be operative whenever hiring, promotion, training, and so forth are going on, this assessment of future use also indicates substantial resistance to this policy. Even if the policy is interpreted narrowly—for example, in terms of minorities and women—it is hard to argue that almost one-third of the supervisors should be so certain that they would have relatively infrequent occasion to use this policy, with 17 percent of these feeling that they would "almost never" use it. Such responses indicate tendencies to view jobs as unlikely to attract or be suitable for minorities or women. Again the policy seems far from full implementation.

We did not, of course, expect full implementation of either policy. The literature on change and innovations is replete with references to the resistance to change and other factors that can inhibit change efforts. In the following sections we shall therefore report the results of analyses attempting to explain why implementation occurred in some cases and not in others. For this explanation, we shall test hypotheses concerning a variety of factors that could be expected to influence efforts toward implementation by supervisors.

FACTORS EXPECTED TO INFLUENCE
IMPLEMENTATION BY SUPERVISORS

Three types of variables were identified as possible influences on the implementation of the alcoholism and EEO policies by these supervisors. They included (1) individual characteristics of the supervisors (demographic variables and personal attitudes), (2) variables related to the supervisory role, and (3) variables describing the installation in which the supervisor worked.

Individual Characteristics

The three demographic variables employed in this research were age, sex, and education. There is some disagreement about the possible effect of such individual characteristics on behavior favoring innovation. In a study of the adoption of an innovative computer-based information system by university faculty, Stern, Craig, and Salem (1976) failed to find any significant differences between adopters and nonadopters on demographic variables. Berelson and Steiner (1964:619), on the other hand, argued that younger persons are less likely to be resistant to change and therefore are more likely to be innovators within a society. They also argued that persons of higher social status were more likely to favor innovation. Other studies have indicated that higher levels of professional training of organizational members are likely to be positively related to the adoption of innovations (Kaplan, 1967; Palumbo, 1969; Mytinger, 1968). Discussions of these findings suggest that it is not the demographic characteristic per se that is expected to facilitate or inhibit behavior supportive of change and innovation, but that it is some difference within perceptual and attitudinal constellations closely associated with the demographic variable that is presumed to be related to greater propensity to innovate. Thus the relationship is indirect, and the real predictor variables are the associated underlying factors that are being tapped indirectly through the demographics: such things as perceptual openness, cognitive complexity, and general psychological flexibility (Kaplan, 1967). If these are the factors involved, then it is possible to argue for the following hypotheses:

4.1. Younger supervisors will be more likely to implement these policies.
4.2. Male supervisors will be more likely to implement these policies than female supervisors.
4.3. More educated supervisors are more likely to implement these policies than less educated supervisors.

Younger supervisors are presumed to be more psychologically flexible and to have less developed perceptual sets. Males have generally been considered less conservative than females on matters of social mores; witness the recent greater female than male opposition to both abortion legislation and proposed legislation designed to support equal rights for women. Since the EEO policy is designed to help women, it could be argued that women supervisors would be more likely to implement at least this policy. We are making the negative prediction because the examples given above, and others, indicate substantial opposition by women to measures supposedly to their advantage. Many women do not see such legislation as beneficial, whether because of their resistance to change or because of substantive problems within the legislation. Education was expected to be positively related to implementing behavior because, within the supervisory ranks, greater education almost always meant college education. While not all college education is professional training per se, college training is more likely to lead to or be indicative of general flexibility, cognitive complexity, and perceptual openness (Trent and Craise, 1967).

Three variables measuring attitudes were also hypothesized to be related to implementing behaviors or attitudes. The first of these was the attitude toward change itself. Hage and Dewar (1973) had used a similar measure[6] and reported that positive values toward change among those elite organizational members who participated in decision making were important predictors of program change within the organizations. Mohr (1966) and Kaplan (1967) also found attitudes of chief executives or administrators to be associated with innovation. Although Hage and Aiken (1967) did not find that such attitudes on the part of all job occupants were related to program change, we felt that supervisors in these federal installations could be considered as possible influentials or elites because they have an important and pivotal decision-making role in the implementation of these policies, especially the alcoholism policy. We therefore hypothesized:

4.4. Supervisors who report positive attitudes toward change will be more likely to implement these policies than supervisors with negative attitudes toward change.

In addition, two job-related attitudes were considered relative to the implementing behaviors and attitudes of these supervisors. Job involvement, as defined and measured by Lodahl and Kejner (1965), is a concept used to describe the degree to which an individual's self-esteem and ego are affected by his job performance (1965:25). Persons with high job involvement are presumably more affected by their job performance than persons less job-involved. Other researchers have developed other measures for similar constructs.[7] Although results of studies relating job involvement to performance have yielded mixed findings (Rabinowitz and Hall, 1977), we felt that job-involved bureaucrats would be inclined to be more conscientious in their duties, and thus more likely to implement these policies.

4.5. Supervisors high on job involvement are more likely to implement these policies than supervisors low on job involvement.

Finally, we measured commitment to the organization and commitment to the federal service as the propensity to stay with the organization or federal service. Using Becker's side-bet theory of commitment (1960), Ritzer and Trice (1969a) developed scales to measure organizational and occupational commitment. Variants of this scale have been used by Alutto and his associates (Alutto, Hrebiniak, and Alonso, 1973; Alutto and Hrebiniak, 1975).[8] Earlier, Victor Thompson (1965) had expressed the view that a moderate amount of commitment—neither complete commitment nor alienation from the organization—would be most conducive to innovation. Following his argument would lead to the prediction of a curvilinear relationship between commitment and innovative types of change.[9] However, we felt that these policies were not highly innovative and thus might be more acceptable to the highly committed than change that required more novel behavior. We thus decided upon a simpler hypothesis:

4.6. Those supervisors with greater commitment to the installation in which they are employed and to the federal service will be more likely to implement the policies than those supervisors with lesser commitment.

Role Characteristics

Four aspects of the supervisor's role were expected to affect his or her level of policy implementation. The first of these was tenure within the organization; supervisors with longer tenure are more likely to implement these policies because of greater experience in the managerial role, including learning ways in which such policies can be implemented within existing role demands, and because seniority within the organization may lead to increased tendencies toward conformity with policy directives. Similar factors should be operative with increased tenure in a given position.

4.7. Supervisors with longer tenure within the organization or within their position are more likely to implement these policies than supervisors with shorter tenure.

Managerial level was expected to be related because those supervisors in higher hierarchical positions are expected to identify more closely with objectives from above, in this case from their Washington headquarters and from the Civil Service Commission.

4.8. Supervisors at higher managerial levels are more likely to implement these policies than supervisors at lower managerial levels.

At the same time, the nature of the work supervised may affect the likelihood of implementing these policies. In the case of the alcoholism policy, deteriorating work performance, especially such things as tardiness and absences, are more likely to be detected when employees work in visible job settings, where they have to be in the same place every day at the same time. Other kinds of jobs involve less routine from day to day, and employees in such jobs can use their discretion to help cover up deteriorating job performance. Thus the alcoholism policy may be easier to implement with employees in less skilled jobs, because such jobs are likely to be more visible and more routine.[10] It also seemed likely that the EEO policy might be more easily implemented at lower skill levels, because women and minority workers have customarily been employed at these levels, and therefore the execution of the EEO policy would represent less of a change at these levels.

4.9. Supervisors of less skilled employees will be more likely to implement the policies than supervisors of more skilled employees.

The third aspect of the work role that we expected to affect policy implementation was the degree of work overload experienced by supervisors. Mytinger (1968), especially, has noted that organizational members who are overburdened are less likely to adopt new health programs. We felt that overload was likely to be even more of a barrier to actual policy use.

4.10. The more supervisors report they suffer from conditions of work overload, the less likely they are to implement the policies.

Finally, general psychological theory, including motivation theory, would suggest that supervisory behavior may be affected by the reward structure of the employing organization. Whether because of inherent needs (Maslow, 1954; Herzberg, 1968; McGregor, 1960)

or because of conditioning processes (Skinner, 1953), supervisory
behavior is likely to be shaped by what behaviors supervisors perceive
are rewarded. Schultz and Slevin (1975a:166) found that managers
who expected an operations research model to have a positive effect
on their own performance were more likely to intend to use it than
other managers, suggesting that the appeal of a change may be
strongly determined by "what can it do for me." In this study, if
supervisors felt that performance was important for promotion, they
would be more likely to be concerned to perform well in implementing these policies.[11] If they perceive seniority or technical skills
as more important for promotion, their performance in implementing these policies is less likely to be rewarded, and supervisors
are therefore less likely to implement the policies.

> **4.11.** Supervisors who feel performance is important to promo-
> tion are more likely to implement the policies, while those
> who feel seniority or technical skills are more important
> for promotion are less likely to implement the policies.

Organizational Characteristics

A variety of organizational-level variables have been related by
other writers to innovation and change in organizations. Many of
these variables will be dealt with in more detail in chapter 7, when
we present results from analyses comparing installations with each
other. In this chapter we are investigating factors impinging on the
individual supervisor, and a smaller number of organizational variables were chosen: the organization's size, whether or not a union
was present, the percentage of employees who were supervisors, and
the degree of centralization in decision making.

Size has been related to innovation in organizations by the
findings of Hage and Aiken (1969) and Kaluzny et al. (1974). Both
sets of researchers have argued that size is likely to mean increased
resources for innovation, especially since overall greater resources are
expected to accompany greater size and thus make the presence of
organizational slack more likely. Since it is difficult to measure slack,
in the sense of resources that might be available because they are not
fully committed, size is used to deal rather indirectly with the issue
of resources.[12]

In addition, size has frequently been discussed as a possible
source of impersonality and concomitant alienation and stress for
individuals in organizations. It would thus be expected to have
negative effects on performance, satisfaction, and morale. Richard
Hall (1972:130- 32) stated that empirical results are rather inconclu-
sive, but previous investigators had looked at other facets of job-
related attitudes and performance than were used in this study. Both

of these policies call for universalistically oriented behaviors (Parsons, 1951), in the sense that they ask the supervisor to ignore personal attributes of subordinates and focus on performances or on ability to perform. The impersonality contributed by larger size may be expected to facilitate the use of such universalistic criteria. These arguments suggest that the mixed results obtained across past studies may have been a function of different types of expected behavior measured as performance. Consequently, it seems worthwhile to test the following hypothesis:

4.12. Supervisors in larger installations are more likely to implement the policies than supervisors in smaller installations.

We made the positive prediction because of the findings on innovation cited above, because of the universalistic orientation of policy prescriptions, and because the predicted negative consequences so often expected have not been well demonstrated.

The presence of a union is likely to affect the implementation of these policies because both policies deal with personnel matters. Since the policies exist, supervisors who work where employees are represented by the union must take policy provisions into account when dealing with employees who might be covered by the policies, lest they become involved in a grievance or other conflict with the union on the grounds that they failed to use policy provisions when they were applicable. Besides the unpleasantness involved in such union-management conflicts, the supervisor involved is likely to find that a case which is settled against management will reflect unfavorably on his abilities as a supervisor. Thus we expect:

4.13. Supervisors who work in installations with unions are more likely to implement the policies than other supervisors.

Many organizational researchers and management theorists have been concerned with issues of span of control or supervisory ratios and how these might affect organizational performance (Fayol, 1949; Blau and Schoenherr, 1971; Freeman, 1973). The general notion is that supervisors can only effectively manage a certain number of subordinates, although more recent theorists would argue that the number would vary with the types of tasks performed or other factors. We asked supervisors how many subordinates reported to them (the usual measure of span of control) and specified that they should include only those employees over whom they had direct supervision and whose performance they evaluated. Despite these cautions, we found that comparison between these responses and the known number of employees in installations yielded results too discrepant to assume that the span-of-control measure was accurate. We therefore substituted a measure obtained from personnel records, in which we calculated the percentage of all employees in each installation who were supervisors. This measure might be considered as an average span-of-control measure for each installation.

At a concrete level, it seemed likely that supervisors might have more difficulty in implementing these policies if they had larger spans of control, since they would then be responsible to assess job performance for a greater number of subordinates, refer more employees for training and promotion, and so on. With fewer subordinates, a supervisor is likely to have a greater amount of interaction with each subordinate and therefore to be more familiar with the performance and problems of each. Larger proportions of supervisors yield smaller average spans of control. We therefore hypothesized:

4.14. Supervisors in installations with larger percentages of supervision are more likely to implement the policies than other supervisors.

By centralization in organizations, we mean to describe the location of decision-making authority within organizations. In more centralized organizations, participation and final authority for many decisions are reserved for those organizational members who occupy positions at the top of the organizational hierarchy of authority. In decentralized organizations, those at the lower echelons of the hierarchy of authority are given some participation in making decisions. Since the location of the final authority and the greatest participation may vary with the decision involved, centralization should ideally be measured by a consideration of some range of decisions within the organization(s) studied (Beyer and Lodahl, 1976; Beyer, 1977).[13]

Past arguments relating centralization to innovation and change have pointed out that centralization may inhibit upward communication (Read, 1962; Shepard, 1967), and make it easier to veto proposed changes (Victor A. Thompson, 1969). Hage and Aiken found a positive relationship between participation in decision making (decentralization) and rate of program change (1967:510–11). These findings follow the general prescriptions of many studies and theorists (Coch and French, 1948; Likert, 1961) that participation by organizational members leads to a greater willingness to implement decisions that are reached. These notions are countered by Sapolsky's (1967) finding that decentralization tended to frustrate the implementation of innovations in department stores. These conflicting findings led Zaltman et al. to argue that centralization may affect different stages of the innovative process differently: "Less centralization appears to be more appropriate in gathering and processing the information at the initiation stage. . . . However, at the implementation stage, it may be that more strict channels of authority can reduce potential conflict and ambiguity that could impair implementation" (1973:146).

Recognizing the risks inherent in making predictions on the basis of conflicting results, we nevertheless decided to make a single hypothesis for all three stages of implementation relative to centralization. We felt that individual supervisors were unlikely to exert themselves to implement these policies in installations in which they had little opportunity to participate in decision making because the policies themselves require considerable exercise of judgment and discretion. If supervision is not accustomed to exercising initiative and discretion, it seemed unlikely that they would do so in the case of these two personnel policies. Our argument, then, is perhaps more akin to that of Merton when he discussed "trained incapacity" (Merton, 1952). We argue that supervision that is unaccustomed to taking responsibility in decision making is also unlikely to voluntarily intervene in drinking problems or be conscientious in applying other controversial policies, like EEO. This may be especially true in the federal sector, as opposed to business, because supervisors in the federal sector are protected from easy dismissal by civil service regulations. We therefore predicted:

4.15. Supervisors who report less centralization of decision making will be more likely to implement the policies than supervisors who report more centralization.

Procedures for Tests of Hypotheses

This concludes our list of hypotheses for individual supervisors. These hypotheses were tested through a series of multiple regressions. In each regression, a measure of implementation was employed as the dependent variable, and the entire list of independent variables just discussed was tested simultaneously to see which would be significantly related to the measure of implementation, controlling for the effects of all of the other independent variables. The dependent variables, or measures of implementation, were treated in the stages specified in our three-stage model. This meant that the analyses of the two later stages of the model—the receptivity and use stages—included the implementation variables from the earlier stage(s) of the model, as well as the independent variables, as predictor variables. By this procedure we not only could test the direct effects of all independent variables on a variable in a later stage of implementation, but simultaneously could assess whether any portion of the effects of the independent variables were operating indirectly through another implementation variable from an earlier stage in the model.

For example, organizational size may affect the diffusion of information; but does it also affect attitudes toward the policy directly, or only through the amount of diffusion? Such questions can be answered through the application of path analysis, providing the researcher is willing to make his assumptions of the possible causal order of variables explicit. Since we have already done this in the three-stage model of implementation, we could use path analysis on the data from supervisors to look simultaneously for the direct effects between independent variables and implementation variables that we have hypothesized, as well as for other indirect effects that might emerge.

RESULTS: FACTORS AFFECTING IMPLEMENTATION

Since regressions were run on eighteen dependent variables for each policy, it seemed desirable to summarize the results of all of these equations in two tables—one for each policy. From these tables we can assess the direction of significant relationships for each independent variable across all of the dependent variables studied, thus learning whether and how often hypotheses advanced were confirmed with significant results in the direction hypothesized. Seven diffusion variables were analyzed as dependent variables for each policy: diffusion to supervisors, diffusion to other employees, training hours spent by supervisors, the number of training topics covered in such supervisory training, learning hours spent by supervisors, administrative emphasis that supervisors perceived each policy had received, and their awareness of the union's position on the policy. All of the independent variables already discussed in the formation of hypotheses were simultaneously included in regression equations with each of these diffusion variables as the dependent variable.

Eight receptivity variables were also analyzed as dependent variables; these vary somewhat across policies. For the alcoholism policy, the receptivity variables include familiarity with the policy provisions, zealous agreement, agreement with the medical model, agreement with performance emphasis, propensity to do own counseling, the assessed benefit of the policy, perceived need for the policy, and the ease of administering the policy. (See Appendix for details on operationalizations and scaling of these variables.) The eight receptivity variables for the EEO policy were familiarity, general agreement, zealous agreement (to seek out minorities), agreement with performance emphasis, propensity to do own counseling, assessed benefit, perceived need, and ease of administration. When these variables were used as dependent variables in multiple regressions, both the

prior nineteen independent variables (individual, role, and organizational characteristics) and the seven diffusion and training variables
were included in the regression equations as independent variables.

For both policies, three variables related to use of the policies
were analyzed as dependent variables in these regressions. They were:
whether or not the supervisor has had some occasion to use the
policy in the past, the number of such uses, and the frequency with
which he expected to use the policy in the future. When these
variables were dependent variables in the regression equations, all
nineteen original independent variables, the seven diffusion variables,
and the eight receptivity variables were included as independent
variables in the equations. The results of these analyses are summarized in tables 4.3 and 4.4.

Individual Characteristics

The demographic characteristics of supervisors yield mixed results as predictors of implementation of these two policies. For both
policies, male supervisors report more diffusion of information to
themselves and their subordinates than do female supervisors. They
also report more administrative emphasis given to the EEO policy
and are more aware of the union's position on both policies. Thus
male supervisors score higher than females in the diffusion stage of
these policies. In terms of the receptivity variables, male supervisors
are more likely than female supervisors to have negative attitudes
toward the policies: while they are in zealous agreement with both
policies, and general agreement with the EEO policy, they also see
both policies as difficult to administer, and feel less need for and
perceive less benefit in the EEO policy than female supervisors.
There are no significant relationships between sex and the use of
either policy.

In disagreement with the past literature and our hypothesis, older
rather than younger supervisors tend to be more supportive to
implementation of these policies. While younger supervisors tend to
report more topics covered in EEO training and more administrative
emphasis given to EEO, it is the older supervisors who agree with the
performance emphasis of both policies and see them as easy to
administer. For the alcoholism policy, younger supervisors reported
more perceived need for the policy but were otherwise less favorable
than older supervisors, who reported more training topics, more
familiarity with policy provisions, and more policy use in terms of
the number of times they had actually used the policy in the past.

For education, differences in direction of relationships between
the diffusion and the receptivity stages is most pronounced. While
more educated supervisors report more policy diffusion, their atti-

tudes toward the policies are more negative than are those of less educated supervisors. For the alcoholism policy, more educated supervisors report more training hours spent on the policy, they tend to be more skeptical than less educated supervisors of the zealous agreement statements, but they are also more skeptical of the performance provisions central to this policy's strategy. For the EEO policy, more educated supervisors report more information diffusion to them and to subordinates, more training topics covered in training, and more administrative emphasis. They are less likely to agree that they should do their own counseling, but also less likely to agree with the performance emphasis and to assess the EEO policy as generally beneficial.

Since the hypotheses were not consistently supported, these results demand some reconsideration of the relationships between demographics and change-related behaviors or attitudes. The major reasons given in past literature for relationships between demographic characteristics and change or innovation really centered on psychological variables, with youth, greater education, and being male generally considered to connote greater psychological flexibility and therefore greater propensity toward innovation and change. What our results seem to show is that the expected relationships occur for the diffusion-of-information stage, if at all, and that the attitudinal stage concerned with receptivity to the policies and the use stage produce results opposite to those hypothesized. Before trying to interpret these results further, we shall summarize other results from the tables.

Attitudes toward work also produce mixed results for these policies. Organizational commitment is negatively related to four of the diffusion variables for the alcoholism policy, and to learning hours for the EEO policy. Federal service commitment is positively related to familiarity for the alcoholism policy and learning hours for the EEO policy, and negatively to ease of administration of the alcoholism policy. Overall, these two variables are not nearly so important as predictors as the other two attitudinal variables. Job involvement is positively related to zealous agreement with the alcoholism policy, to agreement with the performance emphasis in that policy, to greater perceived ease of administration, and to greater assessed benefit from the policy. Thus the effects of job involvement on supervisory implementation are all in the receptivity stage for the alcoholism policy. For the EEO policy, job involvement is positively related to the number of training topics and to familiarity with policy provisions, as well as to the receptivity variables of assessed benefit, agreement with the emphasis on performance, perceived ease of administration, and zealous agreement to seek out minority members for employment. Overall, however, the results

T A B L E 4.3 Summary of Significant Results[a] of Path Analyses of Implementation of Alcoholism Policy among Supervisors

Independent Variables	USE			RECEPTIVITY									DIFFUSION					
	Expected use	Number of uses	Part use	Ease of administration	Perceived need	Assessed benefit	Own counseling	Performance emphasis	Medical model	Zealous agreement	Familiarity	Aware union position	Administrative emphasis	Learning hours	Training topics	Training hours	Diffusion to employees	Diffusion to supervisors
Sex (hi=male)		+		−				+		+	+	+			+		+	+
Age		−		+						−		−			−	+	−	
Education								−			+					−		
Organizational commitment																		
Federal commitment		+		−												+		
Job involvement			+	+	+	+	+	+	+	+			−					
Change attitude				−	+	+		+		+			+					
Years in position			−									−	−					
Years in organization																		
Skill level			+		+				+		+		−		−	−		
Overload																		
Managerial level		−								+			+				+	+
Promotion based on performance																		
Promotion based on technical skills				+		+							+		+			
Promotion based on seniority																+		
No. of employees (size)	+		+		+		+		−	+								
Percentage supervisors	+			−	+						−							

TABLE 4.3 (Continued)

DEPENDENT VARIABLE IN REGRESSIVE EQUATION

Independent Variables	DIFFUSION								RECEPTIVITY							USE		
	Difussion to supervisors	Diffusion to employees	Training hours	Training topics	Learning hours	Administrative emphasis	Aware union position	Familiarity	Zealous agreement	Medical model	Performance emphasis	Own counseling	Assessed benefit	Perceived need	Ease of administration	Past use	Number of uses	Expected use
Centralization																		+
Union present			+	+			+					−						
Diffusion to supervisors								+								+		
Diffusion to employees								+										
Training hours																		
Training topics								+							−	+	−	
Learning hours								+										
Administrative emphasis								+				+			+			
Aware union position																+		
Familiarity																		
Zealous agreement																		
Medical model																		
Performance emphasis																		
Own counseling																		
Assessed benefit																+	+	
Perceived need																		+
Ease of administration																		+

+ sign indicates a positive relationship; − sign indicates a negative relationship.

[a] All relationships that reached the .10 level of significance are included above, since the purpose of this table is to detect trends and patterns in the data. Data on the magnitude of the relationships are available in tables 4.5-4.7.

TABLE 4.4 Summary of Significant Results[a] of Path Analyses of Implementation of EEO Policy among Supervisors

Independent Variables	DEPENDENT VARIABLE IN REGRESSION EQUATION																
	USE			RECEPTIVITY								DIFFUSION						
	Expected use	Number of uses	Pase use	Ease of administration	Perceived need	Assessed benefit	Own counseling	Performance emphasis	Zealous agreement	General agreement	Familiarity	Aware union position	Administrative emphasis	Learning hours	Training topics	Training hours	Diffusion to employees	Diffusion to supervisors
Sex (hi=male)				− +	−	−			+			+	+				+	+
Age						−		+ −	−				− +		−		+	+
Education							−	+					+	+	+			
Organizational commitment																		
Federal commitment											+			−				
Job involvement			+	+ −	+ +	+		+ +	+ +	+				+	+		+	+
Change attitude					+			+ +	+ +							+		
Years in position					−							+ −						
Years in organization		+												+ +	+ +	+	+ +	+ +
Skill level		+												+			+	+
Overload									+		+			+	+	+	+	+
Managerial level	+				+	+			+	+		+	+	+		+	+	+
Promotion based on performance												−					+	+
Promotion based on technical skills																		
Promotion based on seniority	−								−	−		−		−	−	−	−	−
No. of employees (size)	+ +	+	+		+ −		+		+		+			+ +	+ +	+ +		
Percentage supervisors										−			+					

TABLE 4.4 (Continued)

DEPENDENT VARIABLE IN REGRESSION EQUATION

Independent Variables	USE			RECEPTIVITY									DIFFUSION					
	Expected use	Number of uses	Past use	Ease of administration	Perceived need	Assessed benefit	Own counseling	Performance emphasis	Zealous agreement	General agreement	Familiarity	Aware union position	Administrative emphasis	Learning hours	Training topics	Training hours	Diffusion to employees	Diffusion to supervisors
Centralization	+		−				−											
Union present												+			+			
Diffusion to supervisors		+		−							+							
Diffusion to employees	+		+	−		+												
Training hours			+					+	+		+							
Training topics					+					+	+							
Learning hours					+		−				+							
Administrative emphasis																		
Aware union position									−									
Familiarity	+		+															
General agreement																		
Zealous agreement																		
Performance emphasis																		
Own counseling																		
Assessed benefit																		
Perceived need			−															
Ease of administration	+		+															

+ sign indicates a positive relationship; − sign indicates a negative relationship.

[a] All relationships that reached the .10 level of significance are included above, since the purpose of this table is to detect trends and patterns in the data. Data on the magnitude of the relationships are available in tables 4.5-4.7.

suggest that the major positive effects of job involvement are in the supervisor's readiness to use the policy, as evidenced by policy-supportive attitudes, and not in the earlier diffusion stage or the later use stage. Thus our hypothesis is supported more for the receptivity than for the other two stages for this variable.

The most important attitude in predicting implementation of the policies by supervisors is clearly their attitude toward change. As in the case of job involvement, the impact of this variable is primarily in the receptivity stage. All of the attitudinal variables except ease of administration are positively related for the alcoholism policy. All but the assessed benefit (no relationship) and ease of administration (negative relationship) variables are positively related for the EEO policy. In addition, those supervisors with more positive attitudes toward change reported more past use of the alcoholism policy. The findings again support our hypothesis for the receptivity stage of implementation, are in only weak support for the other two stages of implementation for the alcoholism policy, and give no support for the other stages relative to the EEO policy.

Overall, the patterning of the results for all of the individual variables suggest that demographics are better predictors of information diffusion and that other attitudinal variables are better predictors of attitudes toward the policies. Results for demographic variables were generally opposite to what was hypothesized on the basis of past research on change and innovation. But, as mentioned frequently, few studies have focused on the implementation stage of change processes. Perhaps youth and education are more facilitative to the initiation or adoption of changes. For the EEO policy, diffusion—the earliest stage of implementation—was greater for younger and more educated supervisors. Otherwise, maturity and less education seemed to aid implementation, at least in securing acceptance of the content of the policies. Either the content of the policies or the fact that they were mandated changes from far above them in the hierarchy could have made these changes less acceptable to the young and highly educated supervisors. In any case, the results indicate that support of certain types of organizational members cannot be taken for granted when contemplating change efforts.

Role Characteristics

Both tenure within a given organizational position and tenure within the employing organizations were hypothesized to be positively related to implementation by these supervisors. The relationships between these variables and the various indicators of implementation are scattered, as shown in tables 4.3 and 4.4, but most of the relationships are in the expected direction. Number of years in the position is positively related to both perceived need and past use of the alcoholism policy; it is also negatively related to training topics and administrative emphasis for this policy. Only two relationships between tenure in the position and implementation were significant for the EEO policy. Again, perceived need was positively related, as were hours spent in training for this policy. For the alcoholism policy only administrative emphasis was significantly related to tenure within the organization, while for the EEO policy both levels of diffusion, awareness of the union's position, and number of past uses were positively related to organizational tenure. Together, the results suggest limited support for the hypotheses, although the findings for the diffusion stage of the alcoholism policy yielded mixed results.

The major impact of these variables seems to be on the perceived need for the policies, and this appears to be accompanied by greater use, since one of each of these tenure variables is significantly related to use of one of the policies. These data suggest that managerial experience may lead to a greater appreciation of need for these policies. The negative results for training and administrative emphasis relative to the alcoholism policy are perhaps best explained by the notion that years in a position may reflect career stagnation, as well as managerial experience. Those supervisors with long tenure in a given position may be those less likely to be promoted, and therefore they may have been omitted from some of the information diffused in this policy. Also, those with long tenure in a single position may simply be poorer and less conscientious supervisors, as evidenced by their lack of promotion, and they may not have paid attention to and therefore remembered all information diffusion that occurred in their installations.

The skill level of subordinates is negatively related to two diffusion variables and one use variable for the alcoholism policy. Supervisors with more skilled subordinates are less likely to be aware of the union's position, less likely to have had as much training on the alcoholism policy, and less likely to have used the policy. For the EEO policy, results by skill level are mixed. Supervisors of more skilled employees are again less likely to be aware of the union's position, and they are also lower on perceived need than other supervisors. In terms of other aspects of information diffusion, however, they are higher, reporting more information diffusion to themselves and to their subordinates, and more time spent in learning about the policy. Thus, hypothesis 4.9 was supported for the alcoholism policy, but received only mixed support for the EEO policy.

The results for work overload are similar to those for skill level. The hypothesis that work overload would negatively affect implementation is supported for the alcoholism policy, producing significant negative relationships with training topics, administrative emphasis, and ease of administration. For the EEO policy, the pattern is reversed, and positive relationships emerge between work overload and training topics and learning hours. These findings seem to relate to the overall levels of administrative emphasis on the two policies. With the policy that is not administratively emphasized—the alcoholism policy—work overload has negative effects on diffusion and the one aspect of receptivity—the concern with administrative ease—most likely to negatively affect an already overburdened supervisor. With the EEO policy, administrative emphasis was high— apparently high enough to override the issues of who was already overburdened, and these very supervisors also received more training and spent more time learning about this policy. It is also likely that supervisors who report themselves to be high on work overload are conscientious, and this may be an additional reason why they report more training and learning about EEO—the administratively emphasized policy.

The results for managerial level are clearly in support of our hypothesis. Higher managerial levels are related to more familiarity with the alcoholism policy, more agreement with the medical model, more perceived need for that policy, and more past use of it. Thus, for the alcoholism policy, higher managerial level was associated with higher receptivity and use. For the EEO policy, results are also positive, but more concentrated in the diffusion stage of implementation. All of the information diffusion, training, and the learning variables are positively and significantly related to managerial level, with the result that these managers also report greater familiarity with this policy. They are also more zealous in their agreement, agreeing that minority members should be sought out to fill vacancies. Interestingly, the greater implementation at the earlier stages for the EEO policy does not lead to greater use of the policy for these higher level managers.

The results for the three factors judged important for supervisors' promotion are very much in accord with our hypothesis for the EEO policy, and more mixed for the alcoholism policy. An emphasis on performance has consistent positive effects on all stages of implementation for the EEO policy, while the importance of seniority has consistent negative effects. The importance of technical skills is also negatively related to awareness of the union position on the EEO policy. For the alcoholism policy, the emphasis on performance in promotion has the hypothesized positive relationships with both diffusion and receptivity variables. For this policy, however, the results for the importance of technical skills and of seniority are also sometimes positive. The importance of technical skills is, however, negatively related to expected use of the alcoholism policy, and the importance of seniority is negatively related to agreement with the medical model of alcoholism. An important point to note about these role variables is that they present consistent relationships with expected use across the two policies. For both policies, the emphasis on performance for promotion is positively related to expected use, while emphasis on seniority in promotion is negatively related to expected policy use in the future. Altogether, the consistency of these findings suggest that the reward structure has effects on the implementation of changes in these federal organizations.

Organizational Characteristics

As predicted, supervisors in larger installations are consistently more likely to implement the policies. For the alcoholism policy, these differences emerge in the receptivity and use stages. Most important, greater size is positively related both to past and future use of this policy. For the EEO policy, the results are even stronger and more consistent: in all three stages of implementation, supervisors in larger installations report more implementation. For the EEO policy, all three measures of policy use are positively and significantly related to installation size.

The presence of a union within the installation produces mixed effects. While it is positively related to diffusion of both policies, the presence of a union appears to produce negative effects on the propensity of supervisors to do their own counseling. Since such counseling is not in strict accord with policy provisions, the results suggest that supervisors are more careful in their interpretation of personnel policies in a situation where a union can call them to account for less than strict interpretation and application of policy provisions. It is far better for the supervisor to avoid taking any risks and to refer the employee to the designated counselor when a union is present. Unions may thus provide the only countervailing weight to the general tendency, already discussed earlier in this chapter, for supervisors to handle personnel matters on their own.

The average span of control of supervisors, measured as the percentage of supervision, is generally positively related to implementation of both policies, as hypothesized, although results are somewhat mixed. The effects on the alcoholism policy are less consistent, with positive relationships with training hours, perceived need, and expected use. Thus, as hypothesized, there are positive relations with at least one variable for each stage of implementation. However, there are also negative relationships with familiarity and with ease of administration for this policy. The results for the EEO policy are consistently positive for the diffusion phase, with positive relations between percentage of supervisors and both training variables, learning hours, and administrative emphasis. The results for the receptivity variables are mixed, with a negative relationship with general agreement, a positive relationship with zealous agreement (seek out minorities), and a negative relationship with ease of administration. However, consistent with the results for the alcoholism policy, there is a positive relationship between the percentage of supervision and expected use. It seems from these findings that low spans of control facilitate diffusion and foster greater expected use, but have negative effects on policy-related attitudes, perhaps because supervisors of smaller work groups have more difficulty accepting the universalistic prescriptions of these policies.

The final structural variable that we tested was centralization of decision making. While this variable has only one significant relationship with implementation of each policy, this relationship is with the important variable of expected use. For both policies, expected use is higher where centralization is higher, in direct contradiction to our hypothesis. These findings appear to support Zaltman and his colleagues (1973) in their discussion of Sapolsky's (1967) findings. In the latter study, decentralization frustrated attempts at implementation. In our study, decentralization does not foster any of the early stages of implementation for individual supervisors, contrary to expectations of the literature, and its reverse—centralization—leads to greater expectations by individual supervisors of future use of both policies.

Summary

In advancing our hypotheses, we chose to make only one hypothesis for each of the independent variables, that is, the individual, role-related, and organizational characteristics already discussed. This was done for some economy and simplicity of presentation and procedure, and also because the literature on innovation and change does not offer many distinctions between how relationships can be expected to differ across the three stages of implementation.[14] As is evident from the results, however, there are different patterns in the relationships for some of the independent variables with the different phases of implementation, and even for measures within a given phase of implementation. As a consequence, the results present a complicated picture—one that is not easy to summarize.

There are really two underlying questions that may help to summarize the detailed results already presented and discussed. The first of these concerns which of the various independent variables are most important in predicting implementation. That is, which of these variables have the most consistent and frequent statistically significant relationships across the stages and various measures of implementation? In a sense, this question returns to the hypotheses and asks which of them were better supported than others and how consistently they were supported. The second question concerns the differential findings for the three phases of implementation. Given these differences, this question asks: Which variables are most important for each phase—that is, for diffusion and training, for receptivity, and for use? In the paragraphs that follow we shall answer each of these questions separately, beginning with the question stated first.

Certain of the independent variables tested produced more consistent relationships than others across all of the various measures of the three stages of policy implementation of these two policies. By looking across the rows of tables 4.3 and 4.4, these variables can be identified. Of the individual characteristics, the attitude toward change was clearly the most important and consistent predictor of implementation. Job involvement was a secondary, positive predictor. While demographic variables were frequent predictors, their results were mixed. Sex was a fairly important predictor for both policies, but age was more important for the alcoholism policy, and education for the EEO policy. The commitment variables were unimportant in predicting implementation of the EEO policy, and generally negative in effect for alcoholism policy diffusion.

Role-related variables produced more scattered effects for the alcoholism policy than for EEO. For both policies, the important predictors were managerial level and the factors considered important in promotion decisions.

Organizational variables most important to implementation were size and the percentage of supervision. While size had the expected positive effects on implementation, the results for the span of control variable were mixed. Although significant results for the other organizational variables were less frequent, they were consistent and thus deserve attention. The presence of a union appears to have some positive effects on diffusion but negative effects on the propensity for supervisors to do their own counseling on policy-related matters. Centralization has a positive effect on future use of both policies. The last two findings together suggest that pressures toward conformity within these installations may lead to increased implementation of these policies, rather than the more participative atmosphere associated with the generation of innovations. This issue will be reconsidered in chapter 7, where the findings for the structural analyses are given.

These results can also be looked at in another way; that is, by considering which variables were most important for each stage of the implementation process. Considering the same findings from tables 4.3 and 4.4, but looking this time down the columns, we can see that being male, the presence of a union, and the criteria for promotion had the most consistent positive effects on diffusion of the alcoholism policy (the first seven columns of table 4.3). The role-related variables of years in position, skill level, and overload had negative effects on the diffusion stage. Organizational commitment also has important negative effects. The results for the EEO policy are similar with these exceptions: education is a more important positive predictor, the role variables tend to have relationships opposite to that for the alcoholism policy, and two organizational variables—size and percentage of supervision—are more important positive predictors for diffusion of the EEO policy.

When we consider the next block of variables—the receptivity variables—we must look not only at the results for the independent variables already discussed, but also at the results for the diffusion variables that were included as predictors in the regression equations for this second stage of the implementation model. For these variables, the attitude toward change is clearly the most important positive predictor. If a supervisor is favorably disposed toward change in general, he is more favorably disposed toward these policies. Job involvement is also an important positive predictor of attitudes that are generally favorable to the policies. Other variables produce rather mixed effects on attitudes, with the exception of size, which has consistent positive effects. Another notable variable is education, with more education leading to more negative attitudes toward the policies, but especially toward the EEO policy. Managerial level is important in predicting attitudes toward the alcoholism policy, but much less important for the EEO policy. Generally, role-related variables are only important for the zealous interpretation of the EEO policy, where role-related factors appear to be consistent in leading supervisors to agree that minority members should be sought for employment vacancies.

None of the diffusion variables are especially important to the receptivity variables except for the strong relationships between diffusion and familiarity with the policies. This dearth of relationships between diffusion and attitudes is especially notable for the alcoholism policy. For the EEO policy, there are scattered positive relationships, and the only negative ones are easily interpreted: those supervisors with more information feel that the EEO policy will not be easy to administer. With the plethora of programs and provisions of this policy, their perceptions are probably right, and so the relationship can be considered a reasonable outcome of diffusion for this policy.

Looking at the three use variables for each policy (the three right-most columns of each table) it is evident that demographics seem to be the best predictor of the number of uses of the alcoholism policy, while role-related factors, organizational characteristics, diffusion variables, and receptivity all contribute to past use. Somewhat the same pattern holds for future use of the policy, except that different variables serve as predictors for past and future use, and diffusion is less important for future use than it was for past use.

For the EEO policy, number of uses was even more difficult to predict, even using all of the independent variables in the table. Apparently, factors not tapped in any of our variables are responsible for the frequency of use of the EEO policy by these supervisors. For past use, demographic, role-related, and organizational factors were much less important for this policy. The most important predictors of past use of EEO were diffusion and receptivity variables; diffusion, training, familiarity, and perceived need. For expected use, largely the same receptivity and diffusion variables were important, but like the alcoholism policy, role-related and organizational variables were also important predictors.

Tables 4.5, 4.6, and 4.7 present the results already summarized in more detail. In these tables, the results of regressions with each of the measures on implementation as a dependent variable are given.[15]

T A B L E 4.5 Significant Relationships from Multiple Regressions of Diffusion of Two Policies on All Independent Variables

	ALCOHOLISM POLICY		EEO POLICY	
	Beta[a]	r	Beta	r
Diffusion to Supervisors				
Sex[b]	.08*	.08	.08**	.14
Promotion based on performance	.16†	.13	.11**	.07
Education			.09*	.22
Years in installation			.10**	.04
Managerial level			.17†	.21
Skill level of subordinates			.12†	.23
Promotion based on seniority			−.17†	−.23
R^2	.05		.16	
Adjusted R^2	.02		.13	
Diffusion to Employees				
Sex[b]	.14†	.13	.13†	.20
Organizational commitment	−.08*	−.04		
Promotion based on performance	.17†	.14	.14†	.10
Education			.09*	.21
Years in installation			.12**	.07
Managerial level			.13†	.20
Skill level of subordinates			.16†	.25
Promotion based on seniority			−.13†	−.17
R^2	.07		.16	
Adjusted R^2	.04		.13	

(continued on next page)

TABLE 4.5 (Continued)

	ALCOHOLISM POLICY		EEO POLICY	
	Beta[a]	r	Beta	r
Training Hours Spent by Supervisor				
Education	.20†	.11		
Organizational commitment	−.09**	−.05		
Attitude toward change	.07*	.08		
Skill level of subordinates	−.11**	−.03		
Percentage supervisors	.15†	.12	.15†	.08
Union present	.08*	.06		
Promotion based on seniority			−.16†	−.19
Promotion based on performance			.10*	.06
Years in position			.09*	.04
Managerial level			.11**	.12
Number of employees in installation			.10**	.04
R^2	.08		.09	
Adjusted R^2	.04		.06	
Training Topics Covered in Supervisory Training				
Age	.12**	.11	−.09***	−.08
Organizational commitment	−.09*	−.03		
Years in position	−.10**	−.02		
Perceived work overload	−.12†	−.10	.15†	.15
Promotion based on technical skills	.10*	.09		
Union present	.11**	.13	.07*	.07
Job involvement	.		.08*	.07
Education			.11**	.22
Managerial level			.09**	.10
Promotion based on seniority			−.17†	−.21
Number of employees in installation			.13†	.10
Percentage supervisors			.10**	.03
R^2	.07		.15	
Adjusted R^2	.04		.12	
Hours Spent Learning About Policy				
Organizational commitment			−.10**	−.06
Federal service commitment			.10**	.02
Managerial level	nothing		.10**	.09
Perceived work overload			.10**	.08
Skill level of subordinates			.13†	.15
Promotion based on seniority			−.15†	−.16
Promotion based on performance	significant		.09*	.09
Number of employees in installation			.08*	.03
Percentage supervisors			.09*	.05
R^2			.09	
Adjusted R^2			.06	

TABLE 4.5 (Continued)

	ALCOHOLISM POLICY		EEO POLICY	
	Beta[a]	*r*	*Beta*	*r*
Administrative Emphasis Given to Policy				
Years in position	$-.13^{**}$	$-.04$		
Years in installation	$.11^{**}$	.07		
Perceived work overload	$-.11^{**}$	$-.11$		
Promotion based on seniority	$.10^{**}$	.14	$-.11^{**}$	$-.16$
Promotion based on perfromance	$.16^{\dagger}$	.14	$.12^{**}$	.06
Age			$-.10^{*}$	$-.10$
Education			$.11^{**}$	.19
Sex			$.09^{**}$	.13
Percentage supervisors			$.14^{\dagger}$	.09
R^2	.08		.10	
Adjusted R^2	.05		.07	
Aware of Union Position on Policy				
Sex[b]	$.13^{\dagger}$	.10	$.09^{**}$	.05
Organizational commitment	$-.08^{*}$	$-.06$		
Skill level of subordinates	$-.15^{\dagger}$	$-.14$	$-.08^{**}$	$-.10$
Union present	$.32^{\dagger}$	.32	$.45^{\dagger}$	.49
Years in installation			$.13^{\dagger}$	.14
Promotion based on seniority			$-.09^{**}$	$-.09$
Promotion based on performance			$.12^{\dagger}$	.12
Promotion based on technical skills			$-.08^{*}$	$-.02$
R^2	.15		.30	
Adjusted R^2	.13		.27	

[a]Beta = standardized regression coefficient.

[b]For this variable, females = 1, males = 2.

$^{*}p < .10$

$^{**}p < .05$

$^{\dagger}p < .01$

From these tables it is possible to assess the magnitude of the relationships, and also easier to look at the predictors of each dependent variable by itself. It was impossible to draw coherent path diagrams for these results because of the large number of variables and significant relationships.

Generally, the equations for the EEO policy account for more variance than those for the alcoholism policy. This was not unexpected, because we were aware before the research began that the opportunities to use the alcoholism policy would probably be relatively infrequent and that this circumstance might affect other aspects of implementation, thus restricting the variance on measures of

T A B L E 4.6 Significant Relationships from Multiple Regressions of Receptivity of Two Policies on All Independent and Diffusion Variables

	ALCOHOLISM POLICY		EEO POLICY	
	Beta	r	Beta	r
Familiarity with Policy				
Age	.13†	.15		
Commitment to federal service	.08*	.15		
Managerial level	.12†	.10	.13†	.17
Percentage supervisors	−.07*	−.12		
Diffusion to supervisors	.14†	.42	.16†	.44
Diffusion to employees	.13**	.40		
Learning hours	.15†	.32	.11†	.29
Training topics	.13†	.33	.13†	.37
Administrative emphasis	.21†	.36	.16†	.36
Aware of union position	.15†	.28	.12†	.20
Job involvement			.07*	.10
Number of employees in installation			.16†	.18
R^2	.39		.37	
Adjusted R^2	.36		.34	
Zealous Agreement with Policy				
Sex	.12†	.11	.09**	.10
Education	−.12**	−.05	−.08*	.03
Attitude toward change	.12†	.13	.13†	.13
Job involvement	.08*	.11	.10**	.12
Promotion based on performance	.14†	.16	.12**	.13
Number of employees in installation	.11**	.11		
Promotion based on seniority			−.12**	−.15
Percentage supervisors			.08*	.05
Managerial level			.11**	.14
Training hours			.13**	.22
Awareness of union position			−.10**	−.03
R^2	.11		.15	
Adjusted R^2	.07		.11	
General Agreement				
Sex			.08*	.08
Attitude toward change		no	.29†	.29
Promotion based on seniority			−.13†	−.16
Promotion based on performance		comparable	.14†	.13
Percentage supervisors			−.11**	−.11
Training topics		measure	.09*	.12
R^2			.17	
Adjusted R^2			.13	

T A B L E 4.6 (Continued)

	ALCOHOLISM POLICY		EEO POLICY	
	Beta	*r*	*Beta*	*r*
Agreement with Medical Model				
Attitude toward change	.09**	.09	no	
Managerial level	.09*	.08		
Promotion based on seniority	−.09*	−.10	comparable	
R^2	.06			
Adjusted R^2	.01		measure	
Agreement with Performance Emphasis				
Age	.12**	.16	.13†	.16
Education	−.12**	−.16	−.13**	−.16
Attitude toward change	.10**	.13	.11**	.13
Job involvement	.10**	.12	.10**	.12
Training hours			.09*	.04
R^2	.10		.10	
Adjusted R^2	.06		.06	
Propensity to do Own Counseling				
Attitude toward change	.10**	.08	.10**	.08
Number of employees in installation	.12**	.08	.12**	.08
Union present	−.10**	−.05	−.09*	−.05
Aware of union position	.10**	.06		
Education			−.09*	−.04
Learning hours			−.09*	−.04
R^2	.07		.07	
Adjusted R^2	.03		.02	
Assessed Benefit of Policy				
Attitude toward change	.15†	.18		
Job involvement	.11**	.13	.09**	.10
Promotion based on technical skills	.11**	.12		
Sex			−.07*	−.09
Education			−.15†	−.13
Promotion based on performance			.20†	.28
Diffusion to employees			.13**	.13
R^2	.09		.17	
Adjusted R^2	.05		.13	
Perceived Need				
Age	−.10**	−.07		
Attitude toward change	.09**	.10	.10**	.10

T A B L E 4.6 (Continued)

	ALCOHOLISM POLICY		EEO POLICY	
	Beta	*r*	*Beta*	*r*
Managerial level	.11**	.04		
Years in position	.11**	.04	.09*	.04
Number of employees in installation	.15†	.11	.12**	.11
Percentage supervisors	.11**	.00		
Sex			−.08	−.04
Skill level of subordinates			−.09*	−.02
Learning hours			.15†	.22
Training topics			.13**	.22
R²	.09		.14	
Adjusted R²	.04		.10	
Perceived Ease of Administration				
Sex	−.11†	−.12	−.13†	−.12
Age	.12**	.13	.09*	.13
Attitude toward change	−.07*	−.05	−.07*	−.05
Job involvement	.11**	.12	.12†	.12
Commitment to federal service	−.08*	.02		
Perceived work overload	−.09**	−.12		
Promotion based on performance	.22†	.23	.21†	.23
Percentage supervisors	−.11**	−.14	−.11**	−.14
Learning hours	−.08*	−.06		
Aware of union position	−.09*	−.08		
Diffusion to supervisors			−.22†	−.09
Diffusion to employees			.19†	.00
R²	.16		.17	
Adjusted R²	.11		.12	

*p < .10
**p < .05
†p < .01

implementation for this policy. However, this tendency is particularly pronounced for the diffusion and training measures presented in table 4.5, rather than for the use variables. In all instances, the amount of variance explained (R^2) is larger for the EEO policy. Nevertheless, looking at the lists of significant predictors, we can see that many are common across the two policies. Training hours, learning hours, and administrative emphasis have the fewest common predictor variables across policies. These are all variables for which there were very large differences in levels of implementation for the two policies.

While there is also a trend for regressions on some of the EEO receptivity variables (table 4.6) to account for more variation than equivalent alcoholism equations, this is not true for all of the

T A B L E 4.7 Significant Relationships from Multiple Regressions of Use of Two Policies on All Independent, Diffusion, and Receptivity Variables

	ALCOHOLISM POLICY		EEO POLICY	
	Beta	r	Beta	r
Past Use of the Policy				
Managerial level	.08*	.08		
Years in position	.12**	.13		
Skill level of subordinates	−.10**	−.09		
Number of employees in installation	.11**	.07	.11**	.14
Diffusion to supervisors	.12**	.22		
Learning hours	.09**	.18		
Familiarity with policy	.17†	.25	.16†	.35
Propensity to do own counseling	.14†	.15		
Organizational commitment			.11**	.11
Union present			−.09*	−.04
Diffusion to employees			.14**	.35
Training topics			.10**	.29
Assessed benefit to policy			−.09**	.04
Perceived need			.14†	.23
R^2	.16		.27	
Adjusted R^2	.11		.22	
Number of Past Uses of Policy				
Age	.09*	.09		
Attitude toward change	.09*	.09		
Organizational commitment	−.08*	−.07		
Administrative emphasis	−.09*	−.04		
Propensity to do own counseling	.08*	.08		
Years in installation			−.09*	−.01
Number of employees in installation			.10*	.10
Diffusion to supervisors			.12*	.11
R^2	.09		.05	
Adjusted R^2	.02		−.01	
Expected Future Use of the Policy				
Promotion based on technical skills	−.10*	−.08		
Number of employees in installation	.09*	.07	.13†	.14
Percentage supervisors	.08*	.04	.11**	.05
Centralization of decision making	.07*	.07	.09**	.07
Perceived need	.22†	.24	.24†	.33
Agreement with performance emphasis	.08*	.10		
Promotion based on seniority			−.11**	−.20
Promotion based on performance			.12**	.13
Diffusion to employees			.11*	.28
Familiarity with policy			.17†	.34
R^2	.14		.27	
Adjusted R^2	.09		.22	

*p < .10   **p < .05   †p < .01

equations. For familiarity, agreement with the performance emphasis, and perceived ease of administration, the results are similar across
the two policies.

Looking at the results for variables relating to use (table 4.7), we
see that the EEO equations are again superior in explaining more of
the variance. Neither set of results explains much of the variance in
number of uses of the policy.

INTERRELATION OF PHASES OF IMPLEMENTATION

To follow through the analyses begun in the previous chapter, it
was necessary to try to assess the degree to which the three phases of
the implementation process are interrelated. Looking at table 4.6, we
see that relatively few of the diffusion or training variables are
significantly related to the receptivity variables. The big exception is
familiarity, with six of the seven diffusion-stage variables related to
familiarity with the alcoholism policy, and five of the seven significantly related for the EEO policy. The only other equations in which
diffusion variables were significant predictors of receptivity to the
alcoholism policy is that explaining the perceived ease of administration, and in that equation both learning hours and awareness of
union position have negative effects. One or two diffusion variables
are significant in almost all of the equations for the EEO policy; they
are important predictors of zealous agreement, need, and perceived
ease of administration. While greater information also has a negative
effect for ease of administration for the EEO policy, learning and
training have positive effects on perceived need. Number of training
hours also has a positive effect on zealous agreement, although
awareness of the union position has a negative effect. Thus training
without awareness of the union position can lead to overreactions to
policy provisions, while awareness of the union position leads to
more careful interpretation of the policy.

When we consider these results together with those in table 4.7,
it is clear that the main effects of the diffusion and training variables
on past use are mediated through familiarity with the policies. Two
diffusion variables also have direct effects on past use of the alcoholism policy: learning hours—for which there were no significant predictors in table 4.6—and diffusion to supervisors. For the EEO
policy, interestingly, it is diffusion to employees and training topics
that are directly related to past use. Diffusion to supervisors is
significantly related to the number of uses of the EEO policy,
although the equation itself is not significant, and the level of
significance for the regression coefficient is marginal ($p = .10$).

In explaining future use of the policy, familiarity is important for
the EEO policy, but not for the alcoholism policy. For both policies,

perceived need is the most important predictor of future use, and since no diffusion variables are significantly related to perceived need for the alcoholism policy, there are no indirect effects of diffusion variables for that policy on future use. For the EEO policy, diffusion to employees is also related to future use.

Considering the receptivity variables as predictors of use, we find that few variables are related to use in these equations. The effects of the receptivity variables where they appear are generally in the predicted direction, but not always. As noted in chapter 3 and elsewhere in this chapter, assessed benefit of the EEO policy is negatively related to past use of that policy. In addition, administrative emphasis is negatively related to the number of uses of the alcoholism policy.

Apparently, use of these policies does not require uniformly favorable attitudes toward the policies. It is also possible that use has led to less favorable attitudes; that is, that use of the alcoholism policy leads to perceptions of less administrative ease in applying the policy, and that use of the EEO policy leads to less perceived benefit from that policy. Longitudinal research would be needed to determine which of these explanations is correct.

A COMPOSITE PROFILE

From these results, we can abstract a tentative composite profile of the supervisor most likely to implement these policies. For the alcoholism policy, the supervisor likely to implement is male, somewhat older than average, of high organizational status, supervising relatively low-skilled employees, in a large organization, who believes his promotion will depend on his performance as a supervisor and that he should counsel his own employees, who positively values change, and who is less than fully committed to his employing organization but involved in his job.

The profile of the supervisor likely to implement the EEO policy would be similar, except that being male and being older than average have some negative as well as positive effects on implementation, and that education seems to have more positive effects on diffusion for this policy and negative effects on attitudes toward the policy. While the amount of variance explained is larger for the EEO policy than for the alcoholism policy, the mixture of results suggest that this policy has caused sharper reactions than the alcoholism policy, so that the same variables can have positive effects in one stage of implementation, and largely negative effects elsewhere. Undoubtedly, the greater pervasiveness, magnitude, and innovativeness of the EEO policy combined with the greater administrative emphasis accorded this policy best account for these rather ambivalent findings.

CONCLUSIONS: DIFFERENTIAL RESULTS ACROSS POLICIES

As in the previous chapter, the results for the EEO policy show more connectedness between the phases of the implementation process, and the results for that policy generally explain more of the variance than for the alcoholism policy. Again we attribute these results to the greater pervasiveness of the EEO policy.

While it is disappointing not to be able to explain more of the variance of the various indicators of implementation with such an array of independent variables, the results account for substantial variance and must be considered in the context of other findings in the study of organizations. We are not aware of any other studies that have attempted to simultaneously consider individual, role-related, and organizational variables to account for both behaviors and attitudes of organizational members. Results from this comprehensive systems approach demonstrate that all of these types of variables are significantly related to individual attitudes and behavior concerning the complex phenomena of organizational change.

5. Installation Director: Ambivalence at the Top

WHILE SUPERVISORS HAD the key role in implementation of these policies because they were the organizational actors who had to apply the policies in most concrete instances, or at least whose cooperation was required if the application of the policy was to be successfully carried out, there are other members of the installations who had important roles to play in the implementation process.

All of the installations had someone who acted as the chief executive locally and who, as such, represented the highest levels of supervisory authority within the installation. A central principle of bureaucracy and of formal organizations generally is that some attempt is made to centralize control and accountability through a chain of command that culminates in the chief executive. We have called this person the director (for uniformity) of the installation throughout this book.

Directors can be viewed in two major ways. First of all, they are supervisors and, as the highest level of supervision within an installation, can be viewed as potential role models for other supervisors. They also, of course, encounter many of the same problems and role demands as other supervisors.

Second, they are chief executives, and since they occupy the highest formally designed position within the organization, they have control over various resources not available to other organizational members or supervisors. This, of course, gives them power and reinforces their positional authority.

Directors can also be viewed as having two other important functions: as potential opinion leaders and as boundary spanners.

Each of these roles, although identified with different literatures, is concerned with the relaying and diffusion of information to relatively uninformed others.

We will assess the directors in our sample from each of these vantage points. First we will ask whether they were typical implementers among supervisors, or whether they were better implementers and therefore good role models as far as these policies are concerned. We will then investigate various factors that might explain what makes some directors better implementers than others. Second, we will assess the degree to which directors used their power and other resources as chief executives to implement the policy themselves and to encourage implementation by others. In the process of these two major analyses, we will also assess the director as opinion leader and boundary spanner when those vantage points are appropriate.

GENERAL LEVELS OF IMPLEMENTATION AMONG DIRECTORS

Information Diffusion and Training

As with the lower-level supervisors, directors had received more written information about EEO than about the alcoholism policy although the differences were not as pronounced for the directors. The chief difference was that EEO insertions for policy manuals exceeded those for alcoholism: 68 percent had received manual insertions for EEO, while 47 percent had received them for the alcoholism policy. Regarding oral communications, however, the differences were even more obvious: 41 percent of the directors reported hearing of the alcoholism policy in a meeting, while 82 percent indicated hearing about the EEO policy changes in this manner. Thus directors learned about EEO at 1 1/2 to 2 times the rate they learned about the alcoholism policy from manual insertions and question-asking meetings. In contrast, they received about the same amount of other forms of information—special brochures (26 percent), word of mouth (21 percent), and bulletin boards (4 percent)—for both policies. No director reported receiving no information at all about either policy.

Unlike the pattern of sources of information to supervisors, the diffusion to directors was quite similar for both policies. Also unlike that pattern, sources of information about the alcoholism policy did not decline sharply from Washington to regional offices but, like supervisory EEO information, came from those sources in roughly equal proportions: 68 to 70 percent from both sources for both policies. This suggest that higher sources in the federal bureaucracy diffused information to directors rather evenly, but the directors, in turn, selectively passed on more EEO information than alcoholism information to supervisors.

Nonetheless directors in much larger numbers (18 percent) expressed a belief that the information they had received about the alcoholism policy was inadequate to explain their role in policy implementation; only 2 percent expressed this belief about EEO. However, roughly twice as many directors felt the need to seek additional information about the EEO policy as sought it for the alcoholism policy (37 percent and 18 percent respectively).

This difference probably arose from the sharp differences in administrative emphasis that accompanied the introduction of both policies. When asked how the introduction of the alcoholism policy and program compared with other policies, the majority of directors reported they had received less than typical exposure (51 percent), while 32 percent believed that they had received less than typical administrative emphasis and that less than the typical number of informational techniques had been used. Comparing the figures with those for supervisors, directors more often judged the alcoholism policy as receiving more introductory emphasis, which accords with the greater amount of information directors received about the alcoholism policy. Only about 12 percent reported they had received more than typical exposure, emphasis, or informational techniques. The perceptions of directors on how EEO policy changes were introduced were very different. Only 2 percent reported that this policy had received less than typical exposure, administrative emphasis, or methods to inform. Large majorities reported more than typical introductory emphasis for EEO: 68 percent for exposure and administrative emphasis and 52 percent for techniques used to inform.

Quite obviously the alcoholism policy received only a lightweight introduction to installation directors; by contrast the EEO policy was heavyweight, considering the emphasis it received in these directors' eyes. There can be little doubt that this situation played a large part in the paucity of information, training activities, and levels of familiarity among line supervisors relative to the alcoholism policy.

Attitudinal Reactions to the Policies: Receptivity and Readiness to Use

We asked directors to respond to the same policy agreement and assessment items as the supervisors (see chapter 4 and Appendix). At a slightly lower rate, they agreed with statements that exceeded the alcoholism policy intentions and prescriptions, such as "Supervisors should concern themselves with employee's off-the-job drinking."

Also like supervisors, they largely agreed with statements that reflected key provisions in the policy, such as "Alcoholism is a treatable illness." Unfortunately, they also resembled their subordinates in failing to give a majority endorsement to a pivotal feature of the policy: "Supervisors can best help employees with drinking problems by concentrating on their work performance." Only 48 percent agreed to some degree with this statement. This is slightly higher than the percentage of supervisors but still shows a heavy degree of disagreement with this central provision. Directors resembled supervisors on another pivotal issue: strong acceptance of an "I'll do it myself" stance toward counseling the problem-drinking employee.

Directors agreed in overwhelming numbers with statements that reflected the EEO policy provisions and disagreed strongly with one statement contrary to the policy's intent. Thus 90 percent agreed that "supervisors should concern themselves with identifying cases of discrimination"; 84 percent that "supervisors can best help minority employees by concentrating on their work performance"; 82 percent that "discrimination in hiring and promotion can be eliminated"; and 84 percent that "minority members should be sought out for employment vacancies." Furthermore, 51 percent disagreed with a statement contrary to the policy: "A poor employment record by a minority employee hurts the EEO program." At the same time, and in sharp contrast with their reaction to the parallel statement about the alcoholism policy, 86 percent endorsed the statement that "supervisors can best help minority employees by concentrating on their work performance." Like their reaction to the alcoholism policy, they overwhelmingly indicated (88 percent) that supervisors should engage in counseling if an employee appeals to them about an EEO problem; this suggests that directors may attach somewhat less importance to the formal roles assigned to EEO counselors than do lower-level supervisors. Overall, directors agreed more with the EEO than with the alcoholism policy, especially in the "concentration on work performance" provision.

When asked how they assessed the policies, directors were again moderately similar to lower-status supervisors. On the question of the need for the policies in their installations, 82 percent felt the alcoholism policy was not needed, while 44 percent believe the EEO policy was unneeded. Regarding ease of administration, 37 percent generally felt the alcoholism policy was easy to administer, while 31 percent believed this about EEO. This difference between policies had been somewhat greater for line supervisors but in the same direction: the alcoholism policy was seen as largely unneeded and somewhat more difficult to administer despite its simpler wording, fewer provisions, and shorter length. At the same time, like supervisors, directors tended to view both policies as beneficial to their installations and to society, and thought that they were a good idea. They were somewhat less than enthusiastic, however, since the mean values on the 7-point semantic differential remained just below 6.0 on all these items for both policies. In the same vein, they saw both policies as being more of a large rather than a small step for government to take, but EEO as substantially a larger one (means of 4.80 for alcoholism and 5.52 for EEO) and about equally useful as opposed to useless to supervisors (5.54 for alcoholism and 5.56 for EEO). Overall, the alcoholism policy, despite the lesser significance attached to it and the fewer complications it presents, posed more administrative difficulties in directors' minds. Moreover, despite its abstract value to them as a general benefit to their installation and community, it is viewed as only minimally needed in their specific, immediate workplace. This low need assessment for the alcoholism policy, contrasted with a much higher expressed need for the EEO policy, was again demonstrated by the directors' responses to two items regarding the extent to which they believed alcoholism and lack of equal opportunity were problems in their installation and how frequently they believed the policies would be used. Regarding the extent to which they estimated their installations had these problems, the mean for EEO was 4.29 on the 7-point scale; for alcoholism it was 2.28—a sizable difference indeed. The means for estimated frequency of use were 4.89 for EEO and 2.41 for alcoholism. In both cases, the magnitude of the response for EEO was almost double that for alcoholism. Clearly directors, like supervisors, perceive a need for the alcoholism policy "elsewhere," but not in their own bailiwick.

Despite these views, we know from supervisory responses that both policies were implemented to various degrees in all installations. We know that they were actually used and that management had expectations about future use that also varied in degree. Even though there were no instances of installations that "fully" implemented or completely ignored the policies, there was a sizable range of implementation between these extremes. We now turn to an examination of factors associated with implementation and use of these policies by directors themselves as another aspect of overall implementation in these installations.

FACTORS EXPECTED TO INFLUENCE
IMPLEMENTATION BY DIRECTORS

Carrying forward the pattern of analysis used with supervisors, four types of factors could influence the director's attempts to implement these policies: individual and demographic characteristics, variables growing from the director role, organizational features of the installation, and characteristics of the community in which the installation was located. Because of the smaller number of directors, we could not use all of these variables simultaneously in multiple regression equations. We therefore analyzed each family of these independent variables separately, using a series of multiple regression equations with each of the measures of implementation as a dependent variable. Only the results for role-related variables are presented here because of space limitations. Other significant results are summarized in the text and were obtained in analyses similar to those presented in table 5.1.

Individual Characteristics

Of the various personal and demographic variables tested (attitudes toward change, age, sex, minority group membership, job involvement, organizational and federal service commitment, and education) as possible predictors of implementing behavior among directors, the general attitudes toward change proved to be the most influential. This variable was related even more to aspects of policy execution by directors than it was among supervisors. An attitude favoring change was very positively associated with director estimates of how many employees could benefit from the alcoholism policy. In addition, it showed significant positive relationships with perceived benefits from the alcoholism policy for the installation, with the appointment of an alcoholism coordinator, with zealous agreement and agreement with the medical model, and with an awareness of the union's position on the policy. Regarding the EEO policy, receptivity to change was positively related to frequency of expected use of EEO in the future and to both zealous and general agreement with EEO provisions. For both policies, it also related positively with agreement with the emphasis on performance. However, receptivity to change apparently generated some skepticism about the ease of administering policy changes, since it correlated negatively with this assessment for both policies.

Job involvement, as an individual characteristic, ranked next in importance. For both policies, the directors who were job-involved agreed significantly more with job performance emphases. Such directors also reported getting more information about the alcoholism policy, but expressed less agreement with the medical model. Regarding EEO, these more involved directors tended to appoint EEO coordinators more frequently, to perceive more administrative emphasis in the policy's introduction, and to agree that the installation should actively seek out minorities for employment.

Commitment to the installation and to the federal service also produced different significant associations with implementing attitudes and behavior by directors for the two policies. Those committed to their installations perceived greater administrative emphasis on the EEO policy but were less aware of the union's position on alcoholism. Those committed to the overall federal service, on the other hand, reported little perceived administrative emphasis on EEO but a relatively large amount for the alcoholism policy. Apparently directors with high local identifications had a sensitivity to the implications of EEO for their installations but were insensitive to the union and its position on alcoholism. Those who were more national in their work-related commitment, however, perceived an emphasis on the alcoholism policy that probably reflected an "out there" belief about alcoholism, and some indifference to the local implications of EEO. This interpretation is also consistent with the negative relationship between federal service commitment and beliefs that discrimination can be eliminated in hiring and promotion. In sum, a more cosmopolitan orientation was associated with more indifference and skepticism about EEO.

The educational level of directors generated much the same pattern. Directors with higher degrees of education perceived greater administrative emphasis for the alcoholism policy but less emphasis for EEO. Perhaps they interpreted EEO as intended to be used elsewhere or simply felt that a policy about discrimination was not very exceptional. But a policy that officially labels problem drinking as a legitimate illness somehow was more salient and appeared with more emphasis to them than to less educated directors. Perhaps their higher educational attainments made them more sensitive to this shift in definition, possibly because they realized it could pose risks for them vis-à-vis the highly educated subordinates they supervise. In keeping with this attitude, the more highly educated directors were in zealous agreement with the alcoholism policy but were relatively unaware of the union position on either policy compared with the less educated directors.

Finally, both the sex and ethnicity (white versus other) of directors shaped their reactions to the policies. Although only four female directors fell into the sample, they believed that more employees could benefit from the policies than did male directors; also, they more often appointed alcoholism coordinators. Male directors, on the other hand, reported more diffusion to subordinates, agreed more on the performance emphasis in both policies and that supervisors should do their own counseling, and expressed more zealous agreement with EEO (that is, they felt they should seek out minorities for vacancies) than did female directors. The seven nonwhite directors who fell into the sample reported that the policies would be easier to administer than did the white directors, and were more sensitive to the union's position.

Role Characteristics

For the four dimensions (personal, role, structural, and environmental) considered, the results concerning the role of directors were the most revealing; they are presented in table 5.1. The adjusted[1] multiple correlations (R^2) for the personal variables just described above ranged from negligible to a highly significant .27 (agreement with medical model), while few of the R^2's in the structural or environmental analyses to be presented in the next sections were significant. In contrast, role-related variables were much stronger predictors, going from insignificant levels to .55 (agreement with EEO policy), while numerous equations yielded R^2's in the vicinity of .40. Since R^2 represents the proportion of the variance in the dependent variable (the measure of implementation) explained by independent variables in the equation, these role-related characteristics must be considered powerful predictors that represent unusual potential for explaining implementing attitudes and behaviors. They are listed at the bottom of table 5.1. Of these, civil service grade was most frequently associated significantly with the various implementing attitudes and behaviors of directors. There was substantial range on this variable among directors, ranging from G.S. 6 to G.S. 17. This variable was generally a positive predictor, but a few findings were negative: thus the higher the civil service grade, the more likely directors were to view both policies as difficult to administer. Also, higher-status directors reported less administrative emphasis on EEO than did those holding lower ratings—a finding parallel to that for education. On the positive side, high civil service ratings among directors were associated with heightened awareness of the union's position on EEO and with increased agreement with the job performance emphasis on both policies. The director of high rank also showed zealous agreement with both policies, had higher estimates of how many employees could benefit for both the EEO and alcoholism policies, and was more likely to appoint policy facilitators for both policies and to anticipate greater future use for both policies. Clearly, high civil service ratings were accompanied by more implementing attitudes and behaviors than were present at lower grades. Official status could produce security, sensitivity, perspective, and freedom from career concerns that would encourage more implementing behavior. On the other hand, high G.S. grade is associated with a zealousness that could be destructive to the intentions of both policies.

In sharp contrast, seniority in the civil service by itself produced many negative associations. (A low intercorrelation of .12 between rating and seniority indicates relative independence of these variables from each other.) Directors with longer civil service reported lower perceived benefits from the alcoholism policy as well as less agreement with its medical model and with the zealous interpretations of the policy. They also made lower estimates of the number of employees who could benefit from EEO and expressed lower agreement with the EEO policy provisions. Consistent with this attitude, they expected EEO to be used less in their installations in the future than did those with less seniority, and they had less often appointed EEO facilitators. In sum, accumulated years in the service, without accompanying rank, seemed to produce negative, skeptical attitudes toward the innovations present in the policies, making for less implementation and poorer implementers.

On the other hand, years in a specific installation had numerous positive implementing effects. That is, local seniority had, in general, the opposite effect of system seniority. Thus the number of years directors had spent in their current installation correlated positively with a perceived administrative emphasis on EEO, consistent with a similar relationship for local organizational commitment. While directors with local seniority were quite low on idealistic interpretations of EEO, they tended more often to appoint EEO facilitators. Furthermore, the more years in the local installation directors reported, the more they perceived a need for both policies. This was especially true for the alcoholism policy, since years in the installation also correlated positively with the director's estimate of the number of employees who would benefit from the alcoholism policy, the overall benefit of the policy to the installation, its expected future use there, agreement with the medical model in the policy, and the appointment of an alcoholism facilitator. Like high civil service grade, the more years directors spent in a particular installation, the more likely they were to hold implementing attitudes and engage in implementing behaviors. Apparently high local seniority accompanied by high civil service grade provided directors with role characteristics that enabled them to take a positive stance toward the policies and engage in more behavior aimed at carrying them out than if they were low on these role features. Moreover, systemwide seniority alone shows no such influence. Rather it tended to negate implementation. In sum, seniority needs to be accompanied by status and to accrue within a particular installation before it is an implementing force.

Our analysis of the factors judged important by directors for their own promotion opportunities were consistent with the role of system-wide seniority in implementing the policies. When directors placed heavy emphasis on seniority as a criteria for their own promo-

TABLE 5.1 Results of Multiple Regression of Directors' Implementation of Both Policies on Role-related Variables

Role-related Variables:[a]	STANDARDIZED REGRESSION COEFFICIENTS (BETAS)[b]							R^2 (adj)
	1	2	3	4	5	6	7	
Dependent Variables								
Diffusion:								
Diffusion of alcoholism policy	—c	—	—	—	—	—	—	08*
Diffusion of EEO policy	40†	−02	−10*	13	−13	11	12	08*
Administrative emphasis—alcoholism	−37†	46†	−20**	11	07	10	17	09*
Administrative emphasis—EEO	−19	−03	04	20**	00	23†	−23†	—
Aware union position—alcoholism	36**	—	—	—	—	—	—	−02
Aware union position—EEO	—	−23	−08	10	00	03	20**	
Receptivity:								
Agreement with medical model—alcoholism	10	42†	16*	−17*	−20†	17†	07	43†
Overall agreement with EEO	10	57†	07	−16†	−18†	08	08	55†
Zealous agreement with alcoholism	11	32†	16**	−10†	−26†	−03	20†	29†
Zealous agreement with EEO	−26†	86†	−18**	23†	−14	−11	21†	39†
Idealistic agreement with EEO	47†	−25	23†	01	02	−27†	12	12**
Perceived benefit—alcoholism	−02	23	08	−14	−24†	22†	−16	12**
Perceived benefit—EEO	—	—	—	—	—	—	—	—
Agreement with performance emphasis—both policies	05	−12	08	01	−03	−05	20*	07
Agree that supervisors do own counseling—both policies	−18	−06	33†	−00	19*	−09	01	03
Perceived need—both policies	−18	27	−25†	−01	−11	30†	09	06
Perceived ease of administration—both policies	−04	−03	46†	−03	−09	−06	−24†	19†
Assessed scope of problem—alcoholism	10	−06	−02	26†	−13	19**	40†	13**
Assessed scope of problem—EEO	−15	40†	06	18*	−19*	11	35†	15**

TABLE 5.1 (Continued)

Role-related Variables:[a]	Standardized Regression Coefficients (Betas)[b]							R^2 (adj)
	1	2	3	4	5	6	7	
Use of Policy:								
Officially appointed alcoholism coordinator	−13	−03	−08	−16	−14	17*	36†	16**
Officially appointed EEO functionaries	−01	−04	−11	04	−21†	19†	63†	39†
How many could benefit—alcoholism	10	−06	−02	26†	−13**	19**	40†	13**
How many could benefit—EEO	−15	40†	06	18*	−19**	11	35†	15**

[a] As follows:
1. Importance of technical skills for promotion
2. Importance of performance for promotion
3. Importance of seniority for promotion
4. Perceived work overload
5. Years in civil service
6. Years in installation
7. Civil service grade

[b] With decimal points omitted.

[c] No significant results.

* p = .10
** p = .05
† p = .01

tion, they perceived low need and administrative emphasis for both policies, although they assessed the policies as relatively easy to administer. Under these conditions, they also showed less zealous agreement with EEO provisions, while, ironically, endorsing its more idealistic features. While the importance of seniority was associated with agreement with the medical model of alcoholism, it was also associated with the counterpolicy attitude that supervisors should do their own counseling.

When the focus shifts to those directors who put an emphasis on job performance as a criteria for their promotion, a very different picture emerges. They agree with a zealous approach to the alcoholism policy and with its medical model. Also, they perceive a higher administrative emphasis on this policy. In addition, they consistently estimate that more employees could benefit from EEO in their installations, while at the same time showing overall and zealous agreement with EEO provisions. Apparently their orientation to performance criteria in their own jobs and careers is compatible with a similar emphasis in both policies. Those directors who emphasize technical skill as a criterion indicate implementing attitudes exclusively toward EEO. They report low administrative emphasis for the alcoholism policy, while reporting relatively heavy diffusion of information to them about EEO, awareness of the union's EEO position, and an idealistic but not zealous agreement with the EEO policy thrust.

Finally, work overload had somewhat different effects on directors than upon lower-level supervisors. It failed to produce clear negative effects on implementing attitudes and behaviors in the way it did among supervisors. But, like supervisors, directors who felt overloaded perceive more administrative emphasis on EEO. Since this same pattern of association exists at all supervisory levels, perhaps the EEO policy is contributing to perceived overload. Alternatively the data could be interpreted to indicate that the more conscientious supervisors and directors who allow themselves to get overloaded also pay more attention to administrative demands made through new policies like EEO. Overload, however, does have negative impact on directors relative to their overall agreement with EEO, but again is positively related to zealous agreement, indicating they feel they should seek out minority members to hire. With these views, we can see how administrative emphasis on this policy could lead to heightened perceptions of work overload.

Organizational Characteristics

The following variables were considered important possible influences on the implementation of the policies by directors: size of the installation (number of employees), formalization (number and specificity of work rules), centralization of decision making within the installation (the degree to which decisions were made by the director rather than subordinates), resource decentralization (the director's influence over budget and personnel allocations), visibility of consequences (the degree to which it was easy to assess performance of tasks within the installation), the amount of contact the director had with his superior, and the presence of a union. Greater size, resource decentralization, visibility of consequences, contact with superiors, and the presence of a union were all expected to be positive influences on implementation by the director because they either help to make resources available to implement the policies or provide conditions that tend to focus on managerial performance by increasing accountability. Centralization and formalization have generally been found to be inhibiting to innovation and change (Hage and Aiken, 1970) because they tend to remove initiative from supervisors and also may actually interfere with the freedom of action they need to make necessary changes. Highly centralized and formalized structures may also lead to what has variously been called "trained incapacity" (Merton, 1957) or the bureaupathic personality (Thompson, 1961). Both phrases are used to describe the bureaucrat who follows the rules to the exclusion of all other concerns and therefore often behaves irrationally or dysfunctionally in terms of actual organizational objectives.

The contribution of these variables to explaining the three phases of implementation for directors was again assessed using multiple regression. These variables were not as consistently important in predicting directors' behaviors in implementing the policies, as evidenced by generally low R^2 values, as were personal or role-related variables. There were, however, some highly significant regression equations, and many individual variables had statistically significant relationships with the directors' implementing attitudes and behaviors. The variables that were most frequently related to implementation by directors were visibility of consequences (Trice, 1965), resource decentralization, union presence, and size of installation.

Low visibility of consequences is a source of uncertainty for directors, because it indicates a lack of unambiguous criteria by which performance can be assessed. One striking finding was the strong relationships between visibility of consequences and whether or not the director was aware of the union's position on the policies ($\beta = .27$ for the alcoholism policy and .22 for the EEO policy, $p = .05$). It appears that directors who had workers whose performance could be readily measured were more careful to monitor the union's position on such personnel policies. Visibility of consequences was also related to directors' agreement with policy content.

Where work consequences were more visible, directors agreed more with the medical model of alcoholism, showed more zealous agreement with the alcoholism policy, and were in more idealistic agreement with EEO. Such directors also agreed more with the emphasis on satisfactory work performance in both policies, undoubtedly because they saw the performance provisions as more applicable and relevant to their installations than did other directors. Directors with high visibility of consequences also saw more benefits in the EEO policy; probably they felt that they could incorporate minority and female workers into jobs with highly visible outcomes fairly readily, while directors who had low visibility of consequences did not see the EEO policy as beneficial because they already dealt with more uncertainty and were not likely to see any other sources of uncertainty as beneficial. There are at least three reasons why female and minority hiring and/or promotions might be better accepted where consequences are more visible. First, directors and other supervisors would not be so likely to fear that they might lose control of the situation, because they have a ready means of assessing inadequate performance and feedback that helps them to know when things are going well or badly. Second, fellow employees are less likely to complain, and if they do, their complaints can be rationally dealt with when the minority employee's work performance can be documented in a concrete way. Third, directors and others may feel that women and minority group members "suit" such jobs but cannot be trusted in jobs with more uncertainty, because people are generally more likely to trust others with discretion who are like themselves.[2] Some of these same factors could also have influenced their acceptance of the alcoholism policy—directors who enjoyed high visibility of consequences probably saw implementing the alcoholism policy as posing less risk for them than did other directors.

On the negative side, directors who headed installations with visible work consequences reported less administrative emphasis on the alcoholism policy than did other directors. Together with the relatively favorable attitudes toward the policy in these installations, these results are both surprising and distressing. Exactly where the alcoholism policy might have been most easily applied and where it was most likely to be supported it had received relatively less push from those in the higher echelons of the agency. We can only speculate about this finding. It may have been that upper levels of management knew the policy would be supported anyway; otherwise, their lack of administrative oversight in this matter implies that there was some opposition or lack of support for the policy content.

Greater director influence over resources made available to the installation was positively related to agreement with the medical model and perceived benefit of the alcoholism policy, although it was negatively related to zealous agreement with this policy. Most important, these more influential directors perceived more need for the alcoholism policy. Thus the decentralization of some control over resource allocations from upper echelons to the directors was, on balance, favorable to implementation of the alcoholism policy. This was not true for the EEO policy. Although directors with more influence over resources saw more administrative emphasis on EEO, they were less likely to agree with the idealistic statement that discrimination can be eliminated. Resource influence was not significantly related to other aspects of EEO implementation. So decentralization of resources did not seem to aid or hinder implementation of the EEO policy.

Union presence was also negatively related to this same statement; perhaps directors who need to cope with unions in the workplace are more realistic than idealistic and are more aware of factors that perpetuate discrimination.

Size was most importantly related to whether or not the director had appointed coordinators for the two policies. In larger installations, directors had more often made these formal appointments, perhaps because they anticipated more need for formally designated persons with greater work load for the position, perhaps because all matters are handled more formally in larger installations and/or perhaps because they had to delegate these matters formally since they already had greater responsibilities than directors of smaller installations. On the other hand, directors of larger installations reported that they had received less diffusion on the alcoholism policy than other directors. Despite this, they perceived more need for both policies than directors of smaller installations. It is hard to imagine why directors of larger installations should receive less information on personnel policies, unless they were more likely to be informed directly from Washington, while directors in smaller installations received more information from their regional offices in addition to what they received from Washington. Alternatively, perhaps directors of larger installations appointed coordinators relatively early, and some of the information reaching other directors had been routed to the policy coordinator.

Other variables had more scattered effects. As expected, centralization of decision making was negatively related to perceived need for both policies.[3] Not surprisingly, rule specificity was positively related to administrative emphasis on the EEO policy, and contact with superiors was negatively related to appointing an alcoholism coordinator.

The multiple regression equations with the structural variables best explained awareness of the union position (16 percent of the variance for alcoholism, 28 percent for EEO) and perceived need for the policies (14 percent of the variance).

The same analyses were rerun for only those installations in which a union was present (n = 45). Since unions were present in all of these installations, the dummy variable called union presence was eliminated from the regression, and three variables relating to the union were added: union influence, the director's knowledge of union adversary activities, and the director's knowledge of general union activities. (See Appendix for how these variables were measured.) It was generally expected that relatively powerful unions and unions about which directors were better informed would be facilitative to the alcoholism policy but might resist the EEO policy.

In these additional analyses, the bulk of the results for the structural variables were similar to those just reported, despite the smaller subsample and the addition of new variables. Only differences in results will therefore be presented, along with results for the three new union-related variables.

Awareness of the union position on the alcoholism policy was better predicted by the structural variables for all installations than it was for just the installations where unions were present, despite the addition of union-related variables. However, the main predictor of such awareness—visibility of consequences—did not change. The only effect of the union-related variables was negative. Directors who knew more about general union activities were *less* likely to be aware of the union's position on the alcoholism policy. The most probable reason for this finding is that unions that emphasize miscellaneous activities (such as newsletters, social activities, and travel tours) exhibit less of the traditional labor values and concerns that center on employee rights and benefits. In such situations, the union may not have bothered to take a position on the alcoholism policy, and this is why the director is not aware of it.

The directors' perceptions of the benefit of the alcoholism policy, however, is much better predicted for just the unionized installations ($R^2 = .26$, p = .05). The major predictor—visibility of consequences—has an even stronger effect ($\beta = .51$, p = .01) for the alcoholism policy, and the director's knowledge of general union activities also has a significant positive effect. The same pattern was found for the EEO policy, but the relationships, while significant, were not as strong. However, zealous agreement with the alcoholism policy is negatively affected by the director's knowledge of general union activities ($-.22$) and heavily and positively influenced ($\beta = .43$, p = .01) by the director's knowledge of union adversary activities. Centralization also has a negative effect on zealous agreement. Apparently, where unions are militant, directors are likely to believe in a more zealous position toward drinking problems among employees. Moreover, neither centralization of influence in decision making within the installation nor knowledge of other union activities is likely to mitigate this overzealous reaction to the alcoholism policy.

A similar pattern of results is found for administrative emphasis on the EEO policy. The more influential the union and the more militant it is, the more likely the director is to report strong administrative emphasis on EEO. However, two variables are negatively related to administrative emphasis on EEO: the proportion of employees working under written rules, and the director's knowledge of general union activities. Finally, the director's knowledge of union adversary activities is positively related, while size is again negatively related to the amount of diffusion directors have had on the alcoholism policy. Apparently militant unions lead to the sending and receiving of more information on the alcoholism policy because it might be expected to involve unions either through the filing of grievances or in a more positive way, if management is able to elicit union cooperation in helping and supporting management in the constructive confrontation of employees with drinking problems. Unions more active in general employee concerns and greater codification of work procedures act as depressing influences on the administrative emphasis transmitted to installation heads on the EEO policy. The role of the union is discussed in greater detail and additional findings relative to the unions in these installations are presented in chapter 8.

Environmental Characteristics

Finally, we believed it was reasonable to expect that an installation's environment could have an impact on a director's feelings and attitudes about the policies. If formal organizations are open systems, their formal administrative leader should take environmental features, pressures, and influences into account when assessing policies and their probable impacts. To uncover such relationships, we performed multiple regression analyses of director attitudes about the policy on the demographic make-up of the communities in which installations were located. Community characteristics used were size of community, median age, population density, median family income, percentage black, percentage of foreign stock, median education, percentage employed in manufacturing and in government, percentage professionals and managers, and percentage unemployed (U.S. Census 1973). These variables produced few and very weak influences on director attitudes toward alcoholism and EEO policies.

In a later chapter we assess the effects of these variables on implementing behaviors of all supervisors in the installations; but for the above analyses we conceived of the director in the role of boundary spanner, filtering and relaying information from the community to his subordinates. Such information could include expression of community norms and values, as well as the relaying of particular demand factors related to demographic characteristics of the community that could make one or both of these policies more needed, relevant, or politically desirable to implement with employees of that installation. For all practical purposes, we could detect little influence on director attitudes from these features of their organizational environments.

Perhaps one reason that the community did not produce much effect on director attitudes is that advancement through civil service usually involves some transfers in location. While the average director in our sample had been in the civil service for 23 years, he or she had been at that installation for only 8 years and in his or her position as director for 5 years. Thus federal executives are not closely tied to the community in which the installations they head are located, and this tends to minimize the effects of that community upon their values and views.

DIRECTORS AS CHIEF EXECUTIVES IN THE IMPLEMENTATION PROCESS

Up to this point we have been analyzing directors as high-level supervisors, but as supervisors nonetheless. Now we turn to the director as the chief executive officer in the installation, an organizational role and position relatively unique and apart from general line supervision. Fortunately there are reports that focus explicitly on the role of top management in attempting to implement innovations. Baldridge and Burnham (1975) found that department chairmen and school administrators held organizational roles and positions that were highly influential in establishing an innovation for a significant period of time. In a somewhat similar vein, Hage and Dewar (1973) found that "informal elites"—those persons who held informal high-status positions and always participated in decision making in health and welfare organizations—exercised as much, if not more, influence on change processes than those of high formal status. Thus both informal and formal organizational leaders can affect implementation. In addition, they concluded from their analysis that these leadership forces were more influential than organization-level forces such as centralization and complexity.

Radnor and Bean (1974), studying the acceptance and use of operations research findings in companies, concluded that the commitment of top management to the innovation was among the major forces central to implementation. Especially emphatic is the work of

Gross, Giacquinta, and Bernstein (1971). Repeatedly they point to the ever-present possibility that top management's influence in educational innovations will fail to be exercised, leading to unexecuted innovations: "Our findings bring into bold focus the need for leadership in the management of the innovation process and the consequences that follow when it does not exist" (1971:215). They place special emphasis upon the responsibility of top management for maintaining conditions that will facilitate subordinates' use of an innovation: providing trained, knowledgeable, and willing staff; providing materials and equipment necessary; and resolving incompatible situations.

Other writers (Kaluzny et al., 1974; Sapolsky, 1967; Wilson, 1966) supplement this position by pointing out that chief executives need adequate resources so that they can induce subordinates to comply with an innovation and also engage in policy-implementing activities themselves. "Slack" (uncommitted resources) is one form of resource often indicated as affecting top executives' ability to actively implement; their power is another. Still other writers focus on the personal characteristics of administrators. Kaplan (1967) and Mytinger (1968), for example, both report that the level of professionalism, the leadership style, and the cosmopolitanism of the administrator were positively related to the actual use of an innovation. Kaplan also reports that "psychological flexibility," along with discretionary judgment of various sorts, are traits of top administrators significantly related to carrying out an innovation. These personal characteristics can also be viewed as resources available to the director.

Although Rogers and Shoemaker (1971:35) define "opinion leaders" as a type of leadership that is informal rather than a function of formal position or status, there are good reasons for also viewing installation directors in this light. The concept posits a two-stage communication flow about innovations—first from impersonal sources to opinion leaders and then through them to a given population. Opinion leaders can influence followers in the population favorably, unfavorably, or with indifference (Katz, 1957). Installation directors, although formal leaders, appear to fit this general notion quite well, since they tend to act as communication channels from other parts of the federal bureaucracy, and probably from other parts of the environment. Moreover, compared to the population of potential users (lower-level supervisors), they clearly have the higher status. Since these are relatively small organizations—the average having 205 employees and 27 supervisors—directors also have substantial opportunity and reason to have face-to-face communication with lower-level supervisors. Both of these are characteristics of opinion leaders, according to Rogers and Shoemaker (1971:218).

The most interesting recent development of this concept comes from data generated by Becker (1970), who showed that opinion leaders are selective in their sponsorship of innovations, assessing the political climate and supporting low-risk changes.

Turning to studies concerning the importance of support from top management for the specific policies under study, generally comparable findings have been reported. Trice and Belasco (1965, 1970) point to the "policy-practice gap" between itself and subordinates that top management typically fail to overcome even though it formally and informally commits itself to an alcoholism policy. Riley and Horn (1974), reporting on ten industrial alcoholism programs, rank support from top management as the highest prerequisite for successful implementation. Similarly, support is often cited as essential in the successful implementation of EEO programs (Chayes, 1974; Hellriegel and Short, 1972). Francine Hall has provided substantial data that EEO goals will be effectively implemented, in part, when top management "provide direct support for the activities necessary to implement the goals" (Hall, 1976:14). These included resources, psychological support, and the exercising of sanctions that held lower-level managers accountable for implementing the policy.

Director Power and Resources Relative to Supervisory Policy Attitudes and Use

A major theme running through the above review is that of the top executive influencing the attitudes and behavior of his managerial subordinates. That is, there is an assumption that line supervision will reflect to a significant degree the attitudes and behavior of top management. Earlier in this chapter we reported that there was indeed a sizable comparability between the attitudes of directors and line supervisors about key provisions and thrusts of both policies. In and of itself this suggests that directors do set the tone and general orientation for these policy innovations.[4] It leaves unanswered, however, what aspects of director attitudes influence actual and expected policy usage by subordinate supervisors. Also, the influence of the presence of organizational "slack" or other resources available to the director has not yet been considered. In order to address such issues, we performed additional multiple regression analyses in which we assessed the effects of the director's power, professionalization, education, tenure in installation and as director, and possession of organizational slack on measures of supervisory receptivity toward and use of these policies. (Table 5.2 gives a list of these same independent variables with other dependent variables.)

Where directors reported high amounts of professional activity (attending meetings and serving as officers), line supervisors reported significantly higher numbers of forms and sources of information and greater agreement with doing their own counseling. The most influential variable, however, remained the number of years spent in the director position in the installation. As directors reported relatively higher tenure in their jobs (the mean is 5.13 years on this variable), the benefits line supervisors perceived for the alcoholism policy sharply declined, as did their agreement with the medical model. Length of tenure as director was also associated with supervisors taking overzealous positions on the alcoholism policy. Even though longer tenure of directors had these negative associations with policy-supportive attitudes, it was, nonetheless, the only director variable that was significantly and positively related to actual supervisory use of this policy in the past. None predicted expected use.

Despite this ambivalence, long-tenured directors apparently exercised greater leadership for alcoholism policy use than did short-tenured ones. They probably had experience that generated skepticism but also had the security to influence subordinates to conform to a policy about which they all felt ambivalent. Consistent with this interpretation is the absence of any relationships between director characteristics and expected use of the policy. Apparently directors are opinion leaders, but where alcoholism is concerned, they are cautious and uncertain ones—prone to misinterpretation of the policy and vacillation. Interestingly enough, the power of the director showed no direct influence on supervisory use, although one aspect of it (power to transfer personnel) had a negative effect on how supervisors perceived ease of administration, while power to change divisions had positive effects on perceived need, and discretion over budget was positively related to agreement with performance.

Aspects of the director's power, however, did emerge as influences on line supervisor attitudes about and use of the EEO policy. Supervisors' assessments of the perceived benefit of this policy and its ease of administration, for example, were smaller when director power (measured by ability to transfer employees and to create or eliminate new divisions), education, and professional activities were greater. Moreover, supervisors' agreement with EEO provisions was negatively related to the director's years in that position and to budget discretion (ability to decide independently about a sizable proportion of the budget). If directors possessed budget discretion or high tenure in the director role, diffusion to supervisors was less. Also, those directors who read more professional journals tended to have supervisors who felt they should do their own EEO counseling. In these respects, more powerful and professional directors seemed to have a discouraging effect on EEO implementing attitudes among lower-level supervisors. However, directors' ability to transfer person-

TABLE 5.2 Results of Multiple Regression[a] of Directors' Implementation Activities on Characteristics Usually Seen as Related to Innovation

	STANDARDIZED REGRESSION COEFFICIENTS (BETAS)											
	Alcoholism Policy						EEO Policy					
Dependent Variables:[b]	1	2	3	4	5	6	1	2	3	4	5	6
Independent Variables[c]												
Years in position		42*					34*		58**	36**	—29	
Years in installation			19**				46*					17
Power to make structural changes		—26*	41†		—34		—25					
Ability to transfer personnel			11*			20*			40*		—09	33**
Uncommitted monies			—15*	—18		29*			—17	—11	—08	
Budget discretion			41†	—16	09				—38*	—12	—10	
Professional activities		—45*		—43†	—33		—48*	—35*				
Professional membership		—15					19	36**	—26		—33*	
Journals read			—17†		19	16				—28*	—45*	
Education		—26*										
R² (adjusted)	—[d]	10*	89**	19†	19**	11*	08	06*	14*	07	02	12**

[a]Stepwise mode; decimal points omitted.

[b]As follows:
1. Facilitator's tenure in role
2. Facilitator has job description
3. Information diffusion by director to facilitator
4. Staff size of facilitator
5. Official time allocation to facilitator
6. Director's expected use of policy

[c]All independent variables pertain to directors.

[d]No significant results.

* p = .10
** p = .05
† p = .01

nel and their professionalization had positive influences on diffusion of information and on perceived need for the EEO policy among supervisors. It is as if the power and professionalization of directors is accompanied by ambivalence toward this policy. This ambivalent theme became even more pronounced in the actual number of supervisory efforts to use EEO. The power of the director was negatively correlated with these actions, although their professional activities were positively related with actual supervisory use, as was their simple seniority (years in installation). On balance, the powerful director appears to have a dampening effect on EEO implementation efforts at lower supervisory levels, while the less powerful seems to release supervisory tendencies to conform and use the policy.

Director Power and Resources Relative to Support for Facilitators

Another prominent theme about chief executives and innovation is the extent to which they provide facilitating conditions supportive of implementation. Since the policy facilitators and their role constitute a major potential vehicle through which directors could exercise their leadership, we looked at the characteristics of directors, including their power, that might predict their providing resources and other support to facilitators. To the degree that the director takes the steps needed to create and sustain the facilitator role, he is engaging in implementing behavior. Also, the extent to which directors expected the policy to be used in the future reflected their anticipation of continued implementation and constituted a second type of implementing variable. Using the same group of independent variables as before, we regressed these new measures of the director's implementation activities on them (table 5.2). Where the director had power to make structural changes, alcoholism facilitators were more likely to receive a job description and the director diffused more policy information to them. Regarding EEO, this same type of power was related only to greater diffusion of information from director to facilitator. The director's power to transfer personnel was associated with their diffusion of the alcoholism policy to supervisors; for EEO it had no effect, but it was a clear-cut predictor of the extent to which directors expected the policy to be used in their installation in the future—the only variable predicting this director projection. In sum, the more powerful directors did, in fact, take more positive implementing actions regarding facilitators than did the less powerful.

Professionalization among directors, however, had the opposite effect. Consistently, measures of professionalization of directors predicted significantly less implementing behaviors among professionalized directors than among less professionalized ones. Thus the professional activities of directors (attending meetings relevant to their occupation or directorship and serving as officers) tended to predict a neglect of policy-implementing behavior: fewer job descriptions and small staff size for facilitators, as well as less information diffusion to them for the EEO policy. Professional activities did have one positive effect—on diffusion of information on the alcoholism policy to coordinators of this policy. Membership in professional associations alone had no effect one way or the other on directors' behavior relative to alcoholism facilitators; it was, however, significantly related to less diffusion of information and smaller staff size for EEO facilitators. Reading professional journals had the same general effect: those directors who read more journals less often issued job descriptions and diffused information for alcoholism facilitators; they also appointed EEO facilitators more recently and gave less official time allocation to them.

Clearly professionalization among directors had a negative influence on policy implementation. In general, this is consistent with earlier findings about skill level and supervisory use of the alcoholism policy; that is, the higher the skill level of supervised employees, the less likely supervisors were to use the policy (Trice and Beyer, 1977). The current findings, however, strongly suggest that reluctance to implement may also be based upon professional attitudes and behavior. Moreover, they apply to the EEO as well as to the alcoholism policy. In all probability the explanation lies in the chief feature of professionalization: autonomy, or control of as many of the circumstances surrounding job performance as possible (Stewart and Cantor, 1974)—as related to the stage of innovation studied here, the implementation stage. That is, professionals among the directors probably find the initiation of innovations consistent with their expectations of autonomy, but find the implementing of changes imposed from outside their sphere of power highly inconsistent with their autonomy. To implement an externally imposed innovation violates the professional's sense of autonomy, calling forth resistance and/or lack of action. Moreover, professionalization is consistent with a concern for high quality of performance, and it may be that such directors feel that women and minorities, as well as alcoholics, cannot perform at a level of competence they feel is needed in their installations. In short, both policies may be seen by professionalized directors as threats to their installation, to its performance, and to the status quo within it. In this sample, education is only moderately correlated or uncorrelated with professionalization ($r = -.18$ with professional activities, .52 with professional memberships, and .10 with journals read), and it has few independent effects on how directors act to support facilitators: education has a positive effect on their providing EEO facilitators with job descriptions, but a negative one on how much staff they provide.

For the most part the possession of slack resources by directors has a negative effect on implementing activities: uncommitted monies had such an effect on job descriptions for alcoholism facilitators, while budget discretion also worked against diffusion of information to them. Uncommitted monies, however, tended to be associated with a high expected use of the alcoholism policy by the director who had them. Slack had no significant influence on director behavior relative to EEO facilitators.

Again, tenure in both directorship and in the installation had positive effects. This was particularly true for EEO facilitators. Where directors had been in the installation for relatively long periods, facilitators received more information and staff. Where they had been in the director job longer, they tended to appoint EEO facilitators sooner and to diffuse more information about alcoholism to that coordinator.

Interestingly, the predictive power of these equations was largest for this latter implementing behavior—information diffusion by director to facilitator, where the adjusted R^2 reached .89, indicating we had explained almost 90 percent of the variance in that behavior. Other equations account for much less of the variance, although the general trend is for these data to better predict behavior relative to the alcoholism than the EEO policy.

How Director Power and Attitudes
Related to Their Own Implementing Behavior

The ambivalence we found in results already reported raised two questions: in what direction was power going—for or against the policy—and how was the combination of power and favorability of attitudes related to implementation? In order to examine these issues, we decided to use the power to make structural changes in their installations as perhaps the most indicative of directors' actual power. We divided the directors into high- and low-power groups at the mean value of the variable. We then ran a series of analyses designed to assess whether director attitudes were differently related to implementation when they had high versus low power. The first part of these analyses assessed the effect of directors' power and attitudes on their own implementing behaviors. For these analyses, we ran parallel multiple regressions of each group's implementing behavior on their attitudes about the two policies. Implementing behaviors assessed were the same as those in table 5.2.

For the alcoholism policy only scattered themes emerged. The most consistent was that higher need for the policy among both high-

and low-power directors was significantly associated with less formalized behavior such as assigned titles or job descriptions to the
alcoholism coordinator. Evidently need either produces a belief that
formalisms may be dysfunctional to policy implementation,[5] or gives
rise to the "I'll manage the problem myself" attitude (Trice, 1965).
There is a significant trend for powerful directors who agree with the
performance emphasis of the policy to spread information to the
facilitator more vigorously than those who tend to disagree with it.
Low-power directors who show receptivity to change do the same
thing. Overall, a sense of need suppresses formalization of alcoholism
coordinator roles despite director power; the important behavior of
diffusion of information downward, however, is triggered by different attitudes for low- and high-power directors. Also when we
controlled for power, a tendency to ritualize appeared. That is,
among both types of directors, when they were *less* favorable to the
policy, they were much *more* likely to engage in formalisms such as
job descriptions and titles for coordinators. Thus ambivalence continued to appear.

When powerful directors reacted to the EEO policy, their agreement with its performance emphasis had no effect upon their own
implementing behaviors. Less powerful ones, with the same attitude,
in contrast, again resorted to formal job descriptions. High assessed
benefits of the policy produced ambivalence among high-power directors: they provided staff to their facilitators but few official titles.
This attitude had positive effects among low-power directors. When
powerful directors believed the EEO policy was easy to administer,
they were likely to reduce staff for the facilitator and provide few
official titles. Less powerful directors who believed the EEO policy
was easy to administer significantly diffused more information than
their counterparts who believed it was difficult to administer.

When powerful directors held strong feelings of need for the
policy, they significantly allocated larger staff size to the facilitator,
but low-power directors only responded to this felt need by providing more formal job descriptions. In addition, receptivity to
change among powerful directors resulted in significantly large
amounts of diffusion of information to their facilitators. Weaker
ones who were receptive to change showed more ambivalence: they
allocated less official time, but were very generous with official titles.

In summary, the attitudes that were associated with positive
steps toward implementation of the policies among high-power directors included need, receptivity to change, assessed benefit, and agreement with performance emphasis, but effects were inconsistent
across policies. The same attitudes tended to be related to implementation by low-power directors, but their behaviors were also positively affected by how easy they felt the policies were to administer.

How Director Power and Attitudes
Related to Supervisory Implementation

Finally, we similarly assessed supervisory implementation as a function of director power and attitudes. These results are given in tables 5.3 and 5.4.[6] As suggested by the previous results, if a director is a proponent of a policy, he may be able to use his power and authority to persuade subordinates to use the policy. If, on the other hand, his support is lukewarm, or he opposes the policy, he may be able to use his authority to discourage policy implementation.[7] The reverse of this idea is that directors with little real power or authority are less likely to be able to influence their subordinates to behave in accordance with their inclinations. In order to test this idea, we again divided the directors into high- and low-power groups at the mean value for power to make structural changes in their installations. We then ran multiple regression analyses of supervisory implementation of the alcoholism and EEO policies on attitudes of director controlling for director power. This permitted us to contrast the relationship of the attitudes of low- and high-power directors with various measures of supervisory implementation.

Four distinct trends emerged for the alcoholism policy. The most prominently ambivalent results occurred when high-power directors also held feelings of high need for the alcoholism policy. Under these conditions, line managers frequently reported significantly *less* implementing behavior. For example, learning hours about the policy were significantly low, as were training hours. In all, seven of the indexes on supervisory implementation were significantly negative under these conditions, while only two were positive: perceived administrative emphasis on the policy and past usage. Evidently, powerful directors who also have strong feelings of need act to decrease diffusion and implementing attitudes of supervisors while insisting on use of the policy.

Under such circumstances, it seems quite unlikely that such policy use is in conformity with the details of the policy. Perhaps the high-power directors are influencing subordinates to bypass policy provisions in dealing with alcoholic employees, or have so administratively emphasized this policy as to produce a relatively uninformed (since diffusion and training are low) reaction to the policy. This interpretation was reinforced when we examined supervisors with low-power directors who showed high policy need. Here the situation was substantially reversed: supervisors showed not only sizable amounts of implementing activities, such as showing very significant amounts of both past and expected policy use, but also more policy-consonant attitudes. Low-power directors who feel need for

TABLE 5.3 Results of Parallel Multiple Regressions[a] of Supervisors' Implementation of Alcoholism Policy on Attitudes of Director Controlling for Director Power

Independent Variables:[b]	Low Power (n = 45)							High Power (n = 21)						
	1	2	3	4	5	6	R^2	1	2	3	4	5	6	R^2
Supervisory Implementation														
Diffusion to supervisor	—c	—	—	—	—	—	—	-24	61†	—	-29**	-38†	-19	71†
Diffusion to employees	—	—	—	26*	—	17	04	—	40*	41*	-54**	-37*	—	45**
Training hours	-36**	—	—	—	—	—	—	-28	22	-29	-30	-53**	—	42**
Training topics	—	—	—	28*	31**	23**	15**	—	47**	—	-28	-40*	42*	44**
Learning hours	—	—	—	—	—	37**	14**	36	26	—	-26	-51†	25	50†
Administrative emphasis	—	—	—	—	—	-27*	05	—	-24	—	71†	40*	—	40**
Familiarity	—	—	—	—	—	—	—	—	—	—	-42**	-31	32	32**
Agree with medical model	—	15	—	-18	-42†	17	14**	—	—	—	—	—	—	—
Agree with performance emphasis	—	-28*	—	26*	34**	28*	16**	—	—	—	—	—	—	—
Propensity to counsel	—	—	—	29*	—	—	06*	—	—	—	—	—	—	—
Perceived benefit	—	—	—	—	29*	—	06*	-32	42*	22	—	-24	53*	12
Need for policies	—	—	—	26*	28*	-31**	16**	—	22	—	35*	-48**	22	42**
Ease of administration	—	—	—	15	.40†	26*	17**	—	31	45*	-40*	57**	—	19
Past use (1 = yes, 0 = no)	—	—	—	28*	.35**	27*	17**	—	—	—	—	—	—	—
Number of past uses	—	—	—	29*	62†	20	17**	—	—	—	—	—	—	—
Expected use	—	—	-27*	—	—	—	28†	—	—	—	—	—	—	—

[a] Standardized regression coefficients, decimal points omitted; stepwise mode; adjusted R^2.

[b] As follows:
1. Agreement medical model
2. Agreement with performance emphasis
3. Assessed benefits
4. Ease of administration
5. Need for policies
6. Receptivity to change

[c] Nothing was significant in these equations.

*p < .10
**p < .05
†p < .01

TABLE 5.4 Results of Parallel Multiple Regressions[a] of Supervisors' Implementation of EEO Policy on Attitudes of Director Controlling for Director Power

LOW POWER (n = 45) columns 1–6, R^2; HIGH POWER (n = 21) columns 1–6, R^2.

Independent Variables:[b]	Low 1	Low 2	Low 3	Low 4	Low 5	Low 6	Low R^2	High 1	High 2	High 3	High 4	High 5	High 6	High R^2
Supervisory Implementation														
Diffusion to supervisor	—[c]			—18		31**	11**	52**	32	42*		57**		16
Diffusion to employees														19*
Training hours	32**	—33*	19	—30*		—18	04	39	26			45**	31*	13
Training topics		—22		—29*			14**					53**		24**
Learning hours										—28			48**	18*
Administrative emphasis	28*				—31**	—	10**	—49**				—49**	26	29*
Familiarity								38	52*	25		47	33	12
Overall agreement	28*	—27*	—24		—21		11*	35						—
Agree with performance emphasis	—20	—28*		22	39**	31**	17**					—24	—33	—
Propensity to counsel	—	—	—	—	—	—	—	—	—	—	—	—	—	—
Perceived benefits	22				25*		10**					—53†	32*	36†
Need for policies												35	33	11
Ease of administration			—27**	34†		—28**	21†	—40*	19		36**	—63†	36**	54†
Past use (1 = yes, 0 = no)		—27*	33**	—31**		—16	09*			24		40*	38*	16
Number of past uses				29*			06	29	—53†		—41			36**
Expected use							—					51**	35*	27**

[a]Standardized regression coefficients, decimal points omitted; stepwise mode; adjusted R^2.

[b]As follows:
1. Agreement with overall policy
2. Performance emphasis
3. Assessed benefits
4. Ease of administration
5. Need for policies
6. Receptivity to change

[c]Nothing was significant in these equations.

*p < .10
**p < .05
†p < .01

the policy seem to pass this need down to their subordinates, producing fuller compliance with the policy.

A second trend was for powerful directors who agreed with the performance emphasis of the alcoholism policy to have considerable positive effects on implementation by lower-level managers. Low-power directors with similar attitudes failed to do this. Thus, for example, such high-power directors had supervisors who diffused more information to rank-and-file employees and experienced more training topics. Unlike high feelings of need, high agreement with performance emphasis among powerful directors engendered implementing activities among subordinate managers. In sharp contrast, low-power directors who held higher agreement with performance emphasis had supervisors with the reverse attitude. Clearly, power must combine with performance emphasis before it has an effect on lower levels of management.

Third, powerful directors who perceived the alcoholism policy as easy to administer had a repressive effect on implementation by their managers. Four of the six significant effects were negative. Apparently their power serves to communicate their beliefs that the policy is easy to manage, and supervisors become lax about it. Lower-power managers contrasted sharply. When they held such attitudes, their subordinates reported significantly greater agreement with performance emphasis and greater past and expected use. Their lack of power, when joined by a feeling of ease, seems to encourage subordinates to explore and use the policy.

A fourth trend, less distinct, can be detected. Having a powerful director who was receptive to change was less influential than sensitivity to policy need, but also had positive effects on supervisors. Under these circumstances they reported a significantly higher need for the policy and had experienced more relevant training topics. Much the same could be said of those supervisors who worked for lower-power directors with high receptivity to change. But some ambivalence entered in that these supervisors also believed that the policy would be hard to administer.

Overall agreement with the EEO policy (see table 5.4) is another instance of how high power combined with a director attitude to have opposite effects on supervisors. Where these conditions prevailed supervisors tended to behave ambivalently: they significantly diffused more policy information to their managers but perceived significantly less administrative emphasis and policy administrative difficulties. Low-power directors, in contrast, who had overall agreement with the policy generated consistently positive reactions. Their supervisors reported significantly more training hours and topics and thus perceived that there was more administrative emphasis on the EEO policy.

A second contrast came from the influence of agreement with the performance emphasis within EEO. When directors had low power and tended to agree with this emphasis they worked with supervisors who reported significantly less overall agreement with the policy, fewer training hours and topics, and significantly less usage. High-power directors seem to generate more ambivalence: When they agreed with the performance emphasis, their supervisors reported significantly greater familiarity with the policy but also significantly less past usage. In sum, lower-power directors who were in agreement with performance emphasis for both the EEO and alcoholism policies had an adverse effect on their supervisors; high-power ones with a similar view about performance had favorable effects on supervisory implementation for the alcoholism policy but mixed reactions for EEO.

The theme of ambivalence reappears when the impact of director power combined with a sense of policy benefits and needs is analyzed relative to supervisors' implementation of EEO. The most impressive was among high-power directors with high perceived policy need. This combination produced six significantly positive and three negative relations with supervisory attitudes and behaviors. Those powerful directors who expressed high need for the policy had supervisors who diffused more EEO information to their subordinates and reported more training topics and hours; a greater proportion had used the policy in the past and expected to do so in the future; at the same time their supervisors perceived significantly less administrative emphasis, had lower perceived benefit, and believed that the policy would be difficult to administer. The number of significant relations were fewer among the supervisors of lower-power directors for this attitude. A similarly ambivalent pattern emerged for low-power directors, however, when perceived benefits was analyzed. Favorable attitudes about EEO policy benefits among these directors was associated, on the one hand, with beliefs that the policy is hard to administer yet, on the other, with significantly higher use. In contrast, high-power directors with high EEO benefits had supervisors who diffused policy information relatively frequently, but the attitude was otherwise unimportant in predicting supervisory implementation. Only high receptivity to change combined with director power to produce additional impacts on supervisors, and these were quite consistent: High power and high receptivity to change had marked positive effects on supervisory policy implementation. Those supervisors reported more training hours, more learning hours, more perceived benefits, and easier administration, as well as more past and expected use. Among lower-power directors the trend was the same but much less pronounced.

To summarize these findings, the combination of attitudes and power of directors seems to have some ambivalent effects on supervisory implementation of the two personnel policies. These effects are most notable among high-power directors and the attitude of policy need, where they occur for both policies. But other examples were found: with receptivity to change for low-power directors, and ease of administration for high-power directors for the alcoholism policy. Generally, with the exception of the need attitude, effects were more positive for high-power directors' attitudes on supervisory implementation of EEO. The only consistently positive influence by high-power directors on implementation of the alcoholism policy was an agreement with the performance emphasis in this policy.

Another noteworthy pattern in the data is the marked differences in where significant relationships were found for the alcoholism policy. Low-power directors' attitudes had most pronounced and positive impact on supervisory receptivity toward and use of the policy, while high-power directors' attitudes had strong, consistent, and predominantly negative effects on diffusion and training activities, with fewer and more mixed effects on receptivity, and use. It seems that low-power directors have more effect on outcomes of the alcoholism policy, while high-power directors somehow discouraged diffusion and training for this policy. Since these contrasting effects are less in evidence for the more pervasive and administratively emphasized EEO policy, we feel that the contrasting findings for the alcoholism policy could occur because directors felt less accountable for conformity to this policy.

How Director Power and Attitudes Related to Implementing Behavior of Facilitators

Next we assessed how the combination of director power and attitudes were related to the implementing behaviors of policy facilitators. These results are presented in tables 5.5 and 5.6. When the director agreed with the medical model of alcoholism contained in the policy, there was a trend for the facilitators of that policy to be influenced in their implementing behaviors—whether the director was powerful or not. Powerful directors with this attitude, however, had more ambivalent effects on their coordinators. On the one hand, their coordinators made more referrals to internal counselors and more often applied for leave provisions. On the other, they applied significantly less for medical benefits and used the alcoholism policy less often. Evidently, powerful directors who agree with the medical model influence coordinators toward less emphasis on the sick role and a use of internal resources instead of medical benefits. Low-power directors who embrace the medical model influence their facilitators less and also produce less ambivalent behaviors from them. The overall activity level of their alcoholism facilitators was significantly high, they talked to more supervisors in group meetings, and they used leave provisions more frequently.

The effects of the agreement of high-power and low-power directors with the policy's performance emphasis on their facilitators varied markedly. High-power directors who agreed with this provision, in contrast with low-power directors, had facilitators who had more often used the policy, talked with more supervisors about it, held more conferences with affected supervisors, engaged in more disciplinary actions, and made greater use of leave provisions and applications for medical benefits. The effect of this attitude among low-power directors was not significantly related to any behavior by the coordinators. Clearly, power combined with agreement with the job performance emphasis among directors produced more implementing facilitator behavior for the alcoholism policy.

When directors favorably assessed the benefits of the policy, the presence or absence of power seemed to make no difference for alcoholism facilitators. The effect seemed to be overwhelming negative, regardless of power. For example, assessed benefit among low-power directors was strongly associated with facilitators who reported talking with relatively few supervisors about the policy, while high-power directors with favorable attitudes about the benefits of the policy had facilitators who infrequently referred cases to organization counselors. Perhaps such idealistic "helping" attitudes among directors produce a sense of unrealism among pragmatic facilitators who are charged with actually carrying out the policy, making them dubious about whether such high expectations can be met. The data regarding the facilitator's contacts with the union when director power and assessed benefit were both high are consistent with this interpretation. Alternatively, directors who knew their alcoholism coordinators had done little were compensating by unusually favorable assessment of the policy.

There were few effects for beliefs that the alcoholism policy was easy to administer for either power condition. Those facilitators who worked with high-power directors spent little time with groups, probably since it was considered unnecessary. Facilitators working with low-power directors who felt this way about administering the policy contacted the union rather frequently; since the policy was seen as easy to administer, the union was evidently less of a complicating factor for them.

High feelings of need for the policy among low-power directors had a stimulating effect on their alcoholism coordinators, but among high-power directors the same attitude failed to produce the same effect on coordinators. Coordinators who worked with low-power

T A B L E 5.5 Results[a] of Parallel Multiple Regressions of Alcoholism Coordinator's Policy-Implementing Activities on Directors' Attitudes Toward Policy Controlling for Director Power

Independent Variables:[b]	Low Director Power (n = 43)[c]							High Director Power (n = 20)[c]						
Dependent Variables	1	2	3	4	5	6	R^2	1	2	3	4	5	6	R^2
Has coordinator used policy	20*				24		06		40*				23	13
Overall activity level	31*		−24	25	33*		09		23					00
Number of supervisors talked to in group meetings	29*	17	−55*	12	43	−21	20**	−36	30	−07	−48**	−58**	−07	46**
Number of supervisors talked to about policy	23	18	−55†	09	42†	−12	19**	34	46*	−08	−15		68*†	35**
Referrals to community agencies	16				16		01				18			−02
Referrals to organizational counselors		−24		25	16		04	46**		−73†	40			31**
Conferences with affected supervisors	24				22		08*		46*					10
Disciplinary actions	24*	−12	−28	22	22		04	−65**	53*	46	24	33	47	03
Leave provisions	32*		−15	13	25		01	72**		−53*	51	29	−43	12
Applications for medical benefits	24				21		04							09
Contacts with union		−15	−30*	29*	32**		08*	−69*	54	55*	24	30	−20	31**
Number of provisions used	23	−11	−21	19	33*	09	01	70*	60*	−70**				−03
Number of policy uses per 100 employees					30**		06*	−69*	28	−15		25		07
Time in role	21				26		08			47		25	50	05

*p < .10
**p < .05
†p < .01

[a] Standardized regression coefficients, decimal points omitted; stepwise mode; adjusted R^2.
[b] As follows:
1. Agreement with medical model
2. Agreement with performance emphasis
3. Assessed benefit of policy
4. Ease of administration
5. Need for policies
6. Receptivity to change
[c] The directors were divided into high and low power groups at the mean value for power to make structural changes in their installations.

TABLE 5.6 Results[a] of Parallel Multiple Regressions of EEO Functionaries' Policy-Implementing Activities on Directors' Attitudes Toward Policy Controlling for Director Power

Dependent Variables[b]	Low Director Power (n = 44)[c]							High Director Power (n = 21)[c]						
	1	2	3	4	5	6	R^2	1	2	3	4	5	6	R^2
Has coordinator used policy	16	-18	18	-23			02**				31	49**		23**
Overall activity level	32**						08**			37*			40*	09*
Number of supervisors talked to in group meetings					21	15	03							19
Number of supervisors talked to about policy	31*	-33**		22	36**	21	17**		37	33		43*		18
Performance evaluations	24			-19	-24		05	34		40*		32	42*	14
Skill assessments		21		-17	-29		04	24		46**				20**
Reporting procedures	22			16	44†		19†	36*		47**				11*
Extra civil service exams				-15		15	03	30		43	-27	52**		33**
Conferences with affected supervisors	21	22					11*			-67†	46		36	15
Counseling	16**				27*		17†			41*		50**		21*
Recruiting procedures	33**	-24*	-08	-16	40†		05			29	-34	32		00
Formal complaint system	31**			42†	41†	25*	20**		23	22	34			05
Applications for promotion	21			-27*	-23		07			27				02
Training programs	17	-24		-30**	-14	26*	07	30		31*				06
Contacts with union						17	09*		39*	43*				17*
Number of provisions used	22	-32**			-20		11*		15	-28	73†			16
Number of policy uses per 100 employees	25*	-47**				18	21†		31	38*		51**		31**
Time in role		-28					06						-22	-00

[a] Standardized regression coefficients, decimal points omitted; stepwise mode; adjusted R^2.

[b] As follows:

1. Agreement with overall policy
2. Agreement with performance emphasis
3. Assessed benefit of policy
4. Ease of administration
5. Need for policies
6. Receptivity to change

[c] The directors were divided into high- and low-power groups at the mean value for power to make structural changes in their installations.

*$p < .10$
**$p < .05$
†$p < .01$

directors showed six significant implementing behaviors. Despite low power, directors who had a relatively high sense of need had facilitators who engaged in greater implementing efforts. The same results for high-power directors, however, were very different: Actually the only significant effect that a director sense of need combined with power had on their facilitators was to significantly *reduce* the number of supervisors they talked to about the policy in group meetings.

Directors' receptivity to change had little effect on alcoholism facilitators. Only when high-power supervisors were receptive to change did their facilitators increase a key implementing behavior: They talked with larger numbers of supervisors about the alcoholism policy.

Table 5.6 shows that EEO facilitators were more influenced by low-power directors who expressed overall agreement with that policy than high-power directors with the same attitude. The former had a significantly higher overall activity level, engaged in more recruiting activities, made more performance evaluations and applications for promotions, and reported greater policy use. Only skill assessments were positively related to agreement among high-power directors.

A second finding for EEO functionaries was more striking: when low-power directors agreed with the performance emphasis in this policy, facilitators who worked for them were negatively affected. Specifically, they reported significantly lower implementing actions relative to the number of supervisors talked with about the policy, use of the formal complaint system, total number of policy provisions used, less time in the role, and significantly fewer actual uses of the policy. High-power directors with this power "turned off" EEO facilitators. It appears that performance emphasis may be rejected by active EEO facilitators unless there is a relatively powerful director, and even then it has few positive effects.

Equally striking is the effect of favorable assessment of the benefits of EEO by powerful directors on facilitators. Of the seventeen indications of facilitator implementing behavior, eight were positively related and significant. In contrast, low-power directors with a comparable attitude had no significant effects on their facilitators. Where the EEO policy was concerned, powerful directors who firmly believed in the benefits of the policy had very active facilitators.

Potent as that combination was, a heightened sense of need for the EEO policy generated more uniform implementing behavior on the part of facilitators: both low-power and high-power directors who expressed a high sense of need had facilitators who very actively engaged in behaviors directed toward carrying out the policy. For example, both engaged in significantly high reporting procedures and in counseling efforts. Another five implementing behaviors were significantly positive under each power condition when directors expressed high need for the EEO policy. As with the alcoholism policy, a heightened sense of need "at the top" has positive effects regardless of the amount of power.

Relationships with perceived ease of administration vary by director power. The effects for low-power directors suggest ambivalence, since when they perceive the EEO policy as easy to use, their facilitators use the formal complaint system more frequently but use applications for promotion and contacts with the union less frequently. High-power directors who believe the policies are easy to administer produce less ambivalence; their attitude accounts for 50 percent of the variance in the number of policy provisions used by their facilitators. Rather unexpectedly, high receptivity to change showed only modest effects, positive for both low- and high-power directors.

In short, the attitudes of high- and low-power directors had markedly different relationships with the implementing behaviors of policy facilitators. While high assessed need for the policies had generally positive effects, other director attitudes did not. Most puzzling were strong negative associations between assessed benefit for the alcoholism policy and implementation by coordinators. For the EEO policy, the same attitude—assessed benefit—had positive effects only for high-power directors, as did ease of administration for that policy. For the alcoholism policy, it was agreement with the performance emphasis that seemed to lead to implementation by coordinators only in the high-power condition, while this same attitude had negative effects on EEO implementing behaviors in installations with low-power directors. On the whole, positive attitudes toward the policies held by directors had more positive relationships with facilitator implementation when the director's power was high. These results strongly suggest that such directors positively influenced their facilitators toward implementation, although with cross-sectional data, the direction of causality can only be assumed as reasonable and most plausible in explaining the relationships found.

SUMMARY

Although individual characteristics of directors were helpful in explaining their implementing activities, role characteristics were most effective, with organizational aspects also helping. The possession of positive attitudes toward change and job involvement combined with commitment to local installation describe the director more likely to implement the policies. High civil service grade and local seniority were also prime predictors, especially when a director perceived that job performance was the main criteria for promotion. Findings also indicated that policy uses took place more frequently where work consequences were highly visible, in larger installations, and where control of resources was decentralized.

When we analyzed directors as chief executives in their installations, they turned out to be cautious and uncertain opinion leaders for the alcoholism policy, and ambivalent ones for the EEO policy. Power, as a characteristic of the top executive, had a mixed result on policy facilitators and line supervisors. Professionalization among them had a clear-cut negative effect on policy implementation, while simple tenure in the installation had positive effects. The possession of slack resources had very mixed effects, but when directors diffused information, especially to facilitators, it produced an implementing effect that was remarkable. All in all, directors were less than firm, predictable opinion leaders.

When we analyzed director power in conjunction with the policy-related attitudes they held, we found that where they had a relatively high perceived need for a policy, they projected that need into their own implementing behavior, into the behavior of their policy facilitators, and into the behavior of lower-level supervisors, regardless of whether they had high or low power. Thus, perceived need exercised a general implementing influence for both policies. Receptivity to change operated in much the same way; that is, it was a generally positive influence for implementation, whether directors' power was low or high.

In contrast, agreement with the performance emphases on the policies worked selectively with director power. When that power was relatively high, agreement with performance emphasis was a positive implementing force for the directors themselves, for their facilitators, and for their supervisors—especially for the alcoholism policy. Where power was relatively lower, however, the effect of agreement with the performance emphases was largely negative for both policies.

Repeatedly the policy-related attitudes and behaviors of directors was associated with ambivalent attitudes and behaviors among supervisors and facilitators. Thus high-tenured directors had significantly higher supervisory use of the alcoholism policy even though they also showed significantly negative associations with supervisor attitudes toward that policy. Regarding EEO, powerful and professional directors were associated with rather poor implementing behavior among their supervisors; yet these directors seemed to generate significantly more diffusion of EEO policy information and to stimulate higher perceived need. The ambivalent theme was less prominent when we analyzed director-facilitator relations. When their directors were powerful, alcoholism facilitators received more information, and

EEO functionaries expected greater future use of that policy. These findings were in the expected direction, but others were not. The negative relationships between director professionalization and supervisory implementation are puzzling because past research has suggested positive relations between professionalization and innovation.

The ambivalence also took the form of ritualism at times. Thus the less favorable to the alcoholism policy directors were, the more they performed formalisms such as job descriptions and giving titles to facilitators, regardless of their power. Another form was simple inconsistency between the power and attitude of directors and the implementing behavior of line managers. Thus high-power directors who had strong feelings of need for the alcoholism policy had subordinates who engaged in significantly *less* implementing behavior. Where EEO was concerned, high-power directors who held overall agreement with that policy had subordinates who diffused information but felt little administrative emphasis. High-power directors who expressed strong needs for EEO are another good example of ambivalence: Their supervisors reported high amounts of implementing behavior, yet they perceived little benefit from the policy and believed the policy would be difficult to administer. Apparently power overcame ambivalence in this instance.

These examples of ambivalence suggest that directors produced alternating reactions in their subordinates. Rather than a simple, direct influence from the "top," they seemed to send out mixed signals and generate a "reflected" ambivalence among other managers. Thus it is oversimplistic to speak generally of the beneficial value of the support of "top" management for implementation of change. Actually it can be a mixed blessing, ranging from clear-cut, direct, and favorable influence to ritualistic appearances of support that actually mask rejection. All things considered, these findings suggest that the assumption of folk wisdom about the inevitable necessity of support from the top is questionable. It produces undue reliance on power and influence, and may lead to the neglect of other dimensions of implementation such as creating familiarity with the change—a force that can be very potent among lower-status managers and facilitators. In a word, such mixed and ambivalent influences among directors raise substantial doubts about the near-universal belief that support from the top is a prime ingredient in successful policy implementation.

6. Internal Change Agents: A Role Analysis of Policy Facilitators

MANY SOCIAL SCIENTISTS believe that the use of change agents is a major factor in the successful introduction of innovations (Bennis, 1966; Rogers and Shoemaker, 1971). Often change agents are not members of the organization undergoing change, but hired professionals with specific expertise relevant to the content of the change, or with skills in facilitating change processes. Of course, change agents can be internal—that is, members of the organization—but outsiders are often seen as having certain advantages in helping organizations to change. Among these advantages are more objective diagnoses, fewer debts that can be cashed in, less vested interests in the status quo, more expertise, and more legitimate acceptance as change agents (Zaltman and Duncan, 1977).

Perhaps the main virtue of outside change agents, however, is that they bring new information or expertise into the organization, and thus *initiate* change and encourage its adoption (Beckhard, 1969). There is, however, an internal role that may be crucial to many attempts at organizational change (Bennis, 1966:115). This is the role of the internal facilitator—the person who has the duty of setting various specifics in motion to get the change *implemented*.

Since "organizations are now the major adopters of social inventions" (Baldridge and Burnham, 1975), this second type of change agent is receiving additional attention by writers who discuss problems in implementing change (Zaltman and Duncan, 1977). Such agents attempt to facilitate the actual use of an innovation by providing explanation, advice, assistance, suggestions, and support as

152

users try to put the innovation into practice (Radcliffe, 1967). We shall use the term "policy facilitators" for the persons who fill that role in the federal organizations we studied. In broader terms, change facilitators are those organizational members who espouse and set in motion the strategy of an innovation.

While Rogers and Shoemaker (1971:227) insist that "most change is not haphazard but the result of planned, premeditated actions by change agents," other writers argue that there is a "paucity of research evidence in support" of this proposition (Gross, Giacquinta, and Bernstein, 1971). Even less is known about the role and effectiveness of inside facilitators of organizational innovations. For those internal agents who have been largely involved only in the implementation phase of change, such as the policy facilitators in this study, there is, with a few exceptions (Scurrah et al., 1971), practically no social science literature available to review or use as guidelines for research. If, however, inside facilitators are viewed as occupying a role, or a segment of a role, within a formal organization, a conceptual framework is available for use even though research data on facilitators are largely lacking. As Kahn (1974:492) points out, the main issue in organizational development is "change in the enactment of roles." Thus the enactment of a change agent role itself, and its effects on target roles, provide a relevant framework.

CONCEPT OF ROLE APPLIED TO CHANGE FACILITATORS

Since persons who come to maintain and further the change (that has been introduced and adopted, but not implemented) will inevitably occupy a role of some form in an organizational setting, role theory provides a series of concepts for description and analysis. Five basic elements constitute an organizational role, as identified by Gross, Mason, and McEachern (1958): (1) individuals (2) in social locations (3) behave (4) with reference to a set of role expectations (5) in specific situations. Roles are performed in social locations where interactions with others are structural features of a role qualitatively different from the person who occupies it. One common location for both persons and roles is the work organization. Here they become attached to a designated location within the system of social relationships that make up the workplace (Thomas and Biddle, 1966). The core concept of role, however, is that despite individual differences and the social location of roles, persons are expected to perform (behave) according to a set of role expectations governing their behavior in that particular role.

A sixth element, one overlooked in the Gross et al. scheme, is the amount of resources available to the role occupant whereby he or she can actually behave according to a set of role expectations (Bunker, 1972:72). This latter element takes on a major importance within formal work settings, where numerous roles compete for limited resources[1] and are evaluated in terms of various efficiency criteria (Thompson, 1967).

Closely related to the description of a specific role is the notion of "counterposition." Raymond Hunt insists that "a role can be comprehensively described only with reference to other roles associated with positions complementary to that occupied by the role player" (1967:259). The totality of counterpositions is referred to as a "role set" for a given role. Thus a given role not only occupies a specific location but also interacts with other positions, and in so doing it contrasts with them but is also complementary to them. Consequently the social location of a role contains both a position to which it is attached and counterpositions with which it interacts—its relevant others.

Finally, the concept of sanctions should be included in a role analysis. Although a role can be functional without sanctions attached to it, the concept is nonetheless important. To what extent are sanctions present that tend to promote congruence of expectations and behavior? Positive ones (rewards) provide reinforcements for engaging in the desired behavior, while negative ones typically imply some form of punishment for failure to comply.

The crux of the concept of role lies in the congruence between actual performance in the role ("role behavior") and the expected performance of the role (Newcombe, 1951). Since expectations do not ensure behavior, some concept is needed to assess the extent of the difference between the two. The concept of congruence, however, can also be used to assess the similarities and differences between expectations of different members of the role set.

When these concepts were applied directly to the facilitators of the two policies studied, specific questions emerged: (1) How did the individual facilitators compare to and differ from each other and from counterpositions (director and line supervisors) with whom they must interact in implementing the policies? How much consensus and similarity existed between them and these relevant others about policy provisions? (2) How were facilitators who were located in line, staff, and director positions different from one another relative to individual attitudes about job and policy and to policy-related activities? (3) How could adequate role performance be explained; that is, what organizational and individual forces tend to throw light on congruence between expectations and behavior in the facilitator role? (4) Finally, to what extent was role compliance by facilitators associated with appropriate behavior among line supervisors—the major counterpositions?

Before these concepts are applied to alcoholism and EEO coordinators in the federal sector, another distinction should be made. Their roles are "enacted" ones; that is, they came into being instantly and formally by explicit mandate—by congressional acts and policy directives from the Civil Service Commission. Unlike many organizational roles, they did not emerge over time and become shaped by a series of occupants. Rather the roles were explicitly created to sustain, expedite, and put forward the mandated changes. The statement setting up the federal alcoholism program (FPL 792-4) explicitly directed that

> an individual should be designated at each field installation to coordinate local operations of the program. Individuals selected for such assignments should be allocated sufficient official time to effectively implement the agency policy and program including bringing education and information to the work force, arranging or conducting supervisory training, developing and maintaining counseling capability (personnel, medical or other counseling resources), establishing liaison with community education, treatment, and rehabilitation facilities, and evaluating the program and reporting to management on results and effectiveness. (U.S. Civil Service Commission, 1971:5)

In response to Public Law 92-261 (EEO Act of 1972), the Civil Service Commission amended the federal personnel manual (FPM 713-17), repeating, making explicit, and incorporating changes to the following provisions calling for EEO officers and counselors:

> The agency shall designate as many equal employment opportunity officers as may be necessary to assist the director of equal employment opportunity in carrying out his functions in all organizational units and locations of the agency. The agency may designate the bureau or field office manager as the equal employment officer for this activity or may designate another employee to the activity. In the latter event, the person designated as equal employment opportunity officer for the bureau or field office shall be under the immediate supervision of the bureau or field office manager in performing his EEO functions and shall assist that manager in carrying out the agency's EEO program in activities under the manager's jurisdiction. His function in support of the EEO program will involve him in the affirmative action aspect of the program (particularly the maximum utilization of skills, upward mobility, communication with recruitment sources, community action, managerial support, recognition of accomplishments, information to employees, counseling service, and the disposition of complaints) as well as the processing of complaints (counseling, representation, impartial investigation, hearing and decision-making). Each agency shall designate as many equal employment opportunity counselors as may be necessary to assist the director of equal employment opportunity in making readily available, in all

TABLE 6.1 Comparison between Alcoholism Coordinators, EEO Functionaries, Line Supervisors, and Installation Directors on Various Individual Characteristics and Job-related Attitudes

	Line Supervisor $n = 634$	Alcoholism Coordinator $n = 71$	EEO Functionary $n = 71$	Director $n = 71$	Overall Mean	F	p*
Age	41.6	41.5	39.6	46.7	41.08	5.23	.01
Years of education	15.40	15.78	15.22	16.64	15.52	6.01	.001
Percentage female	16.3	18.9	23.6	4.5	16.14	3.31	.05
Civil service grade	11.49	11.42	10.77	14.32[a]	11.66	20.36	.001
Tenure in installation	10.44[a]	7.50	6.67	8.38	9.58	19.20	.001
Tenure in federal service	17.45	17.00	15.37[a]	22.87	17.69	25.49	.001
Receptivity to change	4.35	4.04[a]	4.49	4.53	4.35	4.45	.01
Organizational commitment	3.43	3.53	3.53	3.46	3.46	.20	n.s.
Federal service commitment	4.06	4.10	3.79	3.90	4.03	1.89	n.s.
Work overload (perceived)[c]	3.73	3.98	3.58	3.92	3.75	1.04	n.s.
Job involvement[c]	2.58	2.37	2.20	2.26	2.50	18.58	.001
Importance of career criteria for own promotion[d]							
Performance	.01	−.45	−.98[a]	−.15	−.12	17.20	.001
Seniority	.00[a]	−.39	−.36	−.42	−.10	7.07	.001
Technical Skills	.00	−.10	−.65[b]	−.76[b]	−.12	13.95	.001

n.s. = not significant.

[a] This mean is significantly different from all other means in this row (Winer, 1962: 85-89).

[b] These means form a common cluster that is significantly different from all other means in this row.

[c] This item has been scored in a negative direction, i.e., the higher the score the lower the attitude.

[d] Standardized scale scores with supervisory mean = 0.0.

* As determined by F tests of one-way analysis of variance.

organizational units and locations of the agency, the counseling called for in Executive Order 11478. (U.S. Civil Service Commission, 1972:6)

INDIVIDUAL FACILITATORS AND THEIR RELEVANT OTHERS

We collected the traditional individual data—age, sex, and education—but decided to collect, in addition, individually oriented data relating primarily to the workplace and work role: tenure, organization and federal service commitment, job involvement, work overload, and perceptions of promotion criteria. Because the policies involved organizational change, we also collected data on attitudes toward change. These data were available for four types of role occupants: the two facilitator groups and two types of line managers (directors and lower-level supervisors). In an effort to discover how much like line supervisors the facilitators were, we compared them on these variables, using one-way analyses of variance (table 6.1).

Facilitators had numerous similarities with line supervisors, but not with directors, on the individual characteristics of age, education, and sex. Directors were somewhat older, had higher education levels, and were less often female. Moreover, as might be expected, they had higher civil service grades and longer tenure in the federal service. Line supervisors, however, tended to have more tenure in the specific installation than did either facilitators or directors. All four groups showed similar commitment to both their current installation and the federal service, and similar findings of work overload. Line supervisors differed in expressing less job involvement than others. Consistent with this feeling, and with long tenure in the installation, they also believed seniority was more important in promotion. Alcoholism coordinators[2] differed on only one dimension: They were significantly less receptive to change than any of the other three groups.

In sum, installation directors showed a sizable block of differences from facilitators and line managers: older, more education, less often female, higher grade and system tenure, and slightly more receptivity to change. Line managers had more installation tenure and less job involvement than facilitators, while EEO functionaries sharply rejected performance standards for their own promotion, and alcoholism coordinators were relatively resistant to change. Thus, apart from directors, there is considerable similarity between occupants of various roles, but not homogeneity. Facilitators have much in common with line managers, but differences on a few key issues make it questionable whether "homophily" (Rogers and Shoemaker, 1971:240) exists between these members of their role set and the facilitators on these individual characteristics.

TABLE 6.2 Comparison of Attitudes toward Alcoholism Policy among Alcoholism Coordinators, Line Supervisors, and Installation Directors

	Line Supervisor n = 634	Alcoholism Coordinator n = 71	Director n = 71	Overall Mean	F	p*
Agreement with medical model of alcoholism[d]	.00	.07	-.15	.01	.65	n.s.
Performance emphasis	3.26[a]	3.68	3.60	3.33	2.27	.10
Policy definition of alcoholism	4.84[a]	5.13	5.29	4.89	3.21	.05
Zealousness in seeking out policy cases[d]	.00	-.21[a]	.18	.00	2.31	.10
Supervisors do own counseling	4.63	4.40	4.73	4.62	.58	n.s.
Relapse indicates failure[c]	2.38	1.97[a]	2.45	2.35	2.42	.10
Perceived benefit[d]	.00	-.04	-.13	-.02	.61	n.s.
Need for policy in installation	2.71[b]	4.17[b]	3.13[b]	2.88	18.64	.001
Ease of administration	3.75[a]	4.81	4.77	3.94	12.59	.001

n.s. = not significant.

[a]This mean is significantly different from all other means in this row (Winer, 1962: 85-89).

[b]Each of these means is significantly different from all other means in this row.

[c]This item is worded opposite to policy provisions, i.e., the higher the score, the less the agreement with the policy.

[d]Standardized scale scores with supervisor mean = 0.0.

* As determined by F tests of one-way analysis of variance.

Comparisons were also made between these groups on attitudes related to the policies under study. Tables 6.2 and 6.3 present data that contrasts each facilitator with directors and line supervisors—the counterpositions most likely to be in their role sets. Thus these tables indicate how much similarity exists between facilitators and their relevant others in attitudes about, and perceptions of, each policy. On these tables, the first three items are ones that are consonant with policy provisions, and therefore higher agreement with these statements indicates more agreement with policy content. On two of the three policy-consonant items for the alcoholism policy (table 6.2), the coordinator and director were both in better agreement with the policy than line supervisors. In the statements that depart from policy provisions (the next three items, rows 4-6 in the table), alcoholism coordinators were least likely to agree with an overzealous approach to seeking out policy cases and that relapse indicated a failure of treatment. Apparently the alcoholism policy facilitators were more aware of and in agreement with policy content, including limitations on appropriate role behavior, than their significant others. In addition, alcoholism coordinators were highest in their perceptions of need for the policy and, with the directors, were also higher than line supervisors in their assessment of how easy the policy is to administer. Overall, the facilitators held role-appropriate attitudes and perceptions for the alcoholism policy, directors were closest to them across these dimensions, and line supervisors were most distant from them in these policy-related attitudes and perceptions.

Table 6.3 presents parallel items for the EEO policy and its facilitator. There are no significant differences among occupants of these roles on items agreeing with the policy (rows 1-3). In the items that disagree with policy provisions (rows 4-6 of table 6.3), facilitators were not in clear accord with the policy. It was the line supervisor, rather than either the EEO functionary or director, who was most skeptical of the zealous item relative to the EEO policy,[3] and all three groups were similar in their attitudes toward failures. However, EEO functionaries were least in agreement with supervisors doing their own counseling, perhaps because the value of their own expertise is put into question by this statement. Interestingly, directors were most likely to agree that supervisors should do their own counseling, while the supervisors themselves were somewhat less enthusiastic. Again there were no differences between groups on perceived benefit or ease of administration, but all role incumbents differed significantly in their perceptions of need for the policy, with facilitators perceiving the greatest need, directors next in perception of need, and line supervisors lowest on this item.

Considering the general pattern of these findings, there is evidence of sufficient dissensus between these role positions to question

TABLE 6.3 Comparison of Attitudes toward EEO Policy among EEO Functionaries, Line Supervisors, and Installation Directors

	LINE SUPERVISOR $n = 634$	EEO FUNCTIONARY $n = 71$	DIRECTOR $n = 71$	OVERALL MEAN	F	p*
Overall agreement with policy emphasis	0.00	−0.01	0.11	0.00	0.64	n.s.
Performance emphasis	4.38	4.34	4.58	4.39	.56	n.s.
Discrimination can be eliminated	4.44	4.78	4.61	4.49	1.27	n.s.
Zealousness in seeking out policy cases	3.85[a]	4.76	4.60	4.00	12.49	.001
Supervisors should do own counseling	4.75[b]	4.07[b]	5.16[b]	4.72	6.90	.001
Individual failure = program failure[c]	3.55	3.61	3.54	3.56	.02	n.s.
Perceived benefit[d]	.00	−.02	.00	.00	.02	n.s.
Need for policy in installation	4.49[b]	5.42[b]	4.90[b]	6.83	6.83	.001
Ease of administration	4.32	3.88	4.18	4.27	1.27	n.s.

n.s. = not significant

[a] This mean is significantly different from all other means in this row (Winer, 1962: 85-89).

[b] Each of these means is significantly different from all other means in this row.

[c] This item has been scored in a negative direction, i.e., the higher the score the lower the attitude.

[d] Standardized scale scores with supervisory mean = 0.0.

* As determined by F tests of one-way analysis of variance.

whether congruence existed between the facilitator role and its counterpositions within these agencies. This dissensus is especially evident in the case of the alcoholism policy, where six of the nine measures tested produced significant differences between groups. While the magnitude of the difference was not large for the first four differences, the last two on table 6.2 cannot be dismissed as unimportant differences. In the case of assessed need for the policy within the installation, the response format is a 7-point scale, meaning that anything over 4 (the neutral point) is a positive response, while anything under 4 is a negative response. Thus the average response of alcoholism coordinators is positive in response to this question, while the average response of all other groups is negative, with line supervisors being most negative. The same observation can be made about ease of administration, but this time both coordinators and directors are positive and only the line supervisors are negative, on the average. Such a split of opinion on basic issues between the coordinators and members of their role sets is likely to seriously dilute the effectiveness of coordinators in their role of internal change agents.

While EEO facilitators did not have systematic dissensus over as many issues with members of their role sets as did alcoholism coordinators, the magnitude of the differences tended to be fairly substantial in all instances of disagreement. There was evidence of considerable zealousness among facilitators that went beyond the policy; this was probably reinforced by their greater sense of need, which in turn added to a milieu of differences. As was the case for alcoholism policy facilitators, the findings suggest that a considerable gap exists between the EEO facilitator and those who are immediately involved in policy use.

Fortunately for policy implementation, neither type of facilitator encountered disagreement over the benefits of their policy and some other issues; they may be able to use these shared sentiments to achieve some measure of congruence in role behaviors.

ORGANIZATIONAL LOCATION OF THE FACILITATOR

Clearly facilitators were located in dissensual environments and faced problems of overcoming or reducing substantial amounts of differences between themselves and relevant others. To what extent did a second aspect of social location—organizational position—influence them in performing their role expectations? Under the present federal policies, facilitators can be located in either the line hierarchy or more laterally in staff positions. That is, the role can be attached to a position that is a clearly defined part of the superior-subordinate chain of line authority, or to a position that is lateral to line authority and formally independent of it—often referred to as a "staff" position. Staff positions are distinguished by little direct exercise of authority, yet persons in them may come to wield considerable power as they shape their roles in their relatively unstructured relations with line authorities (Whyte, 1969). Alternatively, the role may be assigned to an installation director or to a line supervisor, who are both part of the line hierarchy.[4] Using this breakdown, we found that for the alcoholism policy 17 percent of the coordinators were directors, 47 percent were from staff positions, and 36 percent were from line supervision; for the EEO policy, the breakdown was 11 percent directors, 59 percent staff, and 30 percent line supervisors.

Being a line supervisor might aid role performance of facilitators. Because the major counterpositions in facilitators' role sets are also line positions, greater congruence might occur than if the facilitator were in a staff position. Many studies have documented a near-universal line-staff conflict that would presumably operate against staff facilitators winning cooperation from line management (Dalton, 1959; Ritzer and Trice, 1969b; Moore, 1962). Consequently if a staff person represents and puts forward a management innovation like these policies, the resistance to him or her could be greater than if that innovation were implemented internally by a line position. That is, some of the resistance might be engendered by circumstances arising from the location of the internal change agent rather than by the content of the innovation.

To test for this possibility, we broke down the data generated from facilitators by organizational location and used one-way analysis of variance to determine how facilitators differed from one another by location. We looked at policy-related activities directed toward implementing the policy, at supervisory usage, at attitudes toward the policy, at attitudes toward change, and at attitudes toward their jobs. Tables of results for these analyses are not presented, because of space limitations, but instead are summarized in the text. Any differences discussed are statistically significant by the same criteria used in tables 6.2 and 6.3.

Relatively few differences emerged between alcoholism coordinators in different locations. Of the fifteen policy-related activities that an alcoholism coordinator could use to implement a policy in a specific case, coordinators located in supervisory positions had done more to develop information and community facilities and had more often referred cases to counselors. Apart from these two differences, alcoholism coordinators did not differ significantly from one another in policy-related activities, regardless of location. Moreover, the organizational location of the coordinators was not associated with different levels of supervisory policy usage—the "payoff" point for policy implementation. Also, there was no evidence that organizational location was associated with different work attitudes or personal characteristics. Alcoholism coordinators showed no differences by location on age, sex, education, civil service grade, attitude toward change, perceived work overload, job involvement, organizational commitment, federal service commitment, or their perceptions of criteria used for promotions.

There were, however, differences by location along other dimensions of the role. Coordinators who were also directors were least likely to be formally appointed to the role, while coordinators who were line coordinators were most likely to have written job descriptions. The appointment of an alcoholism coordinator is usually done by the installation director, and apparently in relatively few instances did he formally designate himself to that role by reporting himself as coordinator to the Civil Service Commission and to his agency headquarters. It is understandable that line coordinators would most often have formal job descriptions, because they were most likely to need them to carry out the role successfully; perhaps they also asked for them, because performing this type of role would be relatively novel for them. On the other hand, coordinators who were in staff or director positions would be accustomed to dealing with personnel matters, and so the various activities of the policy could be seen as an extension of activities already performed.

We also investigated whether there were differences in the number of other policies administered, the time the occupant had served in the role, and the size of the installation in which he or she was located. None of these situational limits on the role were significantly different by location.

Considering resources given to the role, we found that locations had not received significantly different amounts of information or different time allotments, but that line coordinators had been given more staff support than other coordinators, probably because they were least likely of the three types of coordinators to have prior access to appropriate staff assistance.

The greatest number of differences between coordinators in different locations emerged when we compared their attitudes toward the policy. Here the difference between line and staff roles was significant for two issues of policy content. Both types of line coordinators—those who were directors and those who were supervisors—were more supportive in their attitudes toward the definition of alcoholism given in the policy and were less supportive of the statement that a relapse indicated that treatment is a failure. Directors, however, were also most likely to endorse an overzealous interpretation of the policy. Line coordinators, on the other hand, were skeptical of supervisors doing their own counseling and thus were most supportive of actual policy provisions relative to counseling. Considering all of these differences in attitudes, it is clear that coordinators who were also line supervisors held more policy-consonant attitudes than coordinators in other locations.

When we combine this information on attitudinal differences with the earlier differences related to the role itself—information development, referrals, formal appointment, job descriptions, and staff assistance—we must conclude that coordinators in line positions showed more factors consonant with implementation of the alcoholism policy than either coordinators who were directors or in staff positions. Of the latter two, coordinators in staff positions were uniformly undistinguished by any features favorable to policy implementation. Altogether, the results give tentative support to the notion that the location of a facilitator role in a staff position may be less advantageous than its location in a line supervisory position.

When the same comparisons were made between EEO functionaries who were located as directors, staff members, or line supervisors, a larger number of statistically significant differences between groups emerged (25 out of 60 variables tested). Again, location in a staff position was least favorable to policy implementation. Staff facilitators were significantly lower than other facilitators on a whole range of policy-related activities: diffusion of policy-related information to supervisors, applications for promotions, recruiting activities, extra administration of civil service examinations, and use of skill assessment procedures. Director coordinators were highest on training for upward mobility. However, the three types of EEO functionaries did not differ significantly according to supervisory usage of the policy within their installation.

Considering the issue of formal appointments, directors were least likely to have been formally appointed as EEO functionaries. However, they had spent more time in the role than other coordinators (an average of 38 versus 14 and 16 months). Staff facilitators administered a larger number of additional policies than either director or line facilitators, while those EEO functionaries in line positions had received the largest time allotments to fill the facilitator role. Staff facilitators had by far the largest average budget (over $20,000 yearly), yet, as reported above, had lagged behind in actual policy implementation.

Perhaps some of the explanation for these differences can be gleaned from a comparison of the personal characteristics and attitudes of these role incumbents. Line facilitators for the EEO policy were more likely to be female, while director facilitators had the most education. Staff facilitators differed in that they were lowest on receptivity toward change. When we compared job-related attitudes, we found that staff EEO facilitators were highest on federal service commitment, while those in line positions were least likely to see performance and technical skills as criteria important for their own promotions.

When we compared policy-related attitudes, staff EEO facilitators were lowest on their assessment of how easy the EEO policy is to administer, but they were also most skeptical about the statement that supervisors should do their own counseling for this policy, while director EEO functionaries were most likely to endorse that statement. As in the case of alcoholism coordinators, we wonder if this response was less because of agreement with policy provisions than because they did not like the idea of supervisors usurping one of their functions under the policy. It is notable that they are not otherwise so supportive of policy provisions. Director facilitators were lowest on perceived need for the policy within their installation, probably because they are less willing than others to admit that discrimination could occur under their administration of the installation. Line facilitators differ on only one attitude: Perhaps because they are least sanguine about the problem, they are somewhat less sure than other EEO functionaries that discrimination can be eliminated.

We must remember, however, that installations tended to have more than one EEO functionary. It is possible that those EEO functionaries in staff positions played a somewhat specialized role in implementation of the EEO policy that could militate against their being as frequently involved in policy-related activities as EEO functionaries in other locations. But it is hard to imagine what these activities might be, since we asked them about eleven policy-related procedures and activities, as well as their activity in training and diffusion of information to employees and supervisors. We also ran separate tests on the number of cases dealt with under policy provisions, as well as on the number of times each procedure or provision had been used. These differences cannot be the result of more consistent follow-up of some cases by certain types of EEO functionaries because the differences tend to hold whether it is the number of cases or the number of times that the procedure has been used that are compared. The one exception was the assessment of skills, where line-type EEO functionaries had used the procedure more times per case than the staff facilitators. Also, staff coordinators were lowest on the number of contacts with the union per case. This finding is surprising, since we would expect the staff EEO facilitator most frequently to be the personnel manager.

No matter how we examined the data, we could not escape the conclusion that EEO functionaries in staff positions have performed the implementation activities suggested by the policy less well and less often than other EEO functionaries. Since the staff facilitators were both less receptive to change and more wedded to the federal service (as reflected by their federal service commitment), it seems likely that they are more conservative than facilitators who are in other locations. They also had more competing policies to administer, although the average number (1.72 versus 1.08 for other locations) does not seem unduly onerous for a person in a staff position.

As in the case of the alcoholism policy, the most favorable position for a facilitator of the EEO policy seems to be that of line supervisor. It must be noted that more than one-third of the line facilitators for the EEO policy are female and that they have the largest time allotment for policy-related activities. These two factors suggest a specialized role that has emerged for some women in these federal installations, but one in which they are not likely to see either their performance or technical skills as important to their own promotion, as evidenced by the lower scores they gave these criteria for promotion. The situation is rather ironic; perhaps another kind of dead-end job (Kanter, 1977) has been created for women by the EEO policy—that of EEO specialist. To illustrate, one woman explained that she had to leave her EEO functionary role and get back into another position within the installation lest she lose her own chances for promotion. Whatever the problems they encounter in their own careers—both as directors and as other supervisors—the line functionaries tend to be more active than those in staff positions. Directors are notable for their involvement in upward bound activities, probably because such programs need backing at that level.

Whether these results, consistent across the two policies, mean that the policies would be better implemented if facilitator roles were uniformly assigned to line positions is hard to tell. There may be other systematic differences between installations that chose different positions for their facilitators, and since we did not use multivariate analyses in the results just reported, these alternative explanations cannot be totally ruled out. The consistency of the findings is, however, remarkable, and certainly tends to suggest that there may be considerable potential for conflict in administering these policies between line and staff persons if the differences found in these analyses can be generalized to other installation members. In that case, each installation could mirror the differences found here, with a consequent lack of congruence between members of the role sets crucial to implementation of these policies. Certainly there are sufficient differences between the types of facilitators to demonstrate that organizational location can affect enacted role content.

EXPLAINING ROLE PERFORMANCE: SOME HYPOTHESES

As suggested in the previous paragraph, other factors besides location can affect facilitator role performance. Some of these factors may interact with the role location to produce different attitudes or behaviors relevant to policy implementation. The organizational literature and our observations in pretesting and interviewing before data collection suggested a variety of hypotheses that could be tested.

Large organizations are often viewed as possessing more resources, and this, in turn, may increase the likelihood of implementing an innovation (Kaluzny et al., 1974). On the other hand, Mohr (1969) found no relationship between size and the amount of resources assigned to innovations. Richard Hall sums up the influence of size by observing that it has a "variable impact on organizations and it cannot be taken as a simple predictor, as it often is" (1972:137). However, enough discussion has occurred to suggest size as a possible predictor of implementing activities by facilitators.

Next, both pretesting and field observations suggested that most facilitators performed numerous roles. As we have seen, they typically spend the large majority of their time as personnel officers or in other staff positions, as line supervisors, or as installation directors. Also, they often have responsibilities to facilitate two or three other special policies. Consequently there was reason to conclude that they work in positions characterized by a multiple set of expectations or "role segmentation" (Gross et al., 1958:61). Under such conditions it seems reasonable to hypothesize that subjective feelings of work overload would hinder role performance by facilitators.

From pretesting interviews and observing case management, we detected how important it was to be in the role to develop identity with it, to come to accept the implications of that identity, and to gain the experience of actually processing a case and experience closure. Clearly time must elapse for these experiences to occur. In neither policy was there daily opportunity to attempt to implement. Weeks or months could pass without a policy case. Consequently we formulated the hypothesis that the sheer length of time in the role would help explain role performance.

Also, it would seem logical that facilitators would increase their implementing efforts if their role had been explicitly formalized by receiving an official organizational status and a job description. As Hall remarks, "Formalization is a major defining characteristic of organizations, since behavior is not random and is directed by some degree of formalization toward a goal" (1972:182). Thus some writers have argued that formalized roles are necessary to achieve the implementation of innovation (Zaltman et al., 1973; Duncan, 1976). Yet empirical data have indicated that formalization in general militates against innovation (Burns and Stalker, 1961; Hage and Aiken, 1967, 1970; Corwin, 1972; Kaluzny et al., 1974). For example, written rules tended to create a repressive atmosphere relative to new ideas; they acted to decrease communications and thus hinder implementation. Moreover, formalization of the coordinator role could be viewed as a ritualistic way to conform to the formal goals of the policy (Merton, 1957). That is, through formalisms an installation could "play it safe" but show no active striving toward policy implementation.

Two additional explanatory variables were suggested by the literature as likely to influence the extent to which facilitators performed their implementing tasks. Both are resources. One is the amount of explicit information about the policy the facilitator had received, while the other consists of actual time allocated to the role and personnel provided to the facilitator for the explicit purpose of carrying out policy duties. The first is termed "diffusion effect" by Rogers and Shoemaker (1971:161). They review a number of relevant studies that show the impact of increments of new information upon adoption and use of innovations. The second appears obvious: the amount of time and staff help made available to a facilitator for use in implementing activities should sharply influence role performance (Thompson, 1967; Berman and McLaughlin, 1975b).

For these considerations, we formulated the following hypotheses about role performance among facilitators:

6.1. The larger the organization in which the facilitator is located, the more policy-implementing activities he or she will perform.

6.2. Among facilitators who report greater work overloads, behaviors aimed at implementing policies will be fewer than for facilitators with less work overload.

6.3. Among facilitators who have been in that role for a substantial period of time, there will be more implementing behavior than among those of low tenure.

6.4. The more formalized the facilitator roles, the more policy-implementing behaviors the incumbent will perform.

6.5. Implementing behaviors will be positively related to the amount of policy information diffused to the facilitator.

6.6. The more staff support and time allocations the facilitator receives, the more policy-related activities he or she will engage in.

RESULTS OF TESTS OF THESE HYPOTHESES

Tables 6.4 and 6.5 present the results of multiple regression analyses of various specific implementation activities of the facilitators on all of the variables represented by the hypotheses. Installation size (hypothesis 6.1) had no significant influence on alcoholism coordinators, but considerable on EEO functionaries. In larger installations, these functionaries applied for promotions, sought extra administration of examinations, and consulted with the installation's personnel department significantly more often. On the other hand, facilitators engaged in significantly less EEO counseling in larger installations. Apparently in bigger installations there was a tendency for EEO functionaries to use more formal methods of implementation, while in smaller ones they relied more heavily on face-to-face informal counseling. In any event the hypothesis was supported for EEO but not for alcoholism policy facilitators. Laws of probability suggest that there are more problem drinkers and alcoholics in larger work organizations, yet alcoholism facilitators in large installations had no higher rate of implementation.

For both types of facilitator, perceived work overload impeded implementation activities (hypothesis 6.2). For alcoholism coordinators it was negatively associated with holding conferences with affected supervisors; that is, the overworked alcoholism coordinator was less likely to confer with the supervisor of the problem-drinking employee about the problem. Also, perceived work overload had negative effects on assisting the alcoholic employee to secure leave for treatment. EEO facilitators seem to be less impaired by work overload. Although overload was positively associated with recruitment activities, it was negatively associated with formal complaints. Apparently the overworked EEO functionary is the one who does a great deal of recruiting, while the less overloaded EEO functionary handles more formal complaints. Overall, hypothesis 6.2 received modest support from the data on alcoholism coordinators and no clear support from the data on EEO functionaries.

Length of time in the role (hypothesis 6.3) was strongly related to facilitators' efforts to implement their policies with specific cases. For alcoholism coordinators, time in the role was significantly and positively associated with referral of problem-drinking employees to counseling, with holding conferences with affected supervisors, and with contacting and working with the union. Four prominent EEO implementing activities also were significantly greater with time in the facilitator role: assessment of skills, applying for promotion,

TABLE 6.4 Results[a] of Multiple Regressions of Policy-related Activities by Alcoholism Coordinators on Various Structural Features Surrounding the Role

Dependent Variables:[b]	STANDARDIZED REGRESSION COEFFICIENTS											
	1	2	3	4	5	6	7	8	9	10	11	12
Independent Variables												
Installation size	01	06	21	−08	10	−06	−05	07	01	−14	03	09
Work overload	01	03	07	05	09	08	−04	−03	−59†	07	−53†	00
Tenure in role	17	17	16	−06	−12	05	16	31*	31**	20	02	43†
Official status	18	10	12	−06	−07	28	15	06	06	23	06	13
Job description	07	08	25	−10	08	−25	−15	−07	−36**	−25	−42**	−23
Policy diffusion to coordinator	−01	02	−14	−12	−02	18	19	13	−02	07	04	05
Staff size	16	43†	29*	00	−02	45*	10	28	40**	48**	45**	03*
Time allocation	−05	01	−02	−14	−16	−26	06	26	04	−24	10	24*
R^2	09	27**	31**	05	05	20	08	31	47†	23	40†	34**

*p = .10
**p = .05
†p = .01

[a]Standardized coefficients (betas) are presented. Decimal points have been omitted.
[b]As follows:
1. Consult organizational medical personnel
2. Consult with others in the organizational bureaucracy
3. Level of information on community facilities
4. Information diffusion to employees
5. Information diffusion to supervisors
6. Applications for medical benefits
7. Refer alcoholic to community agency
8. Refer alcoholic to counselor in organization
9. Hold conference with alcoholic's supervisor
10. Disciplinary action
11. Assist alcoholic to procure leave
12. Contact with union

TABLE 6.5 Results[a] of Multiple Regressions of Policy-related Activities by EEO Functionaries on Various Structural Features Surrounding the Role

Dependent Variables:[b]	STANDARDIZED REGRESSION COEFFICIENTS														
	1	2	3	4	5	6	7	8	9	10	11	12	13	14	15
Independent Variables															
Installation size	34*	05	10*	06	-38†	53	30	34*	04	-05	-06	05	-27	-08	10
Work overload	13	-22	28*	-32	03	-20	09	-23	10	-27	-07	14	03	02	-15
Tenure in role	43**	06	43†	19	-12	-07	50†	00	-41**	-15	-15	52†	-12	-09	18
Official status	-13	-07	01	-04	00	08	-02	-20	03	-03	-10	09	08	05	22
Job description	09	14	07	13	-01	03	10	04	13	03	-08	13	25	29	07
Policy diffusion to functionary	17	34*	33**	-27	19	13	20	10	34*	09	14	30*	-03**	-07	01
Staff size	-17	-24	-10	12	75†	-13	-12	15	00	-19	-28**	-15	47**	-04	-05
Time allocation	-13	04	-01	09	-01	-27	-17	25	20	07	-36*	-13	04	12	-16
R²	36*	30	41	22	61†	38*	38**	37**	32*	19	17	41**	37*	12	10

[a] Only the standardized coefficients (betas) are presented. Decimal points have been omited.
[b] As follows:
1. Apply for promotion
2. Upward mobility training
3. Recruiting procedures
4. EEO formal complaint
5. EEO counseling
6. Extra administration of civil service exams
7. Performance evaluation
8. Consult organization personnel
9. Information on community facilities
10. Diffusion to supervisors
11. Diffusion to employees
12. Skill assessments
13. Reporting procedures
14. Conferences with affected supervisors
15. Contact with union

*p = .10
**p = .05
†p = .01

recruiting procedures, and performance evaluations. On the other hand, the effect of tenure on information on community facilities was negative, suggesting that as time goes by the EEO functionary tends to work less closely with interested community groups. Overall, hypothesis 6.3 received considerable support from the data.

Our hypothesis about role formalization (6.4) was not supported: The direction of significant relationships obtained were opposite to the hypothesis. For alcoholism coordinators, the possession of a written job description was associated with a significantly lower number of conferences with the alcoholic's supervisor. Moreover, when such descriptions were present, the coordinator was less likely to assist problem-drinking employees in procuring sick leave for treatment. For EEO functionaries, role formalization failed to affect role performance one way or the other. Not only do the data reject the hypothesis, but they suggest another one: namely, that where the alcoholism policy is concerned, formalization of the coordinator role may be detrimental to role fulfillment. Those data are thus in accord with other empirical findings that formalization inhibits innovation and change, and in disagreement with conceptual analyses that suggest that the implementation stage requires formalized roles.[5] Instead the results remind us that formalization is often expected to generate a repressive atmosphere for managerial innovations. Such formalization may well generate supervisory fears about "going formal" with alcoholic workers—that coordinators are "hatchet men." In a broader sense, it supports the findings of Hage and Aiken (1967), Hage and Dewar (1973), and many other researchers that formalization acts to decrease communications and to stymie change efforts.

Hypothesis 6.5 predicted a positive relationship between the amount of policy information diffused to facilitators and the amount of implementing behavior. The results failed to confirm this hypothesis for the alcoholism coordinator. Perhaps their relatively low receptivity to change operates to neutralize the effects of increased information about the policy. In contrast, diffusion is positively and significantly associated with the role performance of the EEO functionaries. Increased diffusion was accompanied by more contact and information from interested community groups, contact with recruiting sources, and use of upward mobility training as well as skill assessments. It seems possible that this is a reciprocal effect; that is, those functionaries who became more involved may have sought more information as a result of their activities, as well as having more information initially. Clearly additional information has accompanied better role performance in the case of the EEO policy.

More information about factors related to greater implementation of policy provisions by alcoholism coordinators comes from our test of hypothesis 6.6. When staff support and time allocations were more generous, alcoholism coordinators more often performed policy-related duties. Staff support was especially helpful; coordinators with larger staffs more often applied for medical benefits, more frequently consulted with various levels of management about the policy, and learned more about community facilities. Their greater role activities also included conferences with affected supervisors and extended to aiding the alcoholic employee to secure sick leave for treatment, or disciplinary action, if needed. With greater time allotments, coordinators tended to reach out for contacts with the union about the policy.

For EEO facilitators, larger staff size had a dramatic effect upon the amount of EEO counseling they performed. In addition, facilitators with greater staff support showed significantly greater compliance with reporting procedures about their activities. One puzzling result, however, was the marginally significant but negative association between time allocation to EEO functionaries and diffusion of policy information to employees. Perhaps as greater amounts of time became available to EEO functionaries, they were less likely to use the more formal means of information diffusion to employees; or perhaps in those installations where time allotments to EEO functionaries were larger, the diffusion process was performed by someone else in the installation.

SUMMARY OF FINDINGS ON FACILITATOR ROLE PERFORMANCE

As we compared results for these two facilitators on the hypotheses, four conclusions about the alcoholism coordinators emerged. First, such simple factors as time in the role and the allocation of the most elementary resources made a very substantial difference in the role performance of alcoholism coordinators. Second, if the assignment as coordinator produced feelings of overload, this could be quite damaging to role performance. Third, the very nature of the problem with which they were identified—alcoholism—seemed to make the formalization of their role a liability rather than an asset. Finally, the role was so poorly supplied with time and resources that more diffusion of information to facilitators apparently failed to help their performance. As discussed in chapter 1, the alcoholism policy is seen as a more lightweight policy: the changes it envisions are less likely to be pervasive, have less magnitude, and are less innovative in content. All of this suggests that the policy initially had limited salience to organizational members, including the person appointed as alcoholism coordinator, unless that person was a recovered alcoholic or the relative of an alcoholic. These are not circumstances that give great impetus toward implementation, especially for persons not too enthusiastic about change. From these results the conclusion seems inescapable that unless some modest resources in the form of time allocations and staff help—especially the latter—are granted to these facilitators, their role performance will be minimal. With this conclusion in mind, it is appropriate to examine in more detail the lamentable lack of resources that characterized the plight of alcoholism coordinators.

Organizational Resources Available to Alcoholism Coordinators

Our data clearly show that most alcoholism coordinators operated with only the most meager resources, if any at all. Almost one-third, as of mid-1974, had no official time allocated to their work with the policy; the remainder averaged less than four hours per week for this purpose. This is less than one-half day per week to perform, develop, and coordinate the alcoholism program—sometimes for more than one installation. Moreover, they typically spent even less time than was allocated—with an average of only one and one-half hours per week on policy-related matters. No wonder our data show that many line supervisors "bypass" them in handling cases of problem drinking. Another possible reason for supervisory bypassing is that more than one-third of the coordinators were appointed less than six months before our visit, and only about half had been officially appointed to that role by the installation director.

Other findings further document the general paucity of resources to support this role. It seems unreasonable to expect the coordinator to be active, for example, unless there is at least a minimal amount of his or her time set aside for policy-related duties. Yet just over half report that no proportion of their time had been officially allocated for them to implement the policy. An even higher percentage (62 percent) reported they spent none, or one percent, of their time actually carrying out their policy-specific tasks. Quite consistent with this is the fact that well over half gave a very low priority to the policy in their day-to-day activities. Also, 80 percent reported no staff help in carrying out the policy, and of those that did report staff help, the vast majority reported having less than full-time assistance.

With a few exceptions, coordinators had no official budget; if they spent any money at all during a year it was likely to be between $40 and $100; most, however, spent nothing. The situation was somewhat better regarding medical facilities available to them, but even here, just under one-quarter were unable to describe the availability of medical facilities. The remainder described units either inside or outside the building or a public health facility nearby. Consequently they believed it was easy to use their medical departments if they wanted to do so. Furthermore, for those with a union (73 percent), there was a strong feeling that the union was in favor of the policy; this was confirmed by their reported absence of any conflicts with the union over the policy and its use. Despite medical availability and favorable union response, less than one-fourth of the coordinators supplemented their programs with additional features that they felt went beyond the minimal requirements of the policy. Perhaps the absence of "hard" resources like time and staff defined the policy as a matter of relatively minor importance.

Because the alcoholism coordinators had received so few resources, we decided to try to determine what would happen to their behavior if modest resources were made available to them. The results in table 6.4 and prior analyses indicated that staff help has been more closely associated with policy implementation than either money or time allocations to the role itself. However, as just discussed, the allocations of time and money were so sparse that it was possible that these variables showed insufficient variance to permit an adequate assessment of their possible impact.[6] With the data reported we can only speculate on their possible contribution to greater use, while we can use the results of the regression analyses reported to project what might happen if staff time were increased by various amounts; this procedure seems justified since we know that staff time was significantly related to various aspects of policy implementation.

In order to make these projections, the coefficients obtained from the past experience of coordinators can be used with new hypothetical values of any independent variable to determine a new value for the dependent variable of interest. Such a procedure is only a gross estimate, since it makes various assumptions about the past data and its relationship with the hypothetical future data that might not be entirely justified. We therefore performed this exercise in a speculative vein, meaning to provide a suggestive example of what impact changes in resources could have.

For the projections, we did not increase either budget or time allocated to alcoholism coordinators. Since the latter averaged about four hours, that was the value used for time allocation of the coordinator. The same procedure was followed for budget, and other relevant variables. Only the values for staff size were changed, as indicated in table 6.6, which gives the results of these projections. As might be expected, when greater staff help is substituted into the equations, results indicate that the policy-relevant activities of coordinators increases. To use a reasonable example, should the

T A B L E 6.6 Projected Percentage of Increase for Various Degrees of Staff Help Upon Alcoholism Coordinator Policy Activities and Supervisor Policy Use[a]

| | STAFF HELP PER WEEK | | | | |
	4 Hours	8 Hours	12 Hours	16 Hours	20 Hours
Finding treatment information	7%[b]	14%	21%	28%	35%
Consulting with key personnel	8	16	24	32	40
Supervisory policy use	9	18	27	36	45
Coordinator case load	14	28	42	56	70
Number of procedures used with alcoholism cases	39	78	11	156	195

[a]Based on average of four hours per week official allocation of time for coordinator.

[b]Confidence limited can be attached to each of these projections; they are not given here because of space limitations, but generally they become very wide as staff hours increase from 4 hours to 20 hours.

coordinator receive and use eight hours of staff help per week, the projections indicate that his performance of policy provisions would improve dramatically.

While these projections do not answer the question of whether increased time allocated to the role and increased budget would also increase implementation efforts, it seems logical to suppose that this might occur, although our data do not permit us to demonstrate such a relationship. Unfortunately, we cannot even estimate in a reasonable way how much implementation would increase with increases in these other resources. Because the installations we studied are relatively small organizations with an average of about 200 employees, and because alcoholism is not a pervasive problem in the sense of the proportion of employees affected, we feel that it is probably sufficient if these installations have part-time coordinators. Budgets would not need to be very large either, since it appears that these installations have good medical facilities available to them, and most communities have treatment centers available.

The same observations do not, however, apply to the EEO policy. EEO functionaries averaged 42 percent of their time officially allocated to EEO duties and reported spending 28 percent of their time on coordinator duties. As might be expected, they gave the EEO policy a very high priority (5.64 on a 7-point scale), and 55 percent reported staff support averaging 1.73 full-time persons to assist them. With this support, EEO functionaries had handled an average of 27.8 cases, while alcoholism coordinators had only handled an average of 3 cases. Also, when we computed the resources per case handled, we found that the alcoholism coordinators had only about one-half the resources per case that the EEO functionaries enjoyed. These results would be even more dismal were we to include monetary resources, which were rarely provided for in the alcoholism policy. It is also interesting to note that for both policies average time allocations reported exceeded the average amount of time that facilitators reported that they actually spent on policy-related matters. This circumstance makes it hard to argue that what facilitators need to make them more active is more time allocation, although we would still argue that *some* rather than zero time allocation should be beneficial for implementation of the alcoholism policy. It has been argued that motivation to engage in the innovative process in the health field is greatly enhanced by the presence of resources (Mohr, 1969). But alcoholism coordinators have so few resources that the fact they achieve anything at all may be a small miracle.

In addition, as would be expected, the longer the coordinator's tenure, the more cases of alcoholic workers he has dealt with under policy provisions and the greater number of other policy-related activities he has engaged in. This suggests that visibility of coordinator and program to supervision can only emerge with time. Furthermore, time may help to reduce the importance of the fact that few, if any, formal rewards come to the coordinator in that role. That is, experienced facilitators may have learned to look for the intrinsic rather than the extrinsic rewards of their role. However, it may be advisable to include in future policy revisions some specific ways in which coordinator efforts can be rewarded extrinsically. Yet their plight is not unique. Recall that the EEO functionaries who were active had rather negative expectations about whether or not either expertise or performance was important for their own promotions. Only some deep ideological commitment would be likely to overcome the lack of reinforcement presented by such a reward structure. Since a substantial proportion of EEO functionaries are women and/or minority group members (38 percent), some of them may have that kind of ideological commitment. In the case of the alcoholism policy, only coordinators who are themselves recovered alcoholics or who have had some sort of personal contact with the problems of alcoholism are likely to hold such ideological commitment for the policy. Although we were made aware that some alcoholism coordinators in our sample were recovered alcoholics, and it is certainly not unusual for such persons to serve as alcoholism coordinators or counselors in work settings, it does not seem advisable or feasible to limit candidates for the role this narrowly.

Alternatively, we can think of educational background as a factor that might make the selection of some persons for the role more suitable than the selection of other persons; education could affect or reflect relevant skills and also motivational commitment to such a program. Given an appointee at an appropriate starting point, the installation and federal service could try to increase both motivation and relevant skills through appropriate training.

The present sample of alcoholism coordinators had too little in the way of appropriate prior training (only 28.7 percent came from social science or health occupation backgrounds, and only 30 percent had prior training relevant to the needs of the alcoholism coordinator role) and too little "in house" training on the policy (only 55 percent had such training). While there are other areas already mentioned where the coordinator needs additional resources, at the very least the coordinator should have a background conducive to acceptance of the coordinator role, especially given the innovative nature of the policy; the opportunity for proper training in the specifics of the role; and minimum time and staff support to effectively develop and implement the policy.

As we have seen, the evidence from our sample of coordinators shows that these as well as numerous other needs for properly developing the coordinator role have been lacking. The result has often been a coordinator who is not in tune with the philosophical demands of such a policy, who lacks complete knowledge of how to deal properly with the clientele, and who, because of lack of time, does not even make the most rudimentary attempts to establish or implement the policy. When 82 percent of the supervisors in our sample respond that they received no policy information from the coordinator, it is not surprising that 53 percent responded that they did not know of the coordinator's existence. Such a record may help to explain why the policy usage rate reported by coordinators in our sample (1.9 percent) is less than 60 percent of an observed prevalence rate of 3.3 percent based upon actual cases of use reported by supervisors.[7]

EEO Functionaries: The Emergence of a Facilitator

While it is quite difficult to conclude that a role actually exists called "alcoholism coordinator," data indicate that EEO officers and counselors occupy a genuine role. Resources have been invested: time officially allocated, money spent, and staff help assigned to the role. Also, the role has crystallized sufficiently to produce distinctive behaviors, outlooks, and policy identities. Moreover, the results indicate the presence of an active role. In larger installations, EEO functionaries were more active. Job overload seemed to have only minor impact. Time in the role appeared to produce "growth"; that is, implementing behaviors were significantly greater. Formalization neither aided nor hindered incumbents in meeting their obligations, but increased information was associated with increased implementation. Furthermore, even though shortage of resources was not nearly the problem it was for alcoholism coordinators, greater resources produced an increase in one of the key behaviors: counseling of cases. It bears repeating that the alcoholism counselors with more resources also showed dramatic increases in a wide variety of implementing behavior—even to extending their efforts to the union.

Obviously the alcoholism coordinator role is in an embryonic stage of formation, while the EEO role is more matured. Also obvious is the need for resources before a facilitating role can emerge. Apparently these can be quite modest, but their virtual absence means that an implementing role will remain largely inchoate even though other ingredients may be operating. These conclusions, combined with the lack of significant relationships between size and implementation of the alcoholism policy, suggest that the amount of organizational resources for use on an innovation at a given time, independent of size, is more predictive of implementation of the innovation (Cyert and March, 1963) than is organizational size itself. The positive relationships between installation size and implementation of EEO probably reflect a demand dimension for use of that policy.

ROLE COMPLIANCE AND SUPERVISORY POLICY USE

In the final analysis, "payoff" for any facilitator role lies in its effect on potential policy users, represented, in this instance, by actual and expected usage by line supervisors. The entire rationale for a facilitator role is that the implementing efforts that emanate from it will be influential in actually getting the innovation into practice. Regardless of how completely a facilitator may fulfill his or her role expectations, unless that performance results in appropriate behaviors among incumbents of complementary roles in the set, the facilitating effort may be thwarted.

In an effort to determine if supervisory actual and expected usage of the policy was related to the alcoholism and EEO facilitators' role compliance activities, we again used multiple regression analysis. To avoid correlating an activity with itself, only those facilitating activities that would logically precede direct policy application to a case could be used relative to actual supervisory use; these were general consultation and diffusion activities. For expected use, however, we assumed that the entire range of implementing behaviors could be analyzed, since their usage could clearly have an impact on expected future use as estimated by a supervisor. Detailed results are not presented here because they can be summarized briefly. When either EEO or alcoholism facilitators more fully fulfilled their roles, it had little if any effect on actual policy usage by supervisors. Neither individual regression coefficients nor overall regression results were statistically significant, except that consulting with the installation's personnel department was associated with expected EEO policy use by supervisors ($\beta = .24$, $p = .05$). When, however, we used the entire range of implementing behaviors in an analysis of expected usage, additional evidence of facilitator influence emerged. Amount of counseling of EEO cases by facilitators was significantly associated with expected policy usage among supervisors ($\beta = .39$, $p = .05$). Moreover, alcoholism coordinators' referrals to community agencies were substantially related to expected use by supervisors ($\beta = .49$, $p = .001$). Apparently role fulfillment has some impact on occupants of counterpositions, but only in terms of expected future use. In a strict sense, however, we must conclude that, as of mid-1974, the facilitators had probably had little if any impact on supervisory policy use until that time. The prospects for them having more impact in the future, however, seemed better because of their effect on supervisory expectations.

It should also be mentioned again that supervisory use may not be as crucial to implementation of the EEO policy, although it would certainly be needed for full implementation. In the case of EEO, policy facilitators can probably do a reasonable amount on their own, or with just the cooperation of affected employees, personnel departments, and installation directors. The cooperation of the supervisor, however, is crucial to the strategies underlying implementation of the alcoholism policy.

On balance, there seems to be little reason to believe that increased facilitator effort had resulted in "changing the patterns of recurring behavior" (Kahn, 1974) that make up the supervisory activities relative to these two policies. This may be due, in part, to the relative newness of the facilitators; as their implementing behaviors accumulate through time their impact may become more discernible. On the other hand, these findings may well coincide with the only substantive study we could find of the effectiveness of various "organizational development" treatments and interventions designed to produce change in organizational behavior (Bowers,

1973). Here the impacts of four different types of interventions ("treatments") were contrasted to determine which one contributed the most to indexes of "organizational development." Two of the treatments consisted of efforts by change agents and differed in that one type used a strategy of interpersonal trust and confidence designed to encourage the client group to set up their own change processes. The other type used private consultations with supervisors combined with task analysis to influence adoption of new objectives and behaviors. The two other methods were survey feedback and laboratory (T-group) training. The O.D. practitioners used these methods in a variety of twenty-three companies, but without any randomization.

One of the treatments associated mainly with individual change agents—"interpersonal process consultation" (Bowers, 1973:33)—was moderately effective, while the other type—"task process consultation"—was not. Survey feedback generated the most desirable changes, while laboratory training was associated with negative changes. Apparently the individual-change facilitators were having moderate success when they acted as group catalysts but little when they attempted to influence managers privately. Combining this with our findings, we can conclude that policy facilitators may reach a point of moderate effectiveness, but rarely one of consistent and significant influence on policy implementation. By contrast, as we shall see in chapter 8, the impact of the union on implementation is probably greater than that of facilitators, even when the union is simply playing its usual adversary role. For that matter, data presented in the previous chapter showed many more significant relationships between characteristics of the director and supervisory implementation of the policies.

This latter point brings into focus yet another conclusion from the Bowers study: the influence of "organizational climate" as a mediating factor (Bowers, 1973:37) on O.D. interventions. The phrase refers to a combination of communication flow, decision-making practices, and the reward system. A favorable climate would be one with well-developed communication flows in all directions, decentralized decision making, and significant rewards for talent and skills. The study finds that the impact of any O.D. intervention is "in part contingent upon the organizational climate in which it occurs" (Bowers, 1973:39), and if this climate is not "changing positively," none of the methods are apt to be of much consequence. Thus autocratic and punitive practices can negate the efforts of change agents, rendering them largely ritualistic. In the next chapter we find that the organizational structure of an installation, especially its centralization, has a sharp, deterrent effect on policy implementation, reemphasizing the point that change agents (internal or external) work within a structural setting that may, or may not, facilitate their efforts.

SUMMARY

We began this chapter by considering the ingredients of roles and the desirable attributes of role sets. One of the important characteristics of role sets that is expected to enhance role performance is homophily with other members of the role set. The two types of policy facilitators and occupants of two of their important counterpositions—supervisors and directors—differ on both demographic characteristics and certain important work-related attitudes. Some demographic differences are what might be expected: directors are older, more educated, and of higher civil service grade. EEO functionaries are more likely to be female, and directors are least likely to be female. But other differences also emerged. EEO functionaries have the shortest tenure in the federal service and are most involved with their jobs. Alcoholism coordinators are lowest on receptivity toward change, while line supervisors have worked at the installation longest. These various groups also perceive the reward structure differently, with line supervisors most likely to believe technical skills are important, and EEO functionaries least likely to believe that performance is important and second least likely to believe that technical skills are important. Overall, while the data do not document large differences on many of the dimensions tested, the differences are numerous enough and of sufficient magnitude to question whether these role-set members can be considered homophilous.

When the exploration of possible differences was carried over into policy-related attitudes, additional differences emerged. Perhaps the most important difference for the alcoholism policy was that coordinators felt the policy was needed, while other members of their role set tended to assess the policy on the negative, or not-needed, side of that scale. A similar pattern was found for the EEO policy, but here all three groups at least had a positive assessment of need. The most notable difference between role occupants was the relative disagreement of EEO functionaries with others relative to need for the policy in the installation. EEO facilitators express a greater sense of need and probably consistently have to work with those less motivated than they are. In sum, both types of facilitators experience dissensus over policy-related matters with occupants of their counterpositions. Clearly, there is insufficient similarities in attitudes, values, and beliefs to appreciably motivate the target systems of these facilitators.

Given this dissensus and the difficulties it can create for implementation efforts, what factors explained the policy-related efforts of the two types of facilitators? Organizational location of the role failed to explain differential role performance for alcoholism coordinators, although it was associated with different resources and levels of formalization of the role. Some differences between policy-related attitudes of alcoholism coordinators in different locations also emerged. Organizational location was more important in explaining role performance of EEO functionaries, with results suggesting that EEO facilitators in staff positions were less effective in their role performance than those in other positions. Nevertheless, the staff facilitators had been granted the largest budgets; we wonder whether they would have done more or less with smaller budgets. Generally, members of line management, but especially directors, were more favorable to the policy and implemented it more extensively than functionaries in staff positions.

When we looked at other factors that might explain differential role performance, we found that formalization of the role and work overload seem to inhibit role performance of alcoholism coordinators, while additional staff help tended to enhance role performance of both facilitators. The sheer amount of time that the person had been in the facilitator role was also associated with more policy implementation efforts by both types of facilitators. The size of the installation also had significant effects on implementation of the EEO policy, perhaps because there was more demand for the program within the larger installations.

When we carried the analysis to its logical conclusion and tested to see what effects the facilitators' role performance had upon supervisory use of the policies, we found few relationships. EEO functionaries who consult more often with other members of the organization have more expected supervisory use within their installations; probably such functionaries have made the EEO policy more salient to supervisors in their installations. For the alcoholism policy, past referrals to community agencies is the best predictor of expected future use by supervisors. Apparently supervisors who have encountered some diagnosed and treated drinking problem in their installations are more likely to believe that such a problem could arise again.

Three general explanations for the paucity of relationships between facilitator and supervisor performance under policy provisions can be offered. One is the dissensus that was detected in analyses of job-related and policy-related attitudes. Perhaps the lack of congruence in attitudes also leads to less than ideal matching of behaviors. It could happen that facilitators became jealous of their special roles and did not actively encourage supervisory participation. A suggestion of this possibility emerged from the results for EEO functionaries. A second possibility is that sometimes each type of role occupant assessed what the other was doing and then let the more active one take the lead and do all of the work. That is, where supervisors were active, facilitators did less, or vice versa. Also, as shown in the previous chapter, directors may have taken the lead away from the facilitator. If such data, with relationships reversed from the usual expectation, were obtained for some number of cases, it would tend to obscure the expected relationships in the other cases.[8] The third possibility is that the roles, especially that of the alcoholism coordinator, have not crystallized sufficiently to have their intended effect.

This lack of connection between coordinator and supervisory behavior is likely to be especially detrimental to implementation of the alcoholism policy because the strategy underlying that policy makes cooperation over issues of work performance very important. In the case of the EEO policy, cooperation is highly desirable, but perhaps not so essential to getting the policy off the ground. Employees can seek out counseling and other programs without supervisory involvement, and thus the lack of connection between facilitator and supervisory role performance may not be as devastating to the implementation of the EEO policy.

As it stands, there is little inducement for role occupants to perform these roles well except for whatever personal satisfactions they can obtain, and these are likely to be related to ideological commitment, which in turn may be rooted in identification with the problems that the policies are designed to ameliorate. Certainly the provision of at least a minimal level of assistance seems advisable for such facilitator roles. Such assistance demonstrates the organization's commitment to the role, and it also serves to create a subjective feeling of support and recognition of needs that may enhance role performance through increased motivation.

Finally, facilitators must work within an organizational structure that may be compatible with the changes they represent and are expected to encourage. In the following chapter we examine in detail the effects of structural variables on the implementation process and show how these block or encourage efforts at policy implementation.

7. Organizational and Environmental Factors: Constraints and Opportunities

IN THE PRECEDING CHAPTERS, we have looked at the factors that have tended to facilitate or inhibit the implementation of the alcoholism and EEO policies by certain key actors within the federal installations. In this chapter we will move to a different level of analysis, focusing on each installation as a formal organization and trying to discover what structural and environmental features distinguish those installations that more fully implemented these policies from those that did not.

The systems approach to the analysis of organizational behavior emphasizes the interconnectedness of various elements within the organization. Individual members of organizations, of course, do the behaving, but their actions may be severely constrained or otherwise affected by organizational features—resources available, discretion allowed within roles, communication channels available, and so on. Many of these organizational features are outside the control of the individual actor, and apply to many actors within the organization. In this sense, it is reasonable to look at the behavior of organizations as a whole, since it is likely that many of the same things would occur in a given organizational structure even if the particular persons occupying the various positions within the organization were to change (Hall, 1972:12-13).

Because organizations depend on the environment for a variety of inputs that are essential to survival, features of the organizational

185

environment also can affect behaviors within the organization. Perhaps the first study to demonstrate the crucial impact of the environment on organizationally executed change was Selznick's study of the TVA (1953). His research uncovered a large number of unintended consequences attributable to environmental pressures and constraints. Yet most of the subsequent literature evaluating organizational change has failed to take account of the environmental setting (Berman and Pauly, 1975:5). Important inputs that each organization must obtain from its environment are its personnel resources to be acquired from the surrounding community. Even in those cases where personnel are hired from outside the immediate community, after they are employed they are likely to live within that community and so be subject to a variety of constraints, opportunities, or pressures emanating from that environment. Many of these will be carried with them into their employing organization as they report to work each day, and others will be experienced by the installation through the actions of other organizations, interest groups, individual citizens, local politics, and so forth. As Berman and McLaughlin (1975a) point out relative to educational innovations, the demographic and political characteristics of the community in which an implementing organization is located affect support for the change to be implemented by producing *pressure* for change, by *constraining* the possibilities of change, and by presenting the *need* to change through the characteristics of the relevant population—in this case, the community work force. While the civil service system was designed to protect members of the federal service from the necessity of wooing support from various constituencies to maintain their jobs, it is unlikely that federal organizations are totally exempt from environmental pressures, nor can they be viewed as exempt from the constraints or opportunities presented by the community, or from the needs of their employees.

In considering how either organizational structure or organizational environments might affect policy implementation, we will again be guided by past literature on change and innovation, as well as by some consideration of the content of the policies themselves. But before we proceed to advance our hypotheses about the relationships of structure and environment to implementation, we will first describe the installations in the sample along the relevant dimensions. This will serve two purposes: it will enable us to introduce the various aspects of structure and environment that were investigated, and it will provide a sort of profile of what these installations and their environments were like so that the subsequent results can be put into perspective relative to other organizations.

STRUCTURAL CHARACTERISTICS

The sampling frame included what the Civil Service Commission calls all "inspectable units" of the federal government falling into nine executive departments, providing the installation had more than 50 employees. The sample was stratified by region, executive department, and size, but the actual list of installations did not have sufficient numbers of installations to fill all cells of the design. Within cells, installations were randomly selected. The numbers of installations in the final sample from the various executive departments were: Agriculture, 9; Commerce, 3; General Services Administration, 12; Health, Education, and Welfare, 15; Housing and Urban Development, 6; Interior, 5; Justice, 6; Transportation, 3; and Treasury, 14. Also, 16 were from the Boston civil service region, 31 from the New York region, and 24 from the Philadelphia region. The reason for stratifying the sample was to guarantee that we would have the full range of executive departments, sizes, and regions represented in the final sample. The implementation of these policies might be expected to vary according to the administrative policies and attitudes of either Washington-level departmental personnel or those in regional offices. Size has been demonstrated to be a pervasive influence on a variety of organizational variables, both structural (Blau and Schoenherr, 1971) and related to organizational change and innovation (Zaltman et al., 1973).

Installations could also be characterized by their administrative level within their executive department. Eleven were regional offices, 38 were area or district offices, and 22 were field offices or posts of duty. The size strata were determined by whether the agency had more or fewer than 150 employees. In the final sample, 39 had less than 150 employees, while 32 had 150 or more employees. The average size was 205 employees, with the largest installation having 1,164 employees and the smallest having only 18 employees.[1] Most employees were full-time; there was an average of only 9 part-time employees per installation.

A variety of structural dimensions of organizations have been identified and measured by past researchers. Some of these are relatively objective characteristics of the organization, such as its size as measured by number of employees. Other relatively objective measures relate to what is called the complexity of the organization. Complexity has both horizontal and vertical dimensions. The vertical dimension refers to the number of levels of authority or supervision there are within the organization. The average installation in our sample had only 3 supervisory levels below the director, which we have called division heads, middle managers, and line supervisors for uniformity throughout this book. But there was considerable variance between installations on this measure; some installations had only one level of supervision under the director and others had 14.

An objective indicator of the horizontal complexity within an organization is the division of labor, or amount of job specialization within the installation. We collected data on job titles of all employees within each installation and considered the number of different job titles as a measure of division of labor. Different levels of the same job title (clerk-typist I and clerk-typist II) were counted as one job title. Installations varied greatly on this measure, with some having as few as 7 different job titles, and one having 189 different job titles. The average was 46 job titles.

Another form of horizontal differentiation is the way in which the various job titles are organized and arranged into administrative subunits within the installation. We counted the number of supervisors reporting to the director as the first level of horizontal differentiation in these installations. Supervisors at this level headed some sort of administrative units themselves, and for uniformity these were arbitrarily dubbed "divisions." The average horizontal differentiation at this level was 6 divisions, but some installations had only one and others had 21 divisions. Such horizontal differentiation can also occur at the next lowest level of supervision within the installations, and we have called the units at this level "sections." The average installation with supervisors at this level had between 9 and 10 sections. Five installations did not have 2 levels of horizontal differentiation.

In most cases (54), horizontal differentiation took place along functional lines; job titles indicated that different divisions performed different functions. For 17 installations, however, division heads had the same or very similar titles, suggesting that their subunits performed parallel duties.

Another concept used to describe organizational structure is formalization, which includes the degree to which job duties are codified in written rules and regulations, and employees are evaluated according to highly codified and specific procedures. We asked directors of installations to evaluate these features of their organization. When directors were asked what proportion of employees must conform to specific rules and procedures for carrying out most of their day-to-day activities, the average response was about 70 percent. As might be expected, many jobs are codified in federal work organizations. Furthermore, in assessing how general or specific these rules and procedures were, the average response was toward the specific end of the scale (mean of 4.6 on a scale in which 1 = very general guidelines and 6 = very specific procedures). Almost all (99 percent) of the installations had a standard procedure for assessing work performance, and the typical form was highly formalized, including both specific factors to be rated and requests for more general comments.

Another important facet of organizational structure is the way in which authority and control are exercised, which is discussed in the organizational literature under the concept of centralization. Two important aspects of organizational control are the issues of who has the authority to make certain decisions and who actually has the most influence over decisions that are made. Organizations where control over decision making is reserved for the top levels of management, giving them "tight" control, are called centralized. Organizations that allow substantial discretion in decision making to lower-level participants are called decentralized.

Both supervisors and directors were asked to assess which levels of supervision had the practical responsibility for making ten different decisions. These data are given in table 7.1. For each decision, the level that received the highest percentage of responses from directors and from supervisors has been printed in boldface type. Supervisors and directors agreed on seven of the ten decisions. On the remainder, supervisors are more likely to assess themselves as most influential. The general pattern of the results shows upper management (including both the director and division heads) as more influential than lower levels of supervision, but first-level supervisors are most influential in two decisions: changes in day-to-day work procedures and approval of annual leave (vacations). The percentage of installations in which lower-level supervision has influence in all or most of the other decisions is not trivial, indicating that some of these federal installations are somewhat decentralized. Supervisors may have given higher estimates of responsibility to division heads than directors because supervisors were not as accurately aware of exactly where those decisions are made that are made by someone superior to them.

We also asked questions designed to assess who had the final authority and who had the most influence in who was hired at the first-line supervisory level. The majority of directors (52 percent) responded that they had the final authority, although 24 percent responded that someone superior to them had final authority in such hiring decisions. When it came to influence, an almost equal number felt that immediate supervisors of the person to be hired had the most influence (31 percent) as felt that they themselves had the most influence (28 percent) in who was hired at this level.

Another crucial aspect of the control structure within organizations is their relative autonomy from parent or other organizations.

TABLE 7.1 Who Has Influence in Which Decisions as Assessed by Directors and Supervisors

| | PERCENTAGE RESPONDING THAT LEVEL HAS PRACTICAL RESPONSIBILITY[a] | | | | | | | |
| | *Directors (n = 70)* | | | | *Supervisors (n = 634)* | | | |
Responses by: LEVEL INVOLVED: *Decision:*	FIRST-LINE SUPERVISOR	MIDDLE SUPERVISOR	DIVISION HEAD	DIRECTOR	FIRST-LINE SUPERVISOR	MIDDLE SUPERVISOR	DIVISION HEAD	DIRECTOR
1. Hire temporary or part-time personnel	39%	45%	46%	40%	36%	45%	62%	44%
2. Approve overtime	21	28	33	63	26	39	59	49
3. Approved change in layout of work area	20	26	54	59	26	38	60	53
4. Approved equipment expense of $100	18	28	47	44	14	32	58	51
5. Approved merit raises	21	25	27	69	29	33	59	63
6. Change day-to-day work procedures	51	42	46	31	64	53	51	37
7. Approved participation in training	33	39	44	56	33	45	64	52
8. Approved annual leave	60	31	43	36	72	50	48	35
9. Approve nonroutine travel	21	29	46	64	25	32	54	56
10. Recommend professional awards	40	37	44	64	49	43	61	61
Mean =	32	33	43	53	37	41	58	55

[a]Percentages equal more than 100 percent because respondents were allowed to check all levels that they felt had practical influence, and most respondents checked more than one level for each decision.

The federal installations in this sample are part of the various executive departments—each with a hierarchy ending in Washington with a cabinet-level officer, and ultimately with the president of the United States. It was important to assess the degree to which installation directors felt autonomous within the huge bureaucracy, that is, the degree to which they felt they could make or influence decisions that were important to their installation. Almost 90 percent of directors reported that they were asked to make recommendations for the operating budget of their installation, and 35 percent felt that their recommendations had a great deal of influence. Another 52 percent felt that their recommendations tended to be followed to a more moderate degree. Only two directors (3 percent) were negative in their assessment of their influence in the budget process. Similarly, 97 percent of directors reported that they were asked to make recommendations in the allocation of personnel to their installations, and 28 percent reported that their recommendations were followed a great deal of the time. Another 61 percent reported positive assessments of their influence on personnel allocations, and only four directors (6 percent) felt less than moderate influence on this item.

Two other aspects of the control structure are the preponderance of supervisory personnel and the preponderance of clerical personnel. Higher ratios of administrators to employees lead to smaller average spans of control for the supervisors and thus to the possibility of closer supervision and control. Also, higher ratios of clerical personnel to other personnel suggest an emphasis on paper work that can be seen as part of the "red tape" syndrome. The presence of so many clerks suggests that much paper work needs to be done, with work completion and other aspects of the job controlled by the necessity to write reports, fill out forms, and so on. The average percentage of supervisors within these installations was 14 percent; the average proportion of clerical employees was 20 percent. These are both lower proportions than Blau and Schoenherr found in state employment agencies, where the average proportion of supervisors was 21.2 percent and the average proportion of clerical workers was 32.1 percent for state headquarters and 21.0 percent and 20.3 percent, respectively, for local offices (Blau and Schoenherr, 1971:375-79). Thus these federal installations are not as bureaucratized on the dimensions of administrative intensity or preponderance of clerical work as are some state offices. Elsewhere (Beyer and Trice, 1976) we have suggested that this sample of government organizations differs from samples in other studies of government organizations in the lower incidence of paper work and the greater diversity of jobs involved in the various missions of the installations.

Finally, the level of expertise or professionalization within a work force provides an important structural constraint upon the organization. A frequently used measure of expertise or professionalization is the number of years of education completed by members of the organization. We asked both directors and supervisors about their years of schooling, and used the surrogate measure of G.S. grade within the civil service system to categorize the nonsupervisory work force, whom we did not interview. The average years of schooling for directors was 16.5 years, indicating slightly more schooling, on the average, than a bachelor's degree from college. The average years of schooling for supervisors was almost as great (15.2 years), indicating at least three years of college completed by the average supervisor.

The average across all installations of the median G.S. rating within the installation was slightly less than a G.S. 7, with a range from G.S. 3 to G.S. 13. This suggests that the heterogeneous nature of the sample includes installations where relatively unskilled employees predominate, as well as other installations with extremely high skill levels. As of spring 1977 the basic salary level for G.S. 3 was $7,408, while that for G.S. 13 was $24,308.

THE SURROUNDING COMMUNITIES

U.S. Census data were used to measure characteristics of the communities surrounding the federal installations studied. All data were taken from the *County and City Data Book* published by the U.S. Bureau of the Census for the year 1972. Data were coded for the municipality in which each installation was located,[2] with the exception of those located in communities with a population of less than 25,000. Since city data were unavailable for such communities, the data on the county were used for these installations.

The community of the average installation in our sample had a population of 906,700 and a population density of 9,823 persons per square mile. However, densities varied widely, from 24 to 37,000 persons per square mile. The median family income for this hypothetical average community was $9,456 for 1974, with a minimum of $4,460 and a maximum of $15,870. The median education completed by persons twenty-five years or older was 11.4 years of schooling (a range of 9.8 to 12.6 years), and the median age was 29.6 years (a range of 23.1 to 35.5).

The average proportion of blacks in the community was 18.7 percent, but some communities had a negligible proportion of blacks (less than 1 percent), while others had over 54 percent. The average proportion of persons of foreign stock was 24.7 percent, ranging from 2.5 to 50.5 percent. The average proportion of females was 52.6 percent, ranging from 46 to over 55 percent.

TABLE 7.2 Comparison of the Average Community Surrounding
Federal Installations in Sample with National Averages
(U.S. Census Data for 1972)

COMMUNITY CHARACTERISTIC	AVERAGE COMMUNITY IN OUR SAMPLE	NATIONAL AVERAGE
Population density (persons per square mile)	9823.3	57.7
Median family income (in dollars)	9456.1	9670.0
Median education (persons 25 years or older)	11.4	12.1
Median age in years	29.6	28.3
Percentage blacks in population	18.7	11.2
Percentage of foreign stock in population	24.7	16.7
Percentage of females in population	52.6	52.8
Percentage of labor force employed in manufacturing	23.7	19.6
Percentage of labor force employed in government units	18.3	15.2
Percentage of labor force employed in professional and managerial jobs	22.3	23.7
Percentage unemployed	4.4	5.6

Data were also recorded on a variety of characteristics of the
labor force chosen for their possible relevance to the policies under
study. In 1972, only 4.4 percent of the labor force in these communities were listed as unemployed, although this varied from a low of
2.2 percent to a high of 6.5 percent. Almost one-quarter (23.7
percent) were employed in manufacturing, and another 18 percent
were in government employment. Of all those employed, slightly
more than 22 percent were in professional or managerial positions.

These data probably present a pretty good composite picture of
the urban northeastern United States; rural areas are undoubtedly
underrepresented. Although we traveled anywhere that a sampled
installation was located, and some were in relatively small communities, the number of truly remote locations was very small. There
may be some smaller local offices or posts of duty of the executive
departments in smaller communities and more rural areas, but these
would have been excluded from our sample because we eliminated all
installations with fewer than fifty employees before the sample was
drawn.

Table 7.2 compares the data on the communities surrounding the
installations with national averages also obtained from the U.S.
Census. The overall profile that emerges is of a rather large, not too
affluent or advantaged urban environment. The proportion of blacks
and foreign-stock is much higher than the national average, as is the
proportion of persons employed in manufacturing. While the propor-

tion of the work force employed in government units is higher than the national average, the proportion in the higher-status jobs (professional and managerial) is somewhat lower. This is echoed in the median family income, which is also lower than the national average, although unemployment was relatively low in the sample communities at that time. Finally, the communities under study had a somewhat older and less educated population than the national average. But the figures presented, with the exception of population density, are not so far from national averages as to suggest that these communities are highly atypical.

Nevertheless, as we proceed to advance and test hypotheses in later sections of this chapter, we will have to remember that the communities in which these installations are located are somewhat disadvantaged—although not in terms of unemployment—compared with national averages.

STRUCTURAL FEATURES RELATED TO IMPLEMENTATION OF CHANGE

In a study of British firms, Burns and Stalker (1961) identified a variety of structural features of organizations that varied in successful firms with the degree of stability of their environment. Unstable environments were seen as requiring organizations to remain more open and flexible so as to be able to adapt appropriately to changing environmental demands and requirements. Successful firms operating in such unstable environments were found to exhibit a constellation of structural characteristics that the researchers grouped under the label "organic," while those dealing with more stable environments exhibited structural features that they termed "mechanistic." The mechanistic features were similar to the monocratic bureaucracy of Weber (1947), while the organic structures departed in important ways from strict hierarchies of authority and communication flow and the rigidities of highly formalized roles and duties that are associated with bureaucracy. Hage and Aiken (1967) further elaborated these ideas when they studied program change within social service organizations. A wide variety of other researchers have investigated the relationship between organizational structure and innovation or change within organizations, with similar results.[3] This study continues trends from earlier research but differs from past efforts in several ways: (1) This study was conducted in organizations within the federal government of the United States, where bureaucracy and mechanistic structures might be considered almost inevitable. (2) The changes studied here were mandated by the U.S. Congress and thus came from outside the organizations whose job it was to implement them. (3) This study focused on the process of the implementation of these changes rather than just their adoption or initiation.

This focus on implementation is an important contribution to the literature on organizational change and innovation because various writers (Wilson, 1966; Shepard, 1967; Zaltman et al., 1973; Petersen, 1976; Duncan, 1976; Pierce and Delbecq, 1977) have suggested that different organizational features may be required for the successful implementation of change than are required for the initiation or adoption of change—calling for what Duncan (1976) has termed the "ambidextrous organization." If these speculations are true, organizations are faced with a difficult problem in organizational design. It is thus important to test such ideas empirically, as we are able to do with data from this study.

Hypotheses

Past research on formal organizations has found relationships between change or innovation and many of the aspects of organizational structure that we have already discussed in this chapter. We will briefly review some of these findings and present the arguments that link change or innovation with each of the structural features of concern.

Many researchers have found positive correlations between size of the organization and some measure of change or innovation (Kaluzny et al., 1974; Thompson, 1965; Mohr, 1969; Aiken and Hage, 1971; Baldridge and Burnham, 1975; Moch and Morse, 1977). The reasons that have been advanced for the relationship vary, but they tend to involve the question of greater resources, whether in terms of persons who have different specializations and form some critical mass (Baldridge and Burnham, 1975) or because large size tends to lead to more general resources and internal differentiation than small size (Aiken and Hage, 1971). Size has been measured both in terms of the number of employees and the size of the budget. While most of the cited studies have focused on the initiation or adoption of innovations, and not on the implementation of change, there is no reason to suppose that resources are any less important to implementation efforts than they are to earlier stages of the change process.

Internal differentiation or complexity is seen as facilitating innovation and change by introducing greater diversity in ideas, which can lead to constructive conflict and away from stifling uniformity of viewpoint. Complexity is introduced through the horizontal differentiation of authority and responsibility between formally designated subunits, through division of labor (job specialization), or through the vertical differentiation of levels of authority (Hall, 1972:143). It is easy to see how complexity might foster the initiation of change efforts, but not so clear that conflict and diversity of viewpoints is advantageous to later stages of change processes. Most empirical research has found that complexity was also associated with greater adoption and implementation of innovations (Aiken and Hage, 1971; Baldridge and Burnham, 1975; Moch and Morse, 1977; Carroll, 1967), although some researchers have suggested that complexity could hinder the adoption of innovations (Barnett, 1953; Aiken and Hage, 1971).

Professionalism has often been found to be associated with greater incidence of innovation and change (Mytinger, 1968; Palumbo, 1969; Hage and Aiken, 1970; Aiken and Hage, 1971). Some writers have argued that professional workers are oriented toward groups outside the organization and thus serve important boundary-spanning roles (Aiken and Hage, 1971; Wilson, 1966). Also, professionals tend to have values and commitments that are consonant with the kinds of changes usually studied.

Finally, professional workers tend to have more education—in fact, this is the measure of professionalization used in this study and elsewhere. As will be discussed in greater length later in this chapter, the process of education appears to lead to greater personal openness and flexibility (Trent and Craise, 1967)—qualities clearly needed in the implementation of change.

Extending the pattern of these results to the implementation of change leads to the following hypothesis for this study:

> 7.1. Organizations that are larger, more complex, and have more professional work forces will be *more* likely than other organizations to implement the alcoholism and EEO policies.

It seems to follow logically that organizations headed by more educated and professional persons should also be more receptive to change, and more successful in implementing it (Kaplan, 1967; Guest, 1962) than other organizations. Hage and Dewar (1973) found that the values of the elite members of organizations had important consequences for innovation.

> 7.2. Organizations headed by more educated leaders are *more* likely than other organizations to implement these policies.

Other organizational features have been found to be less favorable to the initiation and adoption of innovations. Centralization of authority and formalization have both been found to be inhibitors of innovation and change (Burns and Stalker, 1961; Corwin, 1972; Hage and Aiken, 1971; Rosner, 1968; Kaluzny et al., 1974; Thompson,

1965), although—as already mentioned—other writers have argued that change processes require organizations to be ambidextrous in structure, with different stages of the change requiring different structural arrangements (Wilson, 1966; Shepard, 1967; Coughlan et al., 1972; Zaltman et al., 1973; Duncan, 1976; Petersen, 1976; Pierce and Delbecq, 1977). They suggest that the relaxation or absence of bureaucratized organizational features may foster conflict and the generation of a greater range of ideas and viewpoints, leading to the initiation of changes, but that the actual implementation of the changes may require more bureaucratic forms of control—especially centralization of authority, some formalization of roles, a well-defined division of labor, and more specific lines of communication. In essence they are saying that the very processes that facilitate the initiation of innovation—especially individual autonomy, conflict, and diversity of viewpoints—tend to interfere with the successful adoption and implementation of the innovation, because organizational members will tend to adhere to their earlier diversities in the absence of more centralized controls that could ensure more uniformity of action. Thus, they argue, the early stages of a change effort are facilitated by decentralization and little formalization, whereas later stages are helped by centralization and more formalization.

These arguments create a dilemma for organizational designers and management, because they suggest that organizations must either alternate between two opposite features or somehow possess both features simultaneously. Some writers have tried to address how such alterations or alternations in structure can be handled in a practical sense (Duncan, 1976; Zaltman et al., 1973), but these discussions fail to take account of the fact that most organizations are managing a variety of changes and innovations, at different stages, all of the time. Since there is only slight empirical evidence (Palumbo, 1969) to support these arguments, we will base our hypotheses on the earlier cited findings, recognizing that a lack of confirmation of this hypothesis will tend to support the ambidextrous argument:

7.3. Organizations that are formalized and centralized in decision making are *less* likely than other organizations to implement these personnel policies.

Although Pennings (1973) has demonstrated that decentralization and organizational autonomy may be negatively related, we expected more autonomous organizations to be more likely to implement the policies than other organizations for the same reasons that more autonomous work forces are generally seen as more receptive to change; that is, more autonomous actors are more accustomed to exercising initiative and can better marshal the resources and motivation necessary to implement changes than can less autonomous actors accustomed to following the decisions of others. Also, when actors do not have discretion to make decisions, it is likely that they will feel that their responsibility is similarly limited.

7.4. Organizations that are more autonomous will be *more* likely than other organizations to implement these policies.

Finally, other aspects of bureaucratization may be seen as either facilitating or hindering attempts to implement change. A larger ratio of supervisors to other employees (often referred to as the administrative ratio) may facilitate policy implementation because there are more supervisory resources available to use in the implementation effort.

7.5. Organizations with a high percentage of supervisors will be *more* likely than other organizations to implement these policies.

A final aspect of bureaucratization often associated with the inhibition of change is the presence of "red tape." Effort and attention devoted to the production of voluminous paper work may well be inimical to the cultivation and fostering of change efforts. It is assumed for this study that a larger proportion of clerical to other employees reflects an emphasis on paper work and red tape within the installation.

7.6. Organizations with a high percentage of clerical workers will be *less* likely to implement these policies than other organizations.

Results

Stepwise multiple regressions were run with all of the structural variables listed in tables 7.3 through 7.5 included as independent variables and a succession of measures of policy implementation as the dependent variable in each equation. The mean of responses from supervisors within a given installation were used as the measures of the various aspects of implementation for that organization. The stepwise mode of regression was employed because the large number of independent variables made some technique for selecting among them necessary, given the relatively modest number of degrees of freedom available.[4] A separate table has been prepared for each phase of the implementation process: diffusion, receptivity, and use. Comparisons across tables will reveal whether different structural features are associated with different phases of implementation just as initiation or adoption of change may require different structural features than its implementation.

As predicted, the size of the organization tends to be positively related to policy implementation, although it is not a consistent predictor. In the diffusion phase, size is only related to the number of topics covered in training for both policies. Mixed effects occur in the receptivity phase, with size being negatively related to the perceived benefit of the alcoholism policy, but positively related to overzealous agreement with the alcoholism policy and familiarity with the EEO policy. These results suggest that attitudes toward the alcoholism policy are not as favorable in large as in small installations, contrary to the hypothesis. For the EEO policy, greater training efforts eventuate in greater familiarity—positive signs of implementation. Size is most important in actual policy use, being related to the average number of past uses of the EEO policy and the expected frequency of future use of both policies by individual supervisors.

The various indicators of complexity have mixed and scattered relationships with measures of implementation. The most consistent are the negative effects of vertical differentiation, especially on diffusion of the EEO policy, agreement with its provisions, and the number of times supervisors have used it. As hypothesized, horizontal differentiation, functional differentiation, and division of labor seem to have predominantly positive effects, especially on attitudinal receptivity toward the policies. The one significant negative effect is on hours spent in training on the EEO policy, although there are also other negative relationships that are not statistically significant.

The relationship of professionalization to implementation tends to vary across the two policies; effects are more positive for the EEO than for the alcoholism policy, although relationships are mostly negative with variables assessing attitudes toward both policies. The difference between the two policies is clearest in the results on use, where higher education is associated with less use of the alcoholism policy and more frequent past and future use of the EEO policy.

There is no support for hypothesis 7.2. The education of the installation directors is only related significantly to agreement with the EEO policy, and then in a direction opposite to the hypothesis. This finding fits with the generally negative attitudes of more educated supervisors toward the policies, and also with the negative relationships between professionalization of the director and implementation reported in chapter 5.

Centralization clearly has negative effects on implementation, as hypothesized. The influence of upper management (in ten decision areas) is quite consistently and negatively related to the three phases of implementation, while the influence of line supervisors over the same decisions—a measure of decentralization—is positively related. It should be pointed out at this juncture that these findings disagree

TABLE 7.3 Multiple Regression[a] of Diffusion of Policies on Structural Characteristics

	STANDARDIZED REGRESSION COEFFICIENTS (BETAS)[c]											
	Alcoholism Policy						EEO Policy					
DEPENDENT VARIABLES:[b]	1	2	3	4	5	6[d]	1	2	3	4	5	6[d]
Independent Variables												
Size (Number of employees)				30**						31†		
Formalization:												
Specificity of work rules								-30†		-19**	16	23**
Percentage working under rules		-26**	21									
Specificity of evaluations			25**		18		-11				14	
Professionalization:												
Education of director		-30**	21	-23**		23**						
Education of supervisors							35†	24**	19*	35†		-22*
Median G.S. grade of employees							24**	25**	24**	18	25**	
Complexity:												
Division of labor			20									
Functional differentiation		19					-17*	-12*				
Horizontal differentiation			-19				19*	19*	-28†		26**	
Vertical differentiation	-19					18			22*		21*	
Organizational autonomy:												
Director's influence on allocations		-27**				-13						15

TABLE 7.3 (Continued)

DEPENDENT VARIABLES:b	STANDARDIZED REGRESSION COEFFICIENTS (BETAS)c											
	Alcoholism Policy						EEO Policy					
	1	2	3	4	5	6d	1	2	3	4	5	6d
Centralization:												
Decentralization of hiring decisions	-21*					29**		22**	19**			-26**
Influence of upper management	-36†		-20	-25**		10	-28**					18
Influence of first-line management	16	36†		28†	-21*	-14		-29†		-43†	-26**	
Bureaucratization:												
Percentage supervisors		16	19			-24*			18			-32†
Percentage clerical staff		-33†										
R² (adjusted)	16†	26†	13**	21*	06	12**	31†	42†	38†	54†	32†	28†

*p = .10
**p = .05
†p = .01

a Stepwise mode, n = 65 for all tables.

b As follows:
1. Diffusion of information on policy to supervisors
2. Diffusion of information on policy to employees
3. Hours spent in training on policy
4. Number of topics covered in training on policy
5. Hours spent in learning about policy
6. Administrative emphasis given to policy (high=low emphasis)

c Decimal points omitted.

d Reverse coded items, see (6).

TABLE 7.4 Multiple Regression[a] of Receptivity toward Policies on Structural Characteristics

| | STANDARDIZED REGRESSION COEFFICIENTS (BETAS)[a] | | | | | | | | | | |
| | Alcoholism Policy | | | | EEO Policy | | | | Both Policies | | |
DEPENDENT VARIABLES:[b]	1	2	3	4	1	2	5	6	7	8	9
Independent Variables											
Size (Number of employees)		−16	16		19						
Formalization:											
Specificity of work rules				44†							
Percentage working under rules				−36†		14		13			−33†
Specificity of evaluations	14		−14							−13	
Professionalization:											
Education of director	21	−18			24**		−26*	16	−19		
Education of supervisors	−45†		−27**		20*	−17	19			−35†	−28**
Median G.S. grade of employees				12					−25**	−17	
Complexity:											
Divison of labor				17		15	45**	28**			16
Functional differentiation		33**					36**			15	
Horizontal differentiation		29*					−15				
Vertical differentiation	−15			−24	−11		−41**				
Organizational autonomy:											
Director's influence on allocations		−17	−13			11				27**	16
Centralization:											
Decentralization of hiring decisions	−15	−17	13	−24**	15		−13			−29**	
Influence of upper management	−24*	−11	−15	−18	−34†	−15		−32†	−11	−22**	−17
Influence of first-line supervisors	15	24*	27*	12				−11			

TABLE 7.4 (Continued)

| | STANDARDIZED REGRESSION COEFFICIENTS (BETAS)[a] | | | | | | | | | | |
| | Alcoholism Policy | | | | EEO Policy | | | Both Policies | | | |
DEPENDENT VARIABLES:[b]	1	2	3	4	1	2	5	6	7	8	9
Bureaucratization:											
Percentage supervisors	-19		26*			-23*	-17		-15		
Percentage clerical staff	27**			14	15		-16				
R^2 (adjusted)	14**	05	11*	20†	25†	06	19†	22†	13**	35†	18†

[a] Decimal points omitted.

[b] As follows:
1. Familiarity with policy content
2. Perceived benefit of policy
3. Zealous agreement with alcoholism policy
4. Agreement with medical model of alcoholism
5. Overall agreement with EEO policy
6. Perceived need for policies
7. Ease of administration for policies
8. Agreement with performance emphasis in policies
9. Agreement that supervisors should do own counseling

* $p = .10$

** $p = .05$

† $p = .01$

TABLE 7.5 Multiple Regression[a] of Use of Policies on Structural Characteristics

	STANDARDIZED REGRESSION COEFFICIENTS (BETAS)[c]					
	Alcoholism Policy			EEO Policy		
DEPENDENT VARIABLES:[b]	1	2	3	1	2	3
Independent Variables						
Size (Number of employees)			23*		34†	21*
Formalization:						
Specificity of work rules		−40†				
Percentage working under rules						
Specificity of evaluations						
Professionalization:						
Education of director						
Education of supervisors		−35†		27**		30†
Median G.S. grade of employees			−28**			
Complexity:						
Division of labor						
Functional differentiation						
Horizontal differentiation				26**		
Vertical differentiation					−31**	
Organizational autonomy:						
Director's influence on allocations			31†			
Centralization:						
Decentralization of hiring decisions						23*
Influence of upper management	−26**			−22*		
Influence of first-line supervisors		22*				
Bureaucratization:						
Percentage supervisors						
Percentage clerical staff						
R² (adjusted)	05**	19†	17†	16†	11†	19†

a Stepwise mode, n = 65.

b As follows:
    1. Percentage of supervisors who used policy in past
    2. Number of past uses of policy
    3. Expected future use of policy

c Decimal points omitted.

*p = .10
**p = .05
†p = .01

with the findings in chapter 4 that centralization had slight positive effects on expected use of both policies (table 4.7). There are three possible reasons for this discrepancy in results. One is that the organizational and individual level effects in fact operate in opposite ways, as the findings would suggest. The second is that the relatively isolated and modest (betas of .07 and .09) findings in chapter 4 are random errors, and should be considered equivalent to a zero relationship. Third, it must be stressed that the measures of centralization used in the two sets of analyses came from different informants and levels of authority within the organizations. As shown in table 7.1, the pattern of findings between supervisors and directors did not fully agree. It seems to us that this is the most likely reason for the differences between these findings and those in chapter 4.

Two factors must be remembered in assessing the importance of this difference in findings: (1) There was only one variable for each policy that was positively and modestly associated with centralization in chapter 4, while the results for this chapter are more numerous, substantial, and consistently negative. Furthermore, the findings in chapter 4 apply only to what supervisors expect to do in the future, while findings here apply to what has happened in the past for all stages of implementation. (2) As mentioned earlier in the chapter, lower-level supervisors may not be fully aware of who makes certain decisions in their organizations because the decision-making machinery is not fully visible to them. For this reason, directors may be better informants on the actual patterns of decision making used.[5] However, even with this interpretation the positive effects of centralization only apply to what supervisors intend to do, and not what they have actually done or experienced. On balance, we feel the findings on centralization in this chapter are the ones deserving attention.

The results for the decentralization of hiring decisions are mixed. This scale includes two items assessing decentralization beginning at levels above the installation director and ending with the immediate supervisor of the person to be hired; modal responses are at the director level for one item and are bimodal at the director and immediate supervisor level for the other item. The effects of this variable tend to be negative for the alcoholism policy and the performance emphasis in both policies, but positive for the EEO policy, including expected future use of the EEO policy. Apparently, greater discretion within the installation over personnel matters is unfavorable for implementation of the alcoholism policy, while it is more favorable to implementation of EEO. Also, control over hiring has different effects than does control over other decisions.

The results for formalization are not entirely consistent, but those that are significant tend to support the hypothesis (six out of seven relationships); the one exception is that formalized rules are associated with more agreement with the medical model of alcoholism. Overall, hypothesis 7.3 received considerable support.

Organizational autonomy, as predicted, has some positive effects on receptivity and use. Although there are some nonsignificant negative effects for receptivity toward the alcoholism policy, the crucial provision for that policy of acceptance of the importance of performance assessments is positively associated with organizational autonomy. Autonomy is also significantly and positively related to future use of the alcoholism policy, although it is negatively related to diffusion of information to employees about that policy. There are no significant relationships between organizational autonomy and implementation of the EEO policy. Thus, hypothesis 7.4 received limited support for the alcoholism policy and no support for the EEO policy.

Contrary to hypothesis 7.5, a larger supervisory ratio does not facilitate implementation; effects are largely negative except that a higher concentration of administrators seems to lead to perceptions of greater administrative emphasis on both policies. The effects of a large clerical staff (hypothesis 7.6) are few and mixed. While a large clerical staff seems to inhibit diffusion of information about the alcoholism policy to employees, this factor is also associated with greater familiarity among supervisors with policy content. These findings are most easily explained if we assume that most clerical employees are women and that supervisors assume that females are less likely to need information about help with problem drinking, or are less likely to raise such subjects with women. If the clerical staff is largely composed of younger females, statistics available at that time supported this view, since younger females were reported to engage in less problem drinking than other groups (Cahalan, 1970).

Discussion of Results

While the results obtained did not support all of the hypotheses, those based on past empirical results received considerable support. Since many of these past studies involved only the investigation of two-variable relationships, the repetition of some of these findings here is strong confirmation of the earlier results. The use of multivariate statistics puts the most stringent demands on the data, since other possible associated effects are simultaneously controlled for in the multiple regression equation. This also enabled us to better assess various explanations given to past findings, or relationships that were posited but not tested.

An example of this possibility is presented by the results on size and those on complexity. Some authors (Aiken and Hage, 1971;

Baldridge and Burnham, 1975) have suggested that size is related to innovations because size leads to greater differentiation and specialization—both components of complexity. This interpretation would suggest that multivariate results would show more significant relationships between complexity and the implementation of change than between size and implementation. Out of 29 regressions run, size had 5 significant relationships with various indicators of implementation, while division of labor and horizontal differentiation together produced 6 significant relationships. The data fail to support the notion that size is only an indirect measure for other aspects of structure that directly affect organizational change, since the indicators of differentiation and complexity do not emerge as more important predictors than size when size is controlled. Other interpretations of the size relationships are possible; the simplest is that larger size creates more opportunities for change efforts to be needed and effected. This explanation is supported by the findings on use in table 7.6. Clearly, number of past uses and frequency of future uses could both be affected by how many persons there are in the installation. The more employees, the larger the likelihood of problem drinking and of having minority group members to be promoted, vacancies for which they can be hired, and so forth. Probabilities of certain events simply increase with the greater opportunities for interaction that are provided by more persons in the organization. The same could be true for other kinds of innovations and organizations. Larger social service agencies can generate more proposals for new programs than small agencies, for example. At the same time, some support was obtained of hypothesized relations for complexity that reflects task specialization (division of labor) and horizontal differentiation, especially when based on function. All three of these variables have largely positive effects on implementation. The relations found between vertical differentiation and change were opposite to general predictions for complexity, suggesting that this variable might better be viewed as an aspect of hierarchical control, like centralization of decision making.

The findings for professionalization certainly differ from those of past studies. There are two components of the usual explanations for the relationship between professionalization and innovation or change: the first involves the availability of more information and ideas with which to enhance the possibilities of creativity. This aspect of professionalization would seem to be particularly beneficial to the earliest phases of the change effort: the initiation stage involving problem sensing and problem solving. They are not as relevant to the implementation of a specified solution to an already sensed problem such as these policies represent. The second component of professionalization that may aid change and innovation efforts are the attitudes of professional persons. These attitudes would be specific to the particular profession involved, but would include such things as concern for client welfare, valuing new ways of dealing with unsolved problems of professional concern, valuing experimentation and research, identification with a professional group rather than the organization, et cetera. From such values, it might be assumed that professionalization would lead to a generally greater receptivity toward change, because change at least opens the avenue toward improvement in client services, better solutions, and so on. However, professionals also have the responsibility of seeing that client welfare comes first, and it is possible that some proposed changes might be seen as damaging at least some aspect of client welfare. Thus it should not be expected that just any change will be supported by professionals, but only those they judge as beneficial.[6]

Not many respondents in this study were professionals in the sense that they belonged to a profession with a code of ethics, but the educational measure that we used is similar to that used by the U.S. Census and other studies, where a college education tends to indicate a professional level within the occupation—for example, accountants versus bookkeepers, engineers versus technicians. Thus it was reasonable for us to expect that education among supervisors might be related to some of the values that are presumed to be related to professionalization. We found, on the contrary, that more educated supervisors were skeptical of the alcoholism policy while they supported the EEO policy. Obviously, they discriminated between contents of the two policies, approving of one and not the other. Furthermore, this pattern was repeated for the more behavioral measures, with diffusion to employees and training topics being less favorable for policy implementation where supervisors had more education. This was true even though the more educated supervisors felt that this policy had received more administrative emphasis than did less educated supervisors; thus they apparently knew it was supposed to be implemented. On the other hand, findings for the relation of education to diffusion of the EEO policy are all favorable, supporting the hypothesis. The same pattern holds for actual use, with past uses of the alcoholism policy being less frequent where supervisors are more highly educated, and both the proportion of supervisors who used the EEO policy in the past and the frequency with which they expect to use it in the future positively related to education.

We interpret these findings as indicating that past relationships between professionalization and innovation or change were found because the particular changes were congenial to the professional values of organizational participants. When the changes are not congenial, there is no reason to expect that professionals will be likely to implement (or even initiate or adopt) them. We shall return to this important point later in this chapter when we discuss results for community variables.

Also, we looked at the relationship between professionalization and our measure of attitudes toward change to see whether professionalization seemed to foster positive sentiments toward change in general. Among individual supervisors (n = 634), the correlation was -.01. If we look at the attitude toward change by installation, and run a regression on the same structural measures as are used in the analyses in tables 7.2 through 7.4, we do not find a significant relationship between change attitude and education of supervisors, director, or the median G.S. level of employees. Zero order correlations are also not significant, ranging from -.02 to -.05. Instead, the primary predictors of the attitude toward change are size (beta = -.41, p = .10), and division of labor (beta = .32, p = .10). Thus the usual assumptions that increased education may lead to greater flexibility and receptivity toward change are severely questioned by these data. At least among federal government supervisors, education per se does not lead to such a global set of attitudes. If such attitudes are fostered by education, it must be by some specific kinds of education.

Perhaps the most interesting and important findings are those for centralization and formalization. Even in the specific phases of implementation studied here, decentralization seems to foster change efforts, while formalization and centralization, including more vertical differentiation, tend to inhibit change. These findings are in the tradition of the bulk of the literature on change and innovation, and fit nicely into the kinds of models of organic versus mechanistic structures or styles advanced by Burns and Stalker (1961) and by Hage and Aiken (1967) among others. They do not fit the speculations about "ambidextrous organizations" that have been stressed recently: that successful implementation may require centralization, less complexity, and perhaps even role formalization, while the initiation of change requires decentralization, high complexity, and unformalized roles (Shepard, 1967; Duncan, 1976). When Duncan and the other authors discuss why and how more centralization, less complexity, and more formalization will facilitate implementation of change, it is clear that they are talking about the ways in which the structure impinges directly on the implementation of the particular change under study, and they argue that other parts of the organization may be differently structured without ill effect to the implementation process. In fact, other parts of the organization must be differently structured if additional changes and innovations are going to be initiated, according to their analyses.

The policies under study in this research are not totally pervasive to the supervisors who responded to us, as we have already discussed in chapter 1. But they also might be relevant at almost any time, and their use or implementation cannot be conveniently compartmentalized into a certain time period or a certain segment of the organization. Every employee is potentially affected, and therefore every supervisor is a potential user. Thus we cannot segment off some part of the organization concerned with implementing this change and see whether its structure is different from that of the rest of the installation. The closest we have come to that approach was in chapter 6, where we looked at the roles of the policy coordinators. Again we found that greater role formalization was an inhibiter, rather than a facilitator, of policy implementation. Therefore, the weight of the data from this study extends and supports the findings that more organic organizational structures are more favorable to change efforts than more mechanistic structures, even in the implementation phase and even in the federal government.

The only way that the other speculations can be reconciled with these data would be to argue that these organizations are so mechanistic that some relaxation from their extreme rigidity is needed to get just about anything done. If that is so, then those who argue for more centralization and formalization during the implementation phase of change efforts will have to modify their advice and apply it only to organizations that are not presently mechanistic. That is, they would have to posit a curvilinear relationship between centralization, formalization, et cetera and implementation, with too much or too little of either being inimical to the implementation effort. But we are in the realm of speculation here, since the existing data do not document such a curvilinear relationship.

Data from the only other comparable study of implementation of which we are aware—the so-called Rand study that we have mentioned so frequently before—also disagree with the notion that organizations must be rather formalized and centralized in decision making to implement change and innovation successfully. From both quantitative and qualitative data, the Rand study researchers conclude: "In summary, our data show that a receptive institutional setting is a necessary but not sufficient condition for effective implementation. An implementation strategy that promotes *mutual adaptation* is critical [our italics]" (Berman and McLaughlin, 1975:23). It is clear from other data they report that the strategy of mutual adaptation they identify involved teacher participation in decision making and some flexibility within the organization (Greenwood et al., 1975:65- 66; Berman and Pauly, 1975:65). However, on the issue of "democratic" versus "authoritarian" leadership, their qualitative results are more mixed. They found some cases that involved highly participatory decision making that were very successful, and others that were not. They also found some projects that were implemented in highly authoritarian ways that were successful in terms of outcomes, although accompanied by problems of morale. They report:

> We suspect that the relative effectiveness of "democratic" as opposed to "authoritarian" leadership and gradualism as opposed to blitz may well be determined by the situation. The districts in which heavy-handed management led to successful project implementation were also districts where there was little active interest in educational change. "Forcing" innovation may well have been the most effective way to bring about significant change in such circumstances. (Greenwood et al., 1975:40)

These findings are consistent with much that has been written and researched on situational approaches to leadership (Fiedler, 1967; House, 1971).

What the weight of our results and those of the Rand study clearly indicate is that a more mechanistic structure is not necessarily associated with better implementation of change.[7] Our data indicate that a more organic structure facilitated the implementation of the personnel policies studied; the Rand study results are more mixed. Perhaps as other studies on implementation are carried out, this issue will be further clarified.

The other aspects of structure that were investigated—the supervisory ratio and the clerical ratio—have not been considered in previous studies of change and innovation. They proved to be relatively unimportant and are not apparently predictors of the implementation of change.

ENVIRONMENTAL EFFECTS ON ORGANIZATIONAL CHANGE AND INNOVATION

Because formal organizations are open systems interacting with an environment, their environment has impacts on processes occurring within the organization. In the case of the federal organizations studied, the environment would have its major effects through characteristics on the work force employed, and through a general climate of attitudes and values in which workers within the organization live.[8] Zaltman et al. (1973:110) suggest two ways that environments can affect internal organizational change: (1) by creating a situation of stress or pressure to which the organization must respond, or (2) by the way in which the carrying out of the change is viewed in terms of environmental norms.

Hypotheses

The various characteristics of the surrounding communities that have already been discussed were chosen from data available from the U.S. Census as variables most likely to affect the implementation of these particular personnel policies. Berelson and Steiner (1964) reviewed various studies suggesting that innovation and change are more likely to be successful among persons who are relatively younger and of higher social status. They also noted that the larger the cultural base, the more there is stimulus for change and innovation, and found that cities were more likely sites for innovation than rural areas. It is easy to extrapolate these findings to apply to communities, in general, and to apply the logic behind them to the implementation of the personnel policies studied, in particular.

Larger communities—cities—are likely to have more resources in terms of expertise, funding, and a mixture of viewpoints and ideas. A recent theory on urbanism (Fischer, 1975) has been summarized: "Presumably the concentration of diverse people into dense settlements is conducive to a cross-fertilization of ideas, to an awareness of and tolerance of diverse values and lifestyles, and thus to innovation and unconventionality" (Glenn and Hill, 1977:38). Also, larger communities may exhibit to a greater degree the orientations that Parsons (1951) has identified with modern societies: universalism, achievement orientation, affectively neutral relations (relative impersonality), and individualistic orientations. All of these values tend to favor the implementation of these personnel policies, which are based on rather impersonal and highly universalistic prescriptions. Both policies are intended to apply to all employees and to eliminate considerations other than job performance in the handling of drinking problems and/or the hiring and promotion of personnel. Thus the general norms of larger communities may favor the implementation of these policies.

Turning to the other question of environmental pressures for change, we also could expect urban communities to create more pressure for implementation of the alcoholism policy, since Cahalan (1970) found more drinking problems in cities than in rural areas. Also, cities tend to have larger proportions of blacks and other minority groups within their population; this could create similar pressures for implementation of the EEO policy. We therefore hypothesize:

7.7. Installations located in larger communities with higher population densities are more likely than other installations to implement these policies.

According to Berelson and Steiner (1964), younger and higher status populations are expected to favor change generally. The young are expected to have fewer vested interests, and to be psychologically more flexible and less afraid of change than older persons. Stouffer (1955) found that younger persons were more tolerant of political deviance than their elders. Since alcoholism is deviant behavior, younger supervisors may be more tolerant of problem drinking and more inclined and willing to help alcoholics through a formalized policy. Younger supervisors might also be expected to be more favorable to the EEO policy, since much of the push for civil rights has come recently, and younger generations of college students, in particular, have been involved in working for civil rights for women and blacks and other minorities.

In this society, social status or class is often measured by the so-called socioeconomic characteristics of income, education, and occupation. Because both high income and greater education are usual measures of higher social status, we would therefore expect these factors to be favorable to implementation of these policies. More educated persons are likely to have more complex perceptual sets and attitudes that permit them to discriminate better between various possible changes, and to favor those that are rational for their self-interest or for the community welfare. In a longitudinal study, Trent and Craise (1967) showed that young persons who had attended college were more open and flexible than they had been in high school, while young persons who went to work instead of college became less tolerant and open after four years. Also, Kelman and Barclay (1963) have argued that authoritarianism is a function of an individual's psychological capacity and his social opportunities; persons of lower social class move in relatively narrow circles and a limited environment and are accordingly more likely to develop relatively simplistic cognitive styles, characterized by a lack of tolerance for ambiguity, closed-mindedness, prejudice, and so on. Furthermore, in their study of children, Kutner and Gordon (1964) produced suggestive evidence that changes in cognitive styles are accompanied by changes in prejudice. Finally, Dohrenwend and Chin-Shong (1967) found that higher-status groups tended to be more tolerant of mental deviation than lower-status groups.

In addition, more prosperous communities are usually expected to be better at innovation because they can afford it. Many of the studies that have been done have been of social service and health programs that require substantial financial resources (Aiken and Hage, 1971; Mytinger, 1967; Mohr, 1969). Of course, more prosperous communities are more likely to have these resources. While the implementation of these policies does not involve any direct expenditure of monies by the communities in which the installations are located, their implementation is likely to be better carried out if the community has certain relevant resources upon which the federal installation may draw for help in implementing the policies. Such resources would include agencies dealing with and facilities for treatment of alcoholism, and agencies dealing with blacks and members of other minorities who could be located for training programs and/or for employment.

Another indicator of social class is occupation. In the United States, professional and managerial jobs are relatively high in status, since they involve either rather independent work that uses high levels of skills and talents, usually accompanied by a college degree, or the supervision and direction of other persons in a work setting.[9] Extending the past discussion of the advantages of status to the occupational sphere, we might also expect persons in such occupations to be relatively favorable to the alcoholism and EEO policies, since these are changes dealing with deviant and disadvantaged groups.

If we assume that the supervisors working in federal installations are likely to be affected by the norms of the surrounding community, in which they are likely to live, it is reasonable to advance the following hypotheses:

7.8. Installations in communities with younger, more prosperous, and more educated populations are more likely than other installations to implement these policies.

7.9. Installations in communities with high proportions of professional and managerial workers are more likely than other installations to implement these policies.

The question of environmental pressures is especially relevant to the relationship between demographics and implementation of the EEO policy. Installations in communities with higher proportions of minority members—notably blacks and women[10]—are likely to experience greater pressures toward equal employment. In such communities, active groups representing minority interests are likely to be more numerous, and these groups would probably watch government agencies rather closely to monitor their implementation of the EEO policy. Also, the presence of a relatively large proportion of unemployed persons within a community may lead to pressures toward implementation of the EEO policy, since the unemployment rates for blacks and other minorities have been higher than that for whites for some time.

7.10. Installations located in communities with high proportions of minority group members (e.g., blacks, or women) or unemployed persons are more likely than other installations to implement the EEO policy.

On the other hand, when the issue of community norms is considered, other community characteristics become relevant to the EEO policy. American blue-collar workers were usually considered to be resistant to various liberalizing social trends within the country in recent years. The "hard hat" worker was seen as opposing various measures intended to increase racial equality, such as busing. The proportion of the labor force employed in manufacturing may reflect this element of relative conservatism within community norms. Also, Cahalan (1970) found a greater incidence of drinking problems among relatively lower-class working men. This suggests that community norms in a community with a high component of manufacturing and blue-collar jobs may favor the alcoholism policy and be resistant to the EEO policy.

Immigrant groups have also been considered to be relatively conservative, especially in matters of racial equality, where they may perceive that disadvantaged groups are competing with them in the marketplace. The Census counts persons who are foreign-born and those who have foreign-born parents as foreign stock. Communities with high proportions of foreign stock may also have relatively conservative attitudes that are not supportive of EEO efforts. To the degree that the more recently arrived groups are disadvantaged in the social and economic structure, they might also be expected to have a greater incidence of alcoholism. [11]

7.11. Installations in communities with high proportions of workers employed in manufacturing and high proportions of persons of foreign stock are less likely to implement the EEO policy and more likely to implement the alcoholism policy than other installations.

The larger the proportion of government workers within a community, the more likely that the community will be embued with consciousness toward government regulations, since employees frequently deal with these regulations in their day-to-day activities, and civil service regulations are all-pervasive in government employment generally. Thus it might be expected that communities with higher proportions of government employees would be more likely to implement both policies as part of their general tendencies to conform to regulations promulgated by government units.

✓   **7.12.** Installations in communities with high proportions of government workers will be more likely than other installations to implement these policies.

Results

As in the structural analyses, stepwise multiple regression was employed to investigate relationships between environmental characteristics and policy implementation. This technique would enable us to control simultaneously for effects from all of the environmental variables while locating those environmental features that were most closely associated with the various phases of implementation. These results are presented in tables 7.6 to 7.8.

Results for those variables that measure whether or not the community is urban or rural do not tend to support the hypothesis. More often than not, community population (or population density) is negatively associated with policy implementation. However, if we consider only the statistically significant relationships, three are positive and two are negative. Community population is positively associated with the administrative emphasis given to the EEO policy and to perceived benefit of the EEO policy. Population density is positively related to administrative emphasis on the alcoholism policy. These results suggest some greater degree of bureaucratic ethos within installations in urban communities, but they also suggest more projected benefit for the EEO policy in urban areas. We might expect this is because of greater expected need within these communities, but that variable is not significantly related to the urban-rural dimension of these communities. Both negative relationships are with diffusion of information of the two policies to supervisors. Apparently, installations in larger communities are poorer in disseminating information, suggesting inactive or overloaded communication channels. Overloaded communication channels would fit with a bureaucratic ethos, and lack of information—if considered indicative of a sort of alienation and extreme impersonality—could also be seen as fitting a trend toward bureaucratization and Parsons's orientations toward modern society.

The effects of the two socioeconomic variables lend mixed support to the hypothesis, with income tending to be favorable to implementation, while education is negatively associated with implementation. Concerning diffusion of the policies, higher income within a community is positively associated with several variables, but only significantly with number of topics covered in training of the EEO policy. Its relationship with administrative emphasis given to the EEO policy is negative. The effects of education are also negative for two aspects of diffusion of the alcoholism policy:

diffusion of information to employees and amount of time supervisors spent learning about the policy.

While the effects of education on attitudes toward both policies tend to be negative, two of these relationships cannot be seen as unfavorable to implementation because the attitudes they represent are not in accord with policy provisions. The third dependent variable in table 7.7 is overzealous agreement with the alcoholism policy, which includes items suggesting attempts to deal with alcoholism out of the job setting and before it has affected job performance. The ninth is agreement with the statement that supervisors should do their own counseling for both policies, while policy provisions set up specific functionaries—the alcoholism coordinator and EEO counselor—to talk to employees about problems that may occur. However, it is clear that supervisors from installations in more educated communities are more skeptical than other supervisors about the benefits of the EEO policy.

When it comes to use of the policies, results are again mixed. While the relationships are positive between income and expected use of both policies, the relationship between education and number of past uses of the alcoholism policy is negative and very substantial in magnitude, accounting for over 20 percent of the variance in number of actual policy uses.

However, the results for the third indicator of social class are more consistently in the hypothesized direction. Clearly a larger proportion of professional and managerial workers in the community is a circumstance favorable to diffusion of the alcoholism policy, and perhaps to receptivity toward these policies, since there are significant and positive relations with familiarity and agreement with the performance emphasis in both policies. Also, there is a very substantial and positive relation between this indicator of community class structure and the number of actual uses of the alcoholism policy.

Overall, we must conclude that there is only very limited support for the hypothesis that installations in higher-income communities are more likely to implement the policies. There is more substantial, if still somewhat mixed, evidence against the hypothesis for the effects of education, since the relationships between education and implementation are predominantly negative. However, the hypothesis is much better supported by the occupational indicators of social class, suggesting that these may be better predictors of change behaviors than either education or income. Particularly when the pattern of findings for this variable are considered relative to those for education, we must conclude that social class may indeed have a positive effect on change efforts, but that the effects of education alone, while controlling for professional or managerial occupation, are negatively rather than positively related to implementation. Wil-

TABLE 7.6 Multiple Regression[a] of Diffusion of Policies on Environmental Characteristics

	STANDARDIZED REGRESSION COEFFICIENTS (BETAS)[c]											
	Alcoholism Policy						*EEO Policy*					
DEPENDENT VARIABLES:[b]	1	2	3	4	5	6	1	2	3	4	5	6
Independent Variables												
Urban or rural:												
Community population	−21*					23*	−24*	−17				39†
Population density				17						07		
County (not a city with population ≥ 25,000)												
Socioeconomic Characteristics:												
Median family income	18	20*					16		11	32**		
Median years of education		−28**	−27**	−22*	−29*		08		−19	−29**		
Median age		−24**				−18						−26**
Minority profile:												
Percentage foreign stock				11	−18							
Percentage black							09		25*	16		−06
Percentage female												
Employment Base												
Percentage employed in manufacturing		17	−32**					−26*	−25	−32**		
Percentage employed in government		14	−36**	−20				−32**	−33**	−23		08

TABLE 7.6 (Continued)

| Dependent Variables[b] | Standardized Regression Coefficients (Betas)[c] | | | | | | | | | | | |
| | Alcoholism Policy | | | | | | EEO Policy | | | | | |
	1	2	3	4	5	6	1	2	3	4	5	6
Employment Base (Continued)												
Percentage employed in professional, managerial occupations	38**	59†		16	35**							
Percentage unemployed	29*											
R^2 (adjusted)	12**	23†	11**	09*	12**	05	02	05	08*	14**	—d	16**

[a]Stepwise mode, n = 71.

[b]As follows:
1. Diffusion of information on policy to supervisors
2. Diffusion of information on policy to employees
3. Hours spent in training on policy
4. Number of topics covered in training on policy
5. Hours spent in learning about policy
6. Administrative emphasis given to policy

[c]Decimal points omitted.

[d]Nothing in equation was significant.

* $p = .10$

** $p = .05$

† $p = .01$

TABLE 7.7 Multiple Regression[a] of Receptivity Toward Policies on Environmental Characteristics

| | STANDARDIZED REGRESSION COEFFICIENTS (BETAS)[c] | | | | | | | | | | |
| | Alcoholism Policy | | | | EEO Policy | | | Both Policies | | | |
DEPENDENT VARIABLES:[b]	1	2	3	4	1	2	5	6	7	8	9
Independent Variables											
Urban or rural:											
Community population	−17		−14		−18	22*					
Population density											
County (not a city with population ≥25,000)											
Socioeconomic characteristics:											
Median family income											34**
Median years of education			−22			−25*			−16		−31**
Median age					−09			−12		16	18
Minority profile:											
Percentage foreign stock	19		14		25*		27**		23*		
Percentage black				35†		−19					
Percentage female											
Employment base:											
Percentage employed in manufacturing				10	−29*	25*	21			21	
Percentage employed in government	−12		−14		−36**		17	−27**	−15		

TABLE 7.7 (Continued)

	STANDARDIZED REGRESSION COEFFICIENTS (BETAS)[c]										
	Alcoholism Policy				EEO Policy				Both Policies		
DEPENDENT VARIABLES:[b]	1	2	3	4	1	2	5	6	7	8	9
Employment Base (Continued)											
Percentage in professional, managerial occupations	32**		30**					−18		28*	12
Percentage unemployed	27*									30*	
R² (adjusted)	05	—[d]	03	13†	04*	11*	06	08**	08*	06	10**

[a] Stepwise mode, n = 71

[b] As follows:
1. Familiarity with policy content
2. Perceived benefit of policy
3. Zealous agreement with alcoholism policy
4. Agreement with medical model of alcoholism
5. Overall agreement with EEO policy
6. Perceived need for policies
7. Ease of administration of policies
8. Agreement with performance emphasis in policies
9. Agreement that supervisors should do own counseling

[c] Decimal points omitted.

[d] Nothing in equation is significant.

* p = .10
** p = .05
† p = .01

TABLE 7.8 Multiple Regression[a] of Use of Policies on Environmental Characteristics

| | STANDARDIZED REGRESSION COEFFICIENTS (BETAS)[c] | | | | | |
| | Alcoholism Policy | | | EEO Policy | | |
DEPENDENT VARIABLES:[b]	1	2	3	1	2	3
Independent Variables						
Urban or rural:						
Community population						
Population density						
County (not city with population ⩾25,000)						
Socioeconomic characteristics:						
Median family income		22*				24*
Median years of education		−46†				
Median age						
Minority profile:						
Percentage foreign stock				20*		37†
Percentage black						
Percentage female						
Employment Base:						
Percentage employed in manufacturing						
Percentage employed in government						
Percentage employed in professional, managerial occupations		48†				
Percentage unemployed					28**	
R^2 (adjusted)	—d	18†	03*	03*	06**	11†

[a]Stepwise mode, n = 71.

[b]As follows:
1. Percentage of supervisors who used policy
2. Number of past uses of policy
3. Expected future use of policy

[c]Decimal points omitted.

[d]Nothing in equation was significant.

*p = .10

**p = .05

†p = .01

son (1966) has commented that studies of community variables and the adoption of changes have indicated that communities that favor innovations are least likely to adopt them, presumably because these higher-class communities have difficulty marshaling the political support needed (Banfield and Wilson, 1963; Hawley, 1963; Pinard, 1963). Perhaps, as we suggested in chapter 5, higher levels of professionalization and education present mixed prospects for innovation. The generally higher levels of autonomy that are part of the expectations of more educated and professional workers may tend to increase resistance to change, especially to externally imposed change, and also prevent the successful use of power and influence to bring about the change. This circumstance is only likely to be reversed when the welfare of the educated and professional groups is seen as importantly enhanced by the change (Becker and Geer, 1960); values in the latent social roles defined by class, education, and occupation will then operate to support the change.

While the signs of coefficients for median age are mixed, the significant relationships are confined to table 7.6, where the effects on diffusion are predominantly negative—supporting the prediction that younger communities encourage implementation of change. The one exception is diffusion of information on the alcoholism policy to employees, which was greater in older communities. Otherwise, hours spent in training for the alcoholism policy and topics covered in training on both policies were greater for installations in younger communities.

There is only one relationship between diffusion and variables relating to minority composition of the community. Installations in communities with higher proportions of blacks have spent more hours in supervisory training on the EEO policy. This seems to have paid off, for there is also a positive relationship between the proportion of blacks in the community and supervisory familiarity with the provisions of the EEO policy (table 7.7).

Relative to actual policy use, the percentage of blacks is significantly and positively related to two aspects of use: the proportion of supervisors who have used the policy in the past and the frequency of expected use in the future. The proportion of females in the population failed to have any significant impacts in implementation of either policy, perhaps because in any community the proportion of females is sufficient to create pressures toward implementation of EEO. In summary, there is some support for the hypothesis that the proportion of blacks would be related to implementation of EEO, since there are significant relationships on at least one variable for every stage of the implementation process.

The hypothesized negative relationships between the proportion in manufacturing and the EEO policy are certainly supported for diffusion of the EEO policy and for familiarity with its content. Surprisingly, however, supervisors in such installations tended to rate the possible benefits of the EEO policy higher than other supervisors. This suggests that the resistance to implementation in these installations is coming not necessarily from these supervisors but perhaps from upper management, since supervisors have received so little information about the policy and the diffusion of information is a task of top management. Only one significant relationship was found between this variable and implementation of the alcoholism policy, and this relationship again indicates less diffusion of information in installations in communities with high concentrations of manufacturing. Thus the hypothesis is supported only for diffusion efforts and only for the EEO policy. In the attitudinal aspects of implementation (table 7.7), the percentage of foreign stock is an important positive influence, associated with more agreement with the medical model of alcoholism, overall agreement with the EEO policy, and a perception of relative ease in administering both policies. The results for foreign stock clearly do not support the hypothesis for the EEO policy since they are opposite to the prediction, and those for the alcoholism policy are too slight to consider the data more than suggestively supportive.

The hypothesis concerning the proportion of government employees within the community is resoundingly rejected by the data. Almost all of the relationships obtained are negative, some at quite substantial levels of association. There are negative relations with training hours for both policies, and with diffusion of information to employees for the EEO policy. There are also substantial negative relations with familiarity with the EEO policy, and with the perceived need for both policies. Clearly, living in a community with many other government employees does not necessarily lead upper management or other supervisors to support policies promulgated by the federal government. With upper management failing to inform them, supervisors are, in turn, skeptical of the need for the policies, which is not surprising. Documenting the need for the policies should be a central task of supervisory training, which has obviously been neglected in these communities. The only explanation of these findings that can be suggested is that the norms in such communities favor general resistance to their bureaucracy and its directives.

Discussion

The patterning of the results cannot be said to provide overwhelming support for hypotheses, whether based on the past literature on change and innovation or based on our reasoning relating policy content to past findings in social psychology. While occasional relationships between community characteristics and implementation processes are found, most of the relationships are not consistent enough across policies or stages of implementation to form a clear pattern of support. The strongest predictor variables were those that measured the bases of employment within the community, especially those related to government employment and either professional or managerial employment.

It is also interesting to note that the relationships found account for more of the variance in implementation of the alcoholism policy than of the EEO policy, while the opposite held true for findings between organizational structure and implementation of the two policies. Apparently, factors external to the organization are somewhat more important for implementation of the alcoholism policy than they are for implementation of EEO.

Of the two processes that were advanced as possible ways in which such community characteristics could affect implementation of the policies within these federal installations, the normative effects seem to be strongest from the data presented. There is only slight evidence of community demand affecting implementation, and this seems to be largely confined to the EEO policy, with several significant relationships between the proportion of blacks in the community and some aspects of EEO implementation, and another relationship between community population and perceived benefit of that policy.

Regional Differences

Because of the apparent importance of normative factors in accounting for differential implementation of the policies, we decided that it might be appropriate to carry the assessment of possible environmental effects one step further and try to assess whether any effects of the region in which the installation was located could be detected. All of the installations studied were located in the northeastern United States, but even within that region, norms are not necessarily homogeneous over such controversial issues as problem drinking and minority rights. We did not have any ready data available to measure characteristics of the regions, but we could assess whether or not implementation varied significantly between regions. Table 7.9 presents the results of such analyses on the data from supervisors.

The findings show much greater differences between regions in implementation of the alcoholism policy than in implementation of EEO. Furthermore, the results for the alcoholism policy are amazingly consistent: region 2 is uniformly high on all measures of implementation of this policy, while region 1 is low, and region 3

TABLE 7.9 Differences by Region in Supervisory Implementation of Policies

MEASURES OF IMPLEMENTATION	MEANS BY REGION			MEAN OVERALL	p*
	1	*2*	*3*		
	n = 248	*n = 166*	*n = 237*		
Alcoholism Policy:					
Diffusion to supervisors	3.63	4.01	3.67	3.74	n.s.
Diffusion to employees	3.89	4.31	3.50	3.84	.007
Training hours	0.78	3.84	0.82	1.59	.000
Training topics	1.30	1.67	0.68	1.17	.000
Learning hours	3.87	5.13	4.17	4.30	n.s.
Administrative emphasis[a]	−0.05	0.45	−0.30	−0.01	.036
Awareness of union position	0.37	0.33	0.32	0.34	n.s.
Familiarity[a]	0.06	0.09	−0.12	0.00	.017
Agreement with medical model[a]	0.12	0.06	−0.16	0.00	.001
Zealous agreement[a]	0.02	0.09	−0.09	0.00	.070
Perceived benefit[a]	0.07	0.06	−0.11	0.00	.033
Whether have used in past	0.12	0.15	0.08	0.11	.077
Number of past uses	0.26	0.37	0.16	0.25	n.s.
Expected future use	1.63	1.92	1.50	1.66	.001
Both Policies:					
Agreement with performance emphasis[a]	0.05	0.01	−0.06	0.00	n.s.
Agree do own counseling[a]	0.00	0.08	−0.06	0.00	n.s.
Need for policies[a]	−0.04	0.07	0.03	0.02	n.s.
Ease of administration[a]	0.13	0.00	−0.09	0.02	.002
EEO Policy:					
Diffusion to supervisors	6.29	6.80	6.96	6.67	.035
Diffusion to employees	6.14	6.21	6.50	6.29	n.s.
Training hours	9.59	12.43	11.99	11.24	n.s.
Training topics	3.35	4.22	3.54	3.65	.041
Learning hours	21.71	39.05	35.09	31.11	.060
Administrative emphasis[a]	−0.37	0.03	0.38	0.00	.014
Awareness of union position	0.57	0.49	0.60	0.56	.063
Familiarity	−0.05	−0.03	0.09	0.00	n.s.
Overall agreement	0.08	0.13	0.04	0.08	n.s.
Perceived benefit[a]	0.09	−0.02	−0.07	0.00	n.s.
Whether have used in past	0.54	0.63	0.61	0.59	n.s.
Number of past uses	9.12	3.24	8.65	7.39	n.s.
Expected future use	4.10	4.38	4.53	4.33	.077

n.s. = not significant.

* As determined by one-way analyses of variance.

[a] Standardized score with mean = 0.00.

usually falls into an intermediate position. More diffusion is accompanied by more training, more administrative emphasis, more agreement, more perceived benefit and ease of administration, and more past and future use of the alcoholism policy in region 2.

Results for the EEO policy, however, have a different configuration. First of all, the results do not form such a coherent pattern, nor are the significant differences as numerous for this policy. In general, region 3 is high on implementation of this policy, with two exceptions: training topics and ease of administration, on which it is lowest. Region 2 has the moderate position on this policy, while region 1 is again least implementing; perhaps this is why the supervisors from that region think the policies are easy to administer!

Now that we have found regional differences, the question is whether or not we are justified in ascribing them to differing cultural values between the regions or whether they would be better explained by other factors. The most obvious alternative explanation of the findings is that regions are administered by different persons and with different effectiveness. We therefore also looked at data we had collected on the relationships that directors of these installations had with their superiors. If these relations differed significantly by region, we might ascribe the regional differences that we found to administrative practices within the regions. Analyses similar to those in table 7.7 were therefore performed on data obtained from installation directors on the following variables: how often they had regularly scheduled meetings with their superiors, how often they had personal contact with their superiors, whether they had received their information on the policies from Washington headquarters, whether they had received information on the policies from their regional offices, and the administrative emphasis they felt each policy had received. Only one of these variables differed significantly by region; this was the frequency of personal contacts between the director and his superiors, which was much lower in region 2 than in the other regions. This finding is too isolated to put much weight upon in interpreting the many differences found in implementation by region. If it is to be interpreted in connection with the implementation data, it suggests that personal contacts between high-level federal managers is damaging to implementation of the alcoholism policy. There certainly was no evidence to support the notion that more effective regional administration accounted for the differences in implementation given in table 7.9.

We thus return to the importance of prevailing cultural norms and values as a possible explanation for the regional differences found, recognizing that this explanation must remain tentative because the connection between the installation members and community (or regional) values per se has been only inferred, not demonstrated.

Summary and Conclusions

These results reveal two major inhibitors to implementation of the alcoholism policy within installations: higher educational levels within the supervisory work force and a strong centralized control structure within the installation, where the director and the supervisors reporting directly to him or her tend to make most of the decisions. Where control is decentralized and first-line supervisors have more influence in decision making, there was more diffusion and familiarity with policy content, and supervisors expected to use the policy more frequently in the future than at other installations. On the other hand, where upper management was more influential, the installation had performed less diffusion of policy information, supervisors were less familiar with policy provisions and less likely to agree with the medical model of alcoholism, they saw the policy as less beneficial than supervisors at other installations, and, not surprisingly, they had actually used the policy less.

Where supervisors were highly educated as compared with other installations, there was less diffusion of information of the alcoholism policy to employees, fewer topics were covered in supervisory training, and supervisors perceived administrative emphasis on the policy to be low. Supervisors in such installations were also low on familiarity with the policy, on agreement that the policy should concentrate on job performance, and on number of past uses of the policy.

A third negative predictor of implementation of the alcoholism policy was formalization. This variable had negative effects on diffusion to employees, agreement with the medical model, and number of past uses of the policy. There were only scattered positive effects of structural variables on implementation of the alcoholism policy. Larger installations tended to cover more topics in training programs, and supervisors in them tended to expect more future use of the policy. Also, greater complexity in terms of functionally and more differentiated structures had a positive effect on the perceived benefits of this policy.

The findings for the EEO policy were generally similar, with the major exception that higher education among supervisors was positively associated with implementation for this policy. Education among supervisors was positively related to five out of six measures of diffusion, reflecting more diffusion and training and more perceived administrative emphasis for this policy among more educated supervisors. The greater efforts expended to diffuse information about this policy resulted in greater familiarity with policy provisions, but not necessarily with policy-consonant attitudes. Most important, higher education of supervisors was associated with more policy use in the past and more expected policy use in the future.

As was the case for the alcoholism policy, the effects of centralization were negative for implementation of the EEO policy, but for this policy decentralization tended not to be a significant predictor. This suggests that line supervisors do not have to feel personally influential to implement the EEO policy, although a domineering upper management may inhibit policy use. Interestingly, the decentralization of hiring decisions, specifically, had a positive effect on diffusion of the EEO policy and also on its expected future use. Formalization was a much less important predictor for the EEO policy, being significantly related only to administrative emphasis, with more formalization being associated with less emphasis.

Again, except for the findings on education, positive relationships between structural features and implementation were sparse. Only size of the installation was positively related, and then only to topics covered in training, number of past uses, and frequency of expected future use.

Overall, the results of the structural variables were more negative than positive. We seem to have uncovered more barriers to implementation than factors that promote it. The organizational structure that is unfavorable to the implementation of change is one that is centralized and formalized. This finding agrees with findings of other research on earlier phases of the change process and throws much doubt on speculations that the implementation of change requires different structural arrangements than the initiation or adoption of change. Organic, rather than mechanistic, structural arrangements appear to facilitate a wide variety of organizational changes and innovations.

Some characteristics of the supervisory work force are also important for implementation efforts; in this study, the education of supervisors was an important predictor of the implementation of both policies. But the effects of this variable were different for the two policies, suggesting that the content of a change may interact with characteristics of a work force to produce either a climate favorable to the change or one that is unfavorable to the change. These data indicated that installations with more educated supervisors were more likely to implement the EEO policy and less likely to implement the alcoholism policy than other installations. Somehow, even though their attitudes were not necessarily consonant, educated supervisors had been persuaded to implement the EEO policy. We suspect this is because this policy had been given more teeth by Congress and the Civil Service Commission. This is reflected in generally higher perceptions of administrative emphasis for this policy than for the alcoholism policy. On the other hand, such educated supervisors are resistant to the alcoholism policy, probably because they are not convinced that their superiors mean business; they have, after all, learned little about the policy in diffusion efforts, and perceive the policy as receiving little administrative emphasis. Thus we can only conclude that upper management in the installations, or perhaps even management at higher levels, does not recognize the same need for this policy when installations have more educated supervisors. We suspect this is because upper management is less likely to accept policy provisions as appropriate for such workers, or tends to believe that the policy is less needed where educational levels are high.[12] Installations with higher levels of education among supervisors also have more educated directors and higher-status nonsupervisory employees (Beyer and Trice, 1976).

The importance of social class as a factor in influencing the process of implementing change is underlined by findings on the environment, as well as by the strong relationships uncovered between supervisory education and implementation. The usual indicators of social class are education, income, and occupation. For the analyses just summarized—those dealing with internal organizational features—education was the important predictor of implementation. For the analyses that assessed factors external to the organization, namely community characteristics, the strongest predictors of implementation were occupational variables. When education had a significant effect in the environmental analyses, it was again a negative influence. But the effects of a higher preponderance of higher-status occupations within the community were consistently positive. Income was not a consistent predictor, although it was related to future use of both policies, suggesting that relative community affluence may increase anticipated use. Another occupational variable, the proportion of the labor force working in government units, was negatively related to implementation.

How can these findings be reconciled or explained? Perhaps occupational status is a more powerful segregator along community lines than is either education or income. The relative importance of professional and managerial occupations in explaining these findings rather than education or income suggests that the communities where these policies were most implemented may have had rather homogeneous populations with heavy concentrations of higher-status occupations. Such a description best fits modern suburbia.

Looking at the pattern of the other environmental findings, this interpretation receives some support. The only other characteristics of communities that are related to implementation of the alcoholism policy are size of community, population density, age, and percentage unemployed. The communities where implementation is greater are smaller, denser, younger, and tend to have some unemployment.

This configuration may well describe some of the close-in suburban communities.

For the EEO policy, other socioeconomic factors take precedence. The proportion of foreign stock and especially the proportion of blacks were higher in communities where implementation was greater. Although results were somewhat mixed, these tended to be the larger and younger communities, with relatively high incomes yet little manufacturing. Such a configuration best describes some of the larger cities in the East.

From these findings, we can only conclude that the influence of social-class factors on the implementation of change efforts is highly dependent on the content of the change involved. It is likely that both perceptions of need or demand for the change as well as community norms and values relating to the change will have effects on the success of change efforts within organizations.

8. Federal Sector Unions: Pressures Toward Conformity

THUS FAR, the discussion and analyses presented have focused on the federal installations in our sample as the organizational systems involved in implementing the policies under study. In the last chapter, we also assessed the effects of the environment on implementing behaviors and attitudes within the installations. Now we turn to another aspect of the environment and move to another level of analysis: that of interorganizational relations.

"Unions are organizations designed to protect and enhance the social and economic welfare of their members" (Tannenbaum, 1965:710). As such, unions are bound to be concerned about the issues posed by the initiation and implementation of personnel policies like the alcoholism and EEO policies. But unions have unique aspects as organizations, most notably their dependency on the employing organizations[1] and the conflictual nature of their relations with the employing organization (Tannenbaum, 1965:710). Thus recent treatments of union-management relations have adopted an interorganization perspective in which the *relations* between the union and the employing organization are the focus of analysis, rather than either organization in and of itself (Kochan, 1975; Schmidt and Kochan, 1977). We have adopted a similar viewpoint in our analysis, being concerned to assess the possible effects that relations between the federal installations in our sample and the unions that represented their employees might have on the implementing behaviors and attitudes going on within the installation.

Despite the recent attention given by the cited authors to unions, and despite some literature on unions as organizations, any reader of most textbooks on organizations or organizational behavior will have difficulty finding a systematic consideration of unions. Few empirical studies of work organizations include variables concerned with the union, despite the recent emphasis on the systems approach and multivariate modeling. This omission is even more glaring in the case of the studies of change and innovation in organizations; a quick survey of several of the most important books in the field failed to uncover even one mention of unions in their indexes (Burns and Stalker, 1961: Bennis, 1966; Hage and Aiken, 1970; Rogers and Shoemaker, 1971; Zaltman et al., 1973; Gross et al., 1971; Zaltman and Duncan, 1977). This study thus is breaking new ground, and so we will admit in advance that our approach here is exploratory. No specific formal hypotheses will be advanced, although the previous literature and our knowledge of the policies, unions, and work organizations will lead to some specific questions.

UNIONS IN FEDERAL WORK ORGANIZATIONS

Federal sector unions are a relatively recent phenomena. Although a few isolated cases of federal employee unions occurred before the early 1960s—for example, in the TVA during the late 1930s (Wykstra and Stevens, 1970)—it was not until Executive Order No. 10988 in 1963 that systemwide acceptance of employee unions for nonsupervisory employees (except for military personnel, FBI, CIA, and NSA employees) was legitimated. This was later expanded by Executive Order No. 11491, signed in 1969 (Wykstra and Stevens, 1970; Naumoff, 1971). Recently, federal sector unions, along with other public sector unions, have grown dramatically. For thousands of federal managers the presence of a union is a relatively new experience.

As of November 1974, 984,000 federal employees (49 percent of the eligible work force) were in bargaining units covered by union agreements. Federal white-collar employees were becoming unionized at a rapid rate: the proportion of eligible white-collar employees in units covered by union agreements has risen from 35 percent in 1970 to 48 percent in 1974. With increasing clamor for reduction in the size of the federal bureaucracy, job security of federal employees could come into jeopardy. It therefore appears unlikely that the growth of federal unions will level off in the near future; their continual rapid growth is more likely.

Federal employee unions are more limited in the scope of their powers than are private sector unions. Under the conditions of the various executive orders, federal employee unions are not allowed to strike. Additionally, they cannot bargain over wage levels in the G.S.

(white-collar) pay structure. Blue-collar employees, however, have a more localized wage structure and the union can negotiate for participation in management wage surveys that are used in determining these wage structures. Also, there are strong "management rights" provisions that further limit the scope of bargaining. Thus, negotiated grievance and arbitration procedures may be superseded by special appeal mechanisms written into federal personnel policies and programs (Smith, 1975).

A further limitation to union power in the federal sector is the heterogeneity of the federal government. The complex of occupations, departmental and agency identifications, et cetera have led to a situation in which no one union has been able to assume a dominant position across the entire federal sector. In fact, in only 36 of 200 union contracts in the federal government does a single union have an agencywide contract. In November of 1974, 103 separate national unions were recognized by the federal government. Of these, only eight had 1 percent or more of the federal employees covered by union contracts under their jurisdiction; and only the American Federation of Government Employees had over 5 percent: in this instance, 27 percent (U.S. Civil Service Commission, 1974).

Finally, the existence and functions of the civil service system, as administered by the Civil Service Commission, absorb many of the powers reserved to unions in the private sector. CSC regulations are paramount in determining salary structures, job qualifications, promotion procedures, and a host of other matters that form the core of traditional union concern with private employing organizations.

Thus the power relations between the employing organization and the union are very asymmetrical in the case of federal sector unions. While the employing organization might always be considered the powerful member of the union-management relation because of the dependency of the union on the employing organization for its very existence, a variety of factors—notably size and industrywide jurisdiction—have enabled private sector unions to somewhat balance the relationship by acquiring more power in dealing with private employers. These conditions are obviously lacking in the case of the federal sector unions, and thus the power of federal unions can be viewed as limited compared with that of other unions.

Despite these limitations, federal sector unionization continues to grow because these unions have a number of powers that are important to federal employees. While they cannot negotiate wage increases, they can negotiate with management over many matters of work standards and conditions. Of even greater importance, they can represent employees in actual disciplinary matters. Moreover, professional federal employees are growing militant in their quest for

autonomy (Cohany and Dewey, 1970), and they turn to unionization as a means of winning greater control over work-related decisions. Additionally, recent budget tightening in general has
threatened the traditional security enjoyed in the federal service
(Weisberger, 1973), making unions more attractive. Because federal
sector unions cannot bargain over monetary issues and are limited in
their jurisdiction over grievance matters (such as those in EEO), they
are motivated to "try harder" in other areas in which their influence
is not so restricted. They thus can be expected to concentrate their
efforts on issues such as working conditions, promotion rights, health
and safety, and job opportunities.

Also, since federal unions are limited in their scope of negotiations, we would expect that they would place more emphasis than do
unions in the private sector upon their power to *defend* employees.
While exact figures on grievances filed by federal employee unions
are not available, civil service records indicate that between 1971 and
1974 more than 800 cases were taken to arbitration by federal sector
unions.

UNION PRESENCE

In attempting to assess the effects that federal unions may have
had on the implementation of the policies studied, we shall focus on
several aspects of the relation between these unions and the employing organizations to which they are attached. The first, most
basic aspect of this relation is whether or not it exists; without a
union present, no union-installation relation is possible. Thus the
first step in our analysis will be to determine how the presence of a
union is related to implementing activities within the installation.

As mentioned earlier, federal unions are likely to emphasize the
defense of employees, and thus the presence of a union tends to
create a conflictual relation between supervisors, who represent management, and the union. Specifically, this emphasis upon the union's
role in defending employees can have two countervailing effects
upon use of the federal alcoholism policy, one of which would seem
to outweigh the other. First, it may make it harder for the union to
join management in a cooperative front when confronting the alcoholic employee, since by doing so the union would be violating its
very raison d'être; that is, it would be deserting its own members.[2]
Such a failure to present a united front gives the alcoholic worker a
chance to manipulate both union and management. Under such
circumstances supervisors have more difficulty in dealing with alcoholic workers, making use of the policy less attractive. On the other
hand, having the union as a potential adversary may convince super-

visors of the need to use the policy, since failure to do so would leave
them vulnerable to grievance actions when it becomes necessary to
confront the alcoholic employee. Since the grievance action seems to
be the greater risk for the supervisor, we would predict that having a
union present in an installation would lead to greater use of the
alcoholism policy by supervisors.

Such a prediction is quite consistent with prevailing opinion
about the impact of labor unions on the behavior of management
(Slichter et al., 1960; Wnorowski, 1970). Most observers feel that
unions encourage bureaucratization by generating pressure to conform to formal rules, regulations, and policies through the ever-
present possibility that actions will have to be justified in adversary
proceedings (Ladd and Lipset, 1973). Thus the presence of a union
sensitizes all levels of management to formal personnel policy; that
is, they will tend to know more about a given policy, accept its
strategy, and follow its prescriptions more fully in actual use than
when a union is absent.

The situation is modified in the case of the EEO policy. This
policy includes special appeal mechanisms for discrimination cases
that take precedence over the union contract by replacing grievance
procedures found in most collectively bargained agreements. These
features of the EEO policy greatly reduce the union's ability to
engage in adversary actions when EEO issues might be involved.
Consequently it seems reasonable to predict that the union, in
general, would have less impact on implementation and use for the
EEO policy than for the alcoholism policy.[3]

Of the 71 installations in our sample, 58 were unionized; these
installations included 535 of the 634 supervisors in the sample.
Comparisons between supervisory data from unionized and nonunionized installations supported our belief that the presence of a
union did indeed influence use of the alcoholism and EEO policies.

The mere presence of the union in these federal installations was
sufficient to lead to significantly more use of a policy. Almost 13
percent of supervisors reporting that a union was present in their
installation had actually used the alcoholism policy, while about 6
percent of supervisors in nonunion installations reported actual past
usage ($\chi^2 = 3.12$, 1 df, $p = .077$). This relationship was especially
pronounced for supervisors of lower-skilled employees, where there
were no cases of policy use without a union, and 18 percent of
supervisors with a union present had used the policy ($\chi^2 = 4.00$, 1
df, $p < .05$). Union presence made no difference in past use for
supervisors with skilled employees, while the results for supervisors
of professional employees were similar to those for all supervisors
(over 11 percent with union and 3 percent without union using
policy, $\chi^2 = 3.17$, 1 df, $p = .075$). Differences between supervisors

in unionized installations and other supervisors were even greater for expected future use of the alcoholism policy, and the pattern of differences by skill level was much the same as with actual past use.

Neither past nor future supervisory use of the EEO policy differed significantly between unionized and nonunionized installations. Fifty-eight percent of the supervisors who reported a union in their installation had actually been involved in the use of the policy compared with 63 percent of supervisors in nonunion situations ($\chi^2 = 0.89$, 1 df, p = .345). Also, the marked differentials found by skill level for the alcoholism policy failed to appear for EEO. Union presence made no difference in whether the policy had been used by supervisors with skilled, professional, or unskilled employees. For future use and number of past uses, the presence of a union had a dampening effect on use of the EEO policy. In installations with skilled employees, expected future use was less when a union was present than when a union was absent. Similarly, number of past uses of EEO was greater in nonunionized than in unionized settings.

We also assessed whether information diffusion activities varied according to whether or not a union was present in the installation. The total amount of information diffusion did not differ for either policy between unionized and nonunionized installations, but training activities did. For the alcoholism policy, the number of topics covered in training about the policy was significantly greater in union installations (means = 1.31 vs. 0.53, p < .001), while comparable figures for the EEO policy were not significantly different (3.63 vs. 3.45). Again the mere presence of the union was associated with greater efforts in implementation of the alcoholism policy, but not of EEO.

A second aspect of the relations between the unions and their installations is the amount and effect of influence being exerted by each party on the other. For the purposes of this analysis, our interest was on the effects the union might have on the installation. If the union had such influence, union sentiments toward the policies should be related to implementation efforts by supervisors. The basic idea was that a favorable assessment by the union of the policies would create some pressure on management to implement them.

In order to determine the union's policy position, we asked supervisors to evaluate the union's reaction to a policy in supporting it and in helping to carry it out. These evaluations were made using 7-point semantic differential scales (for policy support: 1 = opposed to, 7 = very much in favor; for helpfulness: 1 = not helpful, 7 = very helpful). Factor analysis indicated that these two items formed a common scale, and a standardized scale score was computed; this became our measure of the supervisor's perception of the union's position on a policy. However, subsequent analyses failed to find much effect of this variable on implementation of the two policies.

Despite the lack of findings relating the union's position on the policies to implementation by supervisors, the results are striking. All of our prior information and comparisons between these federal sector unions and private sector unions led us to expect the unions in our sample to be relatively powerless in their relation with management. Yet their mere presence in an installation was accompanied by substantially more use of the policies. Clearly, the federal sector unions were having some effect on implementation efforts.

SUPERVISORY AWARENESS OF UNION'S POSITION

Since the presence of a union made a substantial difference in policy use, it seemed reasonable to expect that its impact could be still greater under some conditions than under others. As already reported, a union's position on the policies had minimal effects. This finding led us to explore the supervisory responses on the union's position in more detail. Reconsidering the matter, we identified a third characteristic of the union-installation relation: its salience to supervisors. It seemed quite probable that a union could be present and take a position on the policy and that some supervisors would be aware of the position, while others would be unaware. This turned out to be the case: of the 535 supervisors in unionized workplaces, 213 reported being aware of a union's position on the alcoholism policy, while 322 were quite ignorant of it. Many more reported some perceptions of the union's reactions to the EEO policy: 351 of the unionized supervisors were able to do so versus 184 who could be classified as unaware. Clearly the impact of the union's position on the policy had been weakened by much supervisory ignorance of union reaction to the policies, especially the one on alcoholism.

What could explain this ignorance? Several possibilities emerged. Perhaps it simply grew out of a generally low level of information about the policies, as might be indicated by low levels of diffusion and no knowledge of the alcoholism coordinator. Another possible explanation came from data indicating that younger unions (those that have been present in the organization for a shorter period of time) and smaller unions with lower relative levels of membership (as opposed to potential membership) are more militant in dealing with management (Kuhn, 1961; Sayles and Strauss, 1967; Bakke, 1970). If this was true of the federal unions in our sample, it seemed reasonable to believe that the militancy of these unions would have produced more audible and visible reactions for supervisors to hear and see. Put differently, perhaps their opposite types—older and bigger unions—were permitting supervisory ignorance by their relative inactivity. Also, the skill level of union members might account for some of the supervisory unawareness, since Warkov, Bacon, and Hawkins (1965) and Trice (1965; 1966) had found supervisors of lower-skilled employees more apt to know about and use the policy than other supervisors. That is, unions with highly skilled employees might somehow encourage supervisory ignorance, perhaps through a lack of militancy. Data on the size, age, and skill level of membership were available from Civil Service records (see Appendix).

Finally, supervisory unawareness of the union's position on the policy could occur because of general ignorance about the union. If so, supervisors will be in the dark about union adversary activities such as grievances and arbitration, as well as more general union activities (union newspapers, social activities, group insurance and vacation benefits, etc.). Analyses were run to test all of the possibilities advanced to explain supervisory awareness/unawareness; the results are given in table 8.1.

The age of the union, supervisory knowledge of the coordinator, the amount of diffusion, and supervisory knowledge of union general activities differentiated between aware and unaware supervisors for the alcoholism policy. Again it is clear that the spread of information about the policy is important for policy implementation. Apparently supervisors became aware of the union's position on the alcoholism policy by receiving a variety of information about the policy within the managerial system from a variety of sources.

In sharp contrast, all features of the union were associated with supervisory awareness of the union's position on EEO. Diffusion of information again contributed heavily to awareness of the union's position. Opposite to expectation, those supervisors aware of the union's position on EEO worked with larger, older, and more skilled unions. In accord with expectation, they also were significantly more informed of both adversary and other activities of the union, and of the EEO policy facilitator.

Now that we had located some reasonable explanations for supervisory ignorance of the union's position on the policies, it became important to assess whether or not the relative awareness of supervisors was associated with implementation of the policies. These results are given in table 8.2.

Aware supervisors expressed significantly greater need for both policies; similarly, more aware supervisors had actually used both policies in the past, and expected to do so in the future, than had uninformed ones. For the alcoholism policy the number of past uses was significantly greater for aware than for unaware supervisors; the findings were in the same direction for the EEO policy, although not statistically significant. Thus awareness seemed to make more consistent differences in use of the alcoholism policy.

T A B L E 8.1 Comparison of Union Variables and Diffusion Between Supervisors Who Are Aware and Unaware of Union Position on Policies

VARIABLES	ALCOHOLISM POLICY			EEO POLICY		
	Aware $n = 211^c$	Unaware $n = 310$	p^*	Aware $n = 346$	Unaware $n = 175$	p^*
Relative size of union[a]	87.45	87.36	n.s.	89.27	84.91	.036
Age of union	7.01	5.93	.001	6.91	5.31	.000
Skill level of union	3.74	3.78	n.s.	3.86	3.58	.035
Supervisory knowledge of coordinator[b]	0.87	0.74	.014	0.88	0.78	.022
Diffusion of policy information	4.05	3.07	.000	6.99	5.93	.000
Supervisory knowledge of union adversary activities	1.78	1.71	n.s.	1.84	1.50	.000
Supervisory knowledge of other union activities	2.20	1.93	.040	2.21	1.67	.000

n.s. = not significant.

[a] Number of union members divided by eligible employees within the installation.

[b] 1 = knowledge, 0 = no knowledge; n = 106 and 134 for alcoholism policy, n = 276 and 134 for EEO policy

[c] Only supervisors in installations with a union are included in these tables; totals vary somewhat from table to table because of missing data due to nonresponse or inapplicable items.

* As determined by one-way analysis of variance.

TABLE 8.2 Comparison of Receptivity and Use of Policies Between Supervisors Who Are Aware and Unaware of Union Position on Policies

RECEPTIVITY AND USE VARIABLES	ALCOHOLISM POLICY			EEO POLICY		
	Aware n = 206	Unaware n = 312	p*	Aware n = 342	Unaware n = 181	p*
Overall agreement with policies	0.08	−0.02	n.s	0.14	−0.03	.015
Agreement with performance emphasis	0.04	0.01	n.s.	0.05	−0.04	n.s.
Agreement that supervisors do own counseling	0.05	−0.07	n.s.	0.02	−0.10	n.s.
Perceived benefit of policies	0.07	0.01	n.s.	0.01	0.08	n.s.
Need for policies	0.13	−0.01	.063	0.11	−0.08	.015
Ease of administration	0.10	0.02	n.s.	0.04	0.06	n.s.
Have used policy	0.17	0.09	.004	0.62	0.49	.006
Number of policy uses	0.47	0.16	.014	9.14	4.57	n.s.
Frequency of expected use	1.88	1.54	.001	4.44	4.09	.077

n.s. = not significant.

* As determined by one-way analysis of variance.

However, awareness of the union's position was associated with greater agreement among supervisors with central provisions of the EEO policy. Clearly awareness of the union's position did little to make supervisors agree with the alcoholism policy. Yet awareness was significantly associated with both need and use for both policies; obviously management does not have to agree with a policy in order to respond to pressure to use it. In this instance it is possible that awareness of the union led to use of the policy, which in turn led to higher perceptions of need. However, it is also plausible that awareness of the union by itself led to greater perception of need for the alcoholism policy since, as mentioned earlier, supervisors prefer the protection from grievance actions that the policy may provide.

EXPLAINING THE IMPACT OF AWARENESS

In order to explore further the impact of the union, it seemed desirable to investigate how a range of variables might affect implementation under conditions in which supervisors were aware of the union's position and under conditions in which they were unaware. A group of independent variables was selected to use in multiple regression analyses, with the actual and expected policy use of both aware and unaware groups of supervisors for both policies as dependent variables. Independent variables included size, age, skill level, and amount of adversary and other activities of the resident union; supervisory agreement with policy provisions; amount of policy information received by supervisors; their assessment of policy needs; and their knowledge of policy facilitators. The attitudinal receptivity measures included in these analyses were those most relevant to union concerns: general supervisory agreement, agreement with counseling and performance provisions, plus supervisory perceptions of need for the policies.

Past Use

The results of regression analyses for past use of the policies are given in table 8.3. The pattern of findings is quite similar for use of the alcoholism policy by aware and unaware supervisors. The amount of policy diffusion showed a strong relationship with use in both groups, demonstrating again the potency of policy information. A somewhat similar conclusion can be reached about supervisory agreement with the counseling provisions. Among unaware supervisors alcoholism policies were more frequently used in lower skilled situations; this relationship was not significant, however, among aware supervisors, suggesting that an active union that communicates its

T A B L E 8.3 Comparison of Multiple Regression Results of Whether They Have Used Policies in Past on Union Variables, Diffusion, and Receptivity Between Aware and Unaware Supervisors

| | STANDARDIZED REGRESSION COEFFICIENTS (BETAS) | | | |
| | *Alcoholism Policy* | | *EEO Policy* | |
INDEPENDENT VARIABLES	AWARE N = 194	UNAWARE N = 234	AWARE N = 311	UNAWARE N = 121
Relative size of union	−.12	.10	.07	.03
Age of union	.06	−.04	−.07	.15
Skill level of union	−.10	−.13*	.05	.17*
Supervisory knowledge of coordinator	.06	.10	.09*	.20**
Diffusion of policy information	.14*	.14**	.36†	.07
Union adversary activities	.08	.01	.06	−.11
Other union activities	−.06	.07	.04	−.01
Overall agreement with policy[a]	.08	−.04	.02	−.04
Agree supervisors should counsel	.17**	.12*	.06	.18*
Agreement with performance emphasis	−.02	−.09	−.02	−.01
Assessed need for policy	−.01	.14**	.14†	.23**
R =	.34	.31	.47	.43
R² (adjusted) =	.07	.05	.20	.10
p =	< .05	<.05	<.001	< .05

[a]This scale leans toward zealous agreement for the alcoholism policy.
*$p < .10$
**$p < .05$
†$p < .01$

position to supervision can perhaps act to spread policy use into all skill levels. Assessed need was related to past use of the alcoholism policy only among supervisors unaware of the union's position. Apparently, as long as supervisors were aware of the union having a position on the alcoholism policy, it was not necessary for them to feel the policy was needed in order for them to use it. In other words, with a union present, supervisors use the alcoholism policy whether they think they need it or not.

In the case of the EEO policy, the pattern of findings varies more between aware and unaware supervisors. For this policy, policy use was greater at higher skill levels among unaware supervisors, and for supervisors with a propensity to do their own counseling, while these variables were unrelated to use by aware supervisors. The most important predictor of past use among the aware supervisors was diffusion of information. Assessed need and knowledge of the coordinator were positive predictors for both aware and unaware supervisors.

Additional analyses of the number of past uses yielded similar results for both policies, and therefore will not be reported.

Expected Future Use

Since maintaining a readiness to use one of these policies among supervisors is a vital and unique aspect of implementing them, the findings about union awareness and expected policy use are especially important. The R^2 values in table 8.4 indicate that aware supervisors were generally more likely than unaware ones to be influenced by other factors related to the union in assessing their use of the alcoholism policy in the future. Thus, those aware supervisors who worked with smaller unions and who reported knowledge of union adversary activity expected to use this policy more frequently in the future than other supervisors. In addition, the activity of unions in other, more general spheres seemed to have a repressive effect on expectations for use of the alcoholism policy. Assessed need for the policy was potent in predicting future use for both the aware and the unaware supervisors. Like the situation for past use, the awares showed no significant association between skill level and expected policy use, while the unawares showed more use for lower skill levels. Thus, for both actual and expected use of the alcoholism policy, supervisory awareness of the union's position seems to distribute policy use across all skill levels rather than to concentrate it in the lower-skilled and lower-status jobs.

Since assessed need for the policy was significantly associated with future use among both aware and unaware supervisors, new information about the relevancy of the policy may be useful and effective in making needs more salient to supervisors who were low on this dimension. A broader approach that incorporates associated problems such as other drug abuse, and related health problems, both physical and mental, could be incorporated into future policy revisions in order to increase a sense of need.

Future use of EEO also showed contrasts between the two groups (table 8.4). Again, need for the policy was an important predictor: Regardless of knowledge of the union's position, those supervisors who had a high belief in the need for EEO expected to use it more in the future. Among aware supervisors, the amount of

TABLE 8.4 Comparison of Multiple Regression Results of Frequency of Expected Future Use of Policies on Union Variables, Diffusion, and Receptivity Between Aware and Unaware Supervisors

	STANDARDIZED REGRESSION COEFFICIENTS (BETAS)			
	Alcoholism Policy		*EEO Policy*	
INDEPENDENT VARIABLES	AWARE N = 193	UNAWARE N = 231	AWARE N = 311	UNAWARE N = 119
Relative size of union	−.21†	.07	−.02	−.17
Age of union	.12	−.02	.00	.08
Skill level of union	−.05	−.15**	.01	.08
Supervisory knowledge of coordinator	.06	.03	.17†	.07
Diffusion of policy information	−.07	.07	.27†	.07
Union adversary activities	.17**	.01	.06	−.04
Other union activities	−.14*	.11	.10*	.06
Overall agreement with policy[a]	.03	−.03	.05	−.00
Agree supervisors should counsel	.05	.03	.12**	−.02
Agreement with performance emphasis	.04	.10	−.08	.11
Assessed need for policy	.25†	.19†	.27†	.25††
R =	.44	.28	.54	.36
R^2 (adjusted) =	.14	.03	.26	.04
p =	< .001	<.10	< .001	n.s.

n.s. = not significant.

[a]This scale leans toward zealous agreement for the alcoholism policy.

*p < .10

**p < .05

†p < .01

policy diffusion was strongly associated with expected use, adding emphasis to the importance of the role played by the dissemination of information about the policy. Also, supervisory knowledge of the EEO facilitator role was significantly associated with expected policy use for aware supervisors. Since none of the union variables was a significant predictor of expected use of EEO, it appears that EEO facilitators played a larger role in expected future use of this policy than did the union. This finding is not surprising, since the EEO policy contains special appeal mechanisms for discrimination cases

T A B L E 8.5 Comparison of Multiple Regression Results of Assessment of Need for Policies on Union Variables Between Aware and Unaware Supervisors

| | STANDARDIZED REGRESSION COEFFICIENTS (BETAS) | | | |
| | Alcoholism Policy | | EEO Policy | |
INDEPENDENT VARIABLES	AWARE N = 196	UNAWARE N = 236	AWARE N = 314	UNAWARE N = 123
Relative size of union	$-.14^*$	$-.11$	$-.10$	$-.12$
Age of union	.09	.07	$.12^{**}$	.03
Skill level of union	.05	.11	.05	.05
Supervisory knowledge of coordinator	$-.05$	.05	.08	$-.03$
Diffusion of policy information	$.16^{**}$	.02	$.12^{**}$	.08
Union adversary activities	$.16^{**}$	$.13^*$	$.17^†$	.09
Other union activities	$-.03$	.01	$-.05$	.02
R =	.29	.21	.27	.17
R^2 (adjusted) =	.05	.01	.05	$-.03$
p =	$<.05$	n.s.	$<.01$	n.s.

n.s. = not significant.
$^*p < .10$
$^{**}p < .05$
$^†p < .01$

that take precedence over the grievance and arbitration clauses of the union's collectively bargained agreement, and EEO facilitators often play a role in processing such cases.

Assessed Need for Policies

Because the assessment of need for the policy had been a powerful predictor of both actual and expected use for supervisors in unionized installations, we decided to assess it separately as the dependent variable in regressions run for both aware and unaware groups. In short, did awareness combine with some of the characteristics of the union, supervisory knowledge, and information, or with knowledge about the union to explain supervisory assessment of policy need? Table 8.5 gives the results. Both size and activities of the resident union had a strong effect on the extent to which aware supervisors believed the alcoholism policy was needed. When supervisors knew the union was active in adversary activities and when the union was small, their sense of need for the alcoholism policy was significantly greater. Also, higher amounts of policy diffusion among supervisors again joined with awareness to produce a heightened sense of policy need. In addition, those supervisors who reported their unions were more active in adversary activities expressed greater need for the alcoholism policy, whether or not they were aware of the union's position on the policy.

Quite similar forces joined awareness to produce a sense of need for the EEO policy. Once more, diffusion of policy information, combined with awareness, was associated with greater expressed need for the policy. However, for this policy, aware supervisors with older unions reported greater expected use. Again the adversary activities by the union were potent enough to generate a higher sense of need when supervisors knew about the union's position. None of the variables in table 8.5 predicted expected future use of the EEO policy.

Clearly a militant union was associated with a greater sense of need for both policies among supervisors and thus can be seen as a potent force for implementing these policies. Since diffusion was also a consistently important predictor of implementation, perhaps these two forces could be deliberately combined to further implementation efforts. The findings suggest that training about these policies could profit from including sessions on the overall adversary role and rights of the union.

Agreement with Performance Emphasis

Finally, because both policies, but especially the alcoholism one, place strong emphasis upon job performance as a determinant of policy use, we used supervisory agreement with the performance provisions of the policies as the dependent variable in multiple regression analyses with the same independent variables. These analyses produced only scattered significant relationships and therefore can be summarized briefly. Aware supervisors with older unions were more likely to endorse provisions stressing performance for both policies, while larger unions had a similar effect among unaware supervisors for EEO. These results suggest that the presence of better established unions is supportive of an emphasis on the use of performance criteria in dealing with employees. Supervisors with unions that are expected to be more militant—the younger and smaller ones—are therefore *less* likely to agree with the performance provisions—a notable rejection on a policy provision especially important for the alcoholism policy. Perhaps such supervisors felt threatened by the presence of a relatively militant union within their installation and responded by being unwilling or afraid to confront issues of job performance. The activities of the union, however, failed to be related to agreement with this provision for either policy.

SUMMARY AND DISCUSSION

A dramatic rise of federal sector unions has occurred over the last decade. They differ from private sector unions in two basic ways: their inability (1) to bargain over salaries and wages and (2) to insist on the priority of negotiated grievance and arbitration procedures when special appeal mechanisms have been built into a specific federal policy. Such handicaps might lead observers to conclude that these unions cannot exert much influence on their employing organization—that the relation between union and installation is one characterized by extreme dependency of the union, and its relative ineffectualness in matters of importance. Our data do not support such pessimistic views of federal unions. Despite their handicaps, they exert important influences on the implementation of both the alcoholism and EEO policies. This is especially surprising since the EEO policy, and the alcoholism policy to a lesser degree, contain the types of procedures and appeal mechanisms that take precedence over union-bargained procedures. Nevertheless, the mere presence of a union was significantly and positively related to both actual and expected supervisory use of the alcoholism policy. For the EEO policy, union presence had a somewhat dampening effect on past and future use for some subgroups of supervisors. These results strongly suggest that these unions are influential in personnel matters.

Moreover, the presence of a union was also related to the number of training topics covered in supervisory alcoholism training time, suggesting that the presence of a union acted to broaden the base of such training, giving it a more general supervisory training thrust than an exclusive focus upon alcoholism. Trice and Belasco (1968) have shown that such a training strategy produced a greater willingness by supervisors to use an alcoholism policy.

Thus, the most basic aspect of the union-installation relation—the mere existence of the relationship—was demonstrated to have considerable impact on crucial implementing behaviors within the installation. Clearly, these federal unions conformed to Sutermeister's general observation: "The union can affect the formal organization, its climate, efficiency, and its communication effectiveness with employees" (1963:48), despite the unique restrictions under which they operate.

The second dimension of the union-installation relation assessed was the influence exerted by the union for or against the policies. Results showed little relationship, except that supervisors were more

familiar with policy provisions when they felt the union was supportive of the policies. These somewhat surprising findings led to the
identification of the most crucial factor in the union-management
relation affecting supervisory implementation of the policies. This
third dimension was the relative salience of the union's position on
the policies: Were supervisors aware or unaware of the union's
position? When comparisons were made between the aware and the
unaware supervisors, aware supervisors were characterized by higher
perceived need for both policies and by greater past and future use of
the policies.

A series of analyses was then performed to see whether or not
the effect of other variables on implementation varied between aware
and unaware supervisors. These analyses failed to uncover any
startling and consistent differences. Often the same variables were
predictors of policy use whether supervisors were aware or unaware.
The most notable exception was the strong effect that union variables had on expected future use for the alcoholism policy and
assessed need for both policies among aware supervisors.

Union variables also had a variety of effects on supervisory
agreement with performance provisions for both policies, suggesting
that aware supervisors who had more established unions were much
more likely to agree with the performance provision—a pivotal one
for the alcoholism policy.

Throughout these results, union variables were less important in
predicting implementation of the EEO policy; this pattern could
result from a realization by supervisors that EEO machinery super-
sedes the union grievance procedures.

Three factors were notable for their frequent impact on policy
use, regardless of supervisory awareness of union position. Perceived
need was a relatively consistent predictor of implementation for both
policies. The amount of information diffusion on the policies was
also a prominent predictor of implementation. The third factor, the
amount of union adversary behavior, was especially important as a
predictor in the case of the alcoholism policy. Only the last of these
factors was a measure of union-installation relations.

However, where the alcoholism policy is concerned, an important
pattern associated with awareness of the union deserves emphasis:
where supervisors are aware of the union's position, skill level is less
related to policy use, suggesting that concentration of use at the
lower skill levels has been broken up in these instances. This finding
suggests a mechanism for reducing one of the major problems in
occupational alcoholism programming, that is, differential use by
skill level.[4]

Considering the overall pattern of the findings, we must conclude
that the federal sector unions serving the installations in our samples

had significant impacts on implementation of both the alcoholism and EEO policies. Despite a variety of factors depriving these unions of conventional sources of power, their mere presence and supervisory awareness of their position on the policies were significantly associated with greater efforts toward implementation. Thus the almost complete neglect of the unions in studies of change in organizations seems to be a classic example of myopia—not a well-considered view that unions are unimportant in explaining change in organizations.

However, the pattern of findings was somewhat stronger and more consistent for the alcoholism than for the EEO policy. We therefore conclude this chapter with a discussion of implications for only the alcoholism policy. Both the results presented and our general knowledge of EEO suggest that the EEO policy may be less subject to union influence, if for no other reason than that it commands so much attention from other sectors of the public. In any case, the thrust of the discussion that follows can be applied, with appropriate translations, to the implementation of other personnel policies and of other organizational changes.

COMMENTS FROM UNION OFFICIALS

In order to explore the direct reaction of federal unions to the alcoholism policy—in contrast to viewing it through the reactions of supervision—we conducted research interviews with ten local union presidents from installations that had fallen into the sample. Four of these were from the New York region, three from Boston region, and three from the Philadelphia region. Three themes prevailed in their responses. The most predominant one was the "left out" theme. That is, these presidents of locals felt that the policy had been devised, formally launched, and circulated without any inputs from federal unions. Three earlier exploratory interviews with various union officials at the national level had produced a similar complaint. In brief, all of these union officials insisted they found cooperation with federal managers in implementation of the alcoholism policy rather difficult because of this neglect of them in its formative stages.

The second theme carried forward the first and became the expression of disappointment because at bottom they agreed with the thrust of the policy. They, in effect, believed it was an opportunity to secure additional benefits for union members while, at the same time, having a legitimate reason to monitor the behavior of federal managers. Along with these advantages they saw the traditional opportunity to claim that the union had played a part in securing the benefits for their members that they saw in the alcoholism policy.

Third, they tended to put their ultimate reaction to the policy in adversary terms, citing their ability to bring grievances to the point of arbitration and often win them, if necessary. They had communicated to management in various ways, usually oral, both their support of the policy, on the one hand, and, on the other, their willingness to use their adversary power to see that it was used. They felt that the managements with which they interacted had perceived their reaction in this adversary context. That is, they tended to readily agree that supervisors would be prone to "protect their flanks" when they became aware of the union's position and do so by giving the policy more attention and use. Although not a prominent theme, some of the local presidents stated with some glee that the policy provided them with an opportunity to find "chinks in the armor," and they had deliberately expressed to other union members their determination to use it in this manner.

From the viewpoint of these themes, some distinct notions emerge for the development of the labor-management committee. Obviously, it functions better if the union is involved early. Fortunately, a consensual basis exists: Both sides find the basic purpose of the policy desirable. Nevertheless, such committees evidently tend to operate within the usual labor-relations context of ultimate adversary power and possible conflict rather than the "cooperation" frequently attributed to, and expected of, them.

Union officials were much more wary in discussing the EEO policy. They expressed awareness of past problems of discrimination within the labor movement and were concerned that they would again be accused of discrimination. But most importantly, they saw the EEO policy as usurping some of their powers. As one official expressed it, "Another group over which we have no control now has adversary power, too." They thus saw the EEO policy as giving them competition, largely because it gave the EEO "machinery" adversary powers that might be used by union members rather than going through union-initiated procedures.

IMPLICATIONS FOR ALCOHOLISM POLICIES

Quite obviously the implementation of the alcoholism policy will profit from doing what the policy formally calls for, namely, that "management should deal with union representatives on program policy information and use, and maintain open lines of communication with union leaders" (U.S. Civil Service Commission, 1971:5). Clearly these "open lines" should include information to supervision about the union's policy position, its general adversary activities, and the inclusion of the union in policy revision. The evidence suggests, however, that federal unions were left out of policy formulation in the early 1970s and have received only sparse attention since then. This observation in turn leads to consideration of the neglect of the role of unions in alcoholism policies and programs in all sectors of the work world.

Despite the vital role of unions in the strategy underlying alcoholism policies, their role has often been overlooked, neglected, and even rejected by management and others. Since problem drinking was frequently regarded as a disciplinary matter in the workplace, and since this traditionally was management's prerogative, the union tended to be disregarded (or feared) in policy writing and implementation. Habbe (1968), for example, asserted that management often suffers from "oversight" and includes the union only as a last detail in planning. A careful assessment of many company programs clearly showed that there has been a relatively low level of union participation even though much publicity and lip service are given to the role the union should play (Trice et al., 1977).

Another reason for this neglect has been the strong emphasis on the "rush to treatment" by many practitioners in the field of alcoholism. This orientation among persons helping the work world to launch alcoholism programs has led to their overlooking the processes and dynamics of management-union relations. Also, personnel and medical departments are oriented primarily toward management. It seems likely that staff persons are less sensitive to the influence of the union than are line managers, who experience the impact of a union's presence more directly. Furthermore, the preoccupation of alcoholism specialists with referrals to treatment leads them to give lower priority to the longer process of constructive confrontation of problem-drinking employees, often resulting in the bypassing of the necessary participation of both supervision and the union.

Thus, in many cases, the union's part has not been played, and the confrontation process has been drained of its vitality because of the rush to treatment that seems to dominate many job-based programs. In addition, community treatment facilities, which understandably seek to treat as quickly as possible, further reinforce the tendencies to neglect the union. Unfortunately, they may urge staff people in a company to bypass the motivating power of supervision and union in order to get an employee "into treatment." Not only does this effectively remove the power of the workplace, but it exposes the employee to a labeling process that may well hasten the development of a severe health problem. One mechanism that has shown substantial promise of at least partially circumventing this unfortunate process and recognizing the important role of the union is the union-management committee, where both sides oversee the use of a policy in such a way that a balance may be obtained between their interests.

Because of the traditional neglect of the union in the formulation and execution of alcoholism and employee assistance programs, the strategy of these policies will be briefly surveyed with the purpose of highlighting the crucial role of the union. Alcoholism policies developed for work settings are based on a basic premise: To the extent that the developing problem drinker experiences an objective, consistent, united, repeated, and forthright confrontation from all of his significant others about his poor performance, he is more apt to respond by trying to bring his performance back to acceptable levels. For those employees represented by a union, the shop steward, the local union officers, and fellow union workers are "significant others"—they are a meaningful part of his role set on the job. Ideally, then, the alcoholism intervention strategy calls for union officials to join with relevant management persons in providing as constructive a confrontation as possible, so as to weaken the denials, rationalizations, and delusions of the problem-drinking employee about his job performance and his possible job loss, and strengthen his determination to change his behavior. In sum, union officials at all operating levels must cooperate in carrying out this strategy, or the intervention will be damaged. Thus, the strategy requires a cooperative and mutually supportive relation between management and the unions.

Frequently, the problem drinker is well on the road to alcoholism, and in this deviant role he or she has learned to become an effective manipulator. Consequently, the problem drinker readily detects and exploits any opportunity to "divide and conquer." In work-world terms this means "playing the union off against management." This places the union in a crucial role. If a common front is not presented, the strategy for helping the problem-drinking employee will suffer substantially. Beyond doubt it is this helping objective that must take priority if the policy is to be effective. The emphasis on impaired production and performance is primarily a mechanism—a tool. It was in this vein that Leo Perlis of the AFL-CIO Community Services Branch stressed that "while the effects of alcoholism on production and profits must always be a concern, labor feels that an industrial alcoholism program should aim at achieving a well-adjusted human being not as a means to increased production, higher profits, and lower absenteeism rates, but as an end in itself" (Perlis, 1973:18).

The impact of the union in formal grievance and arbitration proceedings is readily apparent. Should a poorly performing employee fail to respond to a series of confrontations so that it becomes increasingly clear that a difficult drinking problem is emerging, the policy strategy calls for introducing what is called "crisis precipitation." That is, in subsequent confrontations, management tells the employee that the company must resort to some form of negative sanctions if work performance does not improve—for example, one week's corrective layoff without pay, a reduction in grade if the employee is a member of management, the loss of a portion of seniority, or even discharge with opportunity for reinstatement. The last resort is to continue offers of help and support for treatment to the employee, but warn him or her that discharge is imminent. Leo Perlis puts the matter as follows: ". . . when everything has been tried and has failed, dismissal as therapy may be in order" (Perlis, 1973:3). Once it is launched, following through on such crisis precipitation is essential.

Clearly, the introduction of disciplinary measures into the confrontation with the alcoholic worker places the union in a paradoxical position. On the one hand, it may accept the need to threaten or implement disciplinary actions against the employee in order to have a successful intervention; on the other hand, it is legally bound to support union members should they seek to file a grievance against management. In a situation where the consequences for the union member are so potentially negative, the union leadership, regardless of its acceptance of the validity of management's case against the alcoholic employee, may be forced (through both legal pressure and "political" considerations, that is, fear that failure to defend the employee may lead to a loss of their positions on the next union election) to oppose management in terms of disciplining the alcoholic worker. This makes the "divide and conquer" strategy of the alcoholic worker even more viable and greatly reduces the likelihood of an effective joint union-management confrontation of the alcoholic employee. Fortunately, formal grievance and arbitration cases appear to be relatively rare. The chances are good that, if the union enters the case while the confrontation is still in its constructive phase and the employee perceives the union as supporting this confrontation effort, he or she will respond by seeking rehabilitation. Thus unions can avoid the double bind of defending a case where they know corrective discipline is justified by helping to motivate the employee to seek help and treatment and thus make such sanctions unnecessary. In this way, unions can help themselves and their employees.

The potential of the labor-management committee to act as a catalyst in bringing together the two parties, and reducing the pressures on both, needs to be emphasized. Although such committees can readily fall into mere ritual, or be dominated by one side or the other, they have been used effectively in safety and retirement issues. Numerous labor-management committees are currently operating, and national labor leaders as well as alcoholism organizations including the National Council on Alcoholism have recommended their use. In some instances they have produced formal memos of understanding about agreed-upon procedures. Whether or not these are attached to formal contracts is a local question, but the possibility is there, making these committees even more viable as devices for continuing union-management cooperation. As Dyer, Lipsky, and Kochan (1977) have pointed out, joint union-management efforts are more feasible if the issues involved are not viewed as ones in which one party gains what the other loses. Thus the situation must be defined by both parties as of potential benefit for effective cooperation to occur.

IMPLICATIONS FOR CHANGE IN ORGANIZATIONS

What implications can be drawn from our data and these observations about the impact of unions on the implementation of organizational change? The most obvious one is the need to recognize that the labor-management relation is a major part of the interorganizational network and the environment of many work organizations. Consequently, some consideration of the union, if one is present, should be built into every phase of a change effort. It is less obvious what form the consideration of the union should take. As our interviews with union leaders indicated, unions react to the content of changes, the historical context in which they occur, and especially to the implications that the change has for the functioning and effectiveness of the union as an organization. Because of the symbiotic nature of the union-management relation, some common cause can often be found to make mutual support of the change feasible.

But even in an atmosphere of substantial consensus, the adversary basis of the relationship will tend to be reasserted, and the tactics and strategies embodied in a change effort must recognize the adversarial tendencies inherent in the relation, yet foster sufficient cooperation to make the change work anyway. In such circumstances, an exchange may be required. Using the alcoholism policy as an example, the union supports management in a potential disciplinary case in exchange for management's assistance to and special consideration of the affected union member, who needs help. Management incorporates the union, and thus shares its control over the situation, in exchange for a reduced probability of a grievance action

and an increased probability of solving a difficult and costly personnel problem. It follows that both members of the exchange must be
perceived by the other as delivering what is promised in order for
cooperation to follow. Different changes and issues, of course, will
dictate different bases of exchange.

When some viable basis for exchange cannot be found, the union
will predictably resist the change, because most changes can be seen
as threats to union effectiveness, especially if initiated by management; the union is always suspicious of management's motives. If for
no other reason, change may be resisted just because it upsets the
status quo, and uncertainty is threatening.[5]

An interesting area for further research is how the structure and
functioning of unions may affect changes carried out within work
organizations. As we have seen in chapter 7, some aspects of the
structure of a work organization seem to facilitate change efforts,
while others tend to be negatively related to change and innovation.
Perhaps structural characteristics of unions are similarly related to
change processes. For example, would change efforts be more successful if *both* work organizations and involved unions were decentralized? What would happen if unions were fully incorporated into
change processes? Would use of an alcoholism policy be greater if
levels of familiarity were high among not only supervisors, but union
officials as well?

Clearly, much more research is needed before the role of the
union in the processes of organizational change has been investigated
adequately. We have been able to provide only a limited demonstration of how fruitful this area of inquiry might be.

9. Evaluating Change in Organizations: Capturing Nonconformity

IN THE PRECEDING CHAPTERS, we have analyzed the implementation of two federal personnel policies by three sets of actors within the adopting organizations, and by considering three types of constraints affecting them. We have looked at supervisors, policy facilitators, the directors who headed the installations, the structure of the installations, their community environment, and finally the presence of unions and their activities. In all of these levels of analyses we have been able to locate various factors that were significantly associated with implementation of the policies. Sometimes different factors were important for implementation of the two policies; sometimes the factors associated with implementation were the same.

In this chapter we shall pull together these somewhat disparate elements and summarize the findings with the intention of gleaning some practical implications for the implementation of such policies in other organizations and for the implementation of change within organizations in general. We shall also address some questions raised by the problems of evaluating change efforts in organizations.

SUMMARY OF RESULTS

Throughout the results presented, we have analyzed the data on implementation in terms of the general model of change presented in chapter 1, and more specifically in terms of the three-stage model of the implementation phase that was discussed and tested in chapter 3.

257

Using this model and a variety of statistical techniques, we have been able to identify factors that were associated with implementation of these policies in the federal organizations in our sample. Since our sample was randomly drawn from a population of all federal installations in three civil service regions in the Northeast, our findings can be generalized to all federal installations in that part of the United States. Because of the rather large variety of tasks performed and skill levels of employees within these installations, we believe that our findings have relevance for other work organizations, including those in the private sector, where policies with the same intent and similar content are also used. While the policies studied have their unique aspects, as we have stressed many times in this book, many findings have sufficient similarity with findings from other studies to suggest that they also have general relevance for the implementation of change in organizations.

Because multiple regression has been the most frequent method of analysis, it should be pointed out that the relationships found are presumably independent of each other; that is, a given beta coefficient indicates the strength of the relationship between two variables—the independent and dependent variable of interest—while controlling for all other independent variables in the same equation. This means that any variable found either negatively or positively related at a statistically significant level to some measure of implementation has importance in and of itself. However, in the summaries that follow, we try to emphasize coherent patterns of relationships. When we do this, we will discuss possible combinations of the variables that would have led to the lowest levels of implementation, and the highest. If, for example, we say that younger and more educated supervisors are poorer implementers than others, this means that either characteristic, in and of itself, was associated with relatively low implementation; it follows that the two characteristics together were likely to be associated with even lower levels of implementation.

Supervisors

Those supervisors who were uncommitted to their installation, female, and relatively young received the poorest diffusion and training on the alcoholism policy. In addition, those supervisors who had remained in their present position for a relatively long time and who felt overloaded with work reported less information on this policy, while those at lower managerial levels were unlikely either to have favorable attitudes toward the policy or to have used it. Also, supervisors of more skilled subordinates were poorer implementers, while those who worked with unionized employees had at least received greater diffusion on the policy. Consistently, those who disagreed with the policy and used it less frequently were conservative regarding change in general. They were also little involved in their jobs and did not believe that their own performance would count heavily toward their own promotion. Also, poorer implementing supervisors tended to work in smaller installations.

All aspects of diffusion were important for familiarity with provisions of the alcoholism policy, and those who were unfamiliar were less likely to have used the policy in the past. Also, supervisors who disagreed that they should counsel employees, who perceived little need for the policy, or who rejected its performance emphasis were less likely to be past or future policy users.

For the EEO policy, demographic characteristics had very mixed effects on implementation. Those supervisors who were female again received less policy diffusion and were therefore less aware of the union's position on this policy and saw less administrative emphasis on it. However, they showed more receptivity toward this policy than other supervisors, especially in the crucial attitudinal components of assessed need, benefit, and ease of administration. Age also had mixed effects for this policy. Although younger supervisors experienced (or remembered) more training topics and perceived more administrative emphasis, they rejected the performance emphasis in the policy and, compared with older managers, saw it as more difficult to administer. Finally, while more educated supervisors received more diffusion, they tended to be unreceptive toward this policy.

Relative newness to the installation and to supervision was negatively associated with diffusion for the EEO policy, as were lower skill levels of employees supervised. Low managerial status was also decidedly a feature of poor implementation of this policy. Less decisive for this policy, but still indicative of the reluctant implementer, was a conservative attitude toward change, but neither a sense of commitment to the installation nor to the federal service in general mattered. What did matter, however, was low job involvement in current supervisory position; it was especially associated with low receptivity among supervisors for EEO. Even more important was the feeling that performance criteria did not matter very much as a basis for their promotion. This variable predicted across all three stages of implementation: diffusion, receptivity, and use. Consistent with this was the assessment by poor EEO implementers that seniority is important as a criteria for their promotion—again across all stages. Little diffusion to employees, low familiarity, and low perceived need also ranked as major characteristics of low implementers, since these variables predicted both past and expected use of EEO.

More than was the case with the alcoholism policy, if a supervisor worked in a smaller installation he was apt to be a poor implementer of EEO; all types of supervisory use of EEO were associated with installation size. The presence of a union had a mixed effect, somewhat like personal demographics, with its presence characterizing somewhat better EEO information diffusion and less actual use.

As indicated for the alcoholism policy, supervisors who are poor implementers of EEO report low familiarity with the policy and engage in little diffusion of EEO information to nonmanagerial employees. Their receptivity and use were especially reduced by these factors. Consistent with these findings, they also reported fewer training topics about EEO and fewer training and learning hours about that policy.

Finally, poor implementers of EEO were characterized by larger spans of control, even though they were more likely to agree zealously with the policy and perceive need for it.

From these brief summaries, limited generalizations can be made about supervisors whose attitudes and behaviors were not consistent with implementation of either policy. They were apt to be younger and therefore relatively new to their installation. Consequently, they tended to be significantly concentrated in low managerial positions. Education had mixed effects; while there was a substantial amount of policy diffusion activities among more educated supervisors, they showed little receptivity to the policies. Low implementing supervisors perceived relatively low levels of need for either policy, held conservative beliefs about change in general, and had low involvement in their supervisory jobs, suggesting a muted alienation. In keeping with the latter, they did not believe performance criteria were important for their own promotion. They also reported fewer training topics and fewer training and learning hours about a policy. Consequently they showed quite low familiarity with policy content. Finally, they were located in small installations where there were no unions to press for implementation.

On the reverse side, supervisors who were implementers of these two policies were older and had been in their installations significantly longer. They had lower educational attainments but were more receptive to change in general. In keeping with this attitudinal stance, they perceived a much greater need for the policies. Moreover, they expressed significantly larger degrees of involvement in their supervisory positions and believed that their own performance as managers rather than technical skill or seniority would be the important criterion for their own advancement. They report having received relevant training topics and hours and more learning hours to absorb the training. Consequently they had greater familiarity with the policies. Finally, they were in much larger installations that were unionized.

The pattern of the findings is striking. Some managers are being left out, or feel left out, of the change processes in these installations. The data show that the young, the lower-status, and females report significantly less diffusion of both policies, supporting the notion that they have been excluded in some respects. When we look at their attitudes, we see that not only have they been left out, but they have turned off. Their attitudes toward the policies tend to be negative and nonsupportive, when significantly different from those of other supervisors. Social change, including these policies, is obviously affecting the relatively powerless supervisors very differently. Or perhaps it is not the issue of power that links being female, young, and low-status to poor implementation of these policies, but a relatively low degree of inclusion, commitment, and identification with their work organizations. Other variables that are associated with poor implementation of these policies are variables that do not augur well for general supervisory performance: low job involvement, a belief that seniority is important while performance is not important for promotion, and a conservative attitude toward change itself. Thus the supervisor who is poor in implementing these policies may well be a generally poorer manager. The findings are more often significant and more consistent in pattern for the more pervasive and administratively emphasized EEO policy, even though this policy probably involves changes of larger magnitude than does the alcoholism policy.

What practical implications can be drawn from these findings? The case of the nonimplementer seems a difficult one indeed. It is hard to change such basic attidues as a general antipathy to change or low job involvement. There are limited possibilities for resocializing employees, and training is the main technique used, although patterns of reward and other techniques can be tried to change behaviors before attitudes.[1] At a minimum, all supervisors must be included in training and diffusion efforts for any envisioned changes, if implementation efforts are needed at all levels of supervision.

Also, time itself may be a helpful factor. Time on the job may erase some of the negative attitudes, if experiences at work negate the validity of those attitudes. It is possible that some nonimplementing supervisors have had insufficient time to be adequately socialized into their managerial roles, and that their difficulties with these policies are only part of their general lack of confidence about that role. Perhaps as they gain experience and earn higher status, they will become more receptive toward change because they will see themselves as having more impact on what occurs in their work organizations; at the present time, their low status may make them feel powerless and the policies seem irrelevant to them.

In any case, it is clear that there is room for improvement in the implementation of both of these policies. An alternative, payoff strategy would be to concentrate on those supervisors who are already implementers; in effect, to "accentuate the positive." Resources could be invested to devise ways in which the supervisor already engaged in implementing these policies could be encouraged and helped. Since this type of supervisor is located in the larger installations, another payoff would be gained automatically, because the investment would be reaching those installations where there are likely to be more alcoholism and EEO cases.

Directors

Installation directors who were implementers of both policies resembled implementing supervisors. They also expressed very positive attitudes toward change, had high job involvement, held higher-status civil service grades within the director role, and had longer installation tenure. They also believed that the quality of performance is the criterion on which their own promotion and careers are judged, rejecting seniority. Implementing directors also enjoyed a decentralized relationship relative to levels of authority above them, but located elsewhere—regionally, for example. Unlike supervisors, female directors were better implementers, especially of the EEO policy.

Directors were in better accord with both policies when they reported high visibility of work outcomes—that is, when the work of subordinates could be evaluated by relatively quantifiable and observable criteria—and also were more likely to be aware of the union's position on both policies. Size of installation was positively related to their appointing policy facilitators, while various measures of union influence and activities tended to have more mixed effects on implementation. For example, where unions are militant, directors are likely to adopt an overzealous interpretation of the alcoholism policy and also to engage in more diffusion of information about that policy. With unions more active in adversary activities, directors also perceive more administrative emphasis on EEO, while the reverse is true if the union concentrates on more general and social activities.

Also, directors had ambivalent effects on implementation by their lower-level supervisors. On the one hand, when directors were both powerful and professional, supervisors experienced more diffusion and had a higher sense of need for both policies. On the other hand, predominant effects of director variables on a variety of other implementing attitudes and actions of line supervisors were negative. The data suggest that directors may be ritualists about the policies, encouraging some important attitudes and motions, but discouraging a follow-through of these thrusts to actual policy use. This ambivalence was especially prominent relative to EEO. Thus, when powerful directors agreed with EEO strategies, they evidently influenced supervisors to be significantly less implementing. This ambivalent result could occur because of resistance by lower-level supervisors to an authority figure. It could also happen because directors pay only lip service to the policies and quietly influence subordinate managers to behave and believe negatively. Analyses that assessed directors' power and attitudes together as influences on supervisory implementation elaborated upon the findings for power alone. Favorable attitudes by powerful directors often had negative effects on supervisory implementation of the alcoholism policy, while favorable attitudes by less powerful directors accompanied greater use of that policy. For the EEO policy, the effects of director attitudes on supervisory implementation were more favorable when directors had relatively high levels of power, and were more evenly divided between positive and negative effects for low-power directors. There was some ambivalence in the findings, however, for both policies at both power levels.

As seems reasonable, the effect of directors upon policy facilitators they had chosen was less ambivalent. When high power and favorable attitudes of directors were combined, they produced largely positive effects on EEO facilitators. The attitudes of low-power directors had more mixed effects for EEO. The ambivalent effects were especially marked among alcoholism facilitators; but even here, director influence was largely positive, especially in the low-power condition.

The only policy-related attitude held by directors that most uniformly generated implementing responses by facilitators was the sense of need for either policy; but this finding did not hold for high-power directors relative to the alcoholism policy. While one relationship was negative and significant, the balance of the coefficients were substantial and positive, although not significant. With that exception, a sense of need was the key to activating the influential directors into exerting a positive influence on facilitators, at least. Unfortunately, the same attitude had more mixed results for supervisory implementation.

These findings suggest an untapped reservoir of potential leadership for implementation of these policies. If special training sessions for directors can convince them of the need for these policies, implementation efforts by facilitators might improve dramatically. On the other hand, influencing directors is *not* a sure-fire way to encourage implementation at other levels. The effects of their attitudes are sufficiently ambivalent to suggest that concentration of efforts at director levels would produce mixed responses, at best, at other levels.

However, the findings also suggest that the director of the small installation and the director who is given little autonomy perform badly in implementation of both policies. Clearly, if the upper echelons of management want to encourage change and conformity to innovative prescriptions, they must allow some discretion to management under them, including heads of even the smallest installations. Directors apparently must have freedom within which to operate, and need the greater responsibility that accompanies more authority before they are active implementers. If upper management wants better performance from directors, it will have to grant them more influence in decisions affecting their installations. In turn, directors will have to grant more autonomy to their subordinates in the supervisory chain before those supervisors are likely to act to encourage implementation.

Finally, we might reiterate that female directors, though very few in number, were significantly better implementers on some dimensions. Whether this is because women who manage to reach such positions are extremely superior managers or because they are more sympathetic, the finding deserves special mention.[2] Perhaps the promotion of more women to positions of comparable responsibility and status will enhance the possibilities for change and innovation in general in work organizations.

Facilitators

The role sets within which facilitators of the policies had to operate were made up of persons substantially different from them. Both demographically and on job-related attitudes, facilitators often differed from line supervisors and directors. There also were similarities, but not enough to overcome the differences and approach homophily within the role set. Prominent among the differences were the tendencies for EEO facilitators to be quite new employees and for alcoholism coordinators to be lowest of the three groups on receptivity toward change in general. Furthermore, some dissensus on actual policy content was apparent. For example, supervisors and directors saw less need for the policies than the policy facilitators did. Dissensus was substantial for both policies, making the facilitator's efforts more difficult.

Despite assumptions that attachment to a staff position would be the best location for the facilitator role, the results suggested that combination with a line manager position was the best for implementation of both policies. Also, formalization and work overload inhibited performance of the alcoholism facilitator, while the addition of staff time sharply improved it. For EEO facilitators installation size had significant results, suggesting more demands on the facilitator in large installations.

Regardless of how facilitators performed, however, they had only slight effects on the policy-related behavior of line supervisors. Perhaps this is due to the dissensus with which they must contend. Equally possible is that these roles have had insufficient time to "jell." Supporting this position was the finding that the simple amount of time a facilitator had been in his or her position significantly predicted more implementing efforts by facilitators. In short, it takes time to "learn the ropes" and shape a role that is only infrequently operative (Trice, 1962).

Growing from this summary are some practical suggestions that could reasonably be considered for relatively large work organizations in the private sector as well as in federal agencies:

Attach alcoholism coordinator roles to a line manager position and to an occupant who is receptive to change in general. Avoid overformalizing this role and double-check to see that it does not generate work overload in the line managers selected. Devise ways to increase a sense of need among both chief executives and lower-level supervisors, making certain that a sense of need is prominent among the attitudes held by the alcoholism coordinator. In this way compatible feelings provide him or her with role-set support. Above all, provide the alcoholism role with reasonable resources—particularly staff support—to carry out the expectations attached to it. This is the most obvious need among facilitators of the federal alcoholism policy; increases in staff time will decidedly improve their efforts to implement despite their own personal feelings about change and the presence of dissensus in their role sets. The data from this study are compelling in this regard.

Find ways to induce alcoholism facilitators to remain in the role for sizable periods of time. Personal reasons, such as being members of Alcoholics Anonymous or having a close relative who has suffered alcoholism, will help. Such persons at times, however, present a risk of overzealousness and are too infrequently available to provide a large corps of motivated facilitators for an enormous, far-flung work system like that within the U.S. Civil Service.

In addition, some reward system is clearly needed for facilitators. There also needs to be some positive and negative sanctions that facilitators could wield in order to secure more recognition of their efforts by busy line managers. Finally, since occasion to use both policies is relatively infrequent, short intense role playing and simulation training is appropriate on a regular basis. Like lifeguards, facilitators ideally must be on the alert for situations that are unlikely to occur frequently. Consequently, their "readiness" needs to be consistently maintained.

Much the same could be said about EEO facilitators. Overzealousness runs the risk of backlash, and although "minorities" are much more numerous than those personally affected by problem drinking, members of minority groups may not be available or equipped for EEO facilitator roles.

The roles of the EEO functionaries were more developed, largely because more resources have been devoted to the development of the role. Some factors do seem to produce beneficial results on implementation by EEO functionaries, however. Increased amounts of information and time in the role were associated with greater implementation. The latter finding presents a dilemma to those appointing these functionaries. It seems both unwise and unfair to hold successful EEO functionaries in their positions too long, because it could then become a dead-end position for them (Kanter, 1977), especially when the incumbent is a minority group member or a woman. Thus, some balance must be struck between the requirements of the facilitator roles and the welfare of the employees filling those roles. One solution is to make the roles part-time ones, attached to other important line management positions. Another solution is to be sure that performance in that role is as rewarded as any other supervisory performance.

We do not mean to imply that members of minority groups are not suitable to facilitate EEO policies, however. Only 23 percent of these facilitators were female, and only 28 percent were members of a racial or ethnic minority group (with some being both female and a member of an ethnic minority), so that we cannot blame minority group members for lack of implementation of the EEO policy; the data do not indicate that minority group membership was strongly associated with implementation one way or the other. What we are suggesting is that *more* than membership in such groups should be considered, and that prior attitudes of any candidate are an important factor to consider in choosing facilitators of change, providing management indeed wants the change carried out.

What seems most clear from the findings is that it is desirable to have facilitators for changes who favor change and who believe in the particular change envisioned and the methods by which that change is going to be attempted. Otherwise it is hard to see how the internal change agent can become involved in and committed to implementing any change.

Organizational Structure

Despite some variations, larger installations clearly had more implementation of both policies. The explanation for this is straightforward: The more employees, the greater the likelihood that alcoholism and equal opportunity problems will emerge. However, it must also be remembered that size was positively related to many aspects of implementation for individual supervisors, where the question of scale of operations is not as relevant. After all, each supervisor has about the same number of subordinates as any other, and so the probabilities for use of the policy are more similar for individual supervisors than they would be for entire installations. What the two findings together suggest is that the greater probability of a problem case arising in the large installation leads to a greater probability of some supervisor or other dealing with one under policy provisions; this may then become a precedent, leading to a kind of snowball effect once the policy has been tried out. This is borne out by the finding that size is less consistent in predicting implementation for the alcoholism policy than for EEO. There are clearly more instances for use of the EEO policy in larger installations than for the alcoholism policy; this means the probability of the ice-breaking tryout of the policy is also greater in those installations.

Also, installations with more job specialization were apt to be more implementing of both policies. Yet, as they became taller in terms of hierarchical levels, they were less implementing. It seems reasonable to conclude that in a more complex division of labor lie opportunities for implementers to act upon their own initiative, particularly when their decisions do not have to go through many levels for approval.

The influence of division of labor was particularly noticeable among professionals, where specialization would tend to be pronounced. Installations with professionalized work forces showed a sharp differentiation between the EEO and alcoholism policies, clearly favoring the former. Manifestly, professionalism is uncongenial to the notion of alcoholism in its midst, but, intellectually at least, professionals tend to embrace the ideologies behind EEO—especially to the point of diffusing information and being receptive to the strategies.

At the same time, the ambivalent note sounded earlier reappears relative to the education of installation directors. Even for EEO, more highly educated directors failed to produce positive associations with implementation of either policy. For the two policies studied here, higher education alone is of doubtful benefit.

Far more consistent as a predictor of a nonimplementing installation are the twin structural features of centralization and formalization. When these are *not* a feature of an installation, policy implementing attitudes and behaviors are *high*. The interpretation seems clear: Formal rules constrict behaviors, especially those that are innovative, while centralization of power and authority at the higher levels reinforces that constriction, largely acting to freeze out change for lack of either opportunity or motivation toward it—even when the changes are mandated, as in the cases studied here. Consistent with this interpretation were our findings concerning the autonomy of an installation: The more its autonomy within the overall system, the more implementing it was.

The practical implications of these findings are clear, and have already been stated. Upper management must allow those managers at lower levels to have some autonomy, or they will not implement change, probably because they feel constricted and probably because they may not feel much stake in the change. Why take the risk in a situation where you have little responsibility anyway?

The fact that greater amounts of education and professionalization does not promote these changes is vexing. No doubt, as we have suggested earlier, professionals only favor change that fits their professional values. If this is the case, efforts must be made to find a fit between the content of changes that are going to be implemented and the existing values of the important managers involved in the implementation process. Perhaps training sessions and diffusion of information about these policies have not been tailored sufficiently to the recipients. Perhaps other arguments can be found that will stress the value to the more educated managers and directors of such policies. Perhaps the problem has arisen because of something relatively simple, like having training and informing done by persons who are less educated than the most educated supervisors. In any case, our findings clearly suggest that upper management cannot count on professionals to automatically favor change and innovation; they may be better at generating change, but they are clearly not always superior at implementing it.

Environmental Variables

Size of the community, unlike that of the installation, tended to discourage implementation efforts, as did high population concentrations. In such settings, diffusion was much less. By contrast, implementing installations tended to be located in traditional suburbia with its more youthful, affluent populations and higher social classes, yet with noticeable unemployment. As expected, however, there emerged some evidence that older populations in the community encouraged more diffusion of the alcoholism policy. More certainty can be attached to the influence of high proportions of blacks in the community. For EEO this demographic feature of an installation's environment, as might be expected, was associated with larger amounts of supervisory training about EEO and more past and expected future use of the EEO policy among supervisors.

Apart from these trends, which are themselves somewhat mixed, the relationships found between community features and policy implementation are of little practical value. Compared with the influence of structural features internal to the installation, the effects of the environmental features are minor. Also, they give rise to few practical suggestions for ways to increase implementation of these policies. Nonetheless, it does seem that any effort to step up policy diffusion might focus initially on installations in locations with high population density.

The Union

The presence of a union, in and of itself, was associated with supervisory use of the alcoholism policy—both actual and expected. This association became even more pronounced when supervisors worked with employees of lower skills. The union's presence was less important for EEO and seemed to have a dampening effect on that policy. Unexpectedly, the position taken by the union on the policy content had little effect on supervisory behavior and attitudes.

We found that supervisory knowledge or ignorance of the union's position, however, was an important variable. For the alcoholism policy, the major factor distinguishing between aware and unaware supervisors was the amount of policy information diffused to them. Apparently, supervisors became aware of the union's position through a variety of information about this policy. For EEO, greater diffusion again accompanied supervisory awareness of the union's position, but union characteristics were also important; aware supervisors worked with larger, older, and more skilled unions. Only union size was related to supervisory awareness of the union's position on the alcoholism policy. Where EEO was concerned all diffusion and union characteristics tested were associated with supervisory awareness.

More important, aware supervisors were superior implementers; they expressed greater need for both policies, expected to use them more in the future than did unaware ones, and had actually used the policies more in the past. Consequently, those forces associated with awareness are important for implementation efforts; higher amounts of policy diffusion evidently trigger awareness of the union's position on a policy and, in turn, implementation by supervisors.

More refined multiple regression analyses of aware and unaware groups of supervisors reaffirmed the prominent role that policy diffusion played in implementation of these policies. The results also demonstrated the crucial effect an active union can have on the pronounced and widespread tendency to implement an alcoholism policy chiefly at lower skill levels. For supervisors aware of the union's position on this policy, skill level was not related to policy use, indicating that implementation of the alcoholism policy was spread across all skill levels among these supervisors, while those unaware supervisors with unskilled employees were more likely to use this policy.

Because occasion to use either policy was typically limited—especially in the alcoholism policy—the finding that awareness of the union's adversary activities predicted expected use of the alcoholism policy is a particularly valuable one. Since unions are relatively new to the federal sector, their influence will probably be mounting as they increase in numbers and grow older, and this projected higher expected use may reflect a projection by supervisors of their increasing influence. Consistent with this point was the finding that where unions were more active in adversary activities, supervisors had higher perceived need for both policies. Also, where unions were older, aware supervisors projected more need for EEO. At the same time, aware supervisors with smaller unions reported more need and more expected use of the alcoholism policy. Also, aware supervisors who worked with older unions agreed with the performance emphasis of the alcoholism policy far more than unaware managers.

The age of the union was related to various facets of implementation of the EEO policy. Thus supervisors working with larger, older, and more skilled unions were more aware of these unions' position on that policy. It may well be that older, more skilled, and larger unions generate concern about EEO matters, as evidenced by the greater expected use of EEO among aware supervisors with older unions. For the alcoholism policy, although aware supervisors had older unions, the age of the union was not a significant predictor of implementation.

Overall, it is difficult to escape the conclusion that the indirect effect of the union on policy implementation by supervisors—especially of the alcoholism policy—was perhaps as influential as were the efforts of the Civil Service Commission and federal managers. The ambivalence about EEO, especially among installation directors, probably comes, in part, from a similar ambivalence among union officials. In sum, they complement each other. Both the managers of the installations and the managers of a union, when one is present, have reasons to deflect and displace EEO goals. In contrast, union officials usually have reasons to espouse the alcoholism policy, since it gives them an excellent chance to force management to perform for the welfare of a union member in a rehabilitative manner rather than a disciplinary one, and they can take much credit for this. In various ways, our results support these inferences and underscore the compelling necessity for the influence of labor unions to be incorporated into efforts to explain and implement changes and innovations in personnel policy.

Coming from this summary are practical suggestions for action that seem to be relevant to many workplaces, both in the public and private sectors. Clearly, line supervisors should be aware of the union's position. Equally clear is the large extent to which the diffusion of policy information generates this awareness. Beyond doubt, the alcoholism policy was underdiffused, but even EEO appears to be underdiffused in this regard. Since a powerful force in union behavior is the reaction of rank-and-file members, it seems reasonable that diffusion might be directed more at nonmanagerial employees, who after all are the rank and file for management as well as for the union.

Next it seems obvious that when managers are informed about the adversary activities of unions in general, and their unions in particular, they become more receptive to these policies and, in general, better implementers. These findings reinforce the value of general supervisory training about unions. For the federal agencies, where unions have dramatically increased recently, an emphasis in such managerial orientations toward the union's rising influence in the future seems particularly appropriate.

Also appropriate would be some practical stance toward older and younger unions. On the one hand, older unions seem to exercise the greater implementing influence. On the other, because unions are rapidly growing in the federal sector, more unions of the future will be young ones. Perhaps one viable approach to this dilemma would be to captialize immediately on the favorable influence of older unions, especially where alcoholism is concerned, but devise ways to encourage policy facilitators to cultivate younger, new unions. It is helpful to recall at this point that the less effective supervisors in implementing either of these policies tended also to be the younger ones. In short, there is a common theme here: Younger unions and younger supervisors generate less implementation. It calls for facilitators to experiment with approaches that might generate a sense of policy need among the more youthful element in their environments—both young managers and young unions.

ALTERNATIVES TO CONFORMITY

Throughout the results already presented, we have analyzed the data on implementation in terms of the general model of change presented in chapter 1, and often more specifically in terms of the three-stage model of the implementation phase that was discussed and tested in chapter 3. The use of this approach has been valuable for an orderly and systematic investigation of possible factors associated with the implementation process. Using it, we have been able to identify a wide range of factors that appear to affect implementation in these federal organizations.

But, as was pointed out in chapters 1 and 3, conformity with policy prescriptions is not the only alternative for members of these organizations. Policies specify both means and goals, and individuals within organizations can accept both, one or the other, or neither. Merton long ago suggested a typology that is convenient for considering such a range of possible reactions to influence processes, and we shall use that typology to perform some further analyses on these data in an attempt to succinctly summarize the key findings of this study, and also to ascertain whether such an approach is better in accounting for the behaviors we have measured in this study than the more straightforward three-stage model on implementation.

The Mertonian Modes of Adaptation

In his paradigm of social structure and anomie, Merton (1938) identified two elements that are important for understanding conformity and deviance. The first of these are culturally defined goals—those purposes or interests that are held out as legitimate objectives for members of society. For the alcoholism and EEO policies, (1) the identification and successful treatment of drinking problems and (2) the elimination of discrimination in hiring and other personnel practices might be considered the ultimate goals of the policies. These goals have been culturally defined through the changes of social values that accompanied and made the passage of relevant legislation possible. The second elements that Merton focused upon are the means to such goals. As he put it, "Every social group invariably couples its cultural objectives with regulations, rooted in the mores or institutions, of allowable procedures for moving toward these objectives" (1969:163). Such regulations have been incorporated in both policies, as discussion in preceding chapters has made clear. Not only do these policies specify ways that the goals should be reached, but they also caution against a variety of methods that are not allowable.

Using American society as an example, Merton went on to analyze the heavy emphasis on goals of success without corresponding emphasis upon legitimate avenues for reaching those goals. He then presented a typology of possible types of adaptation that individual members of society might use to deal with the goals and prescribed means that their culture and society present to them (see table 9.1). The first adaptation he identified was that of the conformist; this adaptation presents the modal response in a stable

T A B L E 9.1 Merton's Typology of Modes of Individual Adaptation[a]

Modes of Adaptation	Culture Goals	Institutionalized Means
Conformity	+	+
Ritualism	−	+
Innovation	+	−
Retreatism	−	−
Rebellion[b]	±	±

[a]Reprinted from Robert K. Merton, "Social Structure and Anomie," *American Sociological Review* 3 (1938): 676, with permission of the publisher and the author.
[b]We do not use this mode in our analyses.

society and is its source of order and predictability. But Merton's main purpose in this analysis was to identify and discuss the various types of deviant adaptations, in which persons achieve socially approved goals through nonprescribed means (innovators), or lose sight of goals and scale them down to what is achievable—a sort of private escape from the pressures (ritualists)—or simply drop out of the competition because they find themselves shut off from means that are both legitimate and effective (retreatists).

This typology can be applied to social systems other than a total society, such as the United States. It seems apparent that work organizations, as formal social systems, also embue their workers with socially approved goals and prescribe certain means as legitimate in reaching those goals. As we have already discussed in the early chapters, the two personnel policies studied can be seen as an attempt to both identify such goals and to specify and institutionalize means to their attainment. Admittedly, the goals and means embodied in these policies are much more specific than those discussed by Merton, but his approach may nonetheless be useful in assessing whether or not the particular modes of adaptation he has suggested do occur in specific situations, can be measured, and then can be associated with other social characteristics that may throw some light on how these modes of adaptation arise.

In adopting such a view of the implementation of these policies, we will be moving away from the rather simple assumptions that governed our earlier analyses. Essentially, the models presented earlier assumed positive relationships between successive stages or steps in a process. But, if we allow for the possibility that a given person (a ritualist) can accept means but not achieve goals, the association between these two successive steps for that individual will be not positive, but negative. The same thing would occur for an innovator, who achieved goals while rejecting prescribed means. If, on the other hand, the organization only included the other two types—the conformists and the retreatists—everything would work out as the models predict: low endorsement of means would lead to little or no achievement of goals, while high acceptance of means would lead to high achievement of goals, and these two types together would produce large positive relations between the two successive phases of the change or implementation process. These relationships are presented graphically in figure 9.1.

In the figure, we have also specified those elements of the implementation process that we have identified as either means or goals of the policies. As discussed in chapter 3, we viewed the diffusion and training stage of implementation as the means prescribed by the policies to realize their goals. Without relevant information, no actors within the installations could be expected to be able to implement the policies. At the same time, we did not feel that the mere diffusion of information was an end or goal in itself. Surely the framers of these policies intended that they should be used. The goals of the policy we have considered to be dual: changing attitudes and changing behaviors. While behavioral change might be considered the *sine qua non* of policy implementation,

Figure 9.1 Association Between Means and Goals in Four Modes of Adaptation.

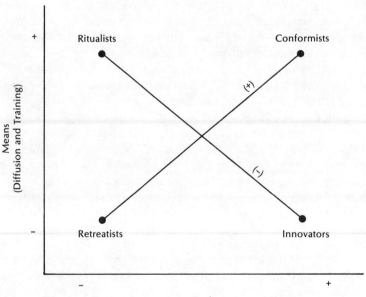

attitudinal change is also important when policies cannot be expected to be in continual use. The intent of the policy, in such instances, must be to create a readiness to use the policy should the occasion for its use arise. We have attempted to tap this readiness to use the policy through our so-called receptivity measures, which assessed a variety of attitudes toward each policy. We have assessed both past and future use of the policies as well.

Our first task in applying the Mertonian typology to our data was to determine which installations were conformist, which were ritualist, which were innovators, and which were retreatist in their implementation of these policies. Accordingly, we decided to divide our installations along two dimensions of possible conformity for each policy, with one grouping determined by the relative position of the installation for diffusion and receptivity of that policy, and the other grouping determined by their positions on diffusion and use. In assessing diffusion and receptivity together, we are looking at attitudinal conformity. In our analyses of diffusion and use, we are analyzing use conformity.

In order to assign installations to the various categories of adaptation, we ranked installations on those individual variables seen as most important and consistent with policy provisions in each phase of implementation. For these analyses supervisory responses were used, since there were multiple responses for all installations, and this was expected to lead to greater reliability in assigning installations to categories. Three variables were ranked for the diffusion phase: diffusion to supervisors, diffusion to employees, and training hours spent by supervisors. The average of the ranks for these three variables determined the overall rank for each installation on policy diffusion—its acceptance of policy means. A similar ranking and averaging procedure was used for variables that measured performance or attainment of policy ends. Two variables were used for the receptivity phase: agreement with the medical model and assessed benefit for the alcoholism policy; and overall agreement and assessed benefit for the EEO policy. Also, three variables were used to compute the overall ranks for use: the proportion of supervisors using the policy, the average number of past uses per supervisor, and the average of supervisors' expected use in the future. After the average ranks had been determined for all three phases, each installation was either judged to be high or low on each phase, depending on the overall ranking in each category. Since there are 71 installations in the sample, ranks at the mid point of 35.5 or above were considered high (+), while those below 35.5 were considered low (-).

Following the scheme presented in table 9.1, those installations high on both means and ends were then classified as conformist; those high on means but low on ends were ritualists; those low on

TABLE 9.2 Basis of Assignment of Installations to Modes of Adaptation

| | ATTITUDINAL CONFORMITY | | USE CONFORMITY | |
MODE OF ADAPTATION	Receptivity (Goals)	Diffusion (Means)	Use (Goals)	Diffusion (Means)
1. Conformist	High[a]	High	High	High
2. Ritualist	Low	High	Low	High
3. Innovator	High	Low	High	Low
4. Retreatist	Low	Low	Low	Low

[a]Where position of installation as high or low is determined by an average of ranks for variables measuring this phase of the implementation process.

means but high on ends were innovators; and those low on both means and ends were retreatists. Codes from 1 to 4 were assigned to the groups in the order given above. Using these procedures, each installation was classified into one of the categories four times: for attitudinal conformity with the alcoholism policy, use conformity with the alcoholism policy, attitudinal conformity with the EEO policy, and use conformity with the EEO policy. These procedures are summarized in table 9.2.

Discriminant analysis was then used to test the degree to which our ranking and averaging procedures had yielded distinct and separable groups.[3] Results of these discriminant analyses classified 83.3 percent of the installations the same as we did for attitudinal conformity with the alcoholism policy, 82.9 percent for use conformity with the alcoholism policy, 75.0 percent for attitudinal conformity with the EEO policy, and 85.3 percent for use conformity with the EEO policy. We judged from these results that our ranking and averaging procedure had been largely successful in grouping the installations in a meaningful way on the basis of the data, and we then proceeded with further analyses.

Explaining Modes of Adaptation

We could now go on to the more interesting phase of this analysis: the identification of those factors associated with the different modes of adaptation to the policies. Since we had already performed extensive analyses of the implementation of the policies, our goal in these new analyses was to profit from what had gone before and to bring together the various findings already obtained in a way that would both summarize and clarify those findings, and perhaps also improve upon the amount of variation in behaviors within the installations that we could account for.

In identifying possible candidates for inclusion in these analyses, we are guided by two considerations: Only variables that had already been shown to be importantly associated with implementation were eligible, and we wanted to try to include variables that had practical implications in that they represented conditions that could conceivably be changed or manipulated by some actors in the organization. We thus hoped to answer one of the frequent criticisms of social science research: that it focuses on factors that cannot be changed or manipulated and thus is of little use to policy makers or administrators (Scott and Shore, 1974). We were not able to realize this last goal entirely; some factors, like size of the installation, were clearly important, but are not easily manipulated at will.

These considerations and the general limitations imposed by the number of installations in our sample[4] led us to the list of predictor variables given in table 9.3, which also presents the results of the subsequent discriminant analyses.

In interpreting these results, the discriminant coefficients presented can be interpreted much like the regression coefficients or betas presented throughout the book—that is, as a measure of association similar to a correlation coefficient—except that the association is now between the particular predictor variable given and an underlying canonical variate or discriminant function that represents all of the variables simultaneously. Also, as in the case of betas, the coefficient should be interpreted like a partial correlation—that is, the association of that single variable with the discriminant function while partialing out the effects of all other independent or predictor variables. Thus the size of the discriminant coefficient is an indicator of how to interpret each of the discriminant functions that underlie the classifications of the groupings according to the four modes of conformity-deviance. For example, for attitudinal conformity with the alcoholism policy, the most important variables on the first discriminant function are size and staff size of the facilitator.[5] On the second function, the most important variables are the director's attitude toward change, community demand (in this case, median age), and the director's assessment of the importance of performance for his or her promotion. (Variables stressed in interpretation of these results have been printed in boldface type in the table.) The best way to assess how these variables actually relate to the various modes of adaptation is to look at a diagram in which each individual installation has been plotted along the dimensions defined by the discriminant functions. This diagram is presented in figure 9.2 for attitudinal conformity with the alcoholism policy. On the diagram each installation is plotted by a symbol that denotes the group to which it was assigned. In addition, group centroids—the center of the plot for each group in two-dimensional space—are indicated. A fur-

TABLE 9.3   Results of Discriminant Analyses[a] of Various Factors Associated with Modes of Conformity and Deviance in Policy Implementation

PREDICTOR VARIABLES	ALCOHOLISM POLICY				EEO POLICY			
	Attitudinal Conformity		Use Conformity		Attitudinal Conformity		Use Conformity	
	1	2	1	2	1	2	1	2
Mean supervisory job involvement	.49	.50	−.59	−.03	.13	.75	.29	−.33
Mean supervisory education	−.46	−.32	.35	.08	−.65	.09	−.62	.43
Size of installation (log)	.67	.26	−.79	.28	−.01	.26	.01	.82
Centralization	−.25	−.41	.29	.14	.71	.23	.64	.13
Percentage employees working under written rules	.06	−.19	−.08	−.16	.14	.04	.26	−.24
Staff size of facilitator	.74	−.41	−.47	−.20	−.05	.42	−.09	.07
Director's attitude toward change	.11	−.57	−.00	.07	−.34	.10	−.39	.01
Importance of performance for promotion of director	−.19	.64	−.05	−.02	−.33	.16	−.24	.10
Director's civil service grade	−.09	−.17	.09	−.40	−.19	.29	−.19	−.64
Administrative emphasis to director	.06	−.17	−.01	.61	.33	.30	.30	.45
Union presence	−.07	−.20	.07	.65	−.12	.02	−.17	−.69
Percentage professional and managerial workers in community	.26	−.12	−.42	−.41	.41	.30	.23	−.08
Community demand	−.13	−.73	.23	.34	.13	.10	−.05	−.13
Canonical correlation	.62	.52	.62	.56	.68	.51	.67	.51
Percentage correctly classified	62.9%‡		70.0%‡		57.1%‡		68.6%‡	
Wilks lambda	.39**		.38**		.35†		.36**	

[a]The first two standardized discriminant functions are presented for each analysis; three were obtained in all analyses, but the last function in each analysis was relatively unimportant in terms of variance accounted for.

[b]Median age for alcoholism policy; percentage of blacks in community for EEO policy.

** p < .05
† p < .01
‡ p = .000

ther aid available for interpreting the plots is the values of the centroids of the various groups, also given in the figure. These values easily indicate the relative position of each group on the two discriminant functions. The arrows on the diagram indicate the direction of key variables that define that function, according to the discriminant coefficients in table 9.3.

Before discussing the diagram and its interpretation, it is worth noting that all of the analyses yielded impressively high percentages of correct classifications of installations and that the relative sizes of the canonical correlations between the first and second discriminant functions for each analyses seem to indicate that there are indeed two underlying dimensions in each analysis. Altogether, the results give most encouraging support for our application of the Mertonian model to the analysis of implementation. The model seems to fit the data well and is quite successful in discriminating between installations in a meaningful way.[6]

Turning to figure 9.2, we can see that attitudinal conformity with the alcoholism policy is associated substantially with resources available, with demand factors, and with attitudes of the installation director. Looking horizontally along function 1, the conformist installations are the largest and have provided the largest amount of staff help to their alcoholism coordinators. These installation characteristics become less prevalent as we proceed through the deviant

Figure 9.2 Plots of Four Modes of Adaptation of Installations for Attitudinal Conformity with Alcoholism Policy

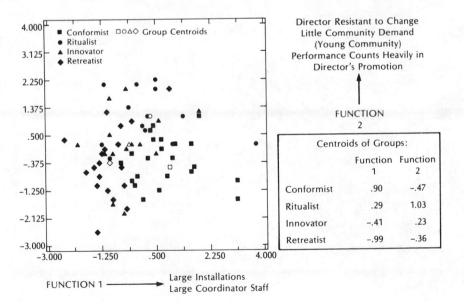

types of adaptation, with retreatist installations being smallest and lowest on staff resources for coordinators. When we look at function 2, the ritualist installations stand out as having directors most resistant to change, least community demand, and directors who believe that performance issues count heavily toward promotion. It is not surprising that such installations diffuse the policy but fail to adopt appropriate attitudes toward it. In communities with a younger median age, the need for the policy is probably not as evident, yet directors want to appear compliant. Innovator installations are relatively close to ritualists on function 2, while both conformist and retreatist installations were more likely to have the opposite characteristics: directors favorable to change, older communities with accompanying demand, and directors less concerned about their performance.

Considering use conformity with the alcoholism policy, as plotted in figure 9.3, we find different factors important in use of this policy. Here the conformist installations are plotted on the left, and rather toward the top of the figure. This indicates, as do the values of the centroids, that the conformist installations are lowest on the values that define function 1 and highest on values that define function 2. Thus the installations conforming with use of the alcoholism policy as well as diffusion are relatively large and are characterized by high job involvement of their supervisors; they also tend

Figure 9.3   Plots of Four Modes of Adaptation of Installations for Use Conformity with Alcoholism Policy

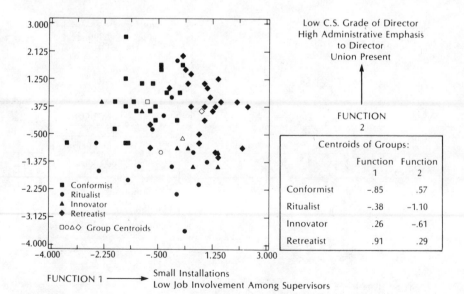

Centroids of Groups:		
	Function 1	Function 2
Conformist	−.85	.57
Ritualist	−.38	−1.10
Innovator	.26	−.61
Retreatist	.91	.29

to be unionized and to have directors who perceived this policy as having relatively high administrative emphasis. Again, retreatist installations that were low on both diffusion and use tend to be like the conformist installations on one factor and least like them on another. That is, the least conforming installations were also high on administrative emphasis and tended to be unionized; however, they were also among the smaller installations with lower supervisory job involvement. The ritualist installations tended to be lowest on perceived administrative emphasis and least likely to have a union present, although they were reasonably large and high on job involvement. Again, the innovator installations were closest to the center of the four groups, being neither highest or lowest on any of the predictor variables. However, it is evident from the diagram that the innovator installations are closest to the ritualists—a rather unexpected finding. The analysis of the details of policy use by supervisors presented in chapter 4 suggested that many uses of this policy did not eventuate in treatment or positive outcomes. Thus, it is possible that the innovators in our sample also redefined policy goals, reporting any action taken about problem drinking as a case of policy use, when perhaps the strategy of the policy was largely ignored in these cases. What is clear from the data presented in chapter 4 is that these innovative approaches may have backfired, because the substituted means did not produce the desired (by the policy) ends.

When we turn to conformity with the EEO policy, we find that some of the same variables are important but the direction of relationships is somewhat different. In figure 9.4 the conformist installations are again on the left, indicating they are not centralized in decision making, have highly educated supervision, and have directors who are receptive to change and concerned about performance. On all of these factors retreatist installations are most opposite. Surprisingly, the installations that are innovative on attitudinal conformity to the EEO policy are not too different from the retreatist installations on function 1, indicating that they are centralized, with lower levels of supervisory education and directors resistant to change. This is hardly the usual picture of innovators. Again, policy ends, as well as means, may have been redefined in reports of policy use.

On the second function, there are other surprises. For this policy, the least conformist installations are apparently highest on facilitator staff and supervisory job involvement, while the conformists are next highest on these dimensions. Apparently, large facilitator staffs do not ensure agreement with the normative prescriptions of the EEO policy and may even provoke resistance to this policy where supervisors are highly job-involved. Innovators are lowest on these dimensions, and ritualists are in a more moderate position. Apparently where job involvement is low, large staffs and diffusion are not needed to bring attitudes into agreement with the EEO policy.

On conformity with use of the EEO policy (figure 9.5), the picture is again different, although some of the same indicators are again important in discriminating between groups. The conformist installations are again the least centralized, have highly educated supervisors, and have directors receptive to change. This finding is exactly the same as that for attitudinal conformity with this policy. On the other function, the innovator installations stand out as largest, without a union, and with relatively low-status directors. The retreatists are most opposite on this dimension, being smallest, being most likely to have a union, and having high-status directors. Conformist and ritualist installations are relatively close together on this function.

In summary, size seems to enhance conformity with the alcoholism policy and use of the EEO policy without much prior training and diffusion effort. Large facilitator staffs enhance attitudinal conformity to the alcoholism policy, while they seem to promote either conformity or complete resistance in the case of EEO. Supervisory attitudes are also important: High job involvement of the supervisory

Figure 9.4   Plots of Four Modes of Adaptation of Installations for Attitudinal Conformity with EEO Policy

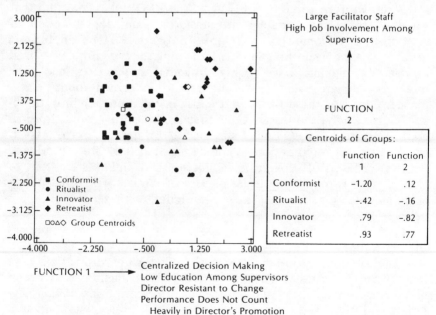

work force is associated with conformity for use of the alcoholism policy, but with both attitudinal conformity and attitudinal retreatism for the EEO policy. In the case of the alcoholism policy, the presence of a union seems to lead to either conforming or retreatist modes of adaptation, while in the case of EEO, the presence of a union is associated with retreatism.

In three of the four analyses, a director whose attitudes are resistant to change is associated with deviant modes of adaptation, while one who is convinced that performance criteria are important to his promotion is likely to ensure only ritualist conformity with the alcoholism policy, stimulating diffusion but little other support for the policy. For the EEO policy, directors' belief that managerial performance is important for their promotion enhances conformity and ritualism. Neither the lowest-status nor the highest-status directors are most likely to be associated with most use conformity with the EEO policy, however, more educated supervisors are favorable to either attitudinal conformity or use conformity with the EEO policy. For the same policy, decentralization of decision making within the installation is also associated with both types of conformity. Finally, the median age of the community is related to attitudinal conformity with the alcoholism policy, older communities being more favorable, perhaps because of different community norms about problem

Figure 9.5　Plots of Four Modes of Adaptation of Installations for Use Conformity with EEO Policy

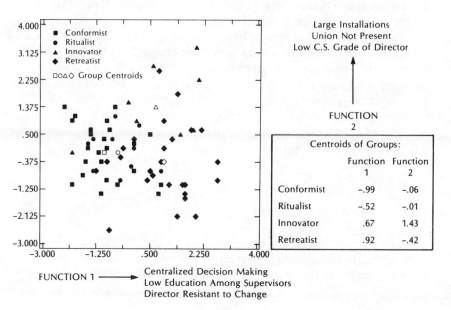

drinking, but also perhaps because more problems with drinking arise in communities of older persons.

Again we find some similarities across the two policies, but also substantial and interesting differences. Overall, the findings suggest that various bureaucratic and supervisory resources available to upper management can have a substantial impact on conformity with the provisions of the alcoholism policy, but that some of the same factors have less clear results for the perhaps more controversial,[7] and surely more pervasive, EEO policy, which also calls for changes of larger magnitude. With the latter type of policy change, some resistance apparently occurs, and this resistance seems to be importantly associated with issues of status and power: civil service grade of directors and educational level of supervisors, and the degree of centralization of decision making within the installation. Attitudes toward work and toward change are also important in determining the mode of adaptation used by the installation in response to more pervasive and controversial changes. Finally, it should be pointed out that these analyses did not correctly classify every single installation. In individual cases, there are exceptions to these generalizations, but the pattern of the findings and the number of correct classifications suggest that a clear trend is present in the data supporting the conclusions drawn above.

Another useful criteria to use in judging these results is to ask: When we consider all of these predictor variables together, how much of the variance in the implementing behavior of these installations can be accounted for? The more variance accounted for, the better the fit between the conceptual scheme used, the predictor variables, and the actual implementing behaviors measured. On this criterion, the results of these analyses are very encouraging. The results in table 9.3 account for 59 and 60 percent of the variance for attitudinal and use conformity with the alcoholism policy, and 63 and 62 percent of the variance for attitudinal and use conformity with the EEO policy.[8] Again, while this is not perfect prediction, the results indicate that we have tapped dimensions of some significance for actual behaviors within these installations.

Comparison of Results of Discriminant Analyses with Earlier Results

All of the independent variables used in the discriminant analyses were chosen because they had rather consistent relationships with the indicators of the three stages of implementation used in earlier chapters. The value of the earlier analyses is supported by the relatively high proportions of correct predictions we were able to make using these variables to discriminate between different modes of response to the policies in the results just discussed. We did not experiment with many combinations of possible independent variables; the results given are those from the first discriminant analyses attempted. We felt the levels of prediction obtained were sufficiently high to confirm the value of this new approach. Because there are so many possible correlates of change in formal organizations, it is difficult to specify in advance of any analysis exactly which variables are most important in predicting organizational response to change effects. Our results thus represent only one of many possible combinations of such variables; future research and theorizing will, we hope, narrow the list of candidates. At the present state of knowledge we must acknowledge that some other combination might have predicted the four modes of response as well as or better than the variables used.

The chief value in these results is thus in identifying variables that are *among* the important predictors of organizational response to change efforts. The question we have tried to answer is what discriminates the organization that conforms from the organization that does not. Additionally we want to know which of the previously identified variables predict more complete implementation—as indicated by conformity—as compared with partial implementation efforts—indicated by two of the deviant modes of response.

The results given in figures 9.2 through 9.5 can be considered as reflecting the patterns illustrated in figure 9.1, where retreatists and conformists are the polar ends of the upward implementation slope, and ritualists and innovators anchor the ends of the opposing slope. It is interesting and important to note (1) that the group centroids on function 1 for all four figures indicate a monotonic relation between the first function and membership in the four groups and (2) that the conformists and retreatists are always at the opposite extremes on the first functions. Since the first functions account for somewhat larger amounts of variance as indicated by higher canonical correlations (table 9.3), the results for these first functions can be seen as supporting the monotonic assumptions used in our three-stage model and in most other research on change. The second functions tend to discriminate the ritualist and innovator modes of response—represented by the declining slope of figure 9.1—from the conformist and retreatist modes. In practical terms, the second functions discriminate those installations with partial implementation from those that did relatively much for all three stages (conformist) or did little or nothing for all stages (retreatist). It is therefore only the results for the second discriminant functions that modify our earlier results.

It is necessary to reconsider the results separately for the two functions in the figures to make this point clear. Looking at figures 9.2 and 9.3, we find that several variables are monotonically associated with the modes of response: The size of the installation is positively related to fuller implementation (conformity versus retreatism) of the alcoholism policy, whether attitudinal or use conformity is considered. More staff assistance for the facilitator is positively related to attitudinal conformity, while supervisory job involvement is associated with more use conformity for this policy. It seems fair to conclude that earlier findings for these variables are thus confirmed in these new analyses.

Considering the variables important in discriminating "deviant" or partial implementation, we find that a director who has a low civil service grade and negative attitudes toward change, but who believes his promotion will depend on performance, and a young community characterize a ritualist response—and to a lesser degree an innovative response—to this policy.

Turning to EEO and figures 9.4 and 9.5, we similarly find that decentralization of decision making, high education of supervisors, and a director receptive to change characterize the conformist, or more fully implementing, installations. For this policy, the director's belief that performance is important for his promotion was also positively related to attitudinal conformity. Function 2 for the EEO analyses in figures 9.4 and 9.5 are important in discriminating innovative response, but not ritualists. The innovator installations for this policy have smaller facilitator staffs and low job involvement among supervisors for attitudinal conformity, and are larger, have no union, and have low-status directors for use conformity with EEO. Since we could not assess fully whether cases of reported policy use were always in full compliance with the policy intent and provision, it is possible that the innovators for this policy are somewhat displacing policy goals in using the policy—an issue already mentioned in connection with the alcoholism policy.

None of the findings resummarized above reverse earlier reported results. On the contrary, they underline again the importance of some of the variables identified as forces encouraging conformity with policies. What the results do is to specify whether the lack of facilitating or supportive factors is more likely to lead to total lack of an attempt to implement (retreatist response) or to some deviant, but partial, effort toward implementation. Two such factors are as follows: (1) The lack of a union and low civil service grades for directors characterize a deviant mode of implementation for use of either policy. (2) Unions and high-status directors clearly produce pressures toward conformity. For other variables, relationships vary by policy. Small size best characterizes the retreatist installation for the alcoholism policy but an innovative response for use of EEO. Low job involvement among supervisors discriminates retreatist response to use of the alcoholism policy and innovative response to attitudinal conformity with EEO. Small facilitator staff characterizes the retreatist response to the alcoholism policy and the innovator response in attitudinal conformity for EEO. A director resistant to change predicts a retreatist response to EEO and a ritualist response to the alcoholism policy. A director who believes performance is important for his or her promotion tends to foster a ritualist response to use of the alcoholism policy and a retreatist response to attitudinal conformity with EEO.

Clearly, the discriminant analyses results refine the earlier findings but do not contradict them. Generally, we would comment that work-related attitudes seem most important in discriminating among responses by installations to the alcoholism policy, while power, status, and professionalization dimensions more importantly characterize modes of response to EEO. Given the differences in pervasiveness and magnitude of change that the policies represent, the findings make sense. With the exception of union presence and director status, important for use of both policies, the findings suggest that just plain better management characterized fuller implementation of the alcoholism policy, whereas the addition of professionalization among supervisors and decentralized decision making was required to create a climate favorable to fuller implementation of EEO.

IMPLICATIONS FOR EVALUATIVE RESEARCH

Because of the current tendency in American society to try to achieve social change through the use of policies and programs, the area of evaluative research has recently received increased attention. Lawmakers who have the formal authority to set up and fund such programs are understandably interested in the outcomes of the new efforts and expenditures. So are taxpayers. The same concern about "results" stimulates increasing efforts at evaluation in the private sector as well.

Traditionally, and as a result of such social pressures, evaluative research is usually viewed as the assessment of *outcomes*. For example, studies of job-based alcoholism programs use a variety of practical measures of outcomes—improvement in supervisory ratings, decrease in lost sick days, and job maintenance—as yardsticks to evaluate program effectiveness (Roman and Trice, 1976; Smart, 1974; Hilker et al., 1972; Franco, 1960). A careful review of the extant evaluative studies of job-based alcoholism programs (Edwards, 1975), however, failed to find any evaluations of the implementation of such programs. This deficiency bears directly on the value of the studies conducted, since, as Edwards comments from his own experience, "in fully half of the evaluation efforts . . . it has been discovered that activities were not being conducted as planned" (1975:64). Apparently the evaluations of program outcomes assume that the intervention strategies inherent in the policy and programs have been implemented with sufficient intensity and over sufficient time to produce the desired outcomes. Results that have been reported here for the federal alcoholism policy make it evident that this is a highly questionable assumption.

While the well-designed and well-executed evaluation of outcomes can answer the question whether or not outcomes have occurred, it often cannot answer the question why such outcomes have or have not occurred, and what needs to be changed to bring about the desired outcomes if the results suggest that present levels of outcomes are not satisfactory. In practical terms, those looking at "unfavorable" results of such an evaluation cannot tell whether the desired outcomes were not obtained because the strategy embodied in the program was deficient or because the strategies were never implemented. As Elmore puts it, "each program model constitutes a 'black box' whose contents are largely unspecified but whose effects are known to some degree" (1976:116). Hyman and Wright (1967) provide an anecdote that dramatizes the importance of determining what has happened in the implementation stage in order to properly judge outcomes. They describe an evaluation study (not their own) of the impact of the use of flyers in a propaganda campaign; the study concluded that the campaign had had little impact. Later it was discovered that the flyers had never been distributed!

The research reported here was an attempt to correct some of the deficiency existing in the literature on job-based alcoholism policies by developing and executing a design for evaluating the implementation process in such programs. It has been apparent for some time that job-based alcoholism programs have tendencies toward instability, because of power struggles, personalities, and other forces (Trice and Roman, 1974:148), and that the reality of existing programs often fails to match what is said about them (Weiss, 1972:33; Hyman and Wright, 1967:744). Bernstein and Freeman (1975:18) and others have described the evaluation of implementation as "process evaluation," which they describe as "determining whether or not the particular program, intervention, or treatment was implemented according to the stated guidelines." Their statement describes very well what we have done, using the content of these policies to develop specific assessments of what had occurred within these federal installations that was in accord with policy provisions and intent. We found that in order to assess the implementation of these policies adequately, it was necessary not only to familiarize ourselves with the history and content of these policies, but also to develop a coherent model of the process of change within organizations, from which we could develop a more specific model of the implementation process itself. It also was necessary to identify the key actors in the implementation process and to collect data from all in order to obtain a relatively complete picture.

Combining our knowledge of details within the policies and our conceptual scheme, we were able to generate very specific and parallel measures of various stages of implementation for each policy appropriate to the various actors. We realize that these measures are not applicable to other types of changes, and probably not even to the same changes in another organizational system.[9] But we feel that the delineation of the concepts and the general approach to measurement should be amenable to alterations that would make the general approach useful for other changes and in other settings.

Process evaluation is "especially appropriate for the initial stages when goals are more apt to shift and objectives remain fuzzy" (Trice and Roman, 1973:13). To evaluate the outcomes of an intervention or change process before the program has had time to "jell" is obviously premature.[10] As mentioned earlier, outcomes are unlikely until implementation has occurred. We felt that this might be the case for the federal alcoholism policy before the research began. The policy was just three years old at the time of our evaluation, and given the size of the federal bureaucracy, we did not feel this was too long a time for the initial stages of the implementation effort. What we found, of course, was rather uneven implementation, with some installations giving evidence of fairly complete implementation and others showing little efforts toward implementation of this policy.

The situation found for the EEO policy was different; this policy had clearly received more extensive implementation in various of these installations. However, there were also cases where little implementation had occurred for this policy, despite the longer history for this social change and the greater administrative emphasis placed upon it. As we have often indicated, changes of greater pervasiveness and larger magnitude may encounter greater resistance, while it is likely that changes of lesser pervasiveness and smaller magnitude may more often suffer mere neglect.

One advantage of assessing the implementation of a new program or policy in its early stages is the opportunity to provide feedback of the results obtained to the system studied. This has been done at the highest levels for the alcoholism policy,[11] the evaluation of which was the primary aim of this research. Thus, the evaluation of implementation of and by itself can be useful to both policy makers and those who have major responsibilities for overseeing execution of the resulting new programs.

Finally, by considering the implementation process as problematical, we early identified a useful approach to the problem of nonconformity to policy prescriptions and intent. Since we focused on implementation itself, we considered that process in considerable detail, and we realized that its progress could be reversed, halted, or slowed, or that there might never be any progress at all. The approach that we used to handle the various possibilities for resistance and nonconformity to these policies was a familiar paradigm that seemed to lend itself to operationalization for this particular research problem. By using Merton's four principal modes of adaptation, we were able to identify the characteristics of installations that are associated with either conformity or nonconformity of various kinds to these policies. Through the combination of classification and the technique of discriminant analysis we were able to account for substantial portions of the variance in implementing behavior within these installations. In the process, we were also able to summarize and synthesize findings from a variety of vantage points taken earlier.

We feel the exercise has been a healthy one. We know more about the implementation of change, and we know more about the implementation of these particular policies. We also feel we know more about how to evaluate the implementation process, and we hope others will follow our lead in viewing all stages of change as problematical and in trying to discover ways to more fully expose the many possibilities and complexities of human behavior inherent in organizational change.

Appendix

THE FOLLOWING ARE brief descriptions of the ways in which our various measures were operationalized. The material is organized by who or what is being characterized and measured: supervisors, directors, facilitators, the installations themselves and their environment, and the unions. Generally, the order of the chapter analyses have been followed in this summary; however, some measures appear in more than one chapter, and they have been listed only once under the person or group being measured.

SUPERVISORS

Diffusion Phase

1. *Diffusion to Supervisors* on each policy: Respondent was asked what he or she had received on alcoholism policy and on changes in EEO policy.
    a. Number of forms of information checked from the following list: memorandum or letter, insertion for policy manual, special brochure, at a meeting, word of mouth, posted on bulletin board.
    b. Number of sources of information checked from the following list: Washington headquarters, regional office, installation head, program coordinator, a fellow worker, public media.
    c. The above were summed for an overall measure of diffusion to supervisors.
2. *Diffusion to Employees* for each policy: Respondent was asked how policies were communicated to employees in his or her

unit, using same format for forms and sources and same procedures for summing them as above.

3. *Training Hours* for each policy: Respondents were asked how many hours they spent in the last two years in training programs directly related to the alcoholism (or EEO) program; number of hours was used as a measure.

4. *Training Topics* for each policy: Respondents were asked what topics they recalled were discussed in training sessions.

   a. For the alcoholism policy, the number of topics checked from the following list: role of alcoholism coordinator, treatment programs, definition of alcoholism, identifying poor work performance, role of medical department, rights of employees, and sick leave provisions.

   b. For the EEO policy, the number of topics checked from the following list: training programs for upward mobility, performance evaluation, recruiting programs, skill assessment, role of EEO counselor and EEO counseling, role of EEO committee, reporting procedures, EEO formal complaint system, and EEO action plan.

5. *Learning Hours* for each policy: Respondents were asked how much time overall they estimated spending learning about the alcoholism (EEO) policy. (The training hours item followed this item several pages later in the instrument. Diffusion items preceded it.)

6. *Administrative Emphasis* for each policy: Respondent was asked to indicate on a 3-point Likert scale how the introduction of the alcoholism (EEO) policy compared with the way other policies or policy changes were introduced: whether each policy had received more, typical, or less exposure, administrative emphasis, and techniques used to inform. Items were standardized and averaged after factor analysis indicated a single factor for each policy. Cronbach alphas: .93 for alcoholism policy; .93 for EEO policy.

Receptivity Phase

7. *Familiarity* for each policy: Respondents were asked to what extent they were familiar with policy aspects on 5-point Likert scales where 1 = totally unfamiliar, 2 = unfamiliar, 3 = relatively unfamiliar, 4 = adequately familiar, 5 = very familiar.

   a. For alcoholism policy, they were asked about the following provisions: medical benefits, disciplinary actions and procedures, definition of alcoholism, situations in which policy applies, leave provisions, union relations, treatment alternatives, reporting procedures, and grievance procedure.

b. For EEO policy, they were asked about the following procedures: formal complaint system, EEO action plan, community action program, incentives program, disciplinary actions and procedures, statistical reporting system, agency self-evaluation, training program, and recruitment program.

c. For each policy, relevant items all loaded satisfactorily together in a factor analysis containing both sets of items. Cronbach alphas: .93 for alcohol; .93 for EEO.

8. *Agreement* with policy provisions: Respondents were asked to assess the degree to which they agreed or disagreed with various policy provisions using 6-point Likert scales where 1 = disagree strongly, 2 = disagree, 3 = disagree slightly, 4 = agree slightly, 5 = agree, 6 = agree strongly. All of these statements for both policies were factor-analyzed together, and the items that loaded satisfactorily together on factors were then standardized, and averaged for individual scale scores (Stevens, 1976). Those items without satisfactory loadings on a single factor were used as single items where appropriate.

a. *Agreement with medical model of alcoholism:* Two-item scale: (1) agree alcoholics should be granted sick leave to obtain treatment and (2) agree that alcoholism is a treatable illness. Alpha = .51.[1]

b. *Zealous agreement with alcoholism policy:* Two-item scale: (1) agree that supervisors should try to identify employees who may be developing drinking problems and (2) agree that supervisors should concern themselves with employees' off-the-job drinking. Alpha = .56.

c. *Performance emphasis* for both policies: Two-item scale: (1) agree that supervisors can best help employees with drinking problems by concentrating on their work performance and (2) agree with the same statement for minority employees. Alpha = .56.

d. *Supervisors should do own counseling* for both policies: Two-item scale: (1) agree that if an employee appeals to a supervisor about a drinking problem, the supervisor should counsel him about it and (2) agree with the same statement for an EEO problem. Alpha = .69.

e. *Overall agreement with EEO policy:* Three-item scale: agree (1) that supervisors should try to identify employees who qualify for promotion, (2) that any denial of equal employment because of race, sex, religion, etc. is a case of discrimination, and (3) that supervisors should concern themselves with identifying cases of discrimination. Alpha = .61.

f. *Zealous agreement with EEO policy:* Single item: agree that minority members should be sought out for employment vacancies.

9. *Assessment* of policies: Respondents were asked to give their assessment of each policy on the following 7-point scales in semantic differential format: (1) not needed in this installation ... widely needed, (2) hard to administer ... easy to administer, (3) harmful to installation ... beneficial to installation, (4) socially harmful ... socially beneficial, (5) minimal step for the government ... giant step, (6) useless to supervisors ... useful, (7) bad idea ... good idea. Items for both policies were then factor-analyzed together, and the same methods were used to derive the following scales.

a. *Perceived benefit* for each policy: Five-item scale: average of responses 3-7 for each policy. Alpha = .82 for alcohol; .88 for EEO.

b. *Ease of administration* for both policies: Two-item scale, average of second response above for each policy. Alpha = .50.

c. *Perceived need* for both policies: Two-item scale: average of first responses above for each policy. Alpha = .49.

Use Phase

10. *Past use* for each policy: Dummy variable. Coded as 1 for those respondents indicating they had had opportunity to use policy procedures with employees they supervise since July, 1971.

11. *Number of past uses* for each policy: Number given by respondent when asked how many employees he or she has dealt with in the period since the relevant policy was issued.

12. *Expected future use* for each policy: Respondent was asked to indicate on a 7-point Likert scale how frequently he or she thought the alcoholism (EEO) policy will be used in his or her unit, with 1 = almost never, 7 = frequently.

Personal Variables

13. *Age:* Approximate age checked from the following categories: 30 and under, 31-40, 41-50, 51-60, 61 and over.

14. *Sex:* Coded by interviewer at time of interview as part of identification code; 1 = female, 2 = male.

15. *Ethnicity:* Dummy variable. Respondent was coded as belonging to various racial (white or nonwhite) and ethnic minority groups on the basis of appearance and surname by the interviewer. These codes were combined so that membership

in any minority group was coded as 1; others were coded as 0.

16. *Education:* Checked from following categories as response to question about educational background: no college, some college, bachelor's degree, some graduate study or professional study beyond bachelor's, master's degree, doctoral degree, other graduate or professional degree. Responses were recoded to reflect approximate years of schooling, with no college = 12, some college = 14, bachelor's degree = 16, some graduate study = 17, master's degree = 18, doctoral degree = 21, M.D. = 24, and other specific degrees as our knowledge indicated.

17. *Attitude toward change:* Sum of five items adapted from Hage and Dewar (1973) and Neal (1965). Respondents indicated agreement with five statements on 6-point Likert scales (same as 8 above): (1) There is really something refreshing about enthusiasm for a change. (2) If I were to follow my convictions, I would devote much time to change movements. This seems to me to be a primary need today. (3) The current situation in our society calls for change; we should do something now (we must respond at once). (4) If you want to get anywhere, it's the policy of the system as a whole that needs to be changed, not just the behavior of isolated individuals. (5) Any organizational structure becomes a deadening weight in time and needs to be revitalized. Alpha = .74.

18. *Job involvement:* Sum of six items developed by Lodahl and Kejner (1965). Respondents indicated agreement with the following four statements on 4-point Likert scales: (1) The major satisfaction in my life comes from my job. (2) The most important things that happen to me involve my work. (3) I'm really a perfectionist about my work. (4) I live, eat, and breathe my job. (5) I am very much involved personally in my work. (6) Most things in life are more important than work (reverse-coded). Alpha = .66.

19. *Commitment* to organization and to federal service: Respondents were asked to indicate whether they would change jobs under the following conditions: no, slight, or large increases in pay, freedom, status, responsibility, and opportunity to get ahead. They could check for each level of each inducement: (1) Yes, definitely change, (2) Undecided, or (3) No, definitely not change. These items were combined into 5-point coding schemes to register increasing levels of commitment, where 1 = change with no increase and 5 = no change with large increase. Tabulations indicated that combinations not used in the 5-point coding scheme were rarely used by respondents, because they were illogical (Beyer, Stevens, and Trice, 1977).

a. *Organizational commitment:* Respondent was asked about

job comparable to present one, but not in the same installation. Alpha = .83.

   b. *Federal service commitment:* Respondent was asked about job comparable to present one, but not in the federal government. Alpha = .93.

Role Variables

20. *Tenure within organization:* Number of years respondent indicated when asked how long he or she had been at this installation.

21. *Tenure in position:* Number of years respondent indicated when asked how long he or she had been in this particular position.

22. *Tenure in federal service:* Respondent was asked how long he or she had been employed in the federal civil service. Response was coded in number of years.

23. *Civil service rating:* Respondents were asked what their civil service rating was. They usually responded in terms of G.S. grades; the code was the number of the grade. Some were commissioned officers, and their ranks were converted to an equivalent G.S. rating.

24. *Managerial level:* Computed from number of levels of supervisors respondent indicated were between him and head of installation; scoring then reversed so that those reporting to director had highest score, those with many levels had lowest score (number of levels was subtracted from six—the highest number of levels reported, plus one).

25. *Skill level of employees:* Coded from response to question asking respondent to describe the work done by employees under his or her supervision. A 6-point scale was derived, with 1 = unskilled only, 2 = unskilled and skilled, 3 = skilled only, 4 = unskilled, skilled, and professional together, 5 = skilled and professional, 6 = professional only. Unskilled work was that judged to require very little training, skilled work would require some special training, and professional work would ordinarily require a college degree in a specific area.

26. *Work overload:* Respondents were asked how often they were bothered by things related to their jobs, using a 5-point scale with 1 = most of the time, 2 = a good deal of the time, 3 = about half the time, 4 = occasionally, 5 = seldom. Three-item scales: mean of standardized responses to the following questions: How often are you bothered by the feeling that you have (1) too little authority to carry out the responsibilities assigned to you, (2) too heavy a workload, one that you can't

possibly finish during an ordinary work day, (3) to take over
the work that others have been unable to finish. These items all
loaded on a single factor, Cronbach's alpha = .54.

27. *Factors Important for Promotion:* Respondents were asked
how much various factors contributed to their career advancement, indicating their assessment on 7-point Likert scales with
1 = unimportant and 7 = important. These items were factor-
analyzed and yielded the following scales:

    a. *Importance of performance in promotion:* Four-item scale:
mean of standardized responses to (1) performance of the
unit you supervise, (2) quality of your performance, (3)
interpersonal skills, (4) administrative skills in applying formal policies. Alpha = .79.

    b. *Importance of seniority for promotion:* Response to single
item on seniority.

    c. *Importance of technical skills for promotion:* Response to
single item on technical skills.

Organizational Variables

28. *Size* of installation: Number of employees in the installation
(part-time are counted as 1/2 employee).

29. *Union presence:* Dummy variable. Coded 0 if respondent indicated no union was present in installation, coded 1 if he or she
gave other response (questions asked whether he or she was a
member of the union.)

30. *Percentage of supervision:* Number of supervisors in installation
divided by total number of employees.

31. *Centralization of decision making:* Following Beyer and Lodahl
(1976), respondents were asked who had influence in ten
decisions: (1) selecting and hiring temporary or part-time personnel after positions are approved, (2) approving overtime, (3)
approving a change in the physical layout of the work area, (4)
approving an expenditure for new equipment costing $100, (5)
approving merit raises, (6) change of day-to-day work procedures, (7) approval of participation in training programs, (8)
approval of annual leave, (9) approval of nonroutine travel,
(10) recommendations for professional awards. Respondents
were allowed to check all of the following levels they judged
had influence in each decision: first-line supervisor, middle-
level supervisor, division head (supervisors reporting to director), and director. Because numbers of levels of supervision
varied across installations, only two levels were used for this
measure. The number of decisions checked for first-line supervision was subtracted from the number made by the director.

DIRECTORS

Diffusion Phase

32. *Diffusion to directors:* Same as 1 for supervisors.
33. *Diffusion by director to facilitators:* Dummy variable. Coded 1 when facilitator checked installation head as a source of his or her information about the policy.
34. *Aware of union position* on policy: Dummy variable. Coded 1 when director answered question asking about union position.
35. *Administrative emphasis* for both policies: Same as 6 for supervisors. Alpha = .91 for alcoholism, .90 for EEO.

Receptivity Phase

36. *Agreement* scales: Same as 8 for supervisors; also *Idealistic Agreement:* Respondents were asked to assess the degree to which they agreed or disagreed with the statement that discrimination in hiring and promotion can be eliminated. Same response format as 8 for supervisors. Alpha = .49 for overall agreement with EEO.
37. *Assessment* scales: Same as 9 for supervisors. Alphas = .81 for alcoholism, .82 for EEO.
38. *Assessed scope of problem* for each policy: Respondents were asked to estimate the degree to which alcoholism (EEO) was a problem within their installations at the present time, and how many employees had been or could be benefiting from the policy. Response formats were 7-point Likert scales with 1 = none and 7 = many.

Use Phase

39. *Appointed facilitator* for each policy: Dummy variable coded 1 when directors indicated they had appointed someone as coordinator of the alcoholism program (EEO officers and counselors).
40. *Formal job description for facilitator* for each policy: Dummy variable coded 1 when facilitator reported having formal job description.
41. *Official time allocation to facilitator* for each policy: What proportion of the facilitator's time he or she reported was officially allocated to the policy involved; it is presumed that director has made or has influence over that time allocation.
42. *Staff size given to facilitator* for each policy: Number of

persons facilitator reported are staff designated to help facilitator in policy-relevant work.

43. *Official title given to facilitator* for each policy: Dummy variable coded 1 when facilitator reported having official title.
44. *Facilitator's tenure in role:* Facilitators were asked when they were appointed to their role. Coded as number of months since appointment.
45. *Expected use* for each policy: Same as 12 for supervisors.

Personal Variables

46. *Age:* Same as 13 for supervisors.
47. *Sex:* Same as 14 for supervisors.
48. *Ethnicity:* Same as 15 for supervisors.
49. *Education:* Checked from following categories in response to question about educational background: no college; some college; B.A.; some graduate study; M.A. or M.S.; M.B.A. or M.P.A.; J.D. (law); Ph.D.; M.D., etc.; other graduate or professional degree. Recoded for number of years of education similarly to 16 for supervisors, except J.D. = 19 years, other graduate or professional degree = 18 years.
50. *Attitude toward change:* Same as 17 for supervisors. Alpha = .73.
51. *Job involvement:* Same as 18 for supervisors. Alpha = .59.
52. *Commitment* to organization and to federal service: Same as 19 for supervisors. Alpha = .84 and .94, respectively.
53. *Professionalization:* Director was asked about professional memberships, professional activity, and journals read.
    a. *Professional memberships:* Number of professional associations director reports belonging to.
    b. *Professional activity:* Two-item scale combining number of meetings attended annually with number of associations in which respondent is officer.
    c. *Journals read:* How many different journals respondent reports having read regularly.

Role Variables

54. *Tenure within organization:* Same as 20 for supervisors.
55. *Tenure in position:* Same as 21 for supervisors.
56. *Tenure in federal service:* Same as 22 for supervisors.
57. *Civil service rating:* Same as 23 for supervisors.
58. *Work overload:* Same as 26 for supervisors. Alpha = .69.
59. *Factors Important for promotion:* Same as 27 for supervisors. Alpha = .88.

Organizational Variables

60. *Size of installation:* Same as 28 for supervisors.
61. *Union presence:* Same as 29 for supervisors.
62. *Union influence:* Three-item scale. Respondents were asked three questions about union influence. The responses to these questions were factor-analyzed and combined into a single scale by averaging standardized scores for each item: (1) Does the union have the support of employees in this installation? Responses ranged from 1 = most of the employees are strongly behind it to 4 = a lot of the employees are opposed. (2) How much influence does the union have in this installation? Response format ranged from 1 = a great deal of influence to 4 = no influence. (3) Do relations with the union affect the way you carry out your supervisory duties? Response format ranged from 1 = I often take the union into account to 4 = I never take the union into account. When constructing scale, coding of items was reversed so that higher numbers = more influence. These items were adapted from some used by Derber et al. (1965). Alpha = .65.
63. *Union activities:* Respondents were asked to check which activities the union had been active in. These responses were factor-analyzed and two factors emerged:
    a. *Union adversary activities:* Three-item scale: whether union engaged in (1) grievance procedures, (2) arbitration, and (3) attempts to influence personnel policies.
    b. *Union employee benefit activities:* Four-item scale. How many of the following activities the union had engaged in: (1) employee facilities and conveniences, e.g., parking, lunchroom, rest rooms; (2) social activities, e.g., bowling, picnics; (3) group benefits, e.g., insurance, vacation tours; (4) union newspapers, bulletins, and newsletters.
64. *Formalization:* Directors were asked about rules and regulations in their installation.
    a. *Percentage working under written rules.* Respondents were asked to estimate the percentage of employees who must conform to specific written rules and procedures for carrying out their day-to-day duties. Response format ranged from 1 = 1-10 percent to 10 = 91-100 percent. When respondent said none, this was coded as 0.
    b. *Specificity of written rules.* Respondents were asked to describe the written rules and procedures for the employees in part (a) above on a 6-point Likert scale where 1 = very general guidelines and 6 = very specific procedures.
65. *Centralization of decision making and director influence:* Ten-

item scale. Centralization of decision making was derived from same question described in 28 for supervisors. The number of decisions that the director checked as one in which he or she had influence was the score of his or her influence in some analyses and was called centralization of decision making in others.

66. *Structural power:* Respondents were asked what changes they could make in internal organization of their installations.

   a. *Director's power:* Two-item scale. Responses to the following items: (1) creating a new division and (2) eliminating a division or combining two into one. Responses were coded 0 = no, 1 = yes under limiting conditions, and 2 = yes. Items were standardized and averaged.

   b. *Director's ability to transfer personnel:* Response to transferring personnel between divisions. Responses coded as above.

67. *Director budget discretion:* Respondents were asked over what proportion of their installations' budget they had some discretion in allocation. Responses were coded from 0 to 100 percent.

68. *Uncommitted monies:* Respondents were asked to what extent there had been uncommitted monies available to their installation during the past year. Response formats were on 5-point Likert scales with 1 = none, 5 = a great deal.

69. *Resource decentralization of installation:* Two-item scale. Respondents were asked to what degree their recommendations on operating budgets and personnel allocations were actually followed. Response formats were on 5-point Likert scales with 1 = not at all and 5 = a great deal. Items were standardized and averaged after factor analysis.

70. *Director contact with superiors:* Two-item scale. Respondents were asked how often they had (1) regularly scheduled meetings or conferences and (2) other contacts with their immediate supervisor. Response formats were in terms of specific time frequencies; for (1) they ranged from 1 = never to 6 = more than monthly; for (2) they ranged from 1 = never to 6 = more than weekly. Items were standardized and averaged.

71. *Visibility of consequences:* Respondents were asked to indicate how installation performance was evaluated by their superiors. The number of the following relatively hard criteria checked is the score for this variable: quotas, errors, client complaints, costs, turnover. Soft criteria that respondents could also check included professional standards, employee satisfaction, compliance with official policies.

FACILITATORS

Diffusion Phase

72. *Diffusion to facilitators:* Same as 1 for supervisors.
73. *Diffusion by facilitators to employees:* Dummy variable. Coded 1 when facilitator checked himself or herself as source of information about policy in diffusion to nonsupervisory employees.
74. *Diffusion by facilitators to supervisors:* Dummy variable. Coded 1 when facilitator checked himself or herself as source of information about policy in diffusion to supervisors.
75. *Administrative emphasis* for both policies: Same as 6 for supervisors. Alphas = .83 for alcoholism, .89 for EEO.

Receptivity Phase

76. *Agreement* scales: Same as 8 for supervisors, except each facilitator was asked only about policy he or she administered. Alpha = .54 for overall agreement with EEO.
77. *Assessment* scales: Same as 9 for supervisors, except each facilitator was asked only about policy he or she administered. Alphas = .77 for alcoholism, .64 for EEO.

Use Phase

78. *Past use:* Dummy variable coded 1 if facilitator reported having had occasion to use relevant policy with employees of that installation.
79. *Number of past uses:* Number given when respondent was asked to estimate the number of employees for whom he or she had applied some aspect of the relevant policy.
80. *Number of policy uses per 100 employees:* Response to 79 above divided by total number of employees in the installation, and the result multiplied by 100.
81. *Number of employees who could benefit per 100 employees:* Response to question asking respondent to estimate the total number of employees who have benefited or could benefit from the relevant policy, divided by the total number of employees in the installation, and the result multiplied by 100.
82. *Who was consulted in setting up program:* Respondents were asked to check all of the following they had consulted in setting up the policy-relevant program: For both policies—personnel department, director of the installation, union repre-

sentatives, fiscal office, Office of Legal Counsel, your immediate supervisor, and supervisors in your installation. In addition, for alcoholism policy—medical department,* regional occupational health representative,* agency alcoholism coordinator at the headquarters level, CSC Office of Retirement, Insurance and Occupational Health*; for EEO policy—EEO agency director,* regional EEO personnel,* CSC EEO personnel,* Women's Program Coordinator,* EEO officer,* 16-point Program Coordinator.*

a. *Number of medical personnel consulted* for alcoholism policy: Number checked from starred items above for that policy.

b. *Number of EEO personnel consulted* for EEO policy: Number checked from starred items for that policy.

c. *Number of others consulted in organizational bureaucracy:* Number checked from items common to both policies above.

83. *Level of information on community facilities:* Respondents were asked whether they kept certain information relevant to each program. The numbers of types of information kept was coded for this item from the following types: location, contact person, description of treatment and cost of treatment for alcoholism policy or function of agency for EEO.

84. *Number of supervisors talked to about policy:* Respondents were asked approximately how many supervisors they had talked with about the relevant policy in the past six months.

85. *Number of supervisors talked to in group meetings:* Respondents were asked how many of these contacts (from 84) were in group meetings.

86. *Policy provisions used:* Respondents were asked to check each of the following policy provisions used, and to estimate the number of times they had used each provision.
    For alcoholism policy:

a. *Application for medical benefits:* Number of estimated times used.

b. *Referral to community agencies:* Number of estimated times used.

c. *Referral to counselors* connected with this installation: Number of estimated times used.

d. *Conferences with affected supervisors:* Number of estimated times used.

e. *Disciplinary actions and procedures:* Number of estimated times used.

f. *Leave provisions:* Number of estimated times used.

g. *Contact with union:* Number of estimated times used.

h. *Number of provisions used in past:* Number of provisions (a) through (g) checked as used in past.

  i. *Overall activity level:* Total of estimated times that all provisions (a) through (g) were used in the past.

For EEO policy (coded as above):

  a. *Applications for promotion.*

  b. *Training programs* to provide upward mobility.

  c. *Recruiting procedures.*

  d. *Formal complaint systems.*

  e. *Counseling.*

  f. *Extra administration of civil service exams.*

  g. *Performance evaluations.*

  h. *Reporting procedures.*

  i. *Conferences with affected supervisors.*

  j. *Contact with union.*

  k. *Number of provisions used in past:* Number of provisions (a) through (j) checked as used in past.

  l. *Overall activity level:* Total of estimated times that all provisions (a) through (j) were used in the past.

Personal Variables

87. *Age:* Same as 13 for supervisors.
88. *Sex:* Same as 14 for supervisors.
89. *Ethnicity:* Same as 15 for supervisors.
90. *Education:* Same as 46 for director.
91. *Attitude toward change:* Same as 17 for supervisors. Alphas = .74 for alcoholism coordinators, .72 for EEO functionaries.
92. *Job Involvement:* Same as 18 for supervisors. Alphas = .51 for alcoholism coordinators, .52 for EEO functionaries.
93. *Commitment* to organization and to federal service: Same as 19 for supervisors. Alphas = .91 and .96 for alcoholism coordinators, .90 and .96 for EEO functionaries.

Role-related Variables

94. *Tenure within organization:* Same as 20 for supervisors.
95. *Tenure in role:* Respondents were asked when they were appointed to their facilitator role. Coded as number of months since appointment.
96. *Tenure in federal service:* Same as 22 for supervisors.
97. *Civil service rating:* Same as 23 for supervisors.
98. *Work overload:* Same as 26 for Supervisors. Alphas = .45 for alcoholism coordinators, .59 for EEO functionaries.
99. *Factors important for promotion:* Same as 27 for supervisors. Alphas = .90 for alcoholism coordinators, .60 for EEO functionaries.

100. *Official status:* Dummy variable. Respondents were asked their official title in connection with relevant policy. Coded 1 if they had official title.
101. *Formal job description:* Dummy variable. Coded 1 if respondent reported receiving official job description.
102. *Official time allocation:* Same as 41 for director.
103. *Staff size:* Same as 42 for director.

Organizational Variables

104. Size of Installation: Same as 28 for supervisors.

INSTALLATIONS

Diffusion Phase

105. *Diffusion to supervisors:* Mean for installation of 1 for supervisors.
106. *Diffusion to employees:* Mean for installation of 2 for supervisors.
107. *Training hours:* Mean for installation of 3 for supervisors.
108. *Training topics:* Mean for installation of 4 for supervisors.
109. *Learning hours:* Mean for installation of 5 for supervisors.
110. *Administrative emphasis:* Mean for installation of 6 for supervisors.

Receptivity Phase

111. *Familiarity:* Mean for installation of 7 for supervisors.
112. *Agreement:* Mean for installation of various measures under 8 for supervisors.
113. *Assessment:* Mean for installation of various measures under 9 for supervisors.

Use Phase

114. *Past use:* Mean for installation of 10 for supervisors; represents proportion of supervisors who have ever used policy in the past.
115. *Number of past uses:* Mean for installation of 11 for supervisors.
116. *Expected future use:* Mean for installation of 12 for supervisors.

Organizational Variables

117. *Size of installation:* Same as 28 for supervisors. Many of the analyses involving structural variables used the logarithm ($\log_{10}$) of size because size tends to have curvilinear relations with other measures of structure (Beyer and Trice, 1976).
118. *Formalization:* Same as 64 for directors.
119. *Professionalization:* Three measures of expertise and education were used:
    a. *Education of director:* Same as 49 for directors.
    b. *Education of supervisors:* Mean for each installation of 16 for supervisors.
    c. *Median G.S. grade of employees:* Median of G.S. grades of all employees in the installation as reported on Personnel Information Summary (PIS).
120. *Complexity:* Four measures of complexity were used:
    a. *Division of labor:* Number of different job titles in an installation as reported on PIS.
    b. *Functional differentiation:* Dummy variable. Coded 1 if the highest level of horizontal differentiation is based on different functions for subunits; coded 0 if subunits have same or similar functions.
    c. *Horizontal differentiation:* Number of subunit heads reporting to installation director, as reported on PIS.
    d. *Vertical differentiation:* Number of levels of supervision in the tallest subunit, as reported on PIS.
121. *Organizational autonomy:* Two-item scale, same as resource decentralization of installation, 69 for directors.
122. *Centralization of decision making:* Three measures were used:
    a. *Influence of upper management:* Based on same question and responses as 65 for directors. Responses were factor-analyzed and two factors emerged. First factor combined influence of installation director with that of his division heads (supervisors reporting directly to him). Therefore this measure is the average of the number of decisions in which the director and division heads have influence in the installation, as reported by the director.
    b. *Line supervisors' influence:* Based on second factor of same responses. This measure is the sum of the number of decisions made by first-line supervisors, as reported by the director.
    c. *Decentralization of hiring decisions:* Two-item scale. Average of director responses to two questions about how influence is exercised in hiring decisions within the installation: (1) Who has the final authority in hiring new personnel at the

first-line supervisory level? (2) Who actually exercises the most influence in who gets hired at this level? Response formats ranged from 1 = someone superior to director to 6 = the immediate supervisor of the person to be hired.

123. *Percentage of supervision:* Number of supervisors divided by the total number of employees, as reported on PIS.

124. *Percentage of clerical staff:* Number of employees with clerical job titles divided by the total number of employees, as reported on PIS.

Environmental Variables

125. *Urban or rural:* Three measures were obtained from U.S. Census data for community in which the installation was located:
    a. *Community population:* Community population in thousands as reported in *County and City Data Book* for 1972 (U.S. Bureau of the Census, 1973).
    b. *Population density:* In tens of persons per square mile.
    c. *County* (not city): Dummy variable. Coded 1 if population is less than 25,000; only county data available and used.

126. *Socioeconomic characteristics:* Three measures from U.S. Census data were used:
    a. *Median family income:* In hundreds of dollars.
    b. *Median years of education:* For persons 25 years or older.
    c. *Median age:* In years for entire community population.

127. *Minority profile:* Three measures were used:
    a. *Percentage foreign stock:* In community population.
    b. *Percentage blacks:* In community population.
    c. *Percentage females:* In community population.

128. *Employment base:* Four measures were used:
    a. *Percentage employed in manufacturing:* Of community labor force.
    b. *Percentage employed in government:* Of community labor force.
    c. *Percentage employed in professional or managerial occupations:* Of community labor force.
    d. *Percentage unemployed:* Of community labor force.

UNION

Diffusion Phase

129. *Diffusion to supervisors:* Same as 1 for supervisors.
130. *Supervisory knowledge of facilitator:* Supervisors were asked

whether they knew if there was a policy facilitator, and who was filling that role. Responses were coded according to a 3-point scale, with 0 = did not know about; 1 = knew facilitator was appointed but could not identify person in that role; 2 = could identify person in facilitator role.

Receptivity Phase

131. *Agreement:* Same as 8 for supervisors.
132. *Assessment:* Same as 9 for supervisors.

Use Phase

133. *Past use:* Same as 10 for supervisors.
134. *Number of past uses:* Same as 11 for supervisors.
135. *Expected future use:* Same as 12 for supervisors.

Union-specific Variables

136. *Relative size of union:* Proportion of nonsupervisory employees represented by a union in supervisor's installation. Data obtained from U.S. Civil Service Commission (CSC) (1974).
137. *Age of union:* Time in years since union received formal recognition from installation, from CSC data.
138. *Skill level of union:* Obtained from CSC data. Unionized employees were classified in ascending order of skill as wage-scale, other G.S., and professional G.S. These data were coded so that 1 = all wage-scale employees; 2 = wage-scale and other G.S.; 3 = all other G.S.; 4 = all three categories of employees; 5 = other G.S. and professional G.S.; 6 = all professional G.S.
139. *Supervisory knowledge of union activities:* Same as 63 for director.
140. *Supervisory perception of union policy support:* Two-item scales. Supervisors were asked how the union has reacted to each of the two policies. Two response formats were provided for each item, with 7-point Likert scales: 1 = very much opposed, 7 = very much in favor; 1 = not helpful, 7 = very helpful. Items were standardized and averaged after factor analysis indicated a single factor for each policy.
141. *Supervisory awareness of union position on policy:* Dummy variable. Responses from 139 above were coded 1 if respondent replied to both response formats for the question, 0 if respondent failed to reply, and as missing data if no union was present.

Notes

INTRODUCTION

1. Zaltman et al. refer to such impetuses to change as performance gaps, which they define as "discrepancies between what an organization could do by virtue of a goal-related opportunity in its environment and what it actually does in terms of exploiting that opportunity" (1973:2). If we generalize this statement to refer to societal goals, broadly defined, and make the comparison between what is being done versus what might be done, then we can reconcile their concept of performance gap with our notion of problem sensing.

2. We recognized that nonsupervisory employees and their behaviors were also important in the implementation of the policies, but we were constrained by funding and other practical considerations to somehow limit the scope of this study. We chose to focus on those actors who were supposed to be active "movers" rather than relatively passive recipients of the implementation of the policies.

3. There is a vast empirical and theoretical literature on the adoption and diffusion of innovations. Much of this research has been summarized by Rogers and Shoemaker (1971).

4. Conceptually their study has remarkable similarity to the research reported here, but we were unaware of their research until after we began to write this book. Since the Rand results have not been published in the usual channels used by academics—journals and books—other readers of this book may also have failed to encounter this example of research on implementation. We wish to thank Richard Elmore for calling this study to our attention.

CHAPTER 1

1. Zaltman et al. (1973:7-16) deal with at least three different meanings of the term "innovation" alone; each of these meanings has different implications for the design of research and the meaning of results. One issue along which usage differs is whether or not innovation involves something merely novel or new to the organization or other adopter, or whether innovation must involve a new invention.

    Zaltman and his co-authors resolve this difference by using "innovation" to refer to "any idea, practice, or material artifact perceived to be new by the relevant unit of adoption" (1973:10). Their definition would include the changes investigated in this book as innovations.

    Knight (1967:479), on the other hand, views innovations as a special case of changes in organizations, with the two differing only in the degree of novelty of outcome.

    A further complication is that while innovation is often defined as an object, as in the above definition, the term will then also be used to denote a process (Zaltman et al., 1973:103). Most of the discussion of innovation in organizations in fact deals with the process, rather than with the object.

2. While these dimensions seemed sufficient to characterize the policy changes discussed in this book, this list may not be exhaustive. Radically different kinds of change may require some additions to this list.

3. Research on the adoption of new inventions, drugs, etc. are less likely to address the issues of process and behavioral change central to this investigation. Studies of new programs (e.g., Hage and Aiken, 1970; Kaplan, 1967) could have attempted to measure the intrinsic characteristics of processes but have tended instead to treat some unknown number of different programs and the processes associated with implementing them as more or less equivalent innovations or changes to be counted. In a sense, they have treated program changes as objects or things, not as processes.

4. We apply these dimensions to organizations in these definitions and in our examples of possible measurements. They could also be used in other social units.

5. The notion of existing programs or routines is used in the same sense here as in March and Simon (1958) and Perrow (1967). The dimension proposed here incorporates the distinction drawn by Zaltman et al. (see note 1) between something new or novel to the organization versus something that is a new invention.

6. Kaluzny and Veney (1977) have used the distinction between means and ends to advance a typology of organizational change: technical (change only in means), adjustment (change only in ends), and adaptation (change in both).

7. In the discussion that follows we focus on conceptual models rather than empirical findings. As mentioned in the Introduction, some phases of the conceptual models—notably implementation and institutionalization—have been neglected in empirical work. Some of these models have never been used in empirical studies.

8. Zaltman et al. also present good summaries of other models of what they call the innovation process, some of them oriented to the individual and some to the organizational level of analysis (1973:61–62).

9. Since its founding twenty-five years ago, the Christopher D. Smithers Foundation has concentrated its efforts on combatting alcoholism.

CHAPTER 2

1. Perhaps it should be made clear that the Hughes Act and the alcoholism policy applies only to government installations within the executive portion of the federal government. This policy does not apply, for example, to employees of the U.S. Congress or U.S. court system.

2. Data were actually collected from 651 supervisors, but further investigation revealed that some did not work within the boundaries defined for the sample installations. Sampling proportions ranged from 50 percent in small installations to 20 percent in large installations.

3. This is probably due to on-the-spot scheduling and person-to-person administration of instruments. Mailed questionnaire studies have generated very low response rates: Habbe (1968) reports a 30 percent response rate in a survey of 520 companies, and the Stanford Research Institute reported that "only 10 of the estimated 300 industrial alcoholism programs were reviewed and only 5 of the 10 companies participated in the mail survey of employee attitudes"; the other five "withdrew" (Riley and Horn, 1974).

4. Training included past experience in similar research, a course of relevant readings and discussions, and the practice and subsequent analysis of role-playing of interviews before closed-circuit television cameras. Interviewers reported these simulated interviews to be more difficult than subsequent "real" interviews in the field. In addition, all field interviewers were observed during actual interviews in the field by one of the authors. Our interviewers were also trained to use a standard introduction stressing that all questions referred to the period since the alcoholism policy was announced by the CSC and the changes in the EEO policy were issued.

5. Kerlinger (1973) has pointed out that the use of multi-item scales with high internal consistency improves this situation further, because the more items there are in the scale, the more likely that the scale will begin to approach interval properties of measurement.

CHAPTER 3

1. There are many examples that could be given, but perhaps three will suffice: the Cole and Cole (1973) study of stratification processes among physicists; the reanalysis of some of the Aston study data by Aldrich (1972); and the study of role commitment among priests by Schoenherr and Greeley (1974). We are well aware of the controversies surrounding use of this method but

feel that it is a valuable tool in analysis and in research design because it makes relationships and assumptions more explicit than multiple regression alone. Readers somewhat familiar with the technique can readily formulate alternative interpretations to the data, if they prefer.

2. Complete path diagrams also indicate the relationships between the exogenous variables (the stage 1 variables here) by placing the product moment (Pearson) correlations between those variables on curved lines with double-headed arrows connecting each of these variables with all others. Because of the number of variables at stage 1 in this model, such a representation here was not practical, requiring fifteen paths between the six variables. Intercorrelations of these variables were, of course, examined, especially to assess whether or not problems of multicollinearity would arise. The two diffusion variables for each policy are most highly correlated (.67 for alcohol; .75 for EEO), whereas other exogenous variables in the model only correlate between .49 and .16. The results given here suggested that the retention of both diffusion variables was desirable; also, their intercorrelations are below the .80 cut-off level often used to avoid multicollinearity problems.

CHAPTER 4

1. In the Rand study, teacher attitudes were conceptualized as part of the "organizational climate" surrounding the implementation of educational innovations; the research found that the morale of teachers and their willingness to spend extra effort significantly affected the percentage of goals achieved. The authors conclude that innovative projects were not "teacher-proof" (Berman and Pauly, 1975:54).

2. Readers are reminded that further details on the operationalizations of all measures are available in the Appendix.

3. In all fairness to the supervisors, we should point out that this may have sometimes been because no alcoholism coordinator had been designated in the installation. Only 63 percent of the coordinators had official appointments, many of these (over one-third) beginning less than six months before our interviews.

4. We were able to obtain data on work outcomes for only 79 of the 85 cases. This shrinkage involved employees who quit their jobs, were fired, or retired, so that supervisors could not judge such outcomes.

5. These percentages add to more than 100 percent because many supervisors took more than one of these actions.

6. Their scale was based on items from Neal (1965).

7. Dubin and his associates (Dubin et al., 1975) studied work in terms of central life interests. Buchanan (1974) used the job-involvement scale as part of a scale of organizational commitment. Lawler and Hall (1970:310) argued that job involvement is a "distinctive job attitude . . . empirically separate from satisfaction attitudes and from intrinsic motivation attitudes," and we follow their views in its use in this research.

8. The measurement of this concept has caused some controversy. These issues

are more fully discussed in other reports from this study (Beyer, Stevens, and Trice, 1977; Stevens, Beyer, and Trice, 1978).

9. We tested this notion by trichotomizing the measures of commitment and performing one-way analyses of variance for each policy, using organizational and federal service commitment as the independent variables and the three measures of use as the dependent variables. Ex post facto tests for differences between means detected no significant curvilinearities.

10. A fuller treatment of just this variable is presented in Trice and Beyer (1977).

11. This statement and others are only expected to be true *et cetibus paribus;* if supervisors felt their supervisors would reward them for *not* implementing the policy, of course this factor might have a reversed effect. We attempt to control for such complexities by the use of multivariate statistics, and we therefore word the hypotheses for each variable without considering moderating effects of other variables, which should be separated out by the simultaneous controls imposed by multiple regression.

   Thompson (1965) has argued that organizational members are not likely to innovate if they perceive the organization as rewarding conformity. He feels they must perceive the organization as an avenue for professional growth if innovation is to be encouraged. As discussed in chapter 1, these policies are better analyzed in terms of dimensions of change than as innovations per se. Clearly, the implementation of these policies is a designated portion of the supervisory role, and thus performing the steps necessary to implement the changes is conformity; since the policies are new and require new behaviors, they also have innovative elements. The professional identity that seems most relevant to implementation of these policies is the supervisory role and performance related to it, rather than the particular technical skills that the supervisor may also possess.

   It should also be noted that when we asked supervisors to rate the importance of six different criteria for their own promotion, the results for an item invoking administrative skill in applying formal policies loaded with other aspects of supervisory performance in factor analysis, while the results for the item on technical skills loaded on two factors and seniority loaded on the second factor. (See Appendix, variable 27.)

12. Mohr (1969), however, failed to find that size was associated with greater resources for innovations in health agencies.

13. Supervisors were asked to check which levels of supervision had influence in a range of decisions (see Appendix). To obtain a measure of centralization for each respondent, the total number of decisions checked for first-line supervisors was subtracted from the number checked for the installation director. The larger this difference, the more centralized the respondent saw the installation.

   Special tests were run on the consistency (or reliability) of these measures by assessing whether the responses of supervisors from the same installation agreed. One-way analyses of variance were performed using the installation code as the independent variable and the measures of centralization as dependent variables (the total decisions of line supervisors, of directors, and their difference); thus we could assess whether there was significantly greater variance between than within installations. All analyses were significant at $p < .001$, indicating significant differences in perceptions of decision making and our centralization measure between supervisors in different installations.

14. A notable exception is the treatment of Zaltman et al. (1973:85–104), who discuss possible sources of resistance to innovation by stages of the innovation process.

15. In these tables, only significant results are presented, although all variables listed in tables 4.1 and 4.2 were included in the equations. Since the tests of significance reported are two-tailed tests, the .10 level of significance is approximately equivalent to a .05 level for a one-tailed test.

CHAPTER 5

1. Such adjustments are conservative, decreasing R^2 according to the number of variables used in the regression equation and the number of observations (or subjects) used.

2. Pfeffer et al. (1976) have shown that social similarity becomes a more important criterion when more certain means of assessment are not available.

3. This finding is opposite in direction to the finding for supervisors in chapter 4 in which centralization was positively related to expected future use. The issue of how centralization is related to implementation is discussed in greater detail in chapter 7.

4. An early recognition of this influence in the organizational behavior literature can be found in Selznick (1949).

5. As will be seen in the next chapter, the formalization of the functionary roles tended to be negatively related to implementation by facilitators.

6. We have chosen to present the standardized regression coefficients here, rather than the unstandardized coefficients which indicate the slope of the regression line. Our major strategy in making comparisons across groups is simply to compare whether or not parallel statistically significant relationships occur in both groups, and not to ascertain whether the exact magnitude of the effect of a given independent variable on a dependent variable differed between powerful and less powerful directors. In our opinion, with samples this small, the coefficients are not likely to be stable enough to make such a comparison advisable.

7. In support of this notion, the Rand study found that administrative support from school district officials, but especially from the school principal, was important for successful implementation of educational innovations. The authors conclude: "Those few schools in which principals were self-proclaimed and dedicated proponents of career education invariably had the best projects" (Greenwood et al., 1975:41–42). Also, their data "show that the principal was especially crucial to implementation" (Berman and Pauly, 1975:59). The data referred to in the last quote were the effects of a variable that measured support from the principal.

CHAPTER 6

1. Berman and McLaughlin found that effective implementation strategies for educational innovations included a "critical mass" of staff working on the innovative project (1975*b*:ix), while actual levels of funding available had less important effects (1975*b*:16) on project outcomes. However, outside funding did provide the impetus to many of the educational projects and made them possible (1975*b*:16). Mohr (1969) also found available resources important in health departments. Thus personnel resources might also be expected to have an especially important role in effective implementation of the federal EEO and alcoholism policies, while the presence of funding might be expected to be less crucial.

2. For the analyses in this chapter, the unit of analysis for policy facilitators was the installation, because facilitators were being compared with other members of their role set in each installation. A few alcoholism coordinators worked for more than one installation, and therefore appear in these analyses more than once (six cases). Their data on personnel demographics, attitudes, roles characteristics, etc. would be the same for all installations they represented in the analyses, but their data on actions taken (cases handled, training performed, etc.) were collected separately for each installation and therefore would differ for the same individual coordinator across installations.

    This situation did not occur with EEO facilitators, because all installations had someone dealing with such matters within the installation.

3. This item read: Minority members should be sought out for employment vacancies.

4. Not all policy facilitators had been formally appointed, although policies called for formal designations to the role. When we made contacts with installations and found that no one had been formally appointed, we asked to interview that person who would handle matters under the policy. Interestingly, as later data will show, formal appointments were not important predictors of how much policy-related activities coordinators had performed.

5. The issue of formalization will be discussed in much greater detail in the next chapter.

6. Money allocations were so infrequent that this variable was dropped from the analyses in table 6.4.

7. This estimated prevalence rate is the ratio between the estimated total number of cases of policy use that had occurred within all installations in our sample and the total number of employees in the sample. Data obtained from each installation on its number of employees were summed to give the total number of employees in the sample. Estimates of the total number of cases of policy use were derived from reports of supervisors, weighted to correct for different sampling ratios used at installations of various sizes. Confidence limits were calculated for the resultant 3.3 percent prevalence rate; results indicated that we can be 95 percent confident that the actual

prevalence rate falls somewhere between 1.9 and 4.7 percent.

8. For an attempt to deal with a similar possibility statistically, see the final chapter of the book.

CHAPTER 7

1. As explained in chapter 2, installation size could change rapidly with layoffs of personnel or some reorganization of units. Despite our best efforts to determine size by telephone before visiting a site, two installations had shrunk to fewer than 50 members by the time we actually conducted interviews. Our measures of size and of other objective structural features of these organizations were based on those of Blau and Schoenherr (1971).

2. In several instances more than one installation that fell in our sample were located in the same city. In these cases, the cities involved are represented more than once in the averages reported here. That is, the data reported are the statistical means of data on the surrounding communities for all installations falling within the sample, with each community counted as many times as there were installations from the community in the sample.

3. See Zaltman et al. (1973:121-55) for a good summary of this literature.

4. Although structural data were collected for all 71 installations, some data were not obtainable because of slight changes in one instrument after interviewing began and difficulties of applying some items in other installations. Complete data on all of the variables included in the regression analyses in this paper were therefore available for only 65 installations.

   Only the measures of implementation came from supervisory responses. Measures of structure generally came from either the responses of directors or from a special instrument designed to collect structural data from the personnel director of each installation. Thus, measures of formalization, centralization, and organizational autonomy used in these analyses were derived from director responses. The only structural measure derived from supervisors' responses was their mean education.

   We also tried to compress the number of independent variables through factor analyzing them and constructing scale items from the factor analyses. These efforts led to masking, rather than strengthening or clarifying, relationships reported here, and so were abandoned.

5. Of course, it could also be argued that both sets of analyses are "right"—that is, that the findings represent the degree of centralization or decentralization experienced by those particular organizational participants. This kind of interpretation would lead to the conclusion that it is better, in implementing change, to have supervisors perceive upper management as having substantial control over decision making, while upper management itself perceives the situation as more decentralized. Perhaps this can be achieved by instilling in upper management sufficient sentiments and cognitions to suggest that decentralization is a good thing.

6. Findings from the analyses of professionalization of directors are more uniformly negative for implementation of both policies. See chapter 5.

7. Recently Moch and Morse also concluded that differing structural arrange-

ments may be associated with the adoption of different types of innovation; they argue that the Burns and Stalker model appears to apply better to some types of innovation than to others (1977:723).

8. Often environments are seen to affect organizations in terms of demands made by the environment that are crucial to organizational survival. Examples are general uncertainty, changing technology, market competition, shortages of raw materials, or changes in demands of consumers. None of these are particularly relevant to the organizations studied, since the federal bureaucracy seems likely to survive as long as the country does. Specific installations usually serve areas that are larger than the surrounding community in which they are located, and their accountability is therefore also broader than to the surrounding community.

9. The U.S. Census combines their occupational groups in the *County and City Data Books*. The professional category includes technical occupations as well as professions: for example, computer programmers, doctors, lawyers, schoolteachers, and social scientists are all included. The managerial category includes all those who are employed in the usual managerial functions in a wide variety of industries, including some self-employed persons.

10. These are the largest "minority" groups, and also groups for whom Census data are available.

11. This, of course, depends to some degree on the prior national origin, since some national groups have markedly lower rates of alcoholism than others (Trice and Pittman, 1958). For purposes of simplicity, however, we will consider the foreign stock group as a whole.

12. Other analyses have documented that the alcoholism policy was more favorably received and was used more frequently in installations where the skill level of employees was relatively low as compared with installations where the skill level was high. Various possible explanations of these findings are advanced and discussed in an earlier paper (Trice and Beyer, 1977).

CHAPTER 8

1. As Tannenbaum points out, unions cannot exist without the employing organizations (1965:710), while numerous employers manage to exist without a union.

2. Dyer et al. found that more than three times as many union activists favored collective bargaining as the "best way" for unions to handle the traditional areas of union concern than favored joint efforts by unions and management. Their research did not include the specific issues of alcoholism or EEO but did include safety in the workplace, job promotion procedures, and grievance procedures. For these three issues, the percentages forming joint programs between unions and management were respectively 41 percent, 38 percent, and 33 percent (1977:164-65). They also found that preferences for joint programs were associated with perceptions that the issues were integrative rather than distributive (1977:167). That is, joint programs represent problems about which both parties are equally concerned—the integrative bargaining model—rather than situations of conflict between the

parties in which "one party wins what the other party loses" (Walton and McKersie, 1965:11)—the distributive bargaining model.

3. Alternatively it would be reasonable to believe that unions would actually impede, even actively block, use of the EEO policy (Wolkinson, 1972).

4. Further data from this study concentrating on this issue appear in Trice and Beyer (1977).

5. The union is far from unique in this regard, of course. Much of the literature on change and innovation is studded with references to the resistance to change, which is almost treated as a given, rather than something requiring explanation. The most frequent prescription for overcoming such resistance is to involve employees in decisions related to the change through participative management—a technique that is difficult if not impossible to implement in the presence of an active and militant union.

CHAPTER 9

1. In a longitudinal study, Hall and his co-workers (1978) found that job involvement of supervisors increased following organizational change.

2. Somewhat the reverse was found among lower-level female supervisors, who were less supportive of the alcoholism policy, but they had received less diffusion on the policies. Thus their negative attitudes may have been a reflection of relative ignorance of the alcoholism policy. Despite lower diffusion on the EEO policy, female supervisors were more supportive of that policy than males.

3. The same variables that were used to rank the installations were used in these analyses. The results then simply verify that the ranking and averaging procedure was reasonably precise, not distorting the data or leading to a hodgepodge of inconsistent results.

4. Readers familiar with statistics will recognize the common problem of dealing with large numbers of possible independent variables in multivariate analysis when the number of degrees of freedom is limited by a moderate-size sample. This problem, of course, has been present throughout our analyses and is the reason that we chose to analyze various levels within the organization separately before attempting an overall synthesis of the findings.

5. There is no hard and fast rule on how to interpret the discriminant functions. We have chosen to interpret them by the variables that have the largest coefficients (or weights) in the function when both the size of the coefficient and its direction are substantially different from one function to another. We are thus interpreting each function in terms of the variables that are associated substantially with only that function.

6. Perhaps we should point out that this is the first attempt of which we are aware to operationalize the Mertonian typology and apply it to the study of organizational behavior. We recognize that this is not exactly the application that Merton originally intended, but we feel that this application may be of

general interest and usefulness just because the application of this typology may be easier within formal organizations than in the general problems of deviance in society at large.

7. More controversial changes would involve changes of larger magnitude, in terms of the dimensions discussed in chapter 1. That is, compliance would involve larger displacements of attitudes and behavior. Since there is no convenient adjective for characterizing this dimension—"large" is too general—we have used the word "controversial" to refer to such changes.

8. To compute this statistic we used the formulas provided by Tatsouka (1970:48–49). The method for determining variance explained for discriminant analysis results is controversial at present. Using more conservative procedures suggested by Paul Lohnes, we summed the redundancies for three factors extracted in canonical correlation analyses in which the classes of the discriminant analyses were represented by three dummy variables. The resultant factor loadings had similarities to the results given in table 9.3, but were not identical. The redundancies equal the variance extracted for each factor multipled by the R^2 for that factor, thus considering both the variance extracted and the fit of the observations around the regression slope for that factor. Using this procedure, we obtained explained variances of 30 percent and 32 percent for the alcoholism analyses, and 28 percent and 29 percent for the EEO results.

9. We have begun such an effort in a large U.S. corporation, where we plan to assess not only the implementation of policy, but outcomes as well.

10. Gramlich and Koshel (1976) provide an excellent example of this problem in their evaluation of educational performance contracting in public schools.

11. Bowers (1973:33) concludes from his evaluation of various organizational intervention techniques that the survey-feedback method tends to be more effective than other highly touted methods. The authors testified in Congress on their findings with co-worker Richard E. Hunt (U.S. Government Printing Office, 1976) and provided various feedback sessions on our survey results to officials in the Civil Service Commission, the unions involved, and other federal agencies. Results of this study have, in turn, been disseminated throughout the federal employment sector by the CSC, through its publications, and through training activities.

APPENDIX

1. For uniformity, Cronbach alphas are given for some two-item scales. We realize that they are not stable with less than three items, and therefore the values in these instances should be considered only broadly suggestive of the level of internal consistency.

References

Aiken, Michael, and Jerald Hage
  1968   Organizational Interdependence and Intraorganizational Structure. *American Sociological Review* 33: 912-31.
  1971   The Organic Organization. *Sociology* 23: 63-82.

Aldrich, Howard K.
  1972   Technology and Organizational Structure: A Re-Examinational of the Findings of the Aston Group. *Administrative Science Quarterly* 17: 26-43.

Alutto, Joseph A., and Lawrence G. Hrebiniak
  1975   Research on Commitment to Employing Organization: Preliminary Findings on a Study of Managers Graduating from Engineering and MBA Programs. Mimeo paper presented at the Academy of Management meetings, New Orleans, August.

Alutto, Joseph, Lawrence G. Hrebiniak, and Ramon C. Alonso
  1973   On Operationalizing the Concept of Commitment. *Social Forces* 51: 448-54.

Argyle, Michael
  1967   The Social Psychology of Social Change. In T. Burns and S. B. Saul (eds.), *Social Theory and Economic Change*. London: Tavistock Publications.

Argyris, Chris
  1962   *Interpersonal Competence and Organizational Effectiveness.* Homewood, Ill.: Dorsey Press.

Bakke, E. Wight
  1970   Reflections on the Future of Bargaining in the Public Sector. *Monthly Labor Review* 93: 21-25.

Baldridge, Victor, and Robert Burnham
  1975   Organizational Innovation: Individual, Organizational, and Environmental Impacts. *Administrative Science Quarterly* 20: 165-76.

Banfield, Edward C., and James Q. Wilson
  1963   *City Politics.* Cambridge, Mass.: Harvard University Press.

Bardach, Eugene
   1977   *The Implementation Game: What Happens After a Bill Becomes a Law.* Cambridge, Mass.: The MIT Press.

Barnett, Homer
   1953   *Innovation.* New York: McGraw-Hill.

Becker, Howard S.
   1960   Notes on the Concept of Commitment. *American Journal of Sociology* 66: 32–40.

Becker, Howard S., and Blanche Geer
   1960   Latent Culture: A Note on the Theory of Latent Social Roles. *Administrative Science Quarterly* 5 (September): 304–13.

Becker, Marshall H.
   1970   Sociometric Location and Innovativeness: Reformulation and Extension of the Diffusion Model. *American Sociological Review* 35: 267–82.

Beckhard, Richard
   1969   *Organization Development: Strategies and Models.* Reading, Mass.: Addison-Wesley.

Belasco, James, and Harrison M. Trice
   1969   *An Assessment of Change Agents in Training and Therapy.* New York: McGraw-Hill.

Bennis, Warren
   1966   *Changing Organizations.* New York: McGraw-Hill.

Berelson, Bernard, and Gary Steiner
   1964   *Human Behavior: An Inventory of Scientific Findings.* New York: Harcourt, Brace, and World.

Berman, Paul, and Milbrey Wallin McLaughlin
   1975a Federal Programs Supporting Educational Change, Vol. I: *A Model of Educational Change.* Prepared for the U.S. Office of Education, Department of Health, Education, and Welfare. R-1589/1, April. Santa Monica, Calif.: Rand Corporation.

   1975b Federal Programs Supporting Educational Change, Vol. IV: *The Findings in Review.* R-1589/4, April. Santa Monica, Calif.: Rand Corporation.

Berman, Paul, and Edward W. Pauly
   1975   Federal Programs Supporting Educational Change, Vol. II: *Factors Affecting Change Agent Projects.* R-1589/2, April. Santa Monica, Calif.: Rand Corporation.

Bernstein, Ilene, and Howard Freeman
   1975   *Academic and Entrepreneurial Research: The Consequences of Diversity in Federal Evaluation Studies.* New York: Russell Sage Foundation.

Beyer, Janice M.
   1977   Power Dependencies and the Distribution of Influence in Universities. Mimeo paper, State University of New York at Buffalo, November.

Beyer, Janice M., and Thomas M. Lodahl
1976 A Comparative Study of Patterns of Influence in United States and English Universities. *Administrative Science Quarterly* 21: 104–29.

Beyer, Janice M., and Harrison M. Trice
1976 A Re-Examination of the Relations Between Size and Various Measures of Organizational Complexity. Paper presented at the Academy of Management meetings, Kansas City, Mo., August.

Beyer, Janice M., John M. Stevens, and Harrison M. Trice
1977 On the Appropriate Application of Tests of Reliability: A Research Note on Measuring Commitment. Working Paper No. 313, School of Management, State University of New York at Buffalo.

Bickel, Alexander
1964 The Civil Rights Act of 1964. *Commentary* 38: 33–39.

Blau, Peter M., and Richard Schoenherr
1971 *The Structure of Organizations.* New York: John Wiley and Sons.

Blau, Peter, and W. Richard Scott
1962 *Formal Organizations.* San Francisco: Chandler Publishing Company.

Bowers, David G.
1973 O.D. Techniques and Their Results in Twenty-three Organizations: The Michigan ICL Study. *Journal of Applied Behavioral Science* 9: 21–43.

Buchanan, Bruce
1974 Building Organizational Commitment: The Socialization of Managers in Work Organizations. *Administrative Science Quarterly* 19: 533–46.

Bunker, Douglas R.
1972 Policy Sciences Perspective on Implementation Processes. *Policy Sciences* 3: 71–80.

Bureau of National Affairs
1973 *The Equal Employment Opportunity Act of 1972.* Washington, D.C.: Bureau of National Affairs.

Burns, Tom, and G. M. Stalker
1961 *The Management of Innovation.* London: Tavistock Publications.

Cahalan, Donald
1970 *Problem Drinkers.* San Francisco: Jossey-Bass.

Carroll, John
1967 A Note on Departmental Autonomy and Innovation in Medical Schools. *Journal of Business* 49: 531–34.

Chayes, Antonia Handler
1974 Make Your Equal Opportunity Program Court-Proof. *Harvard Business Review* 52: 81–89.

Coch, L., and J. R. P. French, Jr.
1948 Overcoming Resistance to Change. *Human Relations* 1: 512–32.

Coe, Rodney, and Elizabeth Barnhill
1967 Social Dimensions of Failure in Innovation. *Human Organization* 26: 149–56.

Cohany, Harry, and Lucretia Dewey
    1970   Union Membership Among Government Employees. *Monthly Labor Review* 93: 15-20.

Cole, Jonathan R., and Stephen Cole
    1973   *Social Stratification in Science.* Chicago, Ill.: University of Chicago Press.

Corwin, Ronald
    1972   Strategies for Organizational Innovation: An Empirical Comparison. *American Sociological Review* 37: 441-54.

Coughlan, Robert J., Robert A. Cooke, and L. Arthur Safer, Jr.
    1972   An Assessment of a Survey Feedback—Problem Solving—Collective Decision Intervention in Schools. Final Report, U.S. Office of Education, Small Grants Division, Contract No. OEG-5-70-0036(509).

Cyert, Richard, and James March
    1963   *A Behavioral Theory of the Firm.* Englewood Cliffs, N.J.: Prentice-Hall.

Dalton, Melvin
    1959   *Men Who Manage.* New York: John Wiley and Sons.

Derber, Milton, W. E. Chalmers, and Milton T. Edelman
    1965   *Plant Union-Management Relations: From Practice to Theory.* Urbana: Institute of Labor and Industrial Relations, University of Illinois.

Dohrenwend, Bruce P., and Edwin Chin-Shong
    1967   Social Status and Attitudes Toward Psychological Disorder: The Problem of Tolerance of Deviance. *American Sociological Review* 32: 417-33.

Dror, Yehezkel
    1968   *Public Policymaking Reexamined.* Scranton, Pa.: Chandler Publishing Company.

Dubin, Robert, Joseph E. Champoux, and Lyman W. Porter
    1975   Central Life Interests and Organizational Commitment of Blue-Collar and Clerical Workers. *Administrative Science Quarterly* 20: 411-21.

Duncan, Robert B.
    1976   The Ambidextrous Organization: Designing Dual Structures for Innovation. Pp. 167-188 in Robert H. Killmann, Louis R. Pondy, and Dennis P. Slevin (eds.), *The Management of Organization Design.* New York: North-Holland.

Dyer, Lee, David B. Lipsky, and Thomas A. Kochan
    1977   Union Attitudes Toward Management Cooperation. *Industrial Relations* 16 (May): 163-72.

Edwards, Daniel
    1975   The Evaluation of Troubled-Employee and Occupational Alcoholism Programs. Pp. 40-135 in Richard Williams and Gene Moffat (eds.), *Occupational Alcoholism Programs,* Springfield, Ill.: Charles C. Thomas.

Elmore, Richard F.
  1976   Follow Through Planned Evaluation. Pp. 101-23 in Walter Williams
          and Richard F. Elmore (eds.), *Social Program Implementation*. New
          York: Academic Press.

Etzioni, Amitai
  1976   *Social Problems*. Englewood Cliffs, N.J.: Prentice-Hall.

Fayol, Henri
  1949   *General and Industrial Management*. Tr. by Constance Storrs. Lon-
          don: Sir Isaac Pitman and Sons.

Fiedler, Fred E.
  1967   *A Theory of Leadership Effectiveness*. New York: McGraw-Hill.

Fischer, Claude
  1975   Toward a Subcultural Theory of Urbanism. *American Journal of
          Sociology* 80 (May): 1319-41.

Franco, S. Charles
  1960   A Company Program for Problem Drinking: Ten Years Followup.
          Journal of Occupational Medicine 2: 157-62.

Freeman, John
  1973   Environment, Technology, and the Administrative Intensity of Manu-
          facturing Organizations. *American Sociological Review* 38: 750-63.

Gibson, Cyrus F.
  1975   A Methodology for Implementation Research. Pp. 53-73 in Randall
          L. Schultz and Dennis P. Slevin (eds.), *Implementing Operations
          Research/Management Science*. New York: American Elsevier.

Glenn, Norval D., and Lester Hill, Jr.
  1977   Rural-Urban Differences in Attitudes and Behavior in the United
          States. *Annals of the American Academy of Political and Social
          Science* 429 (January): 36-50.

Gramlich, Edward M., and Patricia P. Koshel
  1976   Is Real World Experimentation Possible? The Case of Education
          Performance Contracting. Pp. 149-66 in Walter Williams and Richard
          F. Elmore (eds.), *Social Program Implementation*. New York: Aca-
          demic Press.

Greenwood, Peter W., Dale Mann, and Milbrey Wallin McLaughlin
  1975   Federal Programs Supporting Educational Change, Vol. III: *The Pro-
          cess of Change*. R-1589/3, April. Santa Monica, Calif.: Rand
          Corporation.

Greiner, Larry E.
  1967   Patterns of Organizational Change. *Harvard Business Review* 45:
          119-28.

Gross, Neal, Joseph Giacquinta, and Marilyn Bernstein
  1971   *Implementing Organizational Innovations*. New York: Basic Books.

Gross, Neal, Ward Mason, and Alexander McEachern
  1958   *Explorations in Role Analysis*. New York: John Wiley and Sons.

Guest, Robert H.
  1962 Managerial Succession in Complex Organizations. *American Journal of Sociology* 67: 47-54.

Habbe, Steven
  1968 *Company Controls for Drinking Problems.* New York: National Industrial Conference Board.

Hage, Jerald, and Michael Aiken
  1967 Program Change and Organizational Properties. *American Journal of Sociology* 72: 502-19.
  1969 Routine Technology, Social Structure, and Organizational Goals. *Administrative Science Quarterly* 14: 366-75.
  1970 *Social Change in Complex Organizations.* New York: Random House.

Hage, Jerald, and Robert Dewar
  1973 Elite Values vs. Organizational Structure in Predicting Innovation. *Administrative Science Quarterly* 18: 279-90.

Hall, Douglas T., James G. Goodale, Samuel Rabinowitz, and Marilyn Morgan
  1978 Effects of Top-Down Departmental and Job Change upon Perceived Employee Behavior and Attitudes: A Natural Field Experiment. *Journal of Applied Psychology* 63: 62-72.

Hall, Francine
  1976 Implementing Organizational Goals: A Model of EEO Commitment and Effort. Paper presented at the annual meeting of the Academy of Management, Kansas City, Mo.

Hall, Richard H.
  1972 *Organizations: Structure and Process.* Englewood Cliffs, N.J.: Prentice-Hall.

Havelock, Ronald G.
  1970 *Planning for Innovation.* Ann Arbor: Center for Research on Utilization of Scientific Knowledge, University of Michigan.

Hawley, Amos H.
  1963 Community Power and Urban Renewal Success. *American Journal of Sociology* 68: 522-31.

Hellriegel, Don, and Larry Short
  1972 Equal Employment in the Federal Government: A Comparative Analysis. *Public Administration Review*, November/December, pp. 851-58.

Herzberg, Frederick
  1968 One More Time: How Do You Motivate Employees? *Harvard Business Review* 46: 53-62.

Hilker, Robert R. J., Fern E. Asma, and Raymond L. Eggert
  1972 A Company Sponsored Alcoholic Rehabilitation Program: Ten Years Evaluation. *Journal of Occupational Medicine* 14: 769-71.

Hill, Herbert
  1968 *NAACP Labor Manual.* New York: NAACP Special Contribution Fund.

Hollingshead, A. B., and F. C. Redlich
1958   *Social Class and Mental Illness: A Community Study.* New York: John Wiley and Sons.

Homans, George
1950   *The Human Group.* New York: Harcourt Brace.

House, Robert J.
1971   A Path-Goal Theory of Leader Effectiveness. *Administrative Science Quarterly* 16 (September): 321–32.

Hunt, Raymond G.
1967   Role and Role Conflict. In Hollander, Edwin, and Raymond Hunt (eds.), *Current Perspectives in Social Psychology.* New York: Oxford University Press.

Hunt, Richard E., Harrison M. Trice, and Janice M. Beyer
1977   *The Impact of Federal Sector Unions upon Supervisory Usage of Federal Personnel Policies.* Working Paper No. 7, Program on Alcoholism and Occupational Health, School of Industrial and Labor Relations, Cornell University, Ithaca, N.Y.

Hyman, Herbert, and Charles Wright
1967   Evaluating Social Action Programs. In Paul Lazarfeld, William Sewell, and Harold Wilensky (eds.), *The Uses of Sociology.* New York: Basic Books.

Kahn, Robert
1974   Organizational Development: Some Problems and Proposals. *Journal of Applied Behavioral Science* 10: 485–502.

Kahn, Robert L., Donald M. Wolfe, Robert Q. Quinn, J. Diedrich Snock, and Robert A. Rosenthal
1964   *Organizational Stress: Studies in Role Conflict and Ambiguity.* New York: John Wiley and Sons.

Kaluzny, Arnold D., and James E. Veney
1977   Types of Change and Hospital Planning Strategies. *American Journal of Health Planning* 1 (January): 13–19.

Kaluzny, Arnold, James Veney, and John Gentry
1974   Innovations of Health Services: A Comparative Study of Hospitals and Health Departments. *Health and Society,* Winter.

Kanter, Rosabeth Moss
1977   *Men and Women of the Corporation.* New York: Basic Books.

Kaplan, Howard
1967   Implementation of Program Change in Community Agencies. *Milbank Memorial Fund Quarterly,* July, pp. 321–31.

Kast, Fremont E., and James E. Rosenzweig
1974   *Organization and Management: A Systems Approach.* New York: McGraw-Hill.

Katz, Elihu
1957   The Two-Step Flow of Communication. *Public Opinion Quarterly* 21: 73–76.

Kelman, Herbert C.
　　1961　Processes of Opinion Change. *Public Opinion Quarterly* 25: 608-15.

Kelman, Herbert C., and Janet Barclay
　　1963　The F Scale as a Measure of Breadth of Perspective. *Journal of Abnormal and Social Psychology* 68: 608-15.

Kerlinger, Fred N.
　　1973　*Foundations of Behavioral Research.* New York: Holt, Rinehart & Winston.

Kerlinger, Fred N., and Elazar J. Pedhazur
　　1973　*Multiple Regression in Behavioral Research.* New York: Holt, Rinehart & Winston.

King, Martin Luther Jr.
　　1964　The Hammer of Civil Rights. *The Nation* 198: 230-35.

Kochan, Thomas A.
　　1975　Determinants of the Power of Boundary Units in an Interorganizational Bargaining Relation. *Administrative Science Quarterly* 20 (September): 434-52.

Knight, Kenneth E.
　　1967　A Descriptive Model of the Intra-Firm Innovation Process. *Journal of Business* 40 (October): 478-96.

Kuhn, James W.
　　1961　*Bargaining in Grievance Settlement: The Power of Industrial Work Groups.* New York: Columbia University Press.

Kutner, Bernard, and Norman B. Gordon
　　1964　Cognitive Functioning and Prejudice: A Nine-Year Follow-up Study. *Sociometry* 27: 66-74.

Labovitz, Sanford
　　1967　Some Observations on Measurement and Statistics. *Social Forces* 46: 151-60.

Ladd, Everett C., and Seymour M. Lipset
　　1973　*Professors, Unions, and American Higher Education.* Berkeley, Calif.: Carnegie Committee on Higher Education.

Lawler, Edward E., and Douglas T. Hall
　　1970　Relationship of Job Characteristics to Job Involvement, Satisfaction, and Intrinsic Motivation. *Journal of Applied Psychology* 54:305-12.

Lewin, Kurt
　　1947a　Frontiers in Group Dynamics I. *Human Relations* 1: 5-41.
　　1947b　Frontiers in Group Dynamics II. *Human Relations* 1: 143-53.

Likert, Rensis
　　1961　*New Patterns of Management.* McGraw-Hill.

Lippitt, Ronald, Jeanne Watson, and Bruce Westley
　　1958　*The Dynamics of Planned Change.* New York: Harcourt, Brace and World.

Lodahl, Thomas, and Mathilde Kejner
　　1965　The Definition and Measurement of Job Involvement. *Journal of Applied Psychology* 49: 24-33.

Lucas, Henry C. Jr.
1975 Behavior Factors in System Implementation. Pp. 203–16 in Randall
      L. Schultz and Dennis P. Slevin (eds.), *Implementing Operations
      Research/Management Science*. New York: American Elsevier.

McCarthy, Philip J.
1957 *Introduction to Statistical Reasoning*. New York: McGraw-Hill Book
      Co.

McFarland, Dalton
1962 *Cooperation and Conflict in Personnel Administration*. New York:
      American Foundation for Management Research.

McGregor, Douglas
1960 *The Human Side of Enterprise*. New York: McGraw-Hill.

Macy, John W., Jr.
1968 Address to the International Congress on Alcohol and Alcoholism.
      Shoreham Hotel, Washington, D.C., September 18.

Malcolm, D. G.
1965 On the Need for Improvement in Implementation of O.R. *Manage-
      ment Science* 2: B48–B58.

Mansfield, Robert
1973 Bureaucracy and Centralization: An Examination of Organizational
      Structure. *Administrative Science Quarterly* 18: 477–88.

March, James, and Herbert Simon
1958 *Organizations*. New York: John Wiley and Sons.

Maslow, Abraham H.
1954 *Motivation and Personality*. New York: Harper & Row.

Merton, Robert K.
1938 Social Structure and Anomie. *American Sociological Review* 3:
      672–82.
1952 Bureaucratic Structure and Personality. Pp. 361–71 in Robert K.
      Merton, Alisa P. Gray, Barbara Hockey, and Hanan C. Selvin (eds.),
      Reader in Bureaucracy. New York: Free Press.
1957 *Social Theory and Social Structure*. Glencoe, Ill.: Free Press.
1969 Social Structure and Anomie. Pp. 162–183 in Walter L. Wallace,
      (ed.), *Sociological Theory*. Chicago: Aldine Publishing Co.

Mintzberg, Henry
1973 *The Nature of Managerial Work*. New York: Harper & Row.

Moch, Michael K., and Edward V. Morse
1977 Size, Centralization and Organizational Adoption of Innovations.
      American Sociological Review 42 (October): 716–25.

Mohr, Lawrence
1969 Determinants of Innovation in Organizations. *American Political
      Science Review*, March, pp. 111–26.

Moore, Wilbert
1962 *The Conduct of the Corporation*. New York: Random House.

Mytinger, Robert E.
1967 Barriers to Adoption of New Health Programs as Perceived by Local

Health Officers. *Public Health Reports* 82: 108-14.

1968   *Innovation in Local Health Services.* Washington, D.C.: Government
Printing Office, Public Health Publication No. 1664-2.

Naumoff, Benjamin B.
1971   Ground Rules for Recognition Under Executive Order 11491. *Labor
Law Journal* 22: 100-105.

Neal, Sister August
1965   *Values and Interests in Social Change.* Englewood Cliffs, N.J.:
Prentice-Hall.

Neal, Rodney, and Michael Radnor
1973   The Relation Between Formal Procedures for Pursuing OR/MS Activities and Group Success. *Operations Research* 21: 451-74.

Newcombe, Theodore
1951   *Social Psychology.* New York: Dryden Press.

Palumbo, Dennis J.
1969   Power and Role Specificity in Organizational Theory. *Public Administration Review* 29: 237-48.

Parsons, Talcott
1951   *The Social System.* Glencoe, Ill.: Free Press.

Pennings, Johannes
1973   Measures of Organizational Structure: A Methodological Note. *American Journal of Sociology* 79: 686-704.

Perlis, Leo
1973   The Human Equation: An Interview with Leo Perlis. AFL-CIO
Department of Community Services. *Alcohol Health and Research
World,* Fall, pp. 17-21.

Perrow, Charles
1967   A Framework for the Comparative Analysis of Organizations. *American Sociological Review* 32 (April): 194-208.

Petersen, James C.
1976   Organizational Structure and Program Change in Protestant Denomi-
nations. *Organization and Administrative Sciences* 6: 1-13.

Pfeffer, Jeffrey, Gerald R. Salancik, and Huseyin Leblebici
1976   The Effect of Uncertainty on the Use of Social Influence in Organizational Decision Making. *Administrative Science Quarterly* 21 (June):
227-45.

Pierce, Jon L., and Andre L. Delbecq
1977   Organization Structure, Individual Attitudes and Innovation. *The
Academy of Management Review* 2: 27-37.

Pinard, Maurice
1963   Structural Attachments and Political Support in Urban Politics: The
Case of Fluoridation Referendums. *American Journal of Sociology*
68: 513-26.

Pressman, Jeffrey L., and Aaron Wildavsky
1974   *Implementation.* Berkeley: University of California Press.

Rabinowitz, Samuel, and Douglas T. Hall
 1977   Organizational Research on Job Involvement. *Psychological Bulletin*, 84: 265–88.

Radcliffe, Ruth
 1967   Introducing New Mathematics in Northside Elementary School. Pp. 213–27 in Richard I. Miller (ed.), *Perspectives on Educational Change*. New York: Appleton-Century-Crofts.

Radnor, Michael, and Alden Bean
 1974   Top Management Support for Management Science. *Omega* 2: 63–75.

Radnor, Michael, and Rodney Neal
 1973   The Progress of Management Science Activities in Large U.S. Industrial Corporations. *Operations Research* 21: 427–50.

Read, William
 1962   Upward Communication in Industrial Hierarchies. *Human Relations* 15: 3–15.

Riley, Frances, and Don Horn
 1974   *Evaluation of Programs Oriented Toward Alcoholic Persons Employed in Industry*. Final Report. Menlo Park, Calif.: Stanford Research Institute.

Ritzer, George, and Harrison M. Trice
 1969a   An Empirical Study of Howard Becker's Side-Bet Theory. *Social Forces* 48: 475–79.
 1969b   *An Occupation in Conflict: A Study of the Personnel Manager*. Ithaca, N.Y.: Cornell University Press.

Rogers, Everett
 1962   *Diffusion of Innovation*. New York: Free Press.

Rogers, Everett, and Floyd Shoemaker
 1971   *Communication of Innovation*. New York: Free Press.

Roman, Paul, and Harrison M. Trice
 1972   Psychiatric Impairment among "Middle" Americans. *Social Psychiatry* 7: 157–66.
 1976   Alcohol Abuse and Work Organizations. Pp. 445–517 in Benjamin Kissin and Henri Begleiter (eds.), *The Biology of Alcoholism*. New York: Plenum Press.

Rosner, Martin
 1968   Administrative Controls and Innovation. *Behavioral Science* 13: 36–43.

Sampson, Edward E.
 1971   *Social Psychology and Contemporary Society*. New York: John Wiley and Sons.

Sapolsky, Harvey
 1967   Organizational Structure and Innovation. *Journal of Business* 40: 497–510.

Sayles, L. R., and George Strauss
 1967   *The Local Union*. New York: Harcourt, Brace and World.

Schein, Edgar H.
  1964   The Mechanism of Change. Pp. 362–78 in Warren G. Bennis, Edgar H.
          Schein, David E. Berlew, and Fred I. Steele (eds.), *Interpersonal
          Dynamics.* Homewood, Ill.: Dorsey Press.

Schmidt, Stuart M., and Thomas A. Kochan
  1977   Interorganizational Relationships: Patterns and Motivations. *Adminis-
          trative Science Quarterly* 22 (June): 220–234.

Schoenherr, Richard, and Andrew Greeley
  1974   Role Commitment Processes and the American Catholic Priesthood.
          American Sociological Review 39: 407–26.

Schultz, Randall L., and Dennis P. Slevin
  1975a   Implementation and Organizational Validity: An Empirical Investiga-
          tion. Pp. 153–82 in Schultz and Slevin, *Implementing Operations
          Research/Management Science.* New York: American Elsevier.

Schultz, Randall L., and Dennis P. Slevin (eds.)
  1975b   *Implementing Operations Research/Management Science.* New York:
          American Elsevier.

Scott, Robert A., and Arnold Shore
  1974   Sociology and Policy Analysis. *The American Sociologist* 9: 51–59.

Scurrah, Martin, Moshe Shani, and Carl Zipfel
  1971   Influence of Internal and External Change Agents in a Simulated
          Educational Organization. *Administrative Science Quarterly* 16:
          113–21.

Selznick, Phillip
  1953   *TVA and the Grass Roots: A Study in the Sociology of Formal
          Organizations.* Berkeley: University of California Press.

Shepard, Herbert A.
  1967   Innovation-Resisting and Innovation-Producing Organizations. *Jour-
          nal of Business* 40: 470–77.

Skinner, B. F.
  1953   *Science and Human Behavior.* New York: Macmillan.

Slichter, Sumner, James Healy, and E. R. Livernash
  1960   *The Impact of Collective Bargaining on Management.* Washington,
          D.C.: Brookings Institution.

Smart, Reginald
  1974   Employed Alcoholics Treated Voluntarily and Under Constructive
          Coercion. *Quarterly Journal of Studies on Alcohol* 35: 196–209.

Smith, Arthur
  1975   The Impact of Collective Bargaining on Equal Opportunity Remedies.
          Industrial and Labor Relations Review 28: 376–94.

Smith, David B., and A. D. Kaluzny
  1975   *The White Labyrinth: Understanding the Organization of Health
          Care.* Berkeley, Calif.: McCutcheon Publishing Co.

Sorenson, Richard E., and Dale E. Zand
  1975   Improving the Implementation of OR/MS Models by Applying the
          Lewin-Schein Theory of Change. Pp. 217–35 in Randall L. Schultz

and Dennis P. Slevin (eds.), *Implementing Operations Research/Management Science.* New York: American Elsevier.

Stern, Louis, Samuel Craig, and Richard Salem
1976   The Effects of Sociometric Location on the Adoption of an Innovation Within a University Faculty. *Sociology of Education* 49: 90–96.

Stevens, John M.
1976   Managerial Commitment, Policy Receptivity, and Policy Implementation in Public Sector Organizations. Ph.D. thesis, State University of New York at Buffalo.

Stevens, John M., Janice M., and Harrison M. Trice
1976   A Path-Analytic Approach to Managerial Commitment. Paper presented at the Academy of Management meetings. Kansas City, Mo., August.
1978   Organizational, Role, and Individual Predictors of Managerial Commitment. Forthcoming in the *Academy of Management Journal.*

Stewart, Phyllis, and Muriel Cantor
1974   *Varieties of Work Experience.* New York: John Wiley and Sons.

Stouffer, Samuel A.
1955   *Communism, Conformity and Civil Liberties: A Cross-Section of the Nation Speaks Its Mind.* Garden City, N.Y.: Doubleday.

Sutermeister, Marvin
1963   *People and Productivity.* New York: McGraw-Hill.

Tannenbaum, Arnold S.
1965   Unions. Pp. 710–63 in James G. March (ed.), *Handbook of Organizations.* Chicago: Rand McNally.

Tatsouka, Maurice M.
1970   *Discriminant Analysis: The Study of Group Differences.* Number 6, Selected Topics in Advanced Statistics: An Elementary Approach. Champaign, Ill.: Institute for Personality and Ability Testing.

Thomas, Edwin, and Bruce Biddle
1966   *Role Theory: Concepts and Research.* New York: John Wiley and Sons.

Thompson, James
1967   *Organizations in Action.* New York: McGraw-Hill.

Thompson, Victor A.
1961   *Modern Organizations.* New York: Alfred A. Knopf.
1965   Bureaucracy and Innovation. *Administrative Science Quarterly* 10: 1–20.
1969   *Bureaucracy and Innovation.* University, Ala.: University of Alabama Press.

Trent, James W., and Judith L. Craise
1967   Commitment and Conformity in the American College. *Journal of Social Issues* 3: 34–51.

Trice, Harrison M.
1962   *Alcoholism in Industry: Modern Procedures.* New York: Christopher D. Smithers Foundation. (Reissued in 1968 and 1971.)

1965   Reaction of Supervisors to Emotionally Disturbed Employees. *Journal of Occupational Medicine* 7: 177-83.

1966   The Alcoholic Employee and His Supervisor. Pp. 338-46 in R. E. Popham (ed.), *Alcohol and Alcoholism.* Papers Presented at the International Symposium in Memory of E. M. Jellinek. Toronto: University of Toronto Press.

Trice, Harrison M., and James Belasco

1965   The Alcoholic and His Supervisor. *Business Quarterly* 30: 34-43.

1968   Supervisory Training About Alcoholic and Other Problem Employees: A Controlled Evaluation. *Quarterly Journal of Studies on Alcohol* 29: 382-99.

1970   Alcoholism and the Work World. *Sloan Management Review* 12: 67-75.

Trice, Harrison M., and Janice M. Beyer

1977   Differential Use of Alcoholism Policy in Federal Organizations by Skill Level of Employees. Pp. 44-69 in Carl Schramm (ed.), *Alcoholism and Its Treatment in Industry.* Baltimore: John Hopkins University Press.

Trice, Harrison M., and David J. Pittman

1958   Social Organization and Alcoholism: A Review of Significant Research Since 1940. *Social Problems* 5: 294-307.

Trice, Harrison M., and Paul M. Roman

1973   *Evaluation of Training: Strategy, Tactics, and Problems.* Madison, Wis.: American Society of Training Directors.

1974   Dilemmas of Evaluation in Community Health Organizations. Pp. 119-78 in Paul M. Roman and Harrison M. Trice (eds.), *Sociological Perspectives on Community Mental Health.* Philadelphia: F. A. Davis.

Trice, Harrison M., Richard Hunt, and Janice M. Beyer

1977   Alcoholism Programs in Unionized Work Settings: Problems and Prospects in Union-Management Cooperation. *Journal of Drug Issues* 6 (Spring): 103-15.

U.S. Bureau of the Census

1973   *County and City Data Book: 1972.* Washington, D.C.: U.S. Government Printing Office.

U.S. Civil Service Commission

1967   *The First Step: A Conference on Drinking Problems.* Washington, D.C.: U.S. Government Printing Office.

1969   *The Key Step: A Model Program to Deal with Drinking Problems of Employees.* Washington, D.C.: U.S. Government Printing Office.

1971   *Federal Personnel Manual Letter No. 792-4. Federal Civilian Employee Alcoholism Programs.* Washington, D.C.: U.S. Government Printing Office.

1972   *Federal Personnel Manual Letter No. 713-17. Revisions in Equal Opportunity Regulations (Part 713).* Washington, D.C.: U.S. Government Printing Office.

1974   *Union Recognition in the Federal Government.* Washington, D.C.: U.S. Government Printing Office

1975   *Internal Evaluation of Agency Alcoholism and Drug Abuse Programs.*
Bulletin No. 792-15. Washington, D.C.: U.S. Government Printing
Office.

U.S. Code Congressional and Administrative News
1972   Volume 1. Washington, D.C.: U.S. Code Congressional and Administrative News.

U.S. Government Printing Office
1976   *Federal Employee Alcoholism Programs.* Hearings Before a Subcom-
mittee on Government Operations, House of Representatives, 94th
Congress, Second Session, June 25 and 28, 1976.

Van Meter, Donald S., and Carl E. Van Horn
1975   The Policy Implementation Process: a Conceptual Framework.
Administration and Society 6 (February): 445–488.

Walton, Richard E., and Robert B. McKersie
1965   *A Behavioral Theory of Labor Negotiations.* New York: McGraw-
Hill.

Warkov, Seymour, Seldon Bacon, and Arthur C. Hawkins
1965   Social Correlates of Industrial Problem Drinking. *Journal of Studies
on Problem Drinking* 26: 58–81.

Weber, Max
1947   *The Theory of Social and Economic Organization.* Tr. by A. M.
Henderson and T. Parsons. New York: Free Press.

Weiss, Carol
1972   *Evaluative Research.* Englewood Cliffs, N.J.: Prentice-Hall.

Weisberger, Joan
1973   *Job Security and Public Employees.* Ithaca, N.Y.: Institute of Public
Employment, New York State School of Industrial and Labor Relations, Cornell University, Monograph No. 2.

Williams, Walter
1971   *Social Policy Research and Analysis: Experience in the Federal Social
Agencies.* New York: American Elsevier.

Williams, Walter, and Richard F. Elmore (eds.)
1976   *Social Program Implementation.* New York: Academic Press.

Wilson, James Q.
1966   Innovation in Organizations: Notes Toward a Theory. Pp. 194–219 in
Thompson, James (ed.), *Approaches to Organizational Design.* Pittsburgh: University of Pittsburgh Press.

Whyte, William F.
1969   *Organizational Behavior.* Homewood, Ill.: Richard D. Irwin and the
Dorsey Press.

Winer, B. J.
1962   *Statistical Principles in Experimental Design.* New York: McGraw-
Hill.

Wnorowski, A. K.
1970   Once You Have an Agreement (How to Avoid Grievances). *Personnel
Journal* 49: 843–46.

Wolkinson, Benjamin W.
  1972   *The Effectiveness of E.E.O.C. Policy in the Construction Industry.*
          Proceedings of the 25th Annual Meeting of the Industrial Relations
          Research Association, pp. 362–69.

Wykstra, Ronald A., and Eleanour V. Stevens
  1970   *Labor Law and Public Policy.* New York: Odyssey Press.

Zaltman, Gerald, Robert Duncan, and Jonny Holbeck
  1973   *Innovations and Organizations.* New York: John Wiley and Sons.

Zaltman, Gerald, and Robert Duncan
  1977   *Strategies for Planned Change.* New York: Wiley-Interscience
          Publications.

Indexes

Name Index

Aiken, Michael, 9, 21, 24, 82, 85, 87, 125, 168, 172, 194-196, 206, 209, 213, 233
Alonso, Ramon C., 83
Alutto, Joseph A., 83
Argyle, Michael, 8
Argyris, Chris, 8

Bacon, Seldon, 239
Bakke, E. Wight, 238
Baldridge, Victor, 130, 152, 195, 196, 207
Banfield, Edward C., 223
Barclay, Janet, 213
Bardach, Eugene, 9
Barnett, Homer, 196
Barnhill, Elizabeth, 57
Bean, Alden, 130
Becker, Howard S., 83, 130, 223
Beckhard, Richard, 152
Belasco, James, 10, 132, 248
Bennis, Warren, 8, 13, 152, 233
Berelson, Bernard, 81, 212, 213
Berman, Paul, 8, 9, 58, 168, 186, 210
Bernstein, Ilene, 10, 11, 288
Bernstein, Marilyn, 9, 11, 131, 153
Beyer, Janice M., 87, 136, 191, 230
Bickel, Alexander, 35
Biddle, Edwin, 153
Blau, Peter, 49, 86, 187, 191
Bowers, David G., 180-181
Bunker, Douglas, R., 9, 154
Burnham, Robert, 130, 152, 195, 196, 207

Burns, Tom, 13, 168, 194, 196, 209, 233

Cahalan, Donald, 206, 212, 215
Cantor, Muriel, 136
Carroll, John, 196
Chayes, Antonia Handler, 132
Chin-Song, Edwin, 213
Coch, L., 87
Coe, Rodney, 57
Cohany, Harry, 235
Corwin, Ronald, 168, 196
Coughlan, Robert J., 197
Craig, Samuel, 81
Craise, Judith L., 196, 213
Cyert, Richard, 179

Dalton, Melvin, 162
Delbecq, Andre L., 195, 197
Dewar, Robert, 49, 82, 130, 172, 196
Dewey, Lucretia, 235
Dohrenwend, Bruce P., 213
Dror, Yehezkel, 21, 25-26
Duncan, Robert B., 152, 168, 195, 197, 209, 233
Dyer, Lee, 255

Edwards, Daniel, 288
Elmore, Richard F., 288
Etzioni, Amitai, 8

Fayol, Henri, 86
Fiedler, Fred E., 211
Fischer, Claude, 212

339

Subject Index

343